MODERN DIASPORAS IN
INTERNATIONAL POLITICS

Modern Diasporas in International Politics

Edited by
Gabriel Sheffer

ST. MARTIN'S PRESS
New York

Library of Congress Cataloging in Publication Data

Main entry under title:

Modern diasporas in international politics.

Based on papers given at a workshop held at the
Leonard Davis Institute, Hebrew University of Jerusalem,
June 1982, and at an international conference held at
MIT in March 1983. Bibliography: p.
1. International relations — Addresses, essays,
lectures. 2. Ethnic groups — Political activity — Addresses,
essays, lectures. 3. Migrations of nations —
Addresses, essays, lectures. 4. Jews — Diaspora — Addresses,
essays, lectures. I. Sheffer, Gabriel.
JX1391.M57 1986   327'.089   84-40608
ISBN 0-312-53790-5

CONTENTS

Contributors
Acknowledgements
Preface

CONTRIBUTORS

Walker Conner, Visiting Professor of Political Science at the National University of Singapore, has published on comparative nationalism.

Locksley Edmondson, Professor of African Studies at Cornell University, has published on Black history and political problems in the United States, Africa, and the Caribbean.

Daniel J. Elazar, President of the Jerusalem Center for Public Affairs, Professor of Intergovernmental Relations at Bar-Ilan University, and Professor of Political Science at Temple University, is author of books on federalism and Jewish affairs.

Milton Esman, Professor of Government, has published on ethnicity, development and international politics.

Iliya Harik, Professor of Political Science at Indiana University, has published on social and political processes in the Middle East, particularly Lebanon.

Arthur W. Helweg, Associate Professor at Western Michigan University, has published on India and her diaspora, ethnic relations and migration.

Dan Horowitz, Associate Professor of Political Science at The Hebrew University, has published on the Israeli political system, and security and defense issues.

Jacob Landau, Professor of Political Science at The Hebrew University, has published on Turkey, the Arabs in Israel, and ethnic problems in the Middle East.

Gabriel Sheffer, Associate Director of the Leonard Davis Institute of International Relations and Senior Lecturer of Political Science at The Hebrew University, has published on British politics in Palestine and the Middle East, the Jewish diaspora, and superpowers in the Middle East.

Myron Weiner, Professor of Political Science at the Massachusetts Institute of Technology, has published on both international and internal migration and on ethnicity.

ACKNOWLEDGEMENTS

We express our thanks to the Fund for Basic Research, administered by the Israel Academy of Sciences and Humanities, for assistance in this project.

PREFACE

This volume is the result of close collaboration between American and Israeli scholars who have been intrigued by the theoretical and practical aspects of the role and influence of ethnic diasporas on international and trans-state politics. This was the first stage in a comprehensive effort to re-examine a host of questions about trans-state networks and their operation. The next foci of work in this new field of study will be irredentism and the impact of world ideological, economic and religious movements and organizations on international politics.

In its first stage this project consisted of a number of preliminary steps. First, the participants examined the literature on the international aspects of ethnic pluralism. Reviewed for this purpose were those studies dealing with ethnic influence on foreign policy and the growing literature on interdependence, dependence, nonstate nations and other related topics. Within this framework we examined the relevant literature on political theory, such as the attitudes of Marxism-Leninism, national-socialism and various pluralistic democratic theories on the question of ethnicity and its role in international politics. Consequently, we concluded that the subject has been virtually neglected and that systematic research would be needed to shed light on it.

The second preliminary step was the mapping out of existing diasporas. Data were gathered about the various diasporas in most of the countries of the world. These data were organized according to the geographic dispersion of ethnic groups and according to various diasporas. The conclusion was very clear--ethnic diasporas are not disappearing but, rather, increasing.

The third step was an examination of the
internal aspects of a number of diasporas. For
this we examined the ideologies of diasporas, their
sociological characteristics, their political
structures, financial bases, mobilization strategies, channels of influence and access to policy-
making elites. Our conclusion was that there are
pertinent connections between the internal characteristics of diasporas and their trans-state level.

The fourth step, and the main purpose of this
project, was to reexamine the international and
trans-state aspects of diaspora activities. We
focused on the relations between the homelands and
host countries. The results of this research are
presented in this volume.

The theoretical questions dealt with in this
volume include: reasons for solidarity between
diasporas and homelands; the problems of dual
authority and loyalty; the importance and magnitude
of the economic-political dimension of diaspora
relations with host countries and homelands; the
mobilization and manipulation of political power,
and the effectiveness of diaspora activities and
their influence on national and international systems. But the basic question was, of course,
whether these diasporas are stable and influential
trans-state networks that coexist and interact with
states and with international organizations. The
chapters in this volume provide an affirmative
answer.

The work on this volume was also conducted in
a number of stages. The first stage was one of
conceptualization and definition. This was essentially accomplished in a workshop held at the Leonard Davis Institute at The Hebrew University of
Jerusalem, in June 1982. The participants included
Professors Walker Conner, Milton Esman and Myron
Weiner, from the United States, and Emmanuel
Guttman, Dan Horowitz, Jacob Landau and the editor
of this volume, from Israel.

Following this workshop it was decided to commission a number of additional articles from
various area specialists. The principals and other
contributors prepared their topics, testing our
operational definition and hypotheses in relation
to concrete experiences. This stage culminated in
an international conference held at MIT in Cambridge, Massachusetts, in March 1983. The various
papers were presented and reviewed for publication
in book form.

Final versions of the papers were submitted

to the editor early in 1984 and the manuscript prepared for publication in Jerusalem and Ithaca, New York later in 1984.

I would like to take this opportunity to thank all the participants in the project and the commentators on the papers for their cooperation. I would also like to thank the Leonard Davis Institute and its officers for the generous and continuous support given to this project, the directors and staff of the Center for International Studies at MIT for hosting our conference in Boston, Yael Efrati, who helped us very much in the earlier stages of the project, and Noa Padan, who coordinated many of the administrative efforts involved in the project. Finally I would like to thank Martine Halban, for her editorial work, and Linda Woodman, the executive editor of the Leonard Davis Institute, for her share in the preparation of this volume for publication.

Gabriel Sheffer
Jerusalem

A NEW FIELD OF STUDY:
MODERN DIASPORAS IN INTERNATIONAL POLITICS

Gabriel Sheffer

This volume is ambitious in scope. Its intention is to contribute meaningfully and systematically to a new field of study: the study of networks created by ethnic groups which transcend the territorial state. More specifically, this volume focuses on the role of trans-state networks developed by historical and particularly by modern diasporas, as well as on the various influences of these networks on international politics. Generally speaking, trans-state networks are structured connections established by groups, institutions and corporations across national and state boundaries, that evoke loyalties and solidarities inconsistent with and sometimes even contradicting the traditional allegiances to territorial states. The networks created by ethnic diasporas are becoming more important in the international arena, and have peculiar and interesting characteristics due to their being part of complex triadic relations between ethnic diasporas, their host countries and homelands. The study of these networks should also shed light on some general problems pertaining to ethnic diasporas, territorial states and international politics.

The motivation to focus on this subject stems from the observation that while these triadic relations are becoming an integral and, moreover, permanent feature of current national and international politics, they have not been adequately studied. Until now research in the field of trans-state networks has been primarily conducted in regard to other political and economic relations. The best known trans-state activities which have been studied and reported in a large, albeit controversial, body of literature are those formed by multinational corporations. Also examined already

1

are those networks established by certain international organizations, such as the United Nations and its functional agencies (for example the International Monetary Fund, and the International Labor Organization), as well as by regional organizations such as the EEC, Nato, the Warsaw Pact and Comecon. Incidentally, it should be noted here that despite the expectations of politicians and scholars that these regional organizations would flourish and create genuine, significant trans-state political and social networks through the spill-over effect, this has not materialized, and the territorial states are still the main actors in these regions and international organizations. By contrast, it seems that some ethnic diasporas are more successful in establishing significant relations which transcend the traditional boundaries of states.

In fact, for some time scholars have been studying the politics of ethnic, religious and racial groups in pluralistic societies to the point where these studies are emerging as a recognized sub-field of political science. However, most of these studies have dealt primarily with the domestic implications of ethnic pluralism in the West, or with state policies vis-à-vis minorities in the Eastern Bloc or in Third World countries. This category includes studies that emphasize ethnic (or religious, or racial) integration, as well as studies that focus on the regulation or management of domestic conflicts in which ethnic groups are involved. Yet, the various trans-state networks which are based on ethnic solidarity, connections and affinities (which in turn command powerful loyalties, control significant political and economic resources, and exercise influence on the politics of states and on their international relations) have not been sufficiently examined. Thus, this volume tackles a neglected aspect of ethnic politics, namely, the international dimension of the ethnic question.

When thinking systematically about this dimension it becomes clear that a vast range of phenomena can be included under the title of trans-state ethnic networks which influence international politics. Among the various relevant phenomena are: irredentism, the activities of political and cultural world movements, and the activities of modern ethnic diasporas. Irredentism denotes the political efforts made either by ethnic groups or by states to unite ethnically related segments of a population in neighboring countries within a common political framework which is either independent or autonomous. An historical example of this phenomenon is that of the Macedonians--who were studied by one of the contributors to this volume (Weiner 1971) more than a decade ago. Another manifestation of the irredentist phenomenon is the continual struggle of the Kurds, particularly in Iraq, for independence or at least autonomy. In the sub-Saharan region irredentism is currently becoming a major political issue causing tension and unrest. The irredentist phenomenon, like ethnic diasporas, has not been examined systematically.

Probably the most elusive and complex issue in the broader sphere of trans-state networks is the role of global churches, religious denominations and world political movements (which are partly based on ethnic connections) in the politics of territorial states, on the one hand, and in international affairs, on the other. A good example of this aspect of international politics is the recent growing involvement of the Vatican in Polish affairs. Thus, for instance, the Vatican was instrumental in simultaneously facilitating the Polish government's decision in 1984 to grant amnesty to political prisoners and persuading President Reagan to lift the economic, technological and scientific sanctions imposed on Poland by his administration. Although examples of the international activities of ideological and cultural movements such as the Communist parties or the Socialist International are abundant, nevertheless, they have not been studied comprehensively. Therefore, irredentism and the role of cultural, ideological and religious world movements in international politics will be reexamined and elaborated in further volumes resulting from the research project which led to this book.

The Scope of the Modern Diaspora Phenomenon

Modern diasporas are ethnic minority groups of migrant origins residing and acting in host countries but maintaining strong sentimental and material links with their countries of origin--their homelands. It is evident that as a result of recent waves of labor migration to Europe, the Persian Gulf, and North America, new diasporas are constantly being formed. Thus, the Hispanics in the United States, the Pakistanis and Palestinians in the Gulf area, the Turks in Western Europe and the Israelis in the US and Canada are establishing themselves as new diasporas in these countries. Therefore, it seems that modern ethnic diasporas will not disappear, but rather will continue to emerge in various host countries, increasing in numbers, organization and size. Furthermore, due to a growing political awareness of these diasporas resulting from changed attitudes towards them in certain host countries in the West, and due to improved systems of communication, the cultural, political and economic activities of these diasporas at the trans-state level will not diminish, but rather expand. Moreover, within established diasporas new inclinations toward new forms of activities are emerging. In certain respects these activities are not less intensive than those which characterized diasporas established during the period of the large migrations in the nineteenth and early twentieth centuries.

Thus, from a political theory view point, Marxist as well as liberal predictions that diasporas are only a transitory stage of social and political development that will vanish either as a result of cultural, social and political tolerance, or due to the emergence of classless societies, have proven far from correct. In fact, certain ethnic groups which were losing their ethnic identity and their inclination toward continuous and organized existence and action have revived their trans-state activities. An example of such a recent political reawakening is that of the Polish Catholic community in the US. This group, motivated by the emergence of Solidarity in Poland, economic difficulties in their homeland and the visit of the Pope to the US, has renewed its active interest in events in their homeland. Consequently, the Polish diaspora in the US has reactivated dormant organizations, and is reestablishing old networks for activities at the trans-state level. Similarly, substantial elements in the Irish community in the US have become increasingly involved in support of the IRA; the Greeks in the US are engaged in a similar revival in their increased activities on behalf of their homeland; and finally, American Blacks continue to show interest in African matters and especially in developments in South Africa. Consequently, all these ethnic groups have intensified their pressure on US foreign policy makers. Some of these diasporas have also intensified their involvement with third countries, or organizations, which are in turn involved in the affairs of their homelands (for example, the Greek community in the US has stepped up its activities against Turkey in the context of the Cyprus dispute). For several decades other diasporas, such as the overseas Chinese in Southeast Asia, the Lebanese in Latin America and the US, and the Indians in East and South Africa, have maintained their group identity through their communal organizations. Some of these diasporas are now increasing their efforts on behalf of their homelands while during periods of tension certain diasporas which have suffered grave injuries in their host countries have tried to influence or even manipulate their homeland's government to come to their rescue, and by doing so have activated dormant trans-state networks. A good example of the latter pattern was that of the Indian community in Uganda in the early 1980s. Because of their organization and determination, ethnic diasporas can become, in some small states, a significant political factor both domestically and in the foreign affairs of their host country. This was the case with the Palestinians in Lebanon before the 1982 Lebanese war.

It is true that modern diasporas can exist comfortably and flourish in pluralistic societies in the West, especially as far as their trans-state activities are concerned. Thus, despite the deep-rooted reluctance to absorb immigrants, which has been particularly evident in the case of guest workers in Western European countries such as Britain, Switzerland, West Germany, Sweden and the Netherlands, immigrant communities have become permanent features in most of these countries. After the initial settling-down period, some of these new diasporas have started to mobilize and organize for political action both at the domestic and international levels. As a result of relatively large-scale migrations to rapidly developing areas in third world countries such as Saudi Arabia and the Persian Gulf Sheikdoms, various states in this part of the world now host new ethnic diasporas. These new diasporas maintain permanent contact with their homelands through regular visits, remittances, lobbying and pressure, in this way developing trans-state connections. Finally, despite immense inherent political difficulties, ethnic diasporas also succeed in maintaining their group identity in the Eastern bloc. In subtle ways these diasporas are continuously involved in struggles against assimilatory policies of their host countries, (especially the Soviet Union), and in attempts to establish their right to keep contact with their homelands, as well as to obtain the right to emigrate to their homelands or to third countries. The problems of the Jews, ethnic Germans and other ethnic minority groups in the Soviet Union are becoming acute domestic issues as well as international controversies (for example, the attempts at repatriating ethnic Germans from the Soviet Union, and the emigration of East Germans to West Germany have both become acute issues in West Germany's relations with the Soviet Union. On a larger scale, the struggle for the right of Russian Jews to emigrate has become an international question involving not only Israel and the Soviet Union, but also the governments of Great Britain, Austria, France, Italy, and the US, as well as a number of Jewish and non-Jewish organizations).

Even this cursory examination of the behavior of modern organized ethnic diasporas shows that they develop and maintain multilateral connections with various political and social groups in their host countries, homelands and third countries. They exchange information and resources with international organizations, governments, and other relevant groups within the states which serve as their base and, of course, with their homelands. Ethnic diasporas are involved not only in national and trans-state politics, but also in cultural, educational and religious affairs and consequently they establish specialized organizations to promote and defend their linguistic, cultural, religious and economic interests in both their host countries and homelands. Such organizations and networks are highly developed in most of the Jewish and overseas Chinese communities, for example. Newer ethnic diasporas are also showing a great deal of interest and active involvement in these fields which are crucial for their survival. For example, one of the more immediate problems of the Turkish diaspora in various European countries is ensuring education for their younger generation. The solutions adopted are different in various countries, but in all cases much tension is created, and at times the Turkish government has been involved.

As has been mentioned, certain activities of ethnic minorities within their host countries--such as their integration processes, cultural and social assimilation conflicts, and attempts to influence foreign policies--have already been examined in the existing body of literature. But, the international and, in particular, the trans-state activities which usually take place in the grey areas of the international system, or within certain subsystems of the host countries and homelands, as well as in third countries, have hardly been addressed by students of comparative politics, or international relations. The lack of research in this field can be illustrated by the fact that only a handful of relevant published works exists. Noteworthy examples of books which deal partly with some of the issues raised here are those by Rothschild (1981), Bertelsen (1980), Shurke and Nobles (1977), Stack (1979) and Said and Simmons (1976). But even these studies do not deal systematically with the activities of diasporas on the trans-state level; instead they focus on the attempts of ethnic groups to influence the foreign policies of their host countries. In these studies the triadic networks of homeland, (or trans-state organization), host country and ethnic diaspora have not been fully conceptualized and empirically explored. The purpose of this volume is to fill this gap.

A number of important modern diasporas, simultaneously active at the trans-state level and in the domestic affairs of their host countries and homelands are the subject of the various case studies of this volume. The selected diasporas are: the overseas Chinese; Turks in a number of West European countries and especially in West Germany and Sweden; Palestinians in the Middle East; Jews, Indians and Blacks in the US; and labor migrants in Europe and the Persian Gulf area. Some of these diasporas combine religious with ethnic solidarities, lending them special strength and resilience in their domestic and trans-state activities. The Jewish, Turkish and Palestinian diasporas belong to this sub-category. Nevertheless, due to processes of secularization occurring within these groups, the ethnic factor is predominant. It produces the necessary social and political ingredients for the bond with the homeland, and differentiates these diasporas from their host society. This is particularly the case with Palestinians who live in Arab countries. On the other hand, the religious ingredient contributes to the ideological, cultural and emotional identification of the diaspora and thus strengthens the bond with the homeland.

Despite the great historical, cultural and religious variety of the diaspora groups discussed

in this volume, they all share one characteristic
--a continuous involvement in a triadic relationship between the diaspora, the host country and the
homeland. Consequently, all these diasporas are
active in the trans-state arena and all have
acquired a certain influence in international politics.

An Operational Definition of Ethnic Diasporas

The problem of definition arises whenever a new
field of academic study is developed. For a number
of reasons the need for a clear operational definition is particularly evident in the case of ethnic
diasporas, especially since the few existing definitions are inadequate for the research perspective adopted in this volume. The realities of
modern diasporas are more complex than those depicted and analyzed in the few available theoretical
discussions--particularly those focusing on the
role and functioning of historical diasporas in
various multi-ethnic empires. Armstrong (1976)
has suggested a distinction between mobilized and
proletarian diasporas. Now, while some of the
modern diasporas discussed in the present volume
can indeed be described as proletarian, "disadvantaged products of modernized polities"
(Armstrong 1976, p. 343)--especially those created
by guest workers and others during the early stages
of their existence--most of the other diasporas are
in fact "mobilized" ethnic groups which do not
have any advantages in status, but enjoy many material and cultural advantages compared to other
groups. While Armstrong focuses on these historical mobilized diasporas, the present volume starts
with the assumption that even new proletarian diasporas are rapidly establishing themselves, acquiring relatively advantaged positions and are
mobilizing for the maintenance, protection and
promotion of their interests. This volume argues
that an important feature of these processes of
organization and mobilization is the creation of
the diasporas' trans-state networks.
    Some of the existing definitions of ethnic
diasporas are inadequate for our purposes since
their underlying assumption is that diasporas are
transitory and that they are destined to disappear
through acculturation and assimilation. Such a
premise limits the scope of the definition, and

the analysis. Usually these definitions focus on the conditions leading to integration and assimilation. The assumption in this volume is that diasporas and their trans-state relations will continue to exist even as diasporas acculturate. Earlier definitions were based on the examination of single, or very limited cases of traditional diasporas. Therefore, these definitions are not adequate for dealing with recently established diasporas, with diasporas which have experienced a revival, or with diasporas which are extending their trans-state networks.

Rather than an alternative concise definition which might neglect significant features of the phenomenon at hand, a more comprehensive definition is suggested here. This operational definition has served as the starting-point for the various chapters in this volume, and was formulated as a result of preliminary research on a number of diasporas. Further studies in this field may, of course, lead to additions or changes of certain elements of our definition, which stands as follows:

Ethnic diasporas are created either by voluntary migration (e.g., Turks to West Germany) or as a result of expulsion from the homeland (e.g., the Jews and the Palestinians) and settlement in one or more host countries. In these host countries the diasporas remain minority groups (the Anglo-Saxon segment in Canada for example will therefore be excluded from the present study). In their host countries diasporas preserve their ethnic, or ethnic-religious identity and communal solidarity. This solidarity serves as the basis for maintaining and promoting constant contacts among the diasporas' activist elements. These contacts have political, economic, social and cultural significance for the diasporas, their host countries and homelands. This is also the basis for the organized actions of the diasporas. One of the purposes of these actions is to create and increase the readiness and ability of the diasporas to preserve a continuous interest in, and cultural, economic and political exchanges with their homelands. Organized diasporas deal with various aspects of their cultural, social, economic and political needs in a way that either complements or conflicts with the activities of the host government. The emergence of diaspora organizations provides the potential for conflicting pressures and for the development of dual authority and dual loyalty patterns and problems. In order to avoid undesirable conflicts with the norms or laws established by the dominant group in their host countries, the diasporas accept certain rules of the game of these countries. At certain periods, however, real or alleged dual loyalties which are generated by the dual authority patterns may create tension between elements in the host country and the diaspora. This sometimes leads to the intervention of homelands on behalf of their diasporas, or in the affairs of the diasporas themselves. And finally, and most importantly, the capability of diasporas to mobilize in order to promote or defend their interests or the interests of their homelands within their host countries will result in the formation of either conflictual or cooperative triadic networks involving homeland, diaspora and host country. These triadic relations are now an integral part of international politics and influence the behavior of all parties involved.

Several difficulties can immediately be discerned with regard to the application of this operational definition to certain diasporas. First, in certain cases it is not entirely clear where or whether there are discrete homelands, or which are the homelands and which are the diasporas. At least three examples of this possible confusion spring to mind and are discussed in this volume. The first example is the Jewish diaspora. For decades after Israel's independence it is still not clear which is the dominant component in world Jewry, and the debate continues about the centrality of Israel to world Jewry. While most Israelis would claim that, by virtue of its independence, sovereignty and politico-military power, Israel should be viewed as the national center, many Jews in the diaspora argue that, because of Israel's insecure position and cultural mediocrity, the diaspora is in fact in the center. The second example is the Palestinian Arab diaspora. In this case also, the homeland and its boundaries are unclear. Does the homeland include the West Bank? Gaza? Jordan? Certain parts, or the whole, of Israel? Among Palestinians there is also continuous controversy concerning centrality. While some

West Bankers argue that only they themselves should decide their fate and future, the PLO claims to be the sole representative of the Palestinian nation. The third example is the Black community in the US and its relations with Africa. The main question here is whether the whole African continent, or certain countries in Africa, are the homeland of the Blacks. A further complication in this context is whether the Blacks in the US can be regarded as a diaspora since their ties with the "homeland" are only a vague concept among certain limited segments of the Black elite in the US. The majority feel that they are not part of a diaspora and that their homeland is definitely the US.

The second difficulty with this definition is connected to the issue of reciprocity in relations between diasporas and their homelands. While diasporas maintain ties with their homelands, the attitudes of the homelands vis-à-vis their diasporas may be vague or ambivalent. Thus, diasporas are not always supported by their homelands. For example, India did not intervene on behalf of its diaspora when it was persecuted and expelled from Uganda. Furthermore, at times homelands are interested in stopping certain activities of their emigrants--for example, the Cubans in the US who oppose Castro's regime, and the white Russian emigres after the Bolshevik revolution. The corollary of this situation is that diasporas do not always support the current government in their homeland. Consequently, rather than maintaining a facade about their consensus on the legitimacy of the government at home, or on their international policies and activities, splits which are difficult to conceal may occur within diasporas. Illustrations of these patterns are abundant and only three examples will be quoted: lack of consensus was evident among overseas Chinese during the struggle between the Communists and nationalists, as well as during the Cultural Revolution in China; many Cubans in the US disapprove of the Castro regime, and they are mobilized to act against it; and there is a growing lack of consensus among Jews concerning the policies of the Israeli government vis-à-vis the Palestinians.

The Theoretical Perspective

The present volume concentrates on three sets of theoretical problems. The first is the causes for

11

diasporas' greater involvement in international politics. In this context the various studies will elaborate on the following issues: the reasons for the creation of recently established diasporas, their members' motivation for organization and mobilization, the implications of higher rates of participation of the rank-and-file in the activities of the diasporas, and the reasons for the growing influence that diasporas can exert on international politics in general, and on the bilateral relations between host country and homeland in particular. A related question is that of the growing participation of diasporas in multinational corporations and economic and commercial international enterprises. (The overseas Chinese, the Palestinians and the Jews have all created a maze of economic networks which are intended to promote and facilitate the achievement of their goals and interests).

The second theoretical focus is the reexamination of some broad questions about the role of states in the modern political world. In this context this volume will try to clarify the question of relations between states and diasporas, and whether any changes can be discerned in these relations. Furthermore, one of the basic concerns of this volume is the reexamination of the crucial question of the extent to which the existence of meaningful trans-state political networks, such as those created by host countries, homelands and diasporas, will change the perceived theoretical and practical importance usually attached to territorial states as the main building blocks of international politics.

The third theoretical focus is on the conditions in host countries conducive to the maintenance of diaspora solidarities and loyalties as well as the conditions in homelands likely to trigger or muffle their expression. There is a large number of possible combinations of strategies and tactics according to which diasporas can act domestically and internationally; this volume will attempt to identify only the most common so that the patterns of diaspora behavior can be delineated and clarified.

The History and Development of Diasporas

Some of the existing diasporas are quite ancient (Jews, Indians and overseas Chinese), certain diasporas have been created in the more recent past (Poles and Irish in the US) and some diasporas are only now emerging (Turks in West Germany, Palestinians in the Persian Gulf area). Within this context, it is important to differentiate between the development and the history of different diasporas.

The similarities between what earlier analysts called "historical diasporas--namely those which emerged within multiethnic empires such as the Moslem, Ottoman, Austro-Hungarian and Russian empires (Jews, Greeks, and Armenians were most prominent among these diasporas)--and modern diasporas which have emerged and organized in the late nineteenth and twentieth centuries in Eastern and Western Europe must be examined. The basic question is whether there is any crucial meaning in such a distinction, and if so, what theoretical and analytical conclusions can be drawn from it.

Some chapters in this volume will follow current developments of a number of diasporas and analyze the reasons for changes in the structure, organization and activities of these modern diasporas. This is crucial for the assessment of the possible future development of the phenomenon of diasporas. The discussion of this aspect will reveal the effects on trans-state triadic networks of the growing awareness of the existence of these diasporas, the main directions of the development of these groups and their networks, and how migrant workers turn into diasporas. This should provide significant insights into the transformation processes of new diasporas into effective mobilized groups active in international politics.

The Comparative Perspective

The study of modern diasporas in this volume is based upon a comparative framework. The main question examined is how the behavior of diasporas is influenced by the rules existing in the political systems of the host countries and by the foreign policies of the homelands. The comparisons are complex since the essays deal with diasporas widely different in their ethnic and cultural origins, historical experiences, periods of emergence and institutionalization, degree of institutionalization, ethno-national identity, ties to homelands and host countries, ability to influence both the former and the latter, and the degree of internal cohesion and external interaction. The profound differences between the political systems of homelands and host countries and the varying international conditions under which these diasporas operate further complicate the comparisons. Since the emphasis in this volume is not on distinct studies of particular diasporas, but rather on the comparative aspect of their experience and behavior in order to develop a valid theory, each of the case studies was researched in accordance with the general framework presented below.

The dependent variables used in various chapters are: the effects of modern diasporas on international politics and on the foreign relations of homelands and host countries; the effects of relevant international events and processes on the security and status of the diasporas, the influence of diasporas on the domestic politics of the host countries; and finally, diasporas as autonomous actors in international affairs.

The independent variables identified which serve as background information in some of the chapters are: the attitudes of host societies toward the political influence of diasporas; diasporas' access to host countries' governments and public opinion; the inclination of home or host governments to draw on diasporas as political resources to promote their interests in bilateral relations, international politics and organizations, and international and trans-national arrangements which affect the flow and status of migrants.

A number of intervening variables have been sub-categorized as follows: (1) Capabilities of the diasporas, i.e., the scope of their internal organization, the duration of their residence in their host countries, the material and educational resources available to them, their legal status within their host countries, the degree of their acculturation to the host societies and their geographical dispersal in the host countries; (2) The objectives of the diasporas' activities, more specifically, do they intend to influence the behavior of host or home governments, or to provide material, political or moral support to home governments or to competing factions within home societies, or to promote or maintain freedom of international or trans-state action in cultural, political and economic spheres? (3) Sources of mobilization and activation of diasporas: mobilization and activation by home governments or by segments in home societies, by host governments or segments in host countries, or by third parties, such as either friendly or hostile diasporas residing in the same host countries, or self-mobilization and activation; (4) Activities of diasporas which affect international politics, including the collection and allocation of funds, application of pressure on host governments for policies favorable to home governments, or to political factions within homelands, pressure on home governments to intervene on behalf of the rights and status of diasporas in host countries, intervention with regard to issues of political choice in homelands, and transnational, economic (or cultural) enterprises involving co-ethnics living in more than one host country.

References

Armstrong, J. A. 1976. Mobilized and Proletarian Diasporas. **APSR** 70, no. 2: 393-403.

Bertelsen, J. 1980. **Non State Nations in International Politics: Comparative System Analysis.** New York: Praeger.

Rothschild, J. 1981. **Ethnopolitics.** New York: Columbia University Press.

Said A. and C. R. Simmons. 1976. **Ethnicity in an International Context.** New Jersey: Transaction.

Shurke, A. and L. G. Nobles, eds. 1977. **Ethnic Conflict in International Relations.** New York: Praeger.

Stack, J. F. 1979. **International Conflict in an American City.** Westport: Greenwood Press.

Wiener, M. 1970-71. The Macedonian Syndrome: An Historical Model of International Relation and Political Development. **World Politics** 23, no. 4: 665-83.

THE IMPACT OF HOMELANDS UPON DIASPORAS

Walker Conner

The reception accorded diasporas has been traditionally heavily influenced by the ethnographic
composition and the ethno-political myths of the
host society. Despite massive migrations, it is
still the case that all but a relatively small
percentage of the world's population lives within
an ethnic homeland. Indeed, a working definition
of a diaspora might well be "that segment of a
people living outside the homeland."
The ethnic homeland is far more than territory. As evidenced by the near universal use of
such emotionally charged terms as the motherland,
the fatherland, the native land, the ancestral
land, land where my fathers died and, not least,
the homeland, the territory so identified becomes
imbued with an emotional, almost reverential dimension. Poets are far better guides for pene-
trating this emotional dimension of the homeland
than are social scientists. In the eighteenth
century, Robert Burns in **The Lay of the Last Min-
strel** suggested the universality of attachment to
homeland:

> Breathes there the man, with soul so dead,
> Who never to himself hath said,
> This is my own, my native land!
>
> ...
>
> Land of my sires! what mortal hand
> Can e'er untie the filial band
> That knits me to thy rugged strand.

The invulnerability of such sentiments to
time, place, and culture is suggested by the works

of several contemporary poets whose homelands are located in the Muslim Central Asian area of the Soviet Union. A 1970 poem by an Uzbek notes:

> So that my generation would comprehend the
>   Homeland's worth,
> Men were always transformed to dust, it seems.
> The Homeland is the remains of our forefathers
> Who turned into dust for this precious soil.[2]

And in a 1971 poem simply entitled "Homeland," another Uzbek writes of Uzbekistan:

> Oh, Homeland, you are the fountainhead
>   of happiness...
> When you are well there is such joy and
>   contentment in my heart;
> When you are well the radiance of the
>   world dances in my soul.
> When the sun lowers its head toward your
>   evening horizon,
> With a tear of gladness in my eye I place my
>   head against your bosom..
> How happy the moment when I understood
>   your pride,
> And in the world of my heart I enclosed
>   your love.
> Your love became a melody unto my heart,
> And without this melody, how sad,
>   so forlorn my soul...[3]

And in the same year, a young Kirgiz poet colorfully asserted the primordial, prenatal nature of this relationship between human and homeland:

> Remember, even before your mother's milk
> You drank the milk of your homeland.[4]

This emotional attachment to the homeland derives from perceptions of it as the cultural hearth and very often, as the geographic cradle of the ethno-national group. In Bismarckian terminology, "Blut und Boden!", blood and soil have become mixed.[5] The emotionally pregnant concept of "my roots" implies soil.[6] The psychological associations thus made between homeland and one's people are the more--not the less--intense for being emotional and resisting exposition in rational terms. Admittedly, such psychological associations are often predicated upon questionable history. Finns and Germans, for example, are descendants of people who migrated from east of what is today perceived as Finland and Deutschland. As more recently illustrated by the Afrikaners and Quebecois, a people can come to consider as their homeland a region where they have dwelt for only a relatively short time. Moreover, as a people expands outward, so does its concept of the homeland. Thus, though once limited to the region of Muscovy, the Russian homeland is today popularly viewed as encompassing the strip of (ethnically) Russian-dominated land stretching from the western border of the Russian Soviet Federated Socialist Republic to Vladivostok. Somewhat analogously, Poles, in their numerous references to homeland, do not appear to differentiate between traditionally Polish-dominated regions and that large western sector of the contemporary state of Poland which, prior to 1945, was populated principally by Germans.

Such considerations hardly negate the emotional attachment of people to a homeland. As in other aspects of nationalism, it is not "facts" but what people perceive to be "facts" that is of essence. The important point is that the populated world is subdivided into a series of perceived homelands to which, in each case, the indigenous ethno-national group is convinced it has a profound and exclusive proprietary claim. Again, the particular words used to describe homelands are instructive. Who but the Scots could have plenary claim to residence within Scotland, who but Germans to Deutchland, Kurds to Kurdistan (literally "Land of the Kurds"), or Nagas to Nagaland?

In such an environment, diasporas are viewed at best as outsiders, strangers within the gates. They may be tolerated, even treated most equitably, and individual members of the diaspora may achieve highest office. Their stay may be multigenerational, but they remain outsiders in the eyes of the indigenes, who reserve the inalienable right to assert their primary and exclusive proprietary claim to the homeland, should they so desire. Moreover, in a number of cases what superficially might pass for the peaceful acceptance of a diaspora has been due to the lack of means to purge the homeland of an alien presence. Thus, in J.S. Furnivall's (1948, p.304) famous model of colonial "plural society," the indigenous people, a small representation of the mother country, and a large immigrant population resided within the colony in reasonable harmony. But relationships altered perceptibly with the end of colonialism. Indeed, as Furnivall notes, even prior to Dutch withdrawal, the nationalist movement on Java achieved popularity because of its anti-Chinese immigrant activities (1948, p.310). Painting with a broader brush, Milton Esman has noted with regard to Southeast Asia generally that "the indigenous nationalists who succeeded the European colonialists shared none of their predecessors' benign tolerance toward the Chinese in their midst (see Esman's essay in this volume). Similarly, benign tolerance toward the Asian migrant community did not long survive the British withdrawal from East Africa. The tolerance shown by the colonial authorities does not require explanation, since their homeland was not involved; their postcolonial actions indicate an absence of tolerance when it did become involved. The important point is that the indigenous peoples of the colonies did manifest their resentment of an alien intrusion when the opportunity presented itself.

History is liberally sprinkled with cases in which diasporas have appeared relatively secure only to be faced with an unexpected outbreak of xenophobia and nativism. The pattern of such outbreaks appears too complex to lend itself to predictability. In some cases, the targeted diaspora has been accused of controlling the most financially rewarding positions (e.g., the Chinese in Malaysia, Asians in East Africa, Frenchmen in Corsica), while in other cases they have held the poorest and least wanted jobs (the **Gastarbeiter** in in Germany and Switzerland). Nativism has appeared at both low and high points in the business cycle, at times of labor shortage and surplus. In some cases, recent large-scale immigration appears to have been a factor giving rise to nativism. But in other cases, a diaspora which had been resident for generations was suddenly targeted as unwanted aliens. The lack of acculturation and integration was broadly indentified as a key element in the nativist attacks upon the Asians of East Africa, but intense acculturation and integration provided no immunity for Jews within Nazi Germany. While in many instances, nativism has been aimed at foreigners and aliens per se, in other cases it has been directed at particular diasporas.[7]

The complexity of the pattern therefore frustrates attempts to anticipate outbreaks of nativism. But this lack of pattern in itself tells us that such considerations as the business cycle, the rate of immigration, cultural distance, historic animosities and the like are at most potential/ likely triggers or exacerbators but are not the root force. Their relationship to nativism may be caustic, but it is not causal. Explanation ultimately lies in the primal title to a homeland claimed by the indigenous ethno-national group. Though it may never be exercised, the power of eviction that is inherent in such a title to the territory may be translated into action at any time. Members of a diaspora can therefore never be at home in a homeland. They are at best sojourn ers, remaining at the sufferance of the indigenous people.[8]

Homelands and States

The political borders of states have been superimposed upon the ethnic map with cavalier disregard for ethnic homelands. Most states contain several homelands, and their land borders regularly dissect others. Given this lack of coincidence between the borders of states and homelands, the potential for a conflict in outlook with regard to migrations is extremely great. States maintain as an attribute of sovereignty the right to set immigration/emigration policy and to determine what restrictions, if any, are to be applied to internal migration. But, as we have observed, a homeland dwelling people considers itself to possess a primal power to determine who shall and who shall not be permitted to reside therein.

The likelihood of contradiction arising between a state's policies and the predilections of a homeland dwelling people will obviously depend in large part on the degree to which the state apparatus identifies itself exclusively with the interests of that people. An important reflection of the intensity of that identification is the state's ethno-political myth. By myth we mean the image of the state that is fostered and projected by its institutions, symbols, propaganda, and the like.

In a number of cases, the ethno-political myth tends to identify the state politically as the expression or general will of a particular ethno-national group and geographically as coterminous either with that people's homeland or at least with a segment thereof. State names (both popular and/or official) are often a contributing element. In nearly fifty instances, the current state designation identifies it with either a people or its homeland: Albania, Bangladesh, Botswana, Bulgaria, Burma, China (both), Congo, Denmark, Arab Republic of Egypt, Finland, France, Germany (both), Greece, Hungary, Iceland, Ireland, Israel, Italy, Japan, Korea (both), Laos, Lesotho, Libyan Arab Jamahiriya, Mongolia, Nauru, Nepal, Norway, Poland, Portugal, Romania, Western Samoa, Somalia, Swaziland, Sweden, Syrian Arab Republic, Thailand, Tonga, Turkey, United Arab Emirates, Vietnam and the Yemen Arab Republic.

The flag, national anthem, constitution, official history (that version which appears in texts which are sanctioned for educational and other public use), and common allusions and metaphors in the utterances of key officials are other means of conveying the ethno-national myth. Germany's traditional national anthem ("Deutschland, Deutschland uber alles") is a paean to the homeland, and the present constitution of the Federal Republic of Germany makes the reunification of the German homeland a constitutional imperative. Although nationalist sloganeering was taboo in the post-Hitler era, this is obviously no longer the case. Willy Brandt of the Socialist Party made use of the slogan "Be Proud You're German!" in his successful reelection to the Chancellorship in 1972, and Helmut Kohl of the Christian Democrats regularly alluded to "das Vaterland" in his successful campaign of 1983.[9]

In the case of the homeland state--that is, a state which the ethno-political myth links closely to a specific people and its homeland--public policies are apt to reflect concern with maintaining the ethno-national purity of the homeland. That is to say, policies are apt to reflect the outlook of the homeland dwellers and vice versa in a reinforcing pattern. Japan offers the most extreme case. Until well into the nineteenth century, Japanese policies aimed at minimizing contact with foreigners, and the very few Westerners permitted to sojourn in Japan were restricted to enclaves. The determination of the authorities to maintain the ethnic purity of the homeland (99.4 percent Japanese) was most recently highlighted by Japan's refusal to be moved by humanitarian considerations, world opinion, or a series of entreaties from the United States and other allies to respond to the plight of the "boat people" departing Vietnam by accepting a reasonable proportion of them for settlement.[10] South Korea, another homeland state (more that 99 percent homogeneous), while agreeing to serve as a transshipment point, also refused to accept "the boat people" for permanent settlement. In its origins, the Vietnamese refugee problem was itself at least partly traceable to a government's policy aimed at ethnically purifying a homeland. Upon consolidating their power over all of Vietnam, the authorities in Hanoi adopted the baseless myth of a single ancestry common to all the indigenous peoples within the country and embarked upon a policy of extremely rapid assimilation. The relatively large Chinese community (some 1.5 million), by far the largest "alien" element in the country, was encouraged to depart. The Chinese in both the northern and southern sectors of Vietnam became the target of particularly harsh treatment, anti-Chinese sentiment was whipped up among the masses, and those attempting to leave were not impeded from doing so. By 1978, literally hundreds of thousands of Chinese were fleeing the country by boat or by crossing into China, and the Vietnamese homeland was being purified commensurately (Connor 1984, Chapter 10).

The general tendency of homeland states to resist alienizing the homeland would appear to be contradicted by the post-World War II flow of migrants into northwestern Europe. As European economic recovery began to outstrip the indigenous labor supply in the late 1950s, several of the region's states became importers of foreign labor. Two evident homeland states, West Germany and Sweden, were among the major recipients. Surprisingly, however, the policy of immigration was initiated in the anticipation that the influx would not have an enduring impact upon the homelands' ethnic composition. The migrants were officially termed "guestworkers," an apt choice of a word, since good guests never outstay their welcome. They were to visit for only as long as needed and then return to their own states which, for the most part, were near at hand and therefore posed little problem of distance. They were, in effect, to serve as seasonal workers, although the seasons were to be determined more by the business cycle than by the calendar. And if the high-labor-demand phase of the business cycle should prove unreasonably long, it was in any case assumed that the **Gastarbeiter** would be in a constant process of rotation. Guests do not become residents. Given the fact that the guestworkers were making possible a higher standard of living than would otherwise have been the case, and that they were assuming the lowliest, poorest-paying tasks that the indigenous populace eschewed, it might have been anticipated that the guests would be well-received, at least for a time. On the contrary, however, from the outset they faced hostility. In one of the earliest comprehensive studies of the reception accorded to the guestworkers throughout all states of the region, Arnold Rose concluded that, despite some variations, there was everywhere a high incidence of prejudice towards the aliens in both public policies and in the attitudes of the indigenous people.[11] In a 1957 questionnaire, only 16 percent of the respondents in Sweden said that they were favorably disposed toward the liberal Swedish immigration policies (Rose 1969, p. 107). And in Germany, a 1964 poll indicated that 64 percent of all women and 70 percent of all men were willing to work an extra hour per week without added remuneration "if this would make the employment of foreigners unnecessary."[12]

The basic laissez faire attitude of the governments toward immigration and towards the migrants has necessarily altered in the face of such attitudes, plus with the increasing evidence that a substantial portion of the ostensible guests were planning to extend their visit indefinitely. Forcible expulsion was not a viable option for governments in post-Hitler, democratic Europe, but restrictive immigration legislation has followed in all countries.[13] As to those migrants who have elected to remain, legislation concerning their status and rights has been passed, but both the level of rights and their actual implementation vary greatly. Perhaps surprisingly, given its homogeneity, Sweden is without peer in granting liberal rights to the "staygrants." However, as Jane Kramer has sensitively recorded (1976, pp. 48, 50), this support is far more ascribable to a sense that "if they are already here and we cannot get rid of them, we must treat them as well as possible, so as not to make this unhappy situation worse," than it is to a conviction concerning universalism or the innate human worth and dignity of these stay-on guests:

The money is dispensed with obligatory cordiality. So is every service of Sweden's elaborate and bountiful welfare state. The sort of racist hatred that prompted **soi-disant** respectable Frenchmen to murder Algerian workers in Marseilles a few summers back would be unthinkable in Sweden. The open contempt of the Germans for their **Gastarbeiter** would not be tolerated. The Swedes are appalled at the thought that the Swiss could publicly debate expelling foreigners for the simple offense of being foreign. Swedes regard foreigners with a calmer, quieter disapproval. They simply treat foreigness as some sort of congenital indiscretion--as a kind of psychic social disease that by rights should embarrass anyone afflicted with it into lying low until the symptoms have disappeared. The **invadrare** in Sweden soon discover that they are isolated-- and they sense that, somehow, their isolation goes deeper than the volatile, defensive separateness of foreign workers in, say, France and Germany. If those workers are "the niggers of Europe," which is how they have described themselves lately, then the Swedish **invandrare** are a little like the sad, nervous boys in a Strindberg book--well fed, well groomed, well cared for, but unacknowledged as fellow human beings until they have managed a reasonable approximation of grownup attitudes. The confusion the **invandrare** feel is deep and bitter, because they have so few practical complaints to corroborate their eerie sense of being in terrible error by being themselves. Predag, for all his grudges, says that no one in Sweden treats him badly. The problem, he says, is that no one seems willing to admit that he is really there.

Sweden, of course, is a notoriously provincial country. It has no history of cultural multiplicity and no real tolerance for it, and the stolid conformity that confounds tourists who come expecting a nation of sexy girls and broody, philosophical drinking partners is really a reflection of the Swedes' profound uneasiness with difference. Sweden may produce its Strindbergs and its suicides, but the Swedes themselves seem to regard genius and madness alike as object lessons in the lamentable inability of some people to supress their eccentricities and become cheer-

The Impact of Homelands Upon Diasporas

fully, comfortably, the same as everybody
else. Most Swedes, in fact, protectionist for
centuries and secure by now in a benign but
stultifying xenophobia, seem to regard for-
eignness itself as something insulting."

Meanwhile, increasing manifestations of
xenophobia toward the **Gastarbeiter** have
characterized German society.[14] A 1982 poll indicated that 79 percent of all adults felt that there
were too many foreigners (**New York Times** August
2, 1982). The word **uberfremdung** (a sense of being
overwhelmed with foreigners or foreign influence)
is commonly heard, violence against the aliens is
not uncommon, and the Christian Democratic Party
ran a very successful election campaign in 1983 on
a platform pledging a tougher stance toward all
aspects of the **Gastarbeiter** question (**New York
Times**, October 14, 1982 and **Washington Post**, November 18, 1982). As the **Neue Presse** (Hanover) noted
on July 15, 1982: "When one speaks of foreign
worker policies one does not mean anymore possibilities to help them but means a search for ways of
sending them home."

In sum, the **Gastarbeiter** phenomenon within
Western Europe does not bear witness to a
cosmopolitan trend away from homeland and homeland
state-psychology. The influx originated almost
without premeditation, on the naive assumption that
the states could benefit without cost, because the
foreign workforce would expand and contract (disappear) simultaneously with demand. Even before it
became evident that such was not the case and that
large numbers of workers might become permanent
residents, hostility toward the alien presence
arose.

Before leaving the discussion of the
homeland state, it is perhaps worth belaboring the
obvious by noting that a state that cultivates such
an ethno-political myth thereby risks alienating
not just aliens, but all peoples (other than the
dominant group) whose homeland is totally or
partially within the state's confines. A number of
states whose titles identify them with a specific
people contain several homelands. It is hardly
conjectural to surmise that the word "Burma" does
not trigger the same positive vibrations within
Shans and Karens, as it does within Burmese, or
that references to "Mother China" trigger different
associations within Han and Tibetan. Some leaders
have appreciated the sensitive nature of such

25

considerations. Thus, the substitution of Iran for
the much older name of Persia was done so as not to
alienate the non-Persian people in such areas of
the country as Kurdistan, Baluchistan, Turkmenia
and Azerbaidzhan. Similarly, Lenin quite calcula-
tingly omitted any reference to Russia or Russian,
when entitling the Union of Soviet Socialist Republics, so as not to irk the sensibilities of the
non-Russian peoples. The change of name from the
Democratic Republic of the Congo to Zaire was
probably motivated by similar considerations.[15]

In some situations, the incompatibility
between the state's ethno-national myth and reality
has been a source of great stress. Thus, one way
of summarizing Israel's major internal problem
would be the dialectical tension generated between
the state myth of a homeland for the Jewish people
and its large Arab population.[16] Similarly, the
vitriol and cruelty with which the Malaysian authorities responded to the "boat people" from Vietnam
suggests that they perceived in them a dangerous
force for further widening the already badly
stretched relationship between the ethno-national
myth of a Malay homeland state and a population
that was one-third Chinese. Noting that an influx
of the refugees, who contained a large percentage
of Chinese, would "upset the delicate racial balance," a Malaysian spokesman made clear that none
of them would be accepted for permanent settlement,
nor would any children born to them while within
Malaysian territory be eligible for citizenship.
In June 1979, the government refused to allow
Malaysia to be further used as even a transshipment
point for the refugees. The government
acknowledged that it had already ordered hundreds
of boatloads of refugees towed back into
international waters, and it threatened legislation
to empower the navy to shoot at sight any "boat
people" within territorial waters. The Malaysian
Home Minister verbally attacked Hanoi for creating
the problem by "throwing rubbish into its
neighbor's gardens," (**Keesing's Contemporary
Archives**, 1980, p.30079).

Consonant with what has been said thus far,
the leadership of a multi-homeland state that has
not adopted the ethno-political myth of a homeland
state is less the natural enemy of diaporas than is
the leadership of a state that has. This in itself
is obviously no guarantee that such leadership will
not occasionally find it convenient to go scapegoating at the expense of aliens, as occurred

during 1983 in Nigeria, when some two million "illegal aliens" were forcibly expelled on short notice. Nevertheless, it cannot be gainsaid that the central leadership in such multi-homeland states as Ethiopia, Ghana, India, Indonesia, Nigeria, Pakistan, and Zaire had advocated the disappearance of the various ethno-national identities in favor of a single statewide one and has also advocated the erosion of homelands into an undifferentiated statewide territory.[17]

In some extreme cases, central authorities have adopted the myth that a statewide people already exists, creating such a people by simple fiat. Thus, the creation of a Yugoslav state was justified on the grounds that there existed a South-slav (Yugoslav) ethno-nation, of which the Serbs, Croats and Slovenes were merely tribal subgroups and their languages only dialects. Czechoslovakia was justified on the ground that Czechs and Slovaks constituted a single nation. Somewhat similar was Franco's myth concerning a single Spanish people, which justified his outlawing of the languages and other overt national peculiarities of the Basques and Catalans. Yet another somewhat analogous case is offered by France which, until quite recently, nurtured the myth of a single, statewide, French people by prohibiting the publication of news concerning nationalist movements and activities occurring in areas such as Brittany and Corsica.[18] All these myths were ultimately forced to give way before incontrovertible evidence of flourishing ethno-nationalism on the part of substate homeland peoples.[19]

Such extreme actions aside, centrists do, as noted, endeavor to erase the significance of homelands. The right of all citizens to free movement and residence within all parts of the state is viewed by the central authorities as a requisite characteristic of statehood. Typifying this conviction is Article 19 of the Indian Constitution which ordains that all citizens "shall have the right to move freely throughout the territory [and] to reside and settle in any part of the territory of India." But in proclaiming and enforcing such a right, the state's authority directly challenges the primal claim of the homeland dwelling people to protect the homeland from an undesired alien presence. And, as a host of examples make clear, intruders into the homeland are no less alien for being compatriots. Basque and Catalan ethno-

27

nationalism has grown more violent in response to the increased immigration of Castillians. Corsicans have responded similarly to French incursions. An emotional Quebecois slogan proclaiming we must be "Masters in Our Home" reflects the reaction to anglophones within Quebec Province. Polls show that some three-quarters of Slovenia's population oppose further immigration from Yugoslavia's other republics (see, for example, **DANAS**, Zagreb, July 4, 1982). The authorities of the Chinese People's Republic have often admitted that the presence of Han in the non-Han homelands has caused resentment, violence, and a rise in secessionist sentiment. "Russian, Go Home!" has been expressed within such diverse Soviet homelands as Latvia and Uzbekistan. And it is known that leaders of some Soviet republics have discouraged heightened investment in their republics because it would be followed by greater immigration.[20]

Homeland psychology therefore operates within the multi-homeland state, as well as in the homeland state. Whether the former does in fact offer a greater measure of security to diasporas depends upon the will and the capability of the central authorities to ensure the right to reside anywhere within the state. As to will, given the fact that homeland psychology is present in each homeland comprising the state, there is always the danger that the central leadership will essay to bolster its sagging popularity or to deflect blame for catastrophe by suddenly embracing what it knows will be the popular course of scapegoating the alien. This was, as noted, certainly the course of events followed in Nigeria in 1983, when the government--facing both a severe economic downturn and an approaching election--suddenly found more than two million illegal immigrants within the state. Their enforced roundup and expulsion was roundly applauded by the media and the public.[21]

Diasporas also risk the possibility of a revolutionary change of government. Thus, a number of diaspora communities within Iran were afforded protection by the Pahlevi dynasty. As that dynasty began to crumble in the late 1970s, some diaspora members sensed that the revolutionary forces boded ill for them and fled the country. Others were sorely to wish they had.

With the best of intentions, governments may still be unable to protect the right of statewide residence. The earlier cited constitutional right to settle anywhere within India certainly did precious little to protect settlers in Assam from atrocities at the hands of that region's "sons of the soil" in early 1983.[22] As endemic violence in Basqueland, Corisca, and Northern Ireland testifies, it is extremely difficult for the authorities of even a highly integrated state to stamp out violence that is locally perceived as perpetrated "in defense of homeland."

The conclusion is that neither homeland states nor multi-homeland states provide healthy environments for diasporas. The latter is to be preferred over the former if it has a government committed to statewide settlement and the will and capability to enforce that commitment. Even this unlikely combination of forces does not eradicate the danger posed by homeland psychology. The reception accorded to aliens in the homeland is hardly affected by proclamations concerning the rights of citizens, and local xenophobia can surface at any time.

MORE SPECIALIZED SITUATIONS AND THEIR CORRESPONDING MYTHS

There are a number of states whose ethnographic composition and/or ethno-political myths do not fall within the categories of homeland and multi-homeland states. Space precludes adequate treatment, but a skeletal treatment of some of the more important is offered below. Unmistakably the most important to a discussion of the reception accorded to diasporas is the immigrant society.

The Immigrant State and Its Myth

The immigrant state is one essentially devoid of homelands. Small segments of its populated area being homelands does not disqualify it. The United States, for example, having absorbed more than 50 million immigrants in its history, certainly merits inclusion as an immigrant state, despite several Amerindian homelands (reservations) within its confines and despite some indications of a homeland consciousness among Spanish-speaking peoples throughout the southwest. Similarly, non-Quebec Canada merits inclusion, despite Amerindian and Eskimo homelands. The important fact is that most of the population lives in non-homeland territory. As we are reminded by the bleaker aspects of

the treatment historically accorded Amerindians of
the United States, homelands need not always have
been absent. Earlier homeland dwellers may have
been killed or driven out. But whatever the reason
for the absence of homelands, the pattern of
imigration was important for maintaining their
absence. It was essential that the settlers were
diverse in ethnic background. Where large waves of
a people have migrated and settled in a concentrated pattern (for example, Afrikaners and
Quebecois), a new ethnic homeland sprang up. Yet, a
key to the immigrant society is that all legal
settlers have an equal claim upon it, regardless of
their ethno-national background.

All of this is reflected in the ethno-
political myth of "the Americans" as "a nation of
nations." The fictional, archetypal American is
regularly depicted as the progeny of several
diverse ethnic strains, a polygenetic legatee of
the melting pot process. The psychological
importance of such a myth should not be
underestimated. Surely, for example, it would be a
less traumatic step for a Scottish emigre to the
United States to become one of "them," a
polygenetic American, than it would be for a
Scottish emigre to London to become an Englishman.
Psychological receptivity to an ethnically neutral
identity is one thing; to exchange one ethno-
national identity for another is something else.
One can undertake the first with one's emotional
memory-bank intact; there is no need to deny
"one's blood" or one's ancestry. Moreover, the
myth of the polygenetic American undermined
psychological barriers to inter-ethnic marriage.
The ethno-national injunction to "Marry one of your
own kind!", though certainly not unknown in the
United States, could not there, unlike in a
homeland, find support in the publicly espoused
standards of the society. In thus exerting a
restraining influence upon ethnically endogamous
precepts, the melting pot myth contained a self-
fulfilling quality.

It is important here to distinguish between
myth and reality. The history of immigration to
the United States certainly has not been so sublime
a tale as the myth of the melting pot suggests.
The manner in which the immigrant and his des-
cendents were received by "fellow Americans" was
often hardly the type of reception that one would
expect from co-members of the family. As numerous
cultural histories of the United States have docu-

mented, the prejudice and bias against "newcomers" have often been great. And, despite the official myth of the melting pot, this lack of hospitality on the part of descendants of earlier settlers has been predicated upon a notion of ethnic purity. While the vision of the polygenetic, melted-down American was the publicly espoused vision held out to the immigrant and to the world at large, it did not follow that this view was shared by the preponderant number of the dominant group, those who at any one time considered themselves to be "the true Americans."

This self-held ethnic image of "the true Americans" underwent significant changes over time. In the early decades of the country's history, despite the presence of Germans, Dutch, Scots, Irish and others, the English clearly predominated, and the "true American" was quite regularly described as a transplanted Englishman. When in the 1840s this view of self was thought to be threatened by proportionally large-scale immigration of non-English peoples, particularly Germans and Irish, the result was a nativist movement (and the Know-Nothing Party), which aimed at prohibiting such immigration.[23] Later in the century, fresh waves of immigration ignited a similar response. Meanwhile, however, the notion of "the true American" had broadened to include all of the older immigrants from northwestern Europe (with the exception of the Irish), on the presumption that such people shared a common Nordic or Teutonic ancestry. As the descendants of the older, non-English immigrants achieved upward mobility, the respectability accompanying success transformed them into quite acceptable marriage partners. However, while escaping its narrow English base, the new self-image of "the true Americans" retained a sense of ethnic purity, as shown (1) in attempts to prevent immigration by peoples from outside of northwestern Europe and (2) in prejudice toward those who had already emigrated from those other areas.

Prior to 1890, immigration had been almost totally from northwestern Europe. But then a sudden change took place. In the last decade of the nineteenth century, more than half of the total immigration came from eastern and southern Europe, and, in the following decade, the proportion reached almost three-quarters of the total. Meanwhile, oriental immigration had become an issue on the west coast.

Ethnic reaction again followed. Nativist organizations, such as the American Protective Association, appeared, as did a resuscitated Ku Klux Klan, dedicated now not just to white supremacy but to Nordic supremacy as well. Such opinions were restricted to extreme elements of the population. Supporting their arguments with the pseudo-scientific theory of the day (the application of Darwinism to human society), the evident virtues of the Teutonic peoples and the vices of all the others were paraded in the "responsible, socially acceptable literature" almost to the eve of World War II.

The period also saw a number of restrictive immigration measures enacted into law. Oriental immigration was effectively throttled through Chinese exclusion acts, a so-called "Gentlemen's Agreement" with Japan, and the creation of an "Asiatic Barred Zone." Legislation applied to the peoples of southern and eastern Europe, if more subtle in wording, was the same in intent. The intent to exclude was only thinly disguised by various formulae which established quotas for immigrants in terms of the percentage of the United States' population represented by each ethno-national group at some prescribed, previous date. Consonant with their intent, the formulae heavily favored immigration from northwestern Europe. They represented an attempt to freeze the ethnic clock or, indeed, to turn it back to a time when "the true American" was not so endangered by mongrelization.

Although the clamor for a dropping of such quotas grew over the years, and although some of the worst features of the restrictive laws were with time ameliorated, the system of quotas predicated upon national origin remained in effect until the mid-1960s. Its time, however, was well over, for there is ample evidence that in the post-World War II era, the publicly espoused myth of the polygenetic American family finally pervaded the subconscious of a significant proportion of the dominant group.[24] With John Kennedy's election in 1960, there was firm evidence that even the highest elective office in the country was not beyond the reach of non-Nordics. More significant than the numerous examples of success by non-Nordics, however, has been the increasing acceptability of non-Nordics as marriage partners. The jump in the number of intermarriages in the postwar period signifies a major blurring of ethnic lines.[25]

The experience of the United States would

therefore appear to add credence to the thesis that homelands serve as a major determinant of the reception accorded to diasporas. In their absence, the probability of a diaspora finding a safe haven is greatly enhanced. Where the myth of the immigrant society harmonizes rather well with reality, diasporas can come to feel "at home."[26] Their claim is the equal of any other's.

Sub-Homeland States and Their Myths

We have noted that homelands are regularly dissected by state borders. Kurdistan, for example, is divided among Iran, Iraq, Syria, Turkey and the Soviet Union. But since the Kurds are not dominant in any of these states, neither they nor their homeland are reflected in any of the states' ethno-political myths. By contrast, the myth of Ireland, West Germany, and at least seventeen of the eighteen Arab states is that the state forms part of a larger homeland.[27] In the case of Germany and Ireland, myth and behavior are in close accord. West Germany has absorbed large numbers of refugees from the homeland's eastern sector, and Ireland, in effect, refuses to recognize the legality of the border separating the northern and southern sectors.[28] The case of the Arab states is more complex.

With the partial exception of Morocco, the symbols, institutions, and popular allusions of leaders--those elements we have identified as contributing to the ethno-political myth--are designed in the case of the Arab states to foster an image of the state's inhabitants as part of a larger Arab nation and an image of the state's territory as part of a "Great Arab Homeland" extending uninterrupted from the Persian Gulf (called by many Arabs, the Arab Gulf) to the Atlantic. In five of the eighteen Arab countries even the formal title of the state serves to remind the populace of their trans-state ethnic identity. The word Arab appears in the official name of the Arab Republic of Egypt, the Socialist People's Libyan Arab Jamahiriya, the Syrian Arab Republic, the United Arab Emirates, and the Yemen Arab Republic. The liberation front in the Western Sahara (Polisario) also thought it advisable to employ the word Arab when they proclaimed the Saharan Arab Democratic Republic in 1976.

State flags and symbols also often reflect an

Arab-wide, rather than a state-wide, focus. Fifty
percent of the eighteen flags fall into this category. Those of Jordan, Kuwait, and the United Arab
Emirates purposefully flaunt the four colors associated with the Arab revolt against the Ottoman
Empire, while those of Egypt, Iraq, Sudan, Syria,
and both Yemens are intentionally close facsimiles
of the original horizontal tricolor associated with
Nasserism. The two most popular state symbols are
Saladin's eagle and the Hawk of Quraish, both popularly associated with Arab greatness (even though
Saladin was a Kurd).

Emphasis on Arabness rather than on state
identity is also pronounced in the case of state
constitutions. Of the sixteen state constitutions
in existence, twelve explicitly state that the
populace is part of the Arab nation; another
(Algeria) does so implicitly by stipulating that
Arab unity is a goal of the society; and still
another (Sudan) waffles on the issue in an attempt
to assuage the sensibilities of the large black
component of the population.[29] Lebanon and Morocco are the only states whose constitutions make no
reference to an Arab identity. Lebanon's case is
traceable to its heterogeneous population. However, the chaos that has enveloped that society
since 1975 was triggered by the interrelated issues
of "Who is a true Arab?" and the responsibility of
Lebanon to support "the Arab cause" of the Palestinians. Those who have subsequently attempted to
reconcile the major elements of the population have
considered it **de rigueur** to stress the Arab nature
and commitment of the society. Morocco appears to
be the one case where the Arab identity of the
population is played down. Not only does the Constitution refrain from mention of the Arab nation
but, by describing the King as "Leader of the
Faithful, Supreme Representative of the Nation,
Symbol of its unity, guarantor of the perpetuity
and continuity of the State" (Article 19), it implicitly recognizes a Moroccan nation and rejects
the goal of Arab unity. By contrast, seven of the
sixteen constitutions explicitly pledge support for
Arab union (unification of the homeland), thereby
admitting, in the state's most basic document, the
state's provisional, stepping-stone character.[30]

In Saudi Arabia and Oman, neither of which has
a constitution, coronation speeches are the closest
thing to an official statement concerning the fundamental nature and purposes of the state. King
Khalid's coronation address identified Arab unity

as one of the two pillars of the Saudi state.[31]
The Omani sultan was more cautious in his wording
at the time of coronation, but he also tied the
destiny of Oman to the Arab World.[32]
Overall, then, the key documents of seventeen
of the eighteen states stress the Arab nature of
their population, and eight of the eighteen commit
themselves to the pursuit of the union of the Arab
homeland. The ethno-political myth of common Arabness
and Arabdom has been sorely tested in recent years
as a result of the huge numbers of Arabs who migrated from their state to some other region of
Arabdom. Statistics are woefully inadequate, but
there are several million such Arabs today, most of
them having been attracted by opportunities in the
oil-mining states.[33] They represent significant
proportions of the population of Iraq, Libya, Saudi
Arabia, and the Gulf states. In Kuwait and Qatar,
they nearly equal in number the indigenous Arabs
and, in the United Arab Emirates, they outnumber
them.

For a time, the fact of common Arabness and
language made the Arabs preferred immigrants.[34]
But increasingly they came to be viewed by the
ruling cliques as a threat to regime-survival. In
addition to being able to converse individually
with the indigenous Arabs, the Arab migrants (particularly the Egyptians and Palestinians) had become powerful forces in the fields of education and
communication and were therefore able to exert
great influence on public opinion.[35] Bereft of
any traditional ties to the state within which they
were working, these young intellectuals represented
the potential carriers of revolutionary, anti-
regime, pan-Arab sentiments. Consequently, the
regimes have been trying to decrease the number of
immigrant Arabs within their domains, contracting
instead with Far Eastern states to provide labor on
a project-by-project basis.[36]

Here, then, we have the mirror image of the
situation in the multi-homeland state. There the
migrant could invoke the myth of the state and
hopefully look to the government for a champion,
but he risked the wrath of the homeland people.
Here, the migrant could invoke the myth of the
homeland and expect a significant reception from
the local people, but he risked the wrath of the
government. In any case, the Arab migrants have
given rise to real tension between the myth officially propagated by the state apparati and the

behavior of the apparati. Arab freedom to reside
anywhere within the homeland is being circumscribed.

Still Other Myths

The preceding discussion does not exhaust the list
of myths that influence the reception accorded to
diasporas. Among those overlooked are (1) the
postcolonial commonwealth myth propagated by a
number of former colonial powers, according to
which citizens of the commonwealth were to be able
to settle in the mother country, if they so wished;
(2) the Marxist-Leninist myth under which nations
and homelands are presumed to be increasingly
losing their significance within socialist societies and particularly within the current Soviet
society of "developed" or "mature" socialism, and;
(3) the trans-state/trans-homeland myth of freedom
of settlement, such as that associated with the
European Economic Community and the Common Nordic
Labor Market. The first was discarded when
challenged by the reality of former colonials
presumptuously trying to exercise the right to
settle in the mother country. The second is retained as a myth of Marxist-Leninist states, despite a growing gap between it and actual trends.
The third has yet to be tested by significant
migration, although the guestworker experience in
Europe suggests this myth too would prove a poor
reflection of reality.

Global Ramifications

Despite the appalling record of ill-treatment that
diasporas have received at the hands of homeland
peoples, population movement into homelands has
been increasing. Migrations have been a constant
of history, but their magnitude, as Kingsley Davis
has recorded, has been accelerating (1974, pp.93-
105). There are no adequate figures reflecting the
number of people currently living within a territory perceived as a homeland by others. Were the
data available, to arrive at such a number one
would begin by totalling the number of non-indige-
nous residents of all homeland and multi-homeland
states. To this mammoth figure would be added
those many millions of people living within their
own multi-homeland state but outside their particu-

lar homeland. Excluding immigrant states, nearly all countries would contribute to the overall figure. As noted, the already meager list of essentially homogeneous homeland states has been further pared in recent years by the influx of **Gastarbeiter** into such countries as Sweden and West Germany.

The incidents resulting from this massive penetration of homelands will necessarily influence relations among states. Relations between Belgrade and Bonn are affected by the treatment accorded Yugoslavian **Gastarbeiter** in Germany; New Delhi-Colombo relations by the treatment of Tamils in Sri Lanka; Peking-Jakarta relations by the current status of Chinese in Indonesia; and Accra-Lagos relations by the treatment of Ghanaians in Nigeria. Moreover, the diaspora need not have originated in another state for it to have trans-state political ramifications. No longer can serious violations of human rights be shielded by the simple assertion that the matter is one that falls within the internal affairs of the state. The Universal Declaration of Human Rights, the Genocide Convention, the Council of Europe's Commission of Human Rights, the American Declaration of the Rights and Duties of Man, the human rights sections of the Helsinki Accords, a growing number of General Assembly resolutions deploring alleged violations of human rights in one or another country, the Carter administration's tying of U.S. foreign assistance to a state's current record of respect for human rights, a number of bilateral agreements concerning the rights of specific diasporas, and the growing frequency with which governments berate one another for alleged violations of human rights, all attest to a growing consensus that active concern for the protection of people does not constitute "intervention in the internal affairs of a state." The fact that the positions taken by governments on such matters often demonstrate a remarkably flexible standard, suggesting propaganda and expediency rather than principle as the underlying motivation, as well as a tendency to judge the behavior of one's enemies by a stricter yardstick than that of oneself or one's allies, should not obscure the fact that the foreign policy objectives of states are often negatively influenced by the state's image with regard to human rights (South Africa being the outstanding case in point). And governments acknowledge this fact by expending great effort to counter such an image. In sum, given the ubiquity of homelands and the enormity of modern migrations, the homeland-alien syndrome has become a significant factor in global politics. In any case, the discussion presented above is at best exploratory. It has attempted to discern --however dimly--how the degree of congruity between ethnic and political borders helps to shape ethno-political myths which, in turn, affect the fortunes of diasporas. The topic, by nature, has an elusive, will-o'-the-wisp quality to it. Psychological perceptions of homelands and the myths to which they give rise are the stuff that dreams are made of. But it is dreams and perceptions that shape our behavior. And as Harold Isaacs (1975, p. 51) has cogently noted:

> We are not as far as we may think from the myths to which...we keep eternally returning, and these myths have heavily to do with the place with which we identify ourselves.

Notes

1 References to the sacred homeland or sacred soil are quite common elements in nationalist perorations. Thus, a leader in the Guatemalan revolution has stated on Cuban radio: "When we speak of our right to our land, this includes not only an economic factor because land also entails a cultural aspect since the land is sacred to us." (FBIS, July 1, 1982, p. 6). This same ascription of sacredness to the homeland is occasionally found in more dispassionate tracts. About the concept of 'fatherland' see for example, Ziya Gok Alp (1959, p. 178). "It means a sacred piece of land for whose sake people shed their blood. Why is it that all other lands are not sacred, but only that which is called the fatherland? And how does it happen that those who believe this way do not hesitate to sacrifice their lives, their families, their most beloved ones? Evidently, not because of any utilitarian value."

In **Richard II**, Shakespeare described England as "this blessed plot." More recently, the late Cardinal Wyszynski of Poland noted: "Next to God, our first love is Poland. After God, one must above all remain faithful to our homeland, to the Polish national culture." (**International Herald Tribune,** May 29, 1981).

2 Cholpan Ergash "Recognizing the Homeland" as cited by Edward Allworth (1973, p. 15).

3 Jamal Kamal, "Homeland," cited by Robert J.

Barrett (1973, pp. 31-32).

4   Turar Kojomberdiev, as cited by Allworth (1973, p. 16).

5   Some writers have discerned in this attachment to place a sociobiological impulse, termed "the Territorial Imperative." For an exposition on this school, particularly in the works of Konrad Lorenz, Robert Ardrey, and Desmond Morris, see Lowis L. Snyder (1975, pp. 1-21).

6   A series of studies conducted within the multi-homeland Soviet Union establishes that residence within or without one's homeland heavily influences attitudes and behavior. Residence influences, **inter alia**, willingness to learn a second language, willingness to enter into an inter-ethnic marriage, the choice of national identity on the part of children resulting from inter-ethnic marriage, and--what is most germane here--attitudes toward other national groups. Residents of the homeland harbor greater hostility toward members of other national groups. For details, see Walker Conner (1984, Ch. 11).

7   In France, for example, physical and verbal attacks have in recent years been much more aimed at Algerian Arabs than at Blacks from Subsaharan Africa. When Myron Weiner undertook his valuable research on nativism within India (1978), Assamese hostility was aimed principally at Bengali Hindus. The Bengali Muslims were not perceived as a threat and had in effect become allies of the Assamese (pp. 110, 124). And yet, when the genocidal explosion occurred in 1983 in Assam, the principal target was the Bengali-Muslim community.

8   It was the realization of this vulnerability of diasporas, predicated upon centuries of experience in a broad sampling of homelands, that gave rise to the urge for the reinstitution of a Jewish homeland. See Salo Wittmayer Baron (1960, pp. 227 **et seq.**).

9   The growing attachment to a reunified homeland was reflected in a poll published in April 1982 when, for the first time, a majority of West Germans indicated that they would welcome reunification even at the expense of withdrawal from NATO and a policy of rigid neutrality. **New York Times,** April 12, 1982.

10   The maximum that Japan agreed to accept was only five hundred, and this number was never processed. By contrast, the United States agreed to accept 161,000. Ethnically homogeneous Norway, with a population only one-thirtieth that of Japan,

agreed to accept six times more settlers than would Tokyo. For a full listing of receiving states and the numbers accepted, see **Keesing's Contemporary Archives** (1979, p. 30082).

Japan's sole alien community of significant size is that of the Koreans, and this residue of empire suffers from severe prejudice. See James Lewis (1981, pp. 23-30). The only other significant minority, the outcast "Buraku-min," is indigenous, although there have been spurious charges that they are of Korean origin.

11 Arnold Rose (1969). This posthumously published work was completed in 1967, but includes data going back to the 1950s.

12 Stephen Castles and Godula Kosack (1973, p. 168). Rose (1969, p. 110) reports a lower affirmative response to this question in another poll, although a majority (51 percent) were still prepared to make sacrifices in order to remove the alien presence.

13 For the history of the treatment accorded the migrants at both the official and unofficial levels, see Daniel Kubat et al. (1979), which includes contributions covering the experiences of the United Kingdom, Austria, the Benelux states, France, West Germany, Denmark, Norway, Finland, Sweden, and Switzerland; Ronald E. Krane (1979) with contributions on Sweden, Switzerland, West Germany, the United Kingdom, the Netherlands, and France; and Mark J. Miller (1981). See also Cheryl Benard (1978, pp. 277-299); Andrei Markovits and Samantha Kazasinov (1978, pp. 373-391); and Ray Rist (1979, pp. 201-218).

For an interesting discussion of the factors helping to account for guestworkers returning to their own country, see W.R. Bohning (1981, pp. 37-40). After examining a host of variables, including personal data (age, sex, skills, rural/urban origin, previous work experience, status and pay in host country, etc.), whether separated from or united with family in the host society, and even stated intention to return or remain, the author concludes that the only index to prediction is nationality (i.e., whether Italian, Greek, etc.).

14 West Germany had earlier absorbed large numbers of Germans from East Germany and Eastern Europe without serious incident. Unlike the case of aliens, the right of these Germans to settle in or move about the homeland was apparently considered incontrovertible.

15 Czechoslovakia is uniquely titled, since

it draws attention to two ethnic homelands.

16   The diaspora theme of Israel's anthem ("The hope that has lived over thousands of years to be a free nation in our own land, the holy land, the land of Israel") underlines the dichotomy between the myth and the ethnic composition of the population.

17   The central leadership of multi-homeland states will obviously deviate from this behavior pattern where the political system is predicated upon true decentralization of decision-making. Switzerland therefore offers the polar exception to the general tendency of the central leadership to promote integration.

18   See the intriguing article by Christian Coulon (1978, pp. 60-79). The effectiveness of this stratagem is suggested by the fact that at the 1973 annual meeting of the Northeast Political Science Association, two months before the French Government felt compelled to alter its policy and publicly outlaw four national liberation movements operating in Brittany and Corsica, I was criticized for referring to ethno-national strivings in both areas. My critic, a French specialist who annually visited Brittany, had detected no such activity or sentiment and flatly denied their existence.

19   Some similarity may be glimpsed between the above cases and the myth of the "new Soviet man," a transnational image currently propagated by the government of the Soviet Union.

20   For details on the Yugoslav, Chinese and Soviet experiences, see Conner (1984, Chapter 11).

21   See the **New York Times**, February 3, 1983, for numerous references to the expulsion's popularity. It is also pertinent to our theme to note that the government of multi-homeland Ghana, from whence had come most of the migrants, hesitated to accept them back because of the fear that this massive influx would adversely affect the country's political stability. Finally, the government asked each homeland ("tribal") leader to accept those returnees who belonged to its ethno-national group. The government thus showed itself to be very sensitive to homeland psychology. See the **New York Times**, January 30, 1983.

22 The government's failure to offer ample protection while refusing to delay elections that were being attacked by Assamese spokesmen was the more poignant because the outbreak of violence was preceded by months of warning. See, for example, the **New York Times**, December 2, 1982 for an article

entitled "India's Assam Cauldron Bubbles
Dangerously Again." The article notes the
prevalence of the "Deport the foreigners!" sentiment. Weiner (1978) is indispensable reading for
the historical and psychological roots of the situation.
    23 The evolution of anglophone Canada's sense
of identity shows remarkable parallels to that of
the United States. See Carl Berger (pp. 3-26)
and Douglas Nord (1978, pp. 116-133).
    24 Harold Isaacs (1975) has perspicaciously
captured the significance of the myth or, as he
calls it, "the dominant credo":
    Group behavior in America was like all group
    behavior where differences of race, religion,
    origin, and culture were involved. That is to
    say, it was full of hate, fear, contempt, and
    was organized in pecking orders of scales and
    levels of dominating and being dominated.
    Several generations of Jews in America, like
    other immigrant and minority groups, suffered
    much the same apartness, rejection, and exclu-
    sion that was the common lot of the Jews in
    Europe. The difference was that the dominant
    credo of the society was in constant con-
    tradiction with this behavior. It proclaimed
    secular equality; its dominant religion
    preached brotherhood. Weak as the spirit was
    compared to the flesh, it still made life
    different in America from life in Europe.
    25 For some pertinent statistics, see Walker
Conner (1979, pp. 57-67). Somewhat paradoxically,
the increase in intermarriage is occurring simultaneously with a well-documented revival of interest in one's pre-American national heritage (what
has been popularly termed "the new ethnicity"). It
should be pointed out that while the heightened
intermarriage rates include people of Oriental
(mainly Chinese and Japanese) descent, marriages
between blacks and non-blacks, while showing a
small upswing, remain extremely low.
    26 Australia is an immigrant state, but the
evolution of its myth is quite different from the
American and non-Quebec Canadian ones. For generations it practiced a British only immigration
policy and until very recently (1973), a "Whites
Only" one. Its myth has changed to "open to everyone" (subject to restrictions on numbers), but a
gap remains between this myth and reality. New
Zealand's experience and the evolution of its myth
also have unique features (particularly reflecting

the proportionately large indigenous population of
Maori), but it is closer to Australia in experience
and myth than to the United States or Canada.
   27   The eighteen states are Algeria, Bahrain,
Egypt, Iraq, Jordan, Kuwait, Lebanon, Libya, Morocco, Oman, Qatar, Saudi Arabia, Sudan, Syria, Tunisia, the United Arab Emirates, and northern and
southern Yemen.   In addition to these states and
Palestine, the Arab homeland, at least in the opinion of some Arabs, one could also include   the
Western Sahara ("the Saharan Arab Democratic Republic"), part, if not all, of Mauritania, and sections of Iran and Turkey which are contiguous to
Arab states and in which Arabs predominate.
   28   Dublin has not recognized the British
claim to incorporation of the homeland's six
northeastern counties into the United   Kingdom, and
peaceful re-unification remains an official commitment.
   29   Article 1 of the Constitution notes that
Sudan "is part of both the Arab and African enti-
ties."
   30 The Syrian Constitution goes further, intentionally eschewing the word "state" in favor of
describing the unit merely as a "region" of the
Arab World.
   31   On March 25, 1975, in his first major
speech following his coronation, King Khalid noted
that the Kingdom of Saudi Arabia is based upon "two
pillars, Islamic solidarity and Arab unity, [and]
considers itself a source of support to every Arab
and in the service of every Arab, and it aims at
cooperation, solidarity and fraternity."
   32   In his coronation speech of July 24, 1970,
the Sultan pledged "to restore our past glory and
to obtain our prominent place in the Arab world."
   33   Palestinians and Egyptians are the two
largest components.   For U.S. State Department
estimates of the distribution of Palestinians by
state, see the **New York Times**, August 12, 1982.
For a discussion of the Egyptian diaspora, see
Maurice Martin (1981, pp. 1-25).
   34   Several states introduced laws requiring
that preferences be assigned first to indigenous
Arabs, then to other Arabs, and finally to non-
Arabs.   See, for example, Emile A. Nakleh (1977,
pp. 148-150).
   35   Tawfic Farah, Faisal Al-Salem, and Maria
Kolman Al-Salem (1980, p. 25) and Philip L. Martin
and Marion F. Houston (1979, p. 320).
   36   Under these contracts, the labor teams are

not permitted to bring dependents, are kept isolated from the host society, and are repatriated as
soon as the project is completed. In some cases,
the workers return each night to a ship during the
project.

REFERENCES

Allworth, Edward. 1973. Regeneration in Central
Asia. In **The Nationality Question in Soviet
Central Asia,** ed. Edward Allworth. New York:
Praeger Publishers.
Alp, Ziya Gok. 1959. Nation and Fatherland. In
**Turkish Nationalism and Western Civilization,
Selected Essays of Ziya Gok Alp.** London: Allen
and Unwin.
Baron, Salo Wittmayer. 1960. **Modern Nationalism
and Religion.** New York: Meridian Books.
Barrett, Robert J. 1973. Convergence and the Na-
tionality Literature of Central Asia. In **The
Nationality Question in Soviet Central Asia.**
See Allworth 1973.
Benard, Cheryl. 1978. Migrant Workers and European
Democracy. **Political Science Quarterly** 93.
Berger, Carl. The True North, Strong and Free. In
Nationalism in Canada, ed. Peter Russell.
Toronto: McGraw-Hill.
Bohning, W. R. 1981. Estimating the Propensity of
Guestworkers to Leave. **Monthly Labor Review.**
Castles, Stephen and Godula Kosack. 1973. **Immigrant
Workers and Class Structure in Western Eu-
rope.** London: Oxford University Press.
Conner, Walker. 1979. America's Melting Pot: Myth
or Reality. In **Societies in Transition.** Ham-
burg: University of Hamburg Press.
-----. 1984. **The National Question in Marxist-
Leninist Theory and Strategy.** Princeton:
Princeton University Press.
Coulon, Christian. 1978. French Political Science
and Regional Diversity: A Strategy of Silence.
Ethnic and Racial Studies 1.
Davis, Kingsley. 1974. The Migration of Human
Populations. **Scientific American** 231 (Sept):
993-105.
Farah, Tawfic, Faisal Al-Salem and Maria Kolman
Al-Salem. 1980. Alienation and Expatriate
Labor in Kuwait. **Journal of South Asian and
Middle Asian Studies** 4.
Furnivall, J.S. 1948. **Colonial Policy and Practice.**
Cambridge: Cambridge University Press.

Isaacs, Harold. 1975. **Idols of the Tribe: Group Identity and Political Change.** New York: Harper and Row.

Keesing's Contemporary Archives 1979, 1980.

Kramer, Jane. 1976. The Invandrare. **The New Yorker** 52 (May).

Krane, Ronald E., ed. 1979. **International Labor Migration in Europe.** New York: Praeger Publishers.

Kubat, Daniel, et al., eds. 1979. **The Politics of Migration Policies: The First World in the 1970s.** New York: Center for Migration Studies.

Lewis, James. 1981. Korean in Japan. **East-West Perspectives** 2.

Markovits, Andrei and Samantha Kazasinov. 1978. Class Conflict, Capitalism and Social Democracy: The Case of Migrant Workers in the Federal Republic of Germany. **Comparative Politics** 10, no. 3.

Martin, Maurice. 1981. Egyptians Abroad and in the Arab World. In **Arab Society 1978-1979: Reflections and Realities.** Beirut: Center for the Study of the Modern Arab World, Saint Joseph's University, Beirut, Dar El-Mashreq Publishers.

Martin, Philip L. and Marion F. Houston. 1979. The Future of International Migration. **Journal of International Affairs** 33.

Miller, Mark J. 1981. **Foreign Workers in Western Europe: An Emerging Political Force.** New York: Praeger Publishers.

Nakhleh, Emile A. 1977. Labor Markets and Citizenship in Bahrayn and Qatar. **Middle East Journal** 31, no.2.

Nord, Douglas. 1978. The 'Problem' of Immigration: The Continuing Presence of the Stranger Within Our Gates. **American Review of Canadian Studies** 8.

Rist, Ray. 1979. The European Economic Community and Manpower Migrations: Policies and Prospects. **Journal of International Affairs** 33.

Rose, Arnold. 1969. **Migrants in Europe.** Minneapolis: University of Minnesota Press.

Snyder, Louis L. 1975. Nationalism and the Territorial Imperative. **Canadian Review of Studies in Nationalism** 3.

Weiner, Myron. 1978. **Sons of the Soil: Migration and Ethnic Conflict in India.** Princeton: Princeton University Press.

Newspapers and Periodicals

International Herald Tribune
The New Yorker
New York Times
Washington Post

LABOR MIGRATIONS AS INCIPIENT DIASPORAS

Myron Weiner

A new class has emerged in many of the world's industrial and oil-producing economies: the foreign workers. Foreign workers are not immigrants. They are not entitled to become citizens. They are allowed to remain in their host country only to work, and can be forced by the government to leave. Except as allowed by the government, they cannot bring their wives and children, and may not be entitled to the social benefits or political rights given to citizens. Many foreign workers live on the edge of the law: some have entered illegally, changed their jobs illegally, or overstayed their entry visas.

Foreign workers are almost always ethnically distinct. Often they differ from the population of their host country in their race, religion, culture, and almost always in their language. The host society does not encourage foreign workers to assimilate with the native population, change their national identity, or mix socially with the locals. The host society and government prefer that they remain foreign, for it is assumed that someday they will return home to their native country.

Despite the intention of governments and the expectations of nationals, a large proportion of foreign workers remains indefinitely in the host country, living in a state of legal and political ambiguity, economic insecurity and as social outsiders, if not outcasts. The children who have come with them, or have been born within the host country, are in an even more ambiguous position; though more at home in their host country than in the land of their parents, they too are expected to return "home."

This essay explores some of the international relations and domestic political consequences (for both the sending and receiving countries) of this phenomenon of people moving across international borders to work in one country while remaining citizens of another. Though I shall provide a global perspective, I shall pay particular attention to the determinants and consequences of international labor migration to the oil-producing Persian gulf countries and to Western Europe, and the differences and similarities between these two groups of countries.

Global Magnitudes

No one knows for sure how many foreign workers there are in the world, partly because their turnover often precludes accurate record-keeping, partly because some governments have no system of counting and reporting or they deliberately under-report their numbers, partly because many foreign workers are illegal , and partly because the category of "foreign workers" is itself unclear.

Western Europe, it is estimated, now has about five million foreign workers and perhaps another six million dependents, with foreign workers coming mainly from North Africa, Portugal, Yugoslavia, Greece, southern Italy and Turkey. The oil-rich countries of the Middle East have about three million foreign workers, recruited from the non-oil producing Arab countries, South Asia and as far away as the Philippines, Thailand, South Korea and Taiwan. The United States does not admit non-immigrant temporary workers in any significant numbers, but there are an estimated four to six million illegal workers and their families in the country, predominantly from Mexico and elsewhere in Latin America and the Caribbean. Oil-producing Nigeria imported some two million workers, both illegal and legal, from neighboring countries, especially Togo, Benin and Ghana, but expelled large numbers early in 1983. South Africa has about 400,000 miners imported from its neighbors. Venezuela has about a million workers mostly from Columbia. Singapore recruits 50,000 workers from Indonesia and Malaysia. There are an estimated 45,000 Vietnamese employed in Soviet Siberia and in several Eastern European countries. And there are seasonal flows of labor across international boundaries in many parts of central Africa and in South and Southeast Asia. There are also daily flows of workers across some international bounda-

ries. Of particular international importance are
the tens of thousands of Arab workers who cross the
Green Line into Israel daily from the West Bank and
Gaza.

Ordinarily not included in the category of
foreign workers are international refugees, especially when they reside in refugee camps and are
not part of the labor force. But there are instances in which refugees become part of the foreign worker labor force, such as Palestinians in
Kuwait and in the United Arab Emirates, Afghan
refugees in Pakistan and Iran, and many of the
refugees in East Africa.

These categories are imprecise. Refugees may
become temporary workers. "Temporary" workers may
become immigrants, while daily migrants may become
a permanent part of the labor force (Newland 1979).

Even putting daily migrants and refugees
aside, the proportion of the labor force that consists of what are locally regarded as foreign workers can often be quite large: in the Federal Republic of Germany and in France it is 9 percent of
the work force, in Austria and Belgium 7 percent,
and in Switzerland it has been as high as 24 percent. In Bahrain it is 39 percent, in Oman 45
percent, and in Kuwait 71 percent, in Qatar 81
percent, and in the United Arab Emirates 85 percent
of the labor force is foreign.

Why Foreign Workers

To explain the presence of foreign workers one must
answer two questions: why do some countries have
shortages of local laborers, and why do governments
choose to deal with manpower shortages by importing
temporary workers rather than permitting permanent
migrations?

The answer to the first question varies from
country to country. In many industrial countries
the local population is unwilling to accept some
jobs at the prevailing wage rate, particularly when
more attractive opportunities are available. Un-
acceptable jobs may be in unskilled, menial, low
status employment, often in the service sector, in
agriculture, or in dead-end repetitive jobs in
industry. It is less expensive for employers to
recruit foreign workers than to pay local workers
to do menial work, dangerous work (e.g., mining),
or to work on night shifts. Foreign workers can be
employed in an expanding service sector (the res-

taurant industry), or in declining marginal industries (the shoe industry in New England). Even
when there is unemployment these jobs may remain
unattractive, especially if wages are close to what
can be received through unemployment or welfare
benefits. In the oil-producing Arab countries virtually
the entire spectrum of jobs is available to foreign workers--from unskilled construction work to
jobs as engineers and managers. Workers are needed
in the expanding industrial sector, and in the
education and health sector where local skilled
manpower is not available.

Demographic considerations also influence government decisions to import manpower. After World
War II, Western European countries had a labor
shortage partly due to the high wartime mortality
rate and the low fertility rate during the thir-
ties. Moreover, the countryside no longer provided
a reservoir of manpower for the growing urban industrial and service sectors.

In the oil-producing Middle East, population
growth rates are high, but the countries with large
oil supplies--especially Libya, Saudi Arabia and
the smaller Persian Gulf states--have small populations. Moreover, since few women are in the labor
force and the population is very young, labor participation rates for these countries are less than
20 percent of the population.

More interesting than the reasons for labor
shortages are the reasons why these shortages are
met by importing temporary workers rather than
through permanent migrations. One reason is that
the manpower shortages are perceived by governments
as temporary. Western European governments assumed that higher post-war fertility rates would
in the long run be sufficient to meet manpower
needs. The US introduced the bracero program to
import Mexican agricultural laborers during World
War II when a wartime draft created manpower shortages that were particularly acute in the agricultural sector. And the Middle East imported
large numbers of workers after the 1973 oil boom to
handle a construction boom.

Many sociologists and economists have pointed
to deeper structural explanations for the use of
foreign workers. One is that foreign workers can
be a cushion in economies with fluctuations in
employment. As unemployment increases, foreign
workers can be forced to leave. A second explanation is that the use of foreign workers enables

industrial societies to fill manpower needs in low-status, low-wage sectors of the economy without perpetuating sharp class cleavages within the native population. If social policy is directed at providing the national population with dignified jobs, good working conditions, reasonable wages and respectable social status, then one could, in theory, reduce inequalities within one's own society through the use of foreign workers.

For both Western European and Middle Eastern countries one other factor is important: by admitting foreign workers rather than permanent migrants, the kind of long-term ethnic cleavages and conflicts that characterize migrant societies could presumably be avoided. Many Europeans subscribe to the notion that each country should contain a single nationality, sharing a common language and culture (and in some instances, a common religion). The governments of Germany, France, Norway, Denmark, Sweden, Belgium, Holland and Switzerland were not inclined to create or increase their heterogeneity.

The manpower-short, oil-rich Middle Eastern countries did have the option of admitting migrant Arabs from neighboring countries without seriously jeopardizing their homogeneity. Such a policy would have been congruent with a pan-Arab perspective. But evidently the governments feared that Arab migrants would bring with them the anti-monarchical ideologies that pervade the Middle East--Nasserism, Baathism and Islamic fundamentalism--thus undermining existing regimes. Even Palestinians admitted into several labor-short countries were not given the right to become citizens for fear that they might seek to transform the political system.

A fundamental premise behind the policy of admitting foreign workers both in the Persian Gulf and in Western Europe is that as far as possible labor should be treated as a pure commodity. From this point of view the preferred workers are those who come without their families, make no use of public services, and make no economic or political demands either upon the employer or upon the state. Foreign workers seem more likely to conform to this ideal than permanent migrants.

Foreign Workers and the Host Society

If foreign workers are to remain temporarily then a central legal and political issue is the question of what rights and benefits they are given by the host country. How this question is resolved has an important impact on the relationship between the government of the host and that of the sending communities and on the political behavior of the foreign workers. On this issue there are sharp differences between the policies of the Persian Gulf governments and those of Western Europe. Among the five small countries of the Gulf—Kuwait, Qatar, Bahrain, the United Arab Emirates and Oman, approximately two-thirds of the labor force is imported. (The most comprehensive data on Middle East migration can be found in Birks and Sinclair 1979, 1980). Foreign workers are fully incorporated into the economic structure: they are employed as construction workers, household workers, doctors, engineers and administrators, in the health and education sectors, and in the expanding industrial sector. Despite the recent decline in oil prices, economic expansion continues and there are indications that the Gulf states are becoming more, not less dependent upon foreign workers. In Kuwait, for example, a new desalination plant is under construction and the Petrochemical Industrial Company is expanding ammonia production. In Qatar, where only 60,000 of the total population of 158,000 is Qatari, construction is underway for new embassies, government buildings, a Sheraton Hotel, Qatar University, 34,000 new houses and more roads. The United Arab Emirates is expanding Jebel Ali industrial port. Petrochemicals, iron and steel and light industries are planned for Abu Dhabi's industrial zone at Ruwais. Oman has opened its first refinery, and projects are underway in the Rusail industrial zone and at Qaboos University.

The same story holds for Saudi Arabia. Today, according to the Ministry of Finance, there are 297,000 construction workers, compared with only 80,000 five years ago. In the new town of Jubail alone there are some 46,000 workers. But it is not simply construction work that requires foreign workers. Soon to be completed are an 800,000 ton-a-year steel plant, a 500,000 ton fertilizer plant, and a 650,000 ton chemical grated methanol plant in Jibail that will require an industrial labor force. Other plants producing urea, polyethylene and ethylene products are in need of workers. Several hundred secondary and tertiary industries are also expected to emerge in Jubail. On a somewhat smaller scale there is a boom in the new industrial city of Yunbu, which will have an industrial port, terminal workers, a refinery, and secondary down-stream and related manufacturing industries. (For accounts of the economic changes taking place in the Gulf, shaping migration, see Choucri 1979; Holliday 1979, 1977; Keeley 1980; and Weiner 1982).

The World Bank predicts that the percentage of the Arab migrant population will fall from 71 to 56 percent between 1975 and 1985, while the share of Asians will rise from 19 to 31 percent in the oil states (Sirageldin et al. 1981). These predictions are not based solely on expected needs in the construction industry, but involve growing needs in other economic sectors.

Middle Eastern governments are concerned with at least three consequences of present migration trends. One is that migrants may affect the exist-ing social, political and cultural order, either by their own actions or by setting in motion reactions on the part of the local population.

The second is a concern that managerial con-trol of all key sectors of the economy be in the hands of locals even as migrants do much of the work. And the third is that no single national group among the migrant workers be in a dominant position by virtue of either their numbers or place in the economy.

Middle Eastern countries use temporary labor migration to fill permanent jobs within their eco-nomies. Though some employment is temporary, par-ticularly jobs in the construction industry (though even here there are long-term manpower needs), Middle East countries have constructed new indus-tries and service sectors that for any forseeable period will require a labor force larger and more skilled than the one which they themselves can provide.

Each of the Persian Gulf governments has re-jected the notion that foreign workers become inte-grated politically and socially into their own societies. On the contrary, they are each commit-ted to creating a sense of insecurity and imperma-nence among the migrants even though they treat the migration process as an enduring one. Specifical-ly, the following policies are pursued:

1. Foreign workers cannot become citizens no matter how long they reside in the country, nor can their children become citizens. Citi-zenship may be bestowed by the ruling Sheiks, - but is rarely given. The policy is a non-

discriminatory one, applied to Palestinians and to other Arabs who have spent their entire lives within the Gulf states, as well as to non-Arabs (Dib 1979; Nakhleh 1977).

2. Foreign workers are not permitted to own property. They cannot own a business, purchase a house, or acquire land. With the exception of Oman, and, until recently Dubai, only citizens can own these assets. Similarly, import licenses and franchises are only given to citizens, though many businesses are actually financed and managed by foreigners with shadow Arab owners.

3. There is no free labor market. Migrant workers receive work permits only after obtaining No Objection Certificates (NOCs) from the government and may not change jobs without the consent of their employer and the Ministry of Labor and Social Affairs. If they change employment without consent they are liable to deportation. They can also be deported for "incitement of workers to strike or to refrain from working" or "physical or verbal attacks on employers or supervisors." Work permits are of limited duration, renewable by the government at periodic intervals.

4. Foreign workers have no political rights. They may neither form nor join trade unions nor hold public meetings. Associations of migrant workers are limited to social functions. Public manifestations of religious activities such as religious processions among non-Muslims are forbidden. Violations of these rules may lead to expulsion from the country. Law-breakers, including those found guilty of traffic violations, may also be expelled with no legal procedures for appeal.

5. Such benefits given to citizens are not extended to foreigners. Free medical care, free universal education from primary school to university and low-cost housing are provided to the local population, but not to migrant workers. Foreign communities are, however, permitted to create privately-financed schools for their own children while employers often provide medical facilities for their employees.

6. Migrant workers may bring their wives and children, but only if their wages are above a level specified by the government. Few unskilled or semi-skilled workers are able to

bring their families under these rules.
7. While there is declared official preference
for migrant workers from other Arab countries,
there is no evidence that such preferences
are practiced. In the past decade, in fact,
the proportion of non-Arabs in the migrant
labor force has increased. Many government
officials and employers actually prefer Asians
since they do not demand equal facilities with
the local population in housing, education and
health, are less likely to make demands upon
employers and, given language differences, do
not interact socially or politically with the
locals.

These policies do more than simply establish
the temporary position of the migrant workers: they
institutionalize a pattern of dualism (with its
implications of opposing principles) as distinct
from pluralism (with its implications of equality).
These arrangements set boundaries not only for the
conduct of the foreign workers but also for the
way the host and home countries relate to one
another over the issue of foreign workers.
The results are clearer when we consider the
policies of Western European countries toward foreign workers. France, Germany, Switzerland, Belgium, Holland and the Scandinavian countries, like
the countries of the Persian Gulf, also admit foreign workers rather than immigrants. The United
Kingdom is an exception since as a result of its
Commonwealth connection it has admitted large numbers of immigrants from the West Indies, East Africa and South Asia and has not therefore made use
of guestworkers.   Holland also has many immigrants
from its former colonies, Indonesia and Surinam,
but has also admitted foreign workers.
In contrast with the countries of the Persian
Gulf, Western Europe has extended to foreign workers many of the same rights and benefits provided
citizens. Foreign workers are not tied to their
employers but are free to change jobs. They are
entitled to the same health, education, unemployment and social security benefits given to citizens. Schools are provided for their children in
the local language and, in some countries, in the
migrants' mother tongue. When the government provides financial benefits to the children of citizens, these same benefits are provided to the children of migrant workers living within the country.
Migrant workers who have been employed for a spec-

ified period are not required to leave the country when they are unemployed; moreover, the authority of the government to expel a foreign worker is prescribed by law and subject to a variety of legal appeal procedures. (For accounts of foreign workers in Western Europe, see Bohning; Kindleberger 1967; Kritz, Keely and Tomasi 1981; Martin and Miller 1980; Paine 1974; Priore 1979; Rhoades 1978 and Rist 1979b). Indeed, in some countries the rights and benefits given to foreign workers are so substantial that the traditional legal distinction between citizens and non-citizens has become blurred.

Initially, almost every European country extended social and economic benefits to migrant workers equal to benefits provided nationals, but restricted their political rights. Then, in the late sixties, several countries (Belgium, France the Federal Republic of Germany, Switzerland and the Netherlands) created consultative councils with representatives of migrant workers. These advisory bodies enabled migrants to take part in decisions involving education, cultural affairs, sports housing, social and health services and other related matters.

In the mid-seventies, several European governments further extended political rights to migrant workers. In 1975 the Swedish parliament gave all foreigners resident in Sweden for more than three years the right to vote and be elected in local elections. Voting rights were also given in other Nordic countries--Finland, Denmark and Norway. The Germans, French and Swiss have not given voting rights to migrant workers, but do guarantee public liberties, including freedom of expression and the right of association.

In Holland the official policy toward migrants is based on four principles: (1) all inhabitants of the country should be treated alike, accorded the same social benefits, and given the same protection under the law; (2) only citizens have the right to vote; (3) only citizens can join the army and (4 non-citizens can be expelled, but are protected against expulsion for any activities that result from an exercise of their public liberties.

European governments have eased restrictions on the entry of family members and, in the Federal Republic of Germany, public policy has actually induced migrants to bring wives and children. Initially, the German government provided migrant workers with an income supplement for each child including those who remained in the home country. But after government bureaucrats complained of fraud and reported that they had no way of verifying whether a migrant had the number of children claimed, the government declared that income supplements would only be provided when the children resided in Germany. The result was a major influx of migrant children: by 1980 as many as 450,000 Turkish children were in Germany (Hayit 1981).

Some European governments provide additional benefits to migrants. In Holland additional teachers are provided in schools where there are substantial numbers of non-Dutch children. In Norway the government provides funds to migrant organizations to enable them to support cultural and social activities and to publish their own journals. Germany has a supplementary housing program for foreign workers. (On the issue of pluralism see Freeman 1979; Rist 1978).

If the distinction between the rights and benefits provided citizen and non-citizen inhabitants has become muted in European law, in the United states there is a tendency to blur the distinction between illegal and legal residents. In a recent case involving a Texas law which permitted local schools to exclude children of illegal aliens, the Supreme Court declared that all children have the same rights to public education. The Court ruled that the fourteenth amendment to the Constitution provides equal protection under the law to all persons, not simply to citizens and resident aliens. Hence, even illegal inhabitants are entitled to legal protection and to benefits provided under the law.

One of the contradictions for Western European countries and for the United States is that while they remain committed to the notion that foreign workers and their dependents should return home, at the same time they have made it increasingly easier and even attractive for foreign workers to remain. In this respect, the policies of the Persian Gulf states, though illiberal from a Western perspective, are more consistent with the goal of preventing temporary migrants from becoming permanent settlers.

Foreign Workers and Foreign Policy

The export of workers is a foreign policy objective of many developing countries. The remit-

tances sent home by the foreign workers now constitute a significant component of the balance of
payments. In 1978 remittances to the Third World
from migrants totaled $23 billion, a tenth of the
earnings that came from exports. For countries
such as Yugoslavia, Greece, Turkey, Italy, Portugal, Jordan, Morocco, Pakistan, India, Egypt, and
Yemen, remittances were equal to a third or more of
the earnings from exports (Swamy 1981; Ali 1981;
Gilani 1981; Stahl 1982; Shahid 1980).

Some countries see emigration as a way of
reducing unemployment. Nineteen percent of the
total population of Yemen, for example, now works
abroad. India's half million workers in the Persian Gulf constitute a significant proportion of
the labor force in Kerala, from which the largest
number of workers come. Similarly, emigration
provides a safety value for some regions of Pakistan, Greece, Algeria, southern Italy, Turkey and
Mexico.

The migrant families left behind receive substantial benefits as a result of remittances: better housing, more land, improved education, higher
nutrition, more consumer durables. Family con-
sumption is up, even if productive investment is
not. For many parents, sending a son abroad is the
most effective way of improving the well-being of
the family.

Exporting workers is, for many countries,
closely linked to obtaining construction contracts
in the Middle East. Asian construction companies
are heavily involved in the region. The South
Koreans are reported to hold $24 billion worth of
construction business in Saudi Arabia. Engineering
Projects India, and the Indian Road Construction
Corporation have also won major contracts, as have
a number of firms in the Philippines, Indonesia
and Thailand. In some instances the competitiveness
of companies is related to their ability to provide
a skilled, disciplined, organized, efficient and
low-cost labor "package." South Korean companies
have become extremely competitive and at present
some 150,000 South Koreans are employed in Saudi
Arabia, the bulk with South Korean construction
companies. Engineering Projects India has been
able to move teams of workers from Indian construction sites to the Middle East. One factor in its
competitiveness is that the Indian government permits Indian companies to pay lower wages to Indian
employees than to those recruited by foreign companies.

Labor Migrations as Incipient Diasporas

A number of governments in Asia have sent government officials to the Middle East to look at manpower needs and to explore ways to increase recruitment. Ministers from Sri Lanka, Bangladesh, Pakistan and India have met with labor officials in Persian Gulf governments; so too have officials from South East and East Asia, the region from which an increasing proportion of foreign workers now comes.

For the sending countries there are some negative costs: a loss of skilled manpower, a drain on manpower in the construction industry, rising wages, the inflationary effects of remittances, the growth of premature consumerism sustained by imports, and a variety of family and community dislocations. Many members of the middle class resent the higher wages and labor shortages in housing construction and among domestic workers. And nationalist sensibilities are often offended by the exodus of one's people to another country. But on balance the governments of sending countries look upon the emigration of workers as desirable and often to be officially fostered.

In fact, the governments of sending countries are often alarmed by the prospect that their citizens working abroad might suddenly be forced to return home, since a massive return migration is regarded as both economically and politically disruptive.

None of the Western European governments has engaged in any large-scale expulsions of foreign workers, though unemployed workers have been encouraged to return home and several governments have offered financial inducements for them to do so. What is striking is that despite rising unemployment throughout Western Europe, a commitment on the part of governments to encourage return migration, growing domestic opposition to foreign workers and to their children in the local school systems and, in several countries, strong xenophobic and racist sentiments, the bulk of foreign workers have remained. From 1970 to 1978 the number of migrant workers did decline, in Germany from 2.35 million to 1.96 million, in France from 1.95 million to 1.64 million and in Switzerland from 710,000 to 489,000. But the number of dependents in Western Europe has hardly changed and in some countries has actually increased. In the Federal Republic of Germany the number of dependents increased from 1.78 million to 2 million, while declining only slightly in France from 2.17 million to 2.06 million. For Western Europe as a whole there were 10,290,000 foreign residents in 1978, consisting of 5,046,000 foreign workers and 5,244,000 dependents. In 1970 the comparable figures were 11,120,000 foreigners of whom 6,074,000 were workers and 5,046,000 dependents. Though the number of workers declined by 830,000 the number of dependents rose by 200,000 (Kudat and Sabuncuoglu 1980; Martin and Houston 1979).

While foreign policy considerations play some role in Western European thinking about foreign workers--for example France is eager to maintain friendly relations with Algeria, Germany with Turkey, and Western European countries generally with Yugoslavia--there are also strong domestic forces opposed to any large scale deportations (Miller 1979; Adler 1977). There are, for one thing, legal constraints. For another, employers have persuaded governments that foreign workers remain a greater economic asset than liability. And a variety of liberal groups provide a political counterbalance to those who would deport foreign workers. The Persian Gulf countries have similarly not deported significant numbers of foreign workers. Kuwait and the UAE have from time to time rounded up illegals for deportation, but this was a way of warning foreign workers not to leave their employers without permission rather than the first step toward large-scale expulsions. As in Western Europe, the need for migrant workers continues.

Where expulsions have taken place, the sending countries have had little or no influence on the behavior of the host country. India was unable to prevent Burma and Uganda from expelling Indians, many of whom had lived in these countries for generations. And most recently, Ghana was unable to influence Nigeria's decision to expel large numbers of its citizens, nor did the United Nations and the Organization of African Unity make any significant effort to provide for more humane repatriation of the workers.

From time to time foreign workers within the Gulf have protested mistreatment by their employers. In Oman, for example, Indian workers protested when their Cypriot employer did not fulfill contract requirements with respect to wages, living arrangements and medical facilities. And in Kuwait Indian workers struck against an Indian company that had asked the government to deport workers who had left to take higher-paying jobs with other construction companies. Both India and

Pakistan have a "Protector of Emigrants" Act which enables the government to scrutinize labor contracts for workers going abroad, and to oversee conditions for their nationals working abroad. But South Asian embassies in the oil-producing states are more often concerned with facilitating emigration than with protecting emigrants. The embassies want to reduce the noise made by their own citizens in the Gulf for they are acutely aware that if their workers strike or are politically troublesome, local employers and governments will recruit their foreign workers elsewhere.

The sending countries have not sought to influence the policies of the manpower-importing countries of the Middle East, though they are concerned that their own citizens be treated equally to other foreigners and they not be abused. The governments of the sending countries have not encouraged their nationals within the Gulf to seek greater rights or benefits, nor have they pressed international organizations to seek to bring about changes in policies of the Gulf governments.

In contrast, foreign workers in Western Europe and their home governments have attempted to influence the policies of Western European countries on migration issues and on the question of rights and benefits of foreign workers. Sending countries have in some instances (for example, Algeria and France) negotiated directly over the recruitment of foreign workers. There have also been direct negotiations between sending countries and the EEC, and sending countries have sought to influence the policies of the International Labor Organization which formulate guidelines for the treatment of foreign workers.

The EEC, for example, has formulated policies over who can enter, how long foreign workers must stay before they earn the right to remain even if they are unemployed, what benefits should be provided by government, and how the principle of equal treatment applies to foreign workers with respect to health, education and other social benefits. The ILO has considered a broader convention which would end some of the distinctions between EEC members and foreign workers from non-EEC countries. Particular attention has been given to enable migrants to bring their families and to maintain their own culture through state support (Bohning 1979; Kennedy-Brenner 1979; Rist 1979a).

One issue that has not received a great deal of public attention is the question of acquiring

61

citizenship. Neither the international organizations nor the home governments have pressed for liberalizing procedures for becoming citizens, though some European countries continue to have restrictive policies. One particularly striking development is that the home governments and the foreign workers have pressed for legislation which would permit the children of foreign workers born in the host country to retain their parents' citizenship even as they acquire the citizenship of the host country.

Finally, it should be noted that considerable potential exists for influence by the home country through the use of migrant communities. It is well known, of course, that Greek migrants to the United States have played an influential role in US-Greek and US-Turkish relations and that Cubans, Jews, Poles and other groups of migrant origin play an influential role in shaping US foreign policy. Migrant workers to Western Europe have not played a comparable role if only because few have acquired citizenship and voting rights; but as they do one can expect Algerians, Turks, Greeks and other migrant groups in Western Europe to become increasingly vocal on foreign policy issues that affect their country and region of origin.

Small but active bands of terrorists--Iranian, Syrian, Iraqi, Libyan and Palestinian--seek to influence the policies of Western European governments to the Middle East, but these constitute a small fraction of the migrant communities, if indeed any of them have the legal status of migrants at all. In a broader sense, however, the very presence of migrants from a region affects the way people and governments of the host society think about that region; Western Europen media, for example, must increasingly take into account the sensibilities of Arab and Turkish migrant workers in covering events in the Middle East.

Similarly, in the labor-importing countries of the Middle East, governments have been sensitive to the presence of Palestinian migrants in shaping their foreign policies. It is no wonder that Kuwait and the United Arab Emirates, both with large Palestinian populations, have had somewhat different foreign policies than neighboring Bahrain and Oman, neither of which has significant numbers of Palestinians.

Relations between Pakistan and several Gulf states have been strengthened as a result of the presence of Pakistani workers, but especially by the presence of Pakistani military personnel on deputation to Saudi Arabia and Oman. The presence of Iranians in Bahrain has affected that country's relations with Iran as tension increased following an attempted coup by pro-Iranian Shiite elements. The Saudis are also reportedly cautious in their relations with Yemen, particularly following the aborted take-over of the Mecca mosque by a group of Islamic fundamentalists that included Yemenites.

It is again important to emphasize that the migrant communities in the Middle East, unlike the migrant workers in Western Europe, have no legitimate rights to take part in political life nor in any way to seek to influence the foreign policies of the host country. There is some ambivalence, though, with respect to migrants from Arab countries. Arab migrants have no more legal rights than other migrants, but many of them subscribe to the notion that there is a single Arab nation which entitles them to the same rights and privileges given to natives and which sets them apart from non-Arab (and certainly non-Muslim) migrants. This concern for the potential mobilization of Arab migrants, and their possible use by their home country to influence the domestic politics and foreign policies of the host government, may account for the willingness shown by Middle East governments to accept more rather than fewer Asian migrants.

The Illusion of Impermanence

Neither the Gulf states nor the countries of Western Europe are in a position to send their foreign workers home. Far-reaching structural changes in the economies of all the oil-producing states in the Middle East have made them dependent upon an expanded labor force, one that connot in the foreseeable future be met by a growth in the domestic labor force. Similarly, though for different reasons, Western Europe has become dependent upon foreign workers for particular occupations and sectors of the economy. In Europe the determinant is no longer a labor shortage, but a complex set of social policies and the creation of a new status hierarchy that make it difficult for employers to turn to a domestic labor supply. That dependence upon foreign workers is not inherent in the structure of industrial economies is clearly demonstrated by Japan, where foreign workers are not

employed--but that is beside the point. Once foreign workers have become part of the economy and
status hierarchy, it is not easy to redefine jobs
so as to make them financially and socially attractive to the domestic population.

The entrenchment of foreign workers into the
economy has been accompanied by their own attempt
to create the infrastructures of community life.
One sees this even in the Persian Gulf where Asians
have created community structures within the confines imposed by the state. Middle class South
Asians have begun to bring their families. There
are now schools for Indian children wholly financed
by the Indian community. For the Christians from
India and Sri Lanka the churches have become important centers of community life. In the Gulf states
there are now a few temples, though in at least one
instance it is located inconspicuously (if not sur-
reptitiously) inside a private residence on a side-
street. Restaurants and movie houses now reflect
the tastes of the Asians. There are Indian sports
clubs in Kuwait, Bahrain, Dubai, Abu Dhabi and Oman
where the middle class can meet, eat, engage in
sports, and conduct their social life, and all of
these have been expanding as their waiting lists
for membership grow. Throughout the Gulf one can
readily buy Malayalee books and newspapers, see
Hindu films (Bahrain alone imported 130 Indian
films in 1977), and buy imported Indian spices,
fruit, sarees, and cassettes.

Neither the recession in Western Europe nor
the decline in oil earnings in the Middle East
resulted in any significant decline in the size and
character of the foreign worker migrations. Indeed, restrictions on the entry of foreign workers
into Western Europe have virtually ended the earlier rotational patterns of workers spending time in
the host country then returning home for a period
knowing that they could come back to the host
country. Similarly in the Gulf, the increase in
the flow of dependents suggests that an increasing
number of workers choose to remain in the host
country for an extended period, perhaps even for
their entire working lives.

Nonetheless, the illusion of impermanence
persists. Few host governments are prepared to
admit that the foreign workers will remain and
that their children, or at least most of them, will
not return home. The home country does not want to
lose its nationals and certainly does not want to
lose remittances. And the parents themselves often

continue to dream of returning "home" and do not want their children to "lose" their identity or give up their citizenship.

The result of this illusion is that the host countries have yet to come to grips with the implications of having within their societies a foreign population that is not likely to return home, but is neither legally, nor socially incorporated into the host society. The result is a set of contradictions, anomalies, and postponed policy questions.

A central question in Western Europe is whether migrant workers, and especially their children, will be culturally and socially absorbed into the national mainstream. The issue is not whether Greek, Turkish, Algerian and Yugoslav children are permitted to retain their language and cultural identity--few dispute that right--but whether public policy has as its goal the creation of a culturally plural society with separate schools for the children of migrants, conducted in their own mother tongue. The related and perhaps more central question is whether governments positively encourage the migrant workers and their children to acquire citizenship and in every respect identify themselves with their new nationality (Castro-Almeida 1979).

That is not a position advocated by the governments of the sending countries nor is it one supported by most political groups within the home countries who persist in viewing the foreign workers as "guests." So long as this issue remains unresolved--it is more difficult to resolve in a period of recession and unemployment than during a period of prosperity--the migrant communities will remain in their present uncertain status, uprooted from one society, but not transplanted into another.

The issue of "dual loyalties," so often raised with respect to immigrants who have acquired the nationality of their host country, is not an issue for foreign workers since they are required to remain "loyal" to their home country, while required to obey the laws of the host country. The situation is inherently fraught with anomalies. Since Turkish workers in Germany, for example, are Turkish citizens, Turkish political groups send activists to Munich, Cologne and West Berlin, among other centers, to mobilize Turkish workers, to raise funds, seek recruits for political work within Turkey and, in the case of some of the Islamic fundamentalist and radical left groups, recruit terrorists. Former Turkish parties, now banned within Turkey, can operate freely within Germany. The Republican People's Party, the Justice Party, the National Salvation Party and the National Action Party are all active in West Germany. The Republican People's Party publishes its own official newspaper in Cologne and there are now some forty Turkish language newspapers and magazines published in Western Europe (Hayit 1981).

A number of Islamic groups banned in Turkey are also active among Turkish workers in Western Europe. An Islamic Cultural Center has been organized in Cologne. Secular-minded Turks have attacked the Quranic School run by the Center as having been "used by the Turkish reactionary parties for the education of their followers."

The more repressive the home country, the more likely that political organizations become active among the foreign workers within the host country, so long as the host country has an open polity. Thus, Turkish and Arab foreign workers have brought the politics of their home countries into that of their hosts. For these groups the goal is not necessarily to influence the foreign policies of their hosts toward their home governments, but to have a direct involvement in the internal politics of their homeland. A kind of mini-Turkish and mini-Arab polity thus develops within the countries of Western Europe.

For this reason the governments of the host countries--and especially their intelligence and police services--take a keen interest in the internal politics of the countries from which their foreign workers come. The German government must be concerned with what is taking place within Turkey and the French government must be watchful of internal political developments within the Arab world. The intrigues of politics within the sending countries become incorporated into a separate but distinct political arena within the migrant community.

The gap between the foreign workers and their host society is even greater in the Middle East, where policies to make migrants temporary seem no more effective than European efforts to prevent "temporary" guest workers from settling. As we have seen, many Asian migrants show signs of "settling in" by bringing their families. But to a far greater extent than in Europe the Asian migrants do see themselves as temporary, for they know they can never become citizens, their children cannot expect to have jobs in the Middle East, and their social and cultural roots remain in their native country. A major difference in the European pattern lies with the children: the children of Asian migrants in the Middle East do not learn Arabic the way that many Turkish children in Munich learn German or Mexican children in Los Angeles learn English. The pull of Western culture is much greater on Third World migrants in the West than is the pull of Arab culture among Asian migrants.

Most of the settled Asian migrants in the Gulf see themselves as a distinct community living in, but not part of, the local society. Indeed, many Pakistani and Indian migrants see themselves as social pariahs, even though they hold jobs that at home would be considered of socially high status and even though within the Gulf they often hold well paying, highly skilled jobs.

Asian migrants are more concerned with what host governments could do to harm them than they are with acquiring benefits. But they also have more confidence in the benevolence of the host governments and in their willingness to provide them with a modicum of security than with opponents of the government. And they expect little help from their own governments, recognizing that their embassies are more concerned with promoting emigration, facilitating visa renewals and encouraging remittances than with presenting the complaints of migrants to their host governments. There are no indications that the Asian migrants are seeking a larger share of the benefits given by the host society to its native population, though clearly the migrants would like to have security to remain and to have the right to change their employment.

Middle Eastern governments do, however, show concern for the reaction of their own population to an alien Asian presence. There is concern that the local population may become resentful at the "cultural pollution" created by a non-Arab and often non-Muslim population living in its midst (Farah, Al-Salem and Kolman Al-Salem 1980). Of perhaps even greater concern is that the local population may become resentful if foreigners hold the more skilled jobs in the economy. Middle Eastern governments, therefore, want to ensure that the higher managerial positions are held by local persons. In every factory, office and institution it is important that top management be local. For Middle Eastern governments, the training of personnel for

these positions is often of even greater priority
than the training of technically skilled manpower.
Concerned about the possibility that migrants
may seek more rights and benefits, Middle Eastern
governments have discussed placing limits on the
number of migrants that can come from a single
country. The Abu Dhabi Planning Department, for
example, has recently recommended population quotas
for each expatriate community to prevent any single
community (presumably Indians) from becoming dominant. In most labor-importing Middle Eastern countries there have been discussions of whether preferences should be given to "fellow" Arabs or at
least to migrants from Muslim countries. In Qatar
the cabinet recently urged private companies to
recruit at least half their work force from Arab
countries. It is not clear, however, whether these
pronouncements are actual policies or whether they
are merely made to assert a pan-Arab or pan-Islamic
identity, or to provide assurances to the local
population. In any event, there is no evidence
that employers have been guided by such pronouncements and on the contrary, there is considerable
evidence that some employers prefer Asian workers.
Most Asians receive lower wages than Arabs, but
their skill levels, work experience and motivation
are no less than those of the Arabs, and compared
to migrants from Arab countries the Asians, especially South Asians, are more likely to remain.
While government may prefer a rotating labor force,
employers prefer a stable labor force. Only active intervention by government ministries seems
likely to compel employers to replace any of their
present skilled Asian workers with Arab migrants.
At the moment, far more significant in shaping the
composition of the migrant population are the pro-
motional efforts of the governments of sending
countries, the nationality of firms receiving contracts, the preferences of locally based employers
and the existing private migration networks.
      Whether the foreign workers are Arabs or
Asians the central issue remains: will the Middle
Eastern governments permanently exclude their
foreign populations from the benefits and rights
given to citizens and, ultimately, from the possibility of acquiring citizenship? At what point
will the foreign communities seek greater rights
or, perhaps more likely, will the host population
react sharply against their presence? In any assessment of the likely outcome in the Middle East
it is critical not to bring to the analysis the

same assumptions that would guide an assessment of policies and their consequences in the United States or Western Europe. The democratic liberal framework within which policies are formulated in the West does not preclude xenophobic, racist or separatist policies, but it does ensure that within these societies there will be groups to take up the cause of the migrants, and that policies are subjected to legal procedures. In the Middle East one is hard put to find any groups that advocate greater rights for Asian migrants or for an extension of citizenship to non-Arabs. Restrictive government policies--which are hardly unique to the Middle East--are not tempered by the legal system or by liberal claims. Dominant and subordinate relationships among families and ethnic groups are characteristics of Arab societies. There is little support for equal relationships within Arab cultures that would provide the ideological basis for improving the position of non-Arab migrants.

Nor are there strong countervailing pressures from the sending countries. The government, media and political elites of India, Pakistan, Bangladesh, the Philippines, Sri Lanka and Turkey may be critical of how their citizens are treated when they migrate to the United States and Western Europe, but their criticisms of Arab countries are likely to remain muted. Psychologically as well as economically and politically, they are ill-equipped to alienate third world oil-producing countries.

Thus, both the countries of Western Europe and the oil-producing Middle East are confronted with temporary foreign workers who are becoming increasingly permanent, but they seem likely to handle the problem in quite different ways. Separatist policies which distinguish between the rights of indigenes and the rights of migrants, and indigenization policies with their emphasis on preference for locals in education and employment have a legitimacy in the Middle East that they do not now have in the West.

Conclusion

Though initially brought in to fill what was seen as a short-term labor shortage, foreign workers have now become an enduring feature of the economies of both Western Europe and the oil-producing Gulf states. Both regions need the workers they have imported, though for different reasons. In both, employers find it advantageous or even necessary to employ foreigners. In both, a substantial portion of the foreign workers prefers to remain indefinitely in the host country where opportunities of employment and higher incomes are so much greater than at home. In both, many migrants have brought their dependents, an indication that they plan to remain for an extended period. In both, there is an ideology of return--an ideology shared by both migrants and natives--in spite of the overwhelming evidence that large numbers of migrant workers will never voluntarily return home. And in both, it is the governments who decide whether foreign workers should be admitted, whether they can remain, whether they can bring dependents, what rights and benefits they should have, whether they can become citizens, and whether they should be sent home.

For the host countries these policy questions are matters of foreign as well as domestic policy. How these questions are resolved is also of abiding interest for the home countries.

Thus, policies once designed to meet short-term needs are having long-term consequences which are only now beginning to be felt. Policies initially based primarily upon an assessment of economic costs and benefits are now understood to have broader social and political effects.

In Europe the growing permanence of the migrants has raised the question of whether migrants should be fully "integrated" and whether "integration" implies long-term linguistic and cultural (though not religious) assimilation, or alternatively whether the state should nurture pluralism. The migrant presence has opened the question of whether the nation states of Western Europe should reconsider their commitment to a single national culture. Should the ethnic pluralism route be followed, what are the likely consequences for economic and social mobility among the migrants and their children?

Some governments are opting for encouraging the integration of existing migrant workers into their host communities--initially by granting citizenship--but closing the doors to further migration. The dilemma is that if a closed door policy restricts the immigration of family members the pace of integration may itself be slowed.

Paradoxically, by reserving for foreign workers jobs that natives did not want, and by enabling lower class natives to move up the occupational, status and income hierarchies thereby reducing the class cleavages that marked European societies, the countries of Western Europe have inadvertently created new social divisions and inequalities along ethnic lines.

Barring a decision to expel foreign workers and their dependents, the countries of Western Europe will soon have a second generation of European-born permanent residents or citizens of North African, Middle Eastern and Southeastern European extraction with distinct ethnic identities, style of life, political outlook and interests that will make them a significant element in European politics. There are at least four sets of issues likely to shape the politics of the foreign workers and their children:

First is the question of migration policy itself, particularly the issue of the admission of family members of migrants.

Second is the question of the rights and benefits provided workers and their families, including the central question of becoming a citizen and holding dual citizenship, but also including the increasingly volatile issues associated with the education of migrant children.

Third is the question of the policies of the host countries toward the countries of migrant origin. Will future West German governments and parties, for example, have to consider the views of a million or more Turkish-Germans in shaping policies toward Turkey and Greece?

Finally, there is the question of the involvement of the migrant communities in the internal politics of their country of origin.

The response of European countries to the demands of their migrants will vary greatly. Already we can see marked differences on the issues of naturalization and pluralism: paradoxically, the homogeneous Scandinavians are inclined to ease the process of becoming a citizen and to be officially tolerant of cultural pluralism, while the heterogeneous Swiss insist upon linguistic assimilation as a precondition to citizenship.

But the sharpest difference within Europe is still the question of the ideology of return. In the Middle East, as we have seen, there is far less ambivalence on this issue. The ideology of return remains deeply entrenched, among the migrants themselves, the governments of their countries and, most deeply of all, among their hosts. While the erosion of this ideology in Europe has opened the

Labor Migrations as Incipient Diasporas

door to integration (even as it increases the anx-
ieties of many citizens), its strength in the Middle East legitimizes separatist policies and con-
strains both migrants and their home governments
from efforts to influence the policies and politics
of the host societies. And the greatest constraint
of all is the belief that Middle Eastern governments hold a powerful trump card which they are
politically capable of and willing to exercise
against selective groups of migrants even if there
are short-term economic dislocations: forced repatriation.

References

Adler, Stephen. 1977. **International Migration and
Dependence.** Hampshire, England: Gower Publishing Company.
Ali, Syed Ashraf. 1981. **Labor Migration from Bang-
ladesh to the Middle East.** Washington, D.C.:
World Bank Staff Working Paper, no. 454.
Birks, J. S. and C. A. Sinclair. 1979. Migration
and Development: The Changing Perspective of
the Poor Arab Countries. **Journal of International Affairs** 33, no. 2: 285-309.
-----. 1980. **International Migration and Develop-
ment in the Arab World.** Geneva International
Labour Organization.
Bohning, W. R. International Migration in
Western Europe: Reflections on the Past Five
Years. **International Labor Review** 118.
-----. 1979. Immigration Policies of Western European Countries. **International Migration Re-
view** 8, no. 2: 155-64.
Castro-Almeida, Carlos. 1979. Problems Facing
Second Generation Migrants in Western Europe.
International Labour Review 118, no. 6: 763-
75.
Choucri, Nazli. 1979. The New Migration in the
Middle East: A Problem for Whom? **Interna-
tional Migration Review** 11.
Dib, George. 1979. Migration and Naturalization
Laws in Egypt, Lebanon, Syria, Jordan, Kuwait
and the United Arab Emirates, Part II: Natur-
alization Laws. **Population Bulletin** no. 16
(June).
Farah, Tawfic, Fasal Al-Salem and Maria Kolman Al-
Salem. 1980. Alienation and Expatriate Labor
in Kuwait. **Journal of South Asian and Middle
Eastern Studies** 6, no. 1.

Freeman, Gary P. 1979. **Immigrant Labor and Racial Conflict in Industrial Societies: The French and British Experience, 1945-1975.** Princeton, N.J.: Princeton University Press.

Gilani, Ijaz. 1981. **Labor Migration from Pakistan to the Middle East and its Impact on the Domestic Economy.** Islamabad: Pakistan Institute for Development Economics.

Hayit, Baymirza. 1981. The Turks in West Germany. **Journal, Institute of Muslim Minority Affairs** 3, no. 2: 264-75.

Holliday, Fred. 1977. Labor Migration in the Middle East. MERIP Reports, no. 59 (August): 3-17.

-----. 1979. Migration and Labour Forces in the Oil Producing Countries of the Middle East. **Development and Change** 8, no. 3: 263-92.

Keely, Charles B. 1980. **Asian Worker Migration to the Middle East.** New York: Population Council Center for Policy Studies, Working Paper no. 52.

Kennedy-Brenner, Carliene. 1979. **Foreign Workers and Immigration Policy: The Case of France.** Paris: Development Centre of the Organization for Economic Cooperation and Development.

Kindleberger, Charles P. 1967. **Europe's Postwar Growth: The Role of Labor Supply.** Cambridge, MA: Harvard University Press.

Kritz, Mary M., Charles Keely and Silvano M. Tomasi, eds. 1981. **Global Trends in Migration: Theory and Research on International Population Movements.** New York: Center for Migration Studies.

Kudat, Ayse and M. Sabuncuoglu. 1980. The Changing Composition of Europe's Guestworker Population. **Monthly Labor Review** (October): 10-17.

Nakleh, Emile. 1977. Labor Markets and Citizenship in Bahrain and Qatar. **Middle East Journal** (Spring).

Newland, Kathleen. 1979. **International Migration: The Search for Work.** Washington, D.C.: World Watch Paper 33 (November).

Martin, Philip L. and Marion F. Houston. 1979. The Future of International Labor Migration. **Journal of Internatioal Affairs** 33, no. 2: 311-33.

Martin, Philip L. and M. J. Miller. 1980. Guestworkers: Lessons from Western Europe. **Industrial and Labor Relations Review** 33, no. 3 (April): 315-30.

Miller, Mark. 1979. Reluctant Partnership: Foreign

Workers in Franco-Algerian Relations, 1962-1979. **Journal of International Affairs** 33, no. 2: 219-37.

Paine, Suzanne. 1974. **Exporting Workers: The Turkish Case.** Cambridge: Cambridge University Press.

Priore, Michael. 1979. **Birds of Passage: Migrant Labor and Industrial Societies.** Cambridge: Cambridge University Press.

Rhoades, Robert. 1978. Foreign Labor and German Industrial Capitalism, 1871-1978: The Evolution of a Migratory System. **American Ethnologist** 5: 553-75.

Rist, Ray C. 1978. **Guestworkers in Germany: The Prospects for Pluralism.** New York: Praeger Publishers.

------. 1979a. The European Economic Community and Manpower Migrations: Policies and Prospects. **Journal of International Affairs** 33, no.2: 201-18.

------. 1979b. Guestworkers and Post World War II European Migrations. **Studies in Comparative International Development** 14, no. 2: 28-53.

Shahid, Jared Burki. 1980. What Migration to the Middle East May Mean for Pakistan. **Journal of South Asian and Middle Eastern Studies** 3, no. 3: 47-66.

Sirageldin, Ismaeil, James Stocknat, Stace Birks, Bob Li and Clive Sinclair. 1981. **Manpower and International Labor Migration in Middle East and North Africa.** Washington, D.C.: World Bank, Technical Assistance and Special Studies Division.

Stahl, Charles W. 1982. **International Labour Migration and International Development.** Geneva: ILO, International Migration for Employment, Working Paper no. 1.

Swamy, Gurushri. 1981. **International Migrant Workers' Remittances: Issues and Prospects.** Washington, D.C.: World Bank Staff Working Paper no. 481.

Weiner, Myron. 1982. International Migration and Development: Indians in the Persian Gulf. **Population and Development Review** 8, no. 1: 1-36.

DIASPORA AND LANGUAGE[*]

Jacob M. Landau

Introductory Remarks:
Some Definitions and Demarcations

Since an exhaustive examination of the relevance
and functions of language in the diaspora   context
is necessarily multidimensional and over-demanding,
one must be selective in one's considerations   at
this stage, expecting to draw tentative conclusions
only. The fact that so little research with direct
bearing on this subject has yet been published
renders this task rather arduous.

As this article is not intended as a study in
linguistics, I shall refrain from too complicated a
definition of "language," choosing to employ the
term in the sense delimited by J. Lyons (1981, p.
8): "a system of symbols intended for the purpose
of communication." "Diaspora"--as defined by a
workshop of political scientists meeting in Jerusalem in June 1982--will generally refer to "a
minority ethnic group of migrant origin in a host
country which maintains sentimental or material
links with its land of origin." A constant, although not overly rigid, adherence to these definitions will dictate the selection of issues and
cases to be discussed.

*I wish to express my thanks to the Leonard Davis
Institute for International Relations, The Hebrew
University of Jerusalem, for editorial assistance;
to the Israel Academy of Sciences and to the
Netherlands Institute for Advanced Study, for
grants which enabled me to carry out a part of the
research involved.

75

Some additional precautions, however, seem necessary. I shall not attempt to investigate, except in passing, the language aspects of diasporas established by means other than migration, such as those created by annexation of territories, whether by physical force or by binational or international agreements--even though political frontiers have been redefined at times on the basis of linguistic factors (Weinstein 1979). I shall abstain also from dealing with the politics of language as such when they are relevant strictly in an internal context, such as the language issue in India, for example. Nor shall I consider nationalist language politics of minority groups directed solely at the majority language, such as demands for linguistic autonomy or equalization. Furthermore, I shall not analyze such issues as the interrelation of language, religion, tradition and so forth in diasporas. A comparative examination of these promises to be productive--but, alas, is better suited to in-depth, interdisciplinary study by several researchers within the scope of a major joint project.

I shall limit myself, therefore, to subjects with a direct bearing upon diaspora-host country-home country relations in their linguistic contexts. Hence, I will not directly include diasporas which are not related to a home country, such as the Druze in Israel, Lebanon and Syria (Oppenheimer 1977), nor the Kurds in Iraq, Turkey and Iran, although the latter group may be said to possess at least "the image of a homeland"--Kurdistan was allotted to them in the peace settlement which followed World War I, but was never established in practice (Harris 1977). Even so, it is obvious that one should be selective, as an examination of the overall situation requires considerably more space than allocated here.

Diasporas Established by Migration

Emigrants and their families have often had to struggle for their language rights, perhaps because the natural assumption of their hosts, generally the majority of the state's population, has been that the newcomers ought to accept the local language and adapt to it. With the sizable increase in the influx of migrant workers in the last generation, chiefly into Western Europe, the language problems of migrants have grown in relevance. The

European Convention on the Legal Status of Migrant
Workers is silent on their rights to preserve their
mother tongue and have it studied by their children. The Papal Encyclical **Exsul Familia** of 1952
recognized the migrants' rights to have instruction
and religious services in their mother tongue (Verdoodt 1977, pp. 241 ff.), but this, too, was largely ignored. In several cases the home countries of
the migrant workers, such as Turkey, Greece, Italy
and Spain, intervened financially or diplomatically, adding another facet to Europe's complex net
of foreign relations. This, too, has had only a
limited impact.

However, in attempting to derive a typology of
diasporas established by migration, a distinction
should first be made between those patterns of
forced and voluntary migrations which are relevant
in a language context as well. Forced migration,
generally a euphemism for expulsion, does not take
language considerations into account at all. Thus,
the exile of the Jews to Babylon after the destruction of their First Temple, or to Rome after the
destruction of the Second, imposed language hardships, in addition to all others, upon the exiles.
Or, considering a more recent example, the population exchange of one-and-a-half million people
between Greece and Turkey in the 1920s, although
hailed internationally as a great success, imposed
a great deal of hardship on many of the expatriated
people, as those of Turkish origin living in Greece
spoke only Greek and experienced some difficulty in
verbal communication upon their repatriation to
Turkey, as did their counterparts, the repatriated
Greeks hailing from Turkey (Merlier 1972).

On the other hand, in voluntary migration,
language proficiency is a primary consideration
influencing emigrants' selection of the target
country in which they establish a diaspora or join
one extant. The main factors very probably lie in
the domains of economic opportunities, or more
liberal regimes, or both, hence the frequent choice
of the United States, which offers this double
advantage to emigrants. Geographical proximity and
historical relations also influence the emigrant's
decision. However, language plays a crucial role.
Recent examples are the favored choice of France
and the Province of Quebec by French-speaking
Jewish emigrants from Morocco and the relatively
large emigration to the US and Australia by
English-speaking Jews from Israel. Such emigrants
adapt to their new linguistic environment and pre-

sumably also to their cultural surroundings more easily than would otherwise be the case--a situation which militates against very close ties to their home countries.

The language element is significant, however, not only as a factor influencing the decision of voluntary migrants to establish a diaspora (or join an existing one) but in the diaspora's relations with both its host country and its home country. I shall attempt later to suggest several characteristics of this phenomenon, based upon an examination of available data.

In the context of our discussion, the issue is rendered more complex by the evident fact that full equality of language is much more difficult to bring about than is generally assumed, even in avowedly pluralistic societies, due to the effects of the largely unavoidable preponderance of one group and/or one culture. Even in situations like that of Belgium, where official efforts have been made to render Flemish and Wallonian/French as equal as possible (a constitutional amendment on 24 December 1970 determined that the Cabinet ought to comprise an equal division between Flemish and French-speaking Ministers), there is a widespread feeling that equality is not practiced sufficiently.

One might describe the language relations of certain diasporas with their respective home countries as "defensive lingualism"--an approach that considers language not merely as a means of communication, but also as the genius of nationhood. Obviously, defensive lingualism as such, when practiced by a diaspora, often runs counter to the ethno-cultural policies of the host country's majority, particularly in new states. The emphasis of the Kurds on their own language in the Republic of Turkey or in Iraq is considered anathema by the respective majorities of the population; not so in Iran where Kurdish is quite close to Persian, the language of the majority, and one wonders whether this fact did not foster a more tolerant attitude to the Kurds in pre-Khomeni Iran than in Iraq and Turkey (Waddams 1975).

The issue of relating languages and diasporas can become particularly acute in new states which acquire independence through decolonization. Inevitably, the colonial history of such countries plays a part in determining their linguistic situations. Frequently, the passage to independence is relatively smooth, as in India, Pakistan and

many African states, where English or French have
continued to maintain a privileged status. In
certain other situations, however, where independence was achieved only after a crucial struggle
and where a foreign community has remained in
place, this diaspora may have additional if not
wholly unexpected problems: one case in point is
Algeria, where the FLN Government has been attempting to promote Arabic, while the French community,
although much dwindled, is looked at askance because of its French language connections. This is
a "colonial hangover," to borrow a term from R.B.
Le Page of the University of Malaya (1964, pp. 45
ff.), who adduces examples of the Dutch in Indonesia. The Indonesian Government went to great
lengths to expel the Dutch after World War II and
to proscribe their language; those who remained are
said to be careful to use local language in public
as well as all international ones except Dutch. A
policy of decolonizing language thus appears to be
crystallizing in certain parts of the world. This,
incidentally, has also been the case with English
in Israel soon after its independence in 1948.

LANGUAGE NATIONALISM

Language nationalism has thus gained ground among
many minorities, including some diaspora groups.
Its creed consists of a single article, namely that
political borders should coincide with linguistic
ones. Certain majorities in multilingual states
consider multilingualism an aberration. Linguistic
minorities in reply point out that, if so, it is a
very widespread aberration. In the context of our
discussion, language nationalism may be defined as
"the stance taken by individuals or groups for or
against the linguistic milieu in their country of
residence and in their home country, if any."
     The political role of diaspora languages in
contacts between diasporas and their respective
home countries may be seen as one aspect of language nationalism. In recent years, language nationalism has increasingly attracted the interest
of social scientists (Fishman 1973). Their studies
underscore the similarities and differences among
the various language nationalisms. For example,
two detailed papers in recent issues of the **Canadian Review of Studies in Nationalism** deal with
language nationalism in the Germanic and the Romance languages, respectively (Wood 1981; Rogers

1981). The main difference between the two is not surprising, of course, but still merits brief mention: while the Germanic languages essentially form a relatively compact bloc, from the Scandinavian countries to the Netherlands, the Romance ones comprise numerous minority areas in far-flung countries. The result, by and large, is far more noticeable language nationalism--even chauvinism--among several of the Romance diasporas and in their home countries than in the areas using Germanic languages (at least in the years following World War II). In Switzerland, Belgium and elsewhere, German still serves, either as **Kultursprache** or as a preferred vehicle of everyday use for a number of highly visible groups, although with few evident signs of political connotations. On the contrary, there are even some indications that certain diaspora groups in the Germanic language area strive--in the post-Nazi era--in an inverse direction to what one might expect. Thus, in Austrian Carinthia, the Wends, a Slovene language group, reject association with present-day Slovenia and support the German-Austrian nationalist opposition to Slovenian language nationalism. The conflict between German and Italian, for example in South Tyrol, has likewise abated in recent years, while German minorities in Czechoslovakia and other Eastern European countries were largely expelled after 1945.

The German community in Denmark (mainly in Schleswig), on the other hand, has had uneven relations with the Danish majority. While it fostered the German language and culture and drew close to the Third Reich between 1920 and 1945, since 1945 it has been so well-integrated that Denmark can serve as a model of language conflict resolution. While the German community in Schleswig still largely supports its own candidates in elections, a study of the town of Tonder has discovered that, although 80 percent of the German minority there opt for the German-language religious service, only about 50 percent send their children to German-language schools (private, but subsidized by the Danish authorities) and, again, only about half of the married German minority speak German with their spouses (Svalastoga & Wolf 1969). Cultural heterogeneity prevails in this case and language does not present any serious problems in attitude either to majority-minority accommodation in Schleswig or to relations between Federal Germany and Denmark, which are generally cordial.

One of the few cases of language nationalism

persisting in the Germanic language area is the above-mentioned Flemish linguistic frustration in Belgium (Moghan 1983)--an extreme case of a diaspora relating to its mother country chiefly, perhaps solely, via language (otherwise, Flamands consider themselves good, loyal Belgians with few, if any, political or other ties with the Netherlands). No wonder, then, that in 1977 a proposal was published for the establishment of a Dutch Linguistic Union, to link the Flemish-speaking community in Belgium with the Netherlands in an official transnational body. Compared with this situation, the Swedish-speaking minority in Finland is not only much smaller in proportion but also much more integrated. Their cultural ties to Sweden do not impinge on their pronounced identification with Finland--a characteristic case of a diaspora which has adapted on all counts to its host country, preserving a mostly sentimental attachment to its home country on the linguistic and cultural plane.

One knows of several cases of the rather different political attitudes of partisans of Romance languages. There are well-known instances of minority groups, some in the nature of diasporas, which have practiced a very active type of language nationalism, with definite political implications towards their home country. A few examples suffice:

The districts of Alsace-Lorraine were dissociated from France after the French defeat in 1870-1871, and German supplanted French in all official use and schooling for nearly half a century. During that period, the French population of these districts struggled hard for the status of French, employing this struggle as the main legal means of expressing political support for rejoining France. Alphonse Daudet's moving story, **La derniere lecon**, typifies this attitude of a French diaspora. The continuation of this linguistic and cultural conflict has had a rather surprising sequel. The two districts became part of France again at the end of World War I, part of the Third Reich early in World War II, as a result of the French collapse, and again part of France at the end of World War II, following Germany's defeat. It is not clear which group constitutes the diaspora in Alsace-Lorraine today, where nearly everyone is bilingual in two world languages, in a spirit marked by a penchant for accommodation.

In the latter part of the nineteenth century,

several districts inhabited by Romanian speakers which formed part of the Austro-Hungarian Empire-- in present-day Transylvania and Bukovina--assidu- ously campaigned on behalf of the Romanian lan- guage. This was their own way of supporting unifi- cation of the Romanian diasporas in those districts with the new state made up then of Wallachia and Moldavia. In more recent years, however, it ap- pears that such campaigning has been carried out less by the Romance diasporas and more so by coun- tries on their behalf. In the particular case of Romania, the authorities have recently been carry- ing out a well-conceived and persistent campaign among Romanian diasporas. They have been spending large amounts of money (remarkably so for a state hard-pressed financially) on the regular mailing out and complimentary distribution of many thousand copies of specially prepared, expensively printed, illustrated periodicals to expatriate Romanians-- all for the sake of keeping up linguistic and cultural ties between the home country and the Romanian diasporas.

Even in Canada, French speakers in the Pro- vince of Quebec are at odds with the English speak- ers and are not necessarily partisans of a union with France. France itself, however, has long advocated a policy of fostering the French language as a part of its approach in spreading French cultural and political influence abroad. In this case, one feels that perhaps France (at least as led by De Gaulle) was more inclined to consider the French Canadians as one of its diasporas than were the French Canadians themselves.

The more extreme case of the Albanians in Yugoslavia is also edifying. The London Conference of 1913, convened after the Balkan Wars, shaped Albania's new frontiers so that more than 50 per- cent of all Albanians remained outside those bor- ders. The frontiers drawn up after the end of World War I were essentially the same, insofar as Albania and Yugoslavia were concerned. The Alban- ians in Yugoslavia numbered close to half a million in 1921--most of them in the region of Kosovo--and, although joined by immigrants from across the Al- banian border (or perhaps because of this) were generally suspected and culturally discriminated against. In the years between the two World Wars, their national language was non-existent, insofar as the Yugoslav authorities were concerned. Ele- mentary schooling was all in Serbo-Croatian, wholly different from Albanian: since Albanian children

could not overcome the language barrier, the an-
alphabetism of the Albanian diaspora in Yugoslavia
reached 90 percent, according to official figures;
in 1939 there were, in the whole of the Kosovo
region, merely three public libraries, with a total
of 6,000 books, all in Serbo-Croatian.

In the generation following the end of World
War II, there was some improvement in the Albanians' cultural rights, but much less than they
desired, even though in 1980 they numbered 77.5
percent of the total population in the region of
Kosovo. They were granted the right, in 1953, to
offer instruction in Albanian in their elementary
schools, but these remained few: in the 1970-71
school year there were only 824 such schools in the
Kosovo region, with a mere 334 of them being eight-
year ones (Reuter 1982). The discontent of the
Albanian diaspora with Yugoslav policies increased.
Although politics had a part in it, as did economics (they complained of discrimination in this
domain), religion (most Albanians were Muslims),
and ideology (a different brand of communism), so
did sentiments of discrimination in education and
language (Tudjman 1981, pp. 103 ff.). It was no
mere chance that the violence in 1981 started at
the University of Prishtina, where about three
quarters of the students are Albanian. The fact
that Albanian irredentist propaganda in the Kosovo
region was openly supported by the Tirana authorities heightened still further the tension between
Yugoslavia and Albania. The struggle for the linguistic rights of the Albanian diaspora in Yugoslavia had a definite part in these developments.
One can observe the difference in the political
behavior of the Albanian diaspora in Greece, which
seems to have integrated more smoothly, to a large
extent due to a more liberal policy towards its
national language there, which apparently induced
them to learn some Greek (Trudgill and Tzavaras
1977).

Some Comments About the Soviet Union

Perhaps the most critically complex situation regarding language diasporas is that of the Soviet
Union's. Analysis of the situation there is hampered by somewhat selective information published
within the Soviet Union itself, which obviously
has never conceded the possibility that some of its
own ethnic minorities may be considered as dias-

poras of other peoples and states. The official attitude has always been that the Soviet Union has solved all the problems--including linguistic ones--of its minorities (Khanazarov 1982, pp. 54 ff.). This should not be taken to mean that the ruling circles are not deeply concerned with the issue, particularly in view of the fact that the population of minority groups, especially in Central Asia, is increasing at a faster rate than that of the Russians themselves, raising several issues of awesome magnitude, as indicated in a number of Soviet and non-Soviet publications (such as Lewis 1972; Akiner 1983). While fostering written literature in the local languages of the minorities, much of the authorities' main effort was invested in spreading Russian, the language of the majority and a major world language. In the Soviet Census of 1979, the following question was asked for the first time: "Which language of the peoples of the Soviet Union do you speak besides your mother language?" Of the 124,700,000 non-Russians, 61,300,000 (or over 49 percent) replied that they were proficient in Russian.

Over time, however, the respective languages of the minorities in the Soviet Union were accorded some special treatment. An evident case is that of the Turkic groups in the Soviet Union which are larger than the Iranian groups there and reside near the borders of Turkey and the Turkish speaking areas of Iran, such as Tabriz. It is evident that the Soviets have considered at least some of them as potential diasporas, at least on the linguistic level, considering their immense efforts at language planning (Lewis 1972, pp. 217-293). In the 1920s, the official policy was to change the script of their respective languages from the Arabic to the Latin alphabet, doubtlessly to raise barriers between them and their relatives in Turkey and Iran. In 1928, as soon as Mustafa Kemal initiated the reform of the Turkish script by adopting the Latin alphabet, the Soviets--not coincidentally-- began switching the script of their own Turkish languages into the Cyrillic alphabet, introducing many non-essential variants among the various alphabets, very probably in order to encumber mutual contacts (Wheeler 1974). These Soviet moves constituted the official response to earlier manipulations of language nationalism among the Turkic diasporas (Wurm 1954, pp. 45-51). In the last two generations of the Czarist Empire, there was an impressive nationalist revival among the Turkic groups led by the Tatars, in which language was the main vehicle. The basic implication of the nationalists was to regard all Turkic groups as a diaspora of the Turks of the Ottoman Empire. As part of the pan-Turk ideology, a common language was initiated by a Tatar intellectual, Gasprinsky, in the 1880s. He invented and propagated this **lingua franca**, based on a vocabulary combining words and expressions common to all the Turkic dialects and to Ottoman Turkish as well. The periodical he edited, aptly named **Tercüman** (The Interpreter), appeared in that language, reaching a circulation of 6,000, and was read among the Tatars and other diaspora groups in Czarist Russia, as well as in the Ottoman Empire. Furthermore, this **lingua franca** was the language of instruction in quite a few Tatar schools in the Crimea at that time (Landau 1981).

Obviously, in the Soviet case, some minorities differed from the majority not merely in language but also in religion, tradition and social culture. In this context, it is striking to note how some of these diasporas have remained alienated in their host countries, a situation which conditions them towards closer links with their home country. While the degree of identification of minority groups in the Soviet Union with other states beyond the frontiers is open to debate, it is obvious that the Soviet establishment continues to consider at least some of them as potential diasporas, as evidenced by its unceasing propaganda against Islam and pan-Turkism, for example. The misgivings of the establishment in this context may well have occasioned the unexpected elevation of Aliyev to key official positions soon after the selection of Andropov in late 1982.

Since the establishment of the Republic of Turkey in 1923, its governments have circumspectly skirted the issue of what could have been considered Turkic diasporas in the Soviet Union, in order not to induce or exacerbate tensions between the two states. Even the Nationalist Action Party which, while in opposition in Turkey, vociferously advocated the cause of the "Captive Turks" in the Soviet Union, refrained from doing so while participating in Coalition Governments, 1975-1977 (Landau 1982). The case of the German diaspora in the Soviet Union is different once again, insofar as the activities of its home country government are concerned. Encouraged by Catherine II, tens of thousands of German peasants, mostly from Hesse and Southwest Germany, migrated since 1763 to Russia, where they enjoyed preferential treatment: tax and military service concessions; the permission to maintain their own language, schools and cultural life (libraries, theaters and, later, German newspapers). At the beginning of World War I, their number reached approximately 600,000 along the shores of the Volga and another 500,000 (or more) in the Crimea and the Black Sea area, in several thousand villages. Their overall condition deteriorated under Communist rule, with forced collectivization, although they were generally allowed to keep their German schools, theaters and newspapers. Disaster struck soon after the Nazi attack on the Soviet Union in June 1941 when, in the following weeks, Stalin had them deported to Siberia, although many were saved by the advancing German troops in the Ukraine and Black Sea region. While those remaining in the Soviet Union were cleared in 1964 of collaborating with the Nazis, neither the autonomy of the Volga Republic nor their cultural and linguistic privileges were restored. The fate of the Soviet Union's German diaspora, many of whose members wish to emigrate, chiefly to Federal Germany, has been a frequent topic of negotiation between the Soviet and Federal German Governments. While the cultural and linguistic aspects have been included, most of the negotiations concerned emigration. According to the Federal German daily **Die Welt** (9 December 1982), about 66,000 Germans arrived in the Federal Republic from Russia between 1972 and 1981. During 1982, the number decreased drastically--one sign of the increasingly tense relations between the two states, or between East and West in general, in the post-Détente years. Those ethnic Germans remaining in the Soviet Union, numbering about 1,900,000, are so scattered that their assimilation via Russification seems to be merely a matter of time. With little teaching of German in schools and few German cultural institutions, the younger generation particularly appears to consider Russification as a **sine qua non** for professional and social advancement. While in the 1959 census, 75 percent of Germans in the Soviet Union reported German as their mother tongue, only 57 percent did so in the 1979 census. Although the Federal German authorities are aware of the situation, they have placed little emphasis upon it and have hardly requested its improvement, concentrating on the presumably more vital matter of German emigration from the Soviet Union.

Turks, Arabs, Greeks and Jews

The relevance of the language factor in determining the relations of a diaspora with its host country and its home country, respectively, is well illustrated in the case of a relatively new diaspora, the Turks in Western Europe. In contradistinction to such diasporas of migrant workers as the Spaniards, Portuguese or Italians, the Turks have been migrating to seek work in Western and Northern Europe--at least in sizable numbers which allow us to consider them a diaspora--only since the early 1960s. In Federal Germany (on which we have to focus, due to limitations of space), the number of Turkish workers rose from 7,000 in October 1961 to 18,500 in July 1962 and reached a peak of 615,827 in mid-1974 (Abadan-Unat 1976, p. 5), stabilizing somewhat after that. Taking into account workers' families and the fact that some have come illegally (and are not registered statistically), the magnitude of the quantitative problems is evident: close to two million Turks in Federal Germany alone. They constitute the largest contingent among foreigners there, 33 percent as compared to 14 percent Yugoslavs, 13 percent Italians, 6 percent Greeks, 5 percent Asians, 4 percent Spaniards and 25 percent other nationalities (according to the **Frankfurter Allgemeine Zeitung,** 14 May 1982). Other issues are no less relevant, as unemployment is growing in all of Western Europe which, as an urbanized, highly industrialized society, appears more prone to friction with disparate diasporas residing in its larger centers of population than a rural pre-industrialized community.

Much of the current research on the Turkish diaspora in Western Europe has focused on socio-economic issues (Krane 1975; Abadan-Unat 1976), emphasizing their labor relations, residential patterns and acculturation difficulties. The strains imposed upon relations between the government of Turkey and those of Western Europe, primarily that of Federal Germany, have been overlooked. Nevertheless, there is no doubt that the facts of life resulting from the presence of a large diaspora of Turkish workers have already affected responses to Turkey's moves to join the European Common Market; some Western European representatives have intimated that they were apprehensive of being "flooded" by Turkish workers (Landau 1980). Tensions between the Turkish government and several others, which have left an impact on almost all official-level negotiations, are only one side of this coin. The other is individual reactions; one hears a great deal about German personal animosity towards Turkish **Gastarbeiter** and their families (expressed, sometimes, in unfunny jokes), but much less about resentment by Turkish intellectuals, mirrored in the Turkish press and probably fed by the feeling that their government is becoming increasingly dependent upon Western Europe.

Moreover, little to no mention is made of the language factor in this context. Obviously, Turkish is different from German, but so are Portuguese and Serbo-Croation. However, the difference lies not merely in vocabulary or pronunciation, as with Portuguese and Serbo-Croation; Turkish is also worlds apart in its syntax, which may well be the expression of a particular mentality. Turkish is an agglutinative language of the Altaic group, in which word order is disparate and word formation is achieved by the addition of numerous enclytic suffixes. This is why it is so laborious for foreigners to learn Turkish, and for Turks to acquire other languages. One could compare this with a left-handed person having to master physical skills with his right hand; it can be done and it has been done, but with tremendous efforts and with results of which one may only seldom boast. Of course, many, possibly most, educated Turks have achieved fluency in one or more foreign languages. However, these have little representation among the **Gastarbeiter** in Western Europe, many of whom belong to the less educated middle or lower class of the unemployed in their home country. Even if prospective employers select the best of the job-seeking population, most still belong to the peasant or poorer urban groups, with serious cultural and linguistic difficulties of acculturation to their new milieu in Western Europe. The same applies to their families, except for children born abroad or those who migrated at a very early age. It has been well-documented by now that the unavoidable daily contact of Turkish children with their peers in the host country is a constant source of friction.

Hence Turkish diasporas in Western Europe maintain close ties with their home country. This is most understandable concerning Turks intending to spend only a few years in Western Europe and then return home; perhaps these do no not belong essentially to a diaspora. However, even the others regularly listen to Turkey's radio broadcasts; Turkish newspapers are flown in daily in matrixes and printed locally in Federal Germany and the Netherlands; Turkish politicians campaign among them and the Turkish **Gastarbeiter** are much more concerned about Turkish than Western European politics; and their own **imams** lead them in prayer. Of particular interest is that--insofar as it can be ascertained--these patterns continue with their children, that is, in the second generation, all of whom speak Turkish at home and in the "quarter", and many of whom study it as well. In this respect, the Turks in Europe seem to differ from other diasporas in which the second generation adapts and the third assimilates. One example of the latter kind which comes to mind is that the Syrian-Lebanese diaspora in the United States, which arrived there chiefly in the late nineteenth and early twentieth centuries. These Arabs formed a diaspora (**mahjar,** in Arabic) with its own Arabic newspapers and literature (al-Na'uri 1967), but with no meaningful political connections with their home country. Even nowadays, when the political connection of Arab diasporas with their home countries has become noticeable (chiefly since the 1975 civil war in Lebanon), they are nonetheless very low-key and moderate in scope, as is characteristic of assimilated migrants' descendants. However, one must remember that the **mahjar's** first generation was led intellectually by such figures as Jubran Khalil Jubran and his peers. Furthermore, they were Christians and were usually acquainted with at least one foreign language, generally French or English. Also, the United States at the turn of the century was a more pluralistic society than some parts of Europe today. The special case of the Turkish diaspora in Western Europe, in the present generation, is their overall separateness from their host countries in language, culture and religion, as well as in the nature of their sojourn abroad, which some of them consider to be only temporary.

There is another difference between these two cases, even if the Turkish diaspora in Western Europe is too recent to allow us to draw a comprehensive comparison. The Turkish children of this diaspora not only speak Turkish at home, of course, but many also study it in special government-organ-

ized classes, at least in Federal Germany, where
wide-scale experiments have been initiated to teach
these foreign children their own language and culture. We may safely predict that both now and in
the foreseeable future, the second generation will
hardly adapt and will certainly not assimilate in
their host countries. The children of the Arab
mahjar, on the other hand, speedily became part of
society in their adoptive host countries, particularly in the United States, since the late nineteenth century. This was largely brought about by
the fact that most of the second generation--and
the whole of the third--had no opportunity to study
Arabic at school (barring a few exceptional cases),
even if they spoke it at home. Hence the rapid
adaptation and even assimilation into their host
countries. Grants for the study of Arabic, offered
by several of the wealthier home countries, are
primarily awarded to university students and therefore have not yet changed the overall situation.
The relations of Arab immigrants' descendants with
their home countries were maintained, when at all,
on two principal levels: sentimental (family ties)
and economic (business connections). Political
relations with the home countries have been generally rare and sporadic. A comprehensive examination of the Lyndon Baines Johnson archives in Aus-
tin, Texas, revealed the amazing fact that relatively little White House political lobbying on
Middle East affairs was carried out by Americans of
Arab extraction (the few such attempts were practically always accomplished by the same individuals).
No less revealing, Arab **mahjar** fundraising for the
home countries has usually been sporadic, becoming
organized and institutionalized only during the
last decade, when the need arose to assist financially a Lebanon ravaged by civil war.
    The situation varies markedly among Greek
Americans, both in their lobbying in the Cyprus
case (Landau 1979) and in their fundraising. The
facts that Arab Americans are fewer in number than
Greek Americans and that Greece is poorer than some
Arab states provide only a partial explanation of
these differences. While one cannot be certain of
the role of the language factor in the above instances, it is nonetheless interesting to note that
Greek American children seem to devote much more
time than Arab American ones to the study of their
home country language. According to the 1960 US
Census, modern Greek was the mother tongue for
173,031 of the foreign-born. The overall figure is

undoubtedly larger if one considers knowledge of Greek among those born in the United States as well. From a survey of Greek speakers in the United States, carried out at approximately the same time (Anderson & Boyer 1970, vol. 2, pp. 232-34) it emerges that the Greek Orthodox Archdiocese of North and South America operated 16 day schools in the US, in which not only were Greek language studies emphasized, but instruction in subjects like history and religion was usually conducted in Greek. Community churches also maintained about 450 afternoon schools at which Greek history and religious studies were offered in Greek. This situation is actually only one facet, albeit an important one, in a basic controversy internally dividing the Greek American community for the last sixty years. Two major trends, essentially contradictory in nature, were represented since the 1920s by the Greek-American Progressive Association (GAPA), striving for the preservation of Hellenic culture among Greek immigrants to the US and their children, and the American Hellenic Educational Progressive Association (AHEPA), campaigning for smoother and speedier Americanization. In the 1960s, GAPA comprised some 10,000 members and AHEPA about 25,000 (Vlachos 1968, pp. 90-98). These obviously represented basically different orientations on the linguistic and cultural levels towards home country and host country, respectively. Again, perhaps it was not coincidental that GAPA, although smaller than AHEPA, was generally more active in lobbying for the interests of Greece and of Greek diasporas in Turkey and Cyprus (Landau 1979).

A parallel, although not identical, situation prevails among parts of the Greek diaspora in present-day Federal Germany; the issue of schooling Greek children has complicated relations between the two governments. Briefly stated, in the Rhine/Main area, where many Greek **Gastarbeiter** reside, two groups of parents repeat the disputes of Greeks in the US, but more bitterly so. An integration-oriented Association of Greek Parents in Frankfurt and its vicinity has been opting for the education of their children in German schools. Their main argument: many of the children will remain in the Federal Republic, hence they should be proficient in German. A more home-country oriented group of parents, Athena, wish their children to study the Greek language and culture in Greek schools. Their main argument: many Greek children

will want to return home some day and a good knowledge of Greek would be extremely important for
their careers there; meanwhile the authorities
wish to integrate them in German schools in order
to produce uneducated people for cheap labor. Thus
Athena has promoted the establishment of tuition-
free Greek elementary and secondary schools. In
1982, some 34,500 youngsters were enrolled in the
former and another 2,500 in the latter. It is a
sign of the popularity of those Greek schools that
pupils have been commuting up to 50 kms daily to
attend them, sometimes in overcrowded classes of up
to sixty pupils, who huddle together often using
outdated textbooks. The Greek **Gymnasium,** or secondary school, in Stuttgart, inaugurated in 1977,
is one such example out of ten. Its 450 pupils,
all Greeks, aged seventeen to eighteen, study each
afternoon on three levels in 17 classrooms. The
aim of all the students is to obtain the **Abitur,**
the coveted graduation-diploma required for regis-
tration at a German university. Since the German
universities tend to refuse to recognize the validity of the certificates of some of these schools,
the Greek Consulate in Frankfurt has been drawn
into the controversy. It was recalled that the
Greek Government was contributing 15 million marks
annually towards the upkeep of these schools.
Negotiations between the two governments led no-
where; as a result, the government of Andreas
Papandreou recently accorded official recognition
to Greek schools abroad (including about 40 in
Federal Germany), as well as the right of admission
to universities in Greece. Under a previous agreement between the two states, this grants automatic
admission rights to the universities of Munich and
Frankfurt as well (Fussel 1982; Zeiss 1982).
    In this context, Jewish diaspora school-
children should also be mentioned. This group has
apparently been investigated to a greater extent
than several other immigrant groups with regard to
educational pursuits. Although I have been unable
to find detailed overall data regarding their
recent instruction in Hebrew, data are readily
available about Jewish studies, which very
frequently comprise some Hebrew. Recent research
carried out on a world-wide basis (Himmelfarb &
Dellapergola 1982) has established that 37 percent
of the total of 1,325,500 Jewish children (outside
Israel), aged 6-17, were enrolled in Jewish schools
during the late 1970s. A breakdown of this 37
percent indicates that 13 percent were enrolled in

day schools and 24 percent in part-time Jewish education; in other words, of those receiving some Jewish instruction, about one-third were enrolled in day schools and two-thirds were receiving part-time Jewish schooling. The data are heavily dominated, of course, by the figures in North America. They indicate an overall decline of almost one-third since the 1960s, which fits the general trend in many Jewish diasporas. The tantalizing questions, to which no definite answer can be offered by the present state of our knowledge are: Is there any correlation between this study of Jewish subjects and Hebrew in the various diasporas, on the one hand, and political and economic involvement in Israel's affairs, on the other? Does this study of Hebrew have any impact on the attitudes of Jewish diasporas towards their host countries? In other words, one wonders how the generation gap in this particular case affects political lobbying for, and voluntary financing of, the home country. A definite answer is particularly hazardous in this instance in that practically no Jewish diasporas (with the exception of Israeli emigrants who in 1983 numbered about 390,000 world-wide), came originally from the State of Israel--while most Italian diasporas came from Italy, and so forth--although many Jews abroad tend to consider Israel as their home country nonetheless.

Towards Typological Observations

It would be a truism to state that we do not know enough about relations between language factors and diasporas to hazard any universal conclusions. Examining all or even a large number of situations in which all diasporas manifest linguistic connections with their respective home countries and host countries would obviously require long-term research and a massive tome to report it. On the other hand, as situations vary considerably, even a thorough examination of any single case, edifying though it may be, would hardly enable one to make global observations of provable validity. Therefore, I have highlighted several situations in which linguistic relations appeared characteristic. The following offer a few observations (based upon the above and on some general familiarity with the subject), which do not claim to draw up a general typology of diaspora-home country-host country linguistic relationships but, rather, lay the groundwork for future discussion.

93

Diaspora and Language

Conditions tending to lead to linguistic (and cultural) accommodation of diasporas with their host countries and possible weakening of the ties with their home countries.	Conditions tending to encourage linguistic (and cultural) alienation of diasporas within their host countries and a possible strengthening of the ties with their home countries.
a. The diaspora is small in overall number, in both absolute figures and in ratio to the majority in the host country.	a. The diaspora is large in overall number, both in absolute figures and in ratio to the majority in the host country.

While most diaspora groups in the United States are relatively small in number and have tended to lose their identity in the American melting pot and, hence, to maintain chiefly symbolic ties with their original home countries (including a weakening of the linguistic ties), the French diaspora in Quebec, large both in absolute figures and proportionate to Canada's overall population, has preserved its cultural (and especially linguistic) connections with France.

b. The diaspora is dispersed into relatively small distant localities.	b. The diaspora resides in relatively compact sizeable groupings.

Since the nineteenth century, German emigrant groups in several South American countries dispersed in small groups which gradually lost contact with their home country and assimilated into their host countries. By contrast, contemporary Israeli diaspora-groups in the United States have concentrated chiefly in New York City and Los Angeles (there were, in 1983, about 75,000 in the New York City area alone). They keep close to one another and maintain close relations with their home country (some even serving or sending their sons to serve in the Israel Defense Forces).

c. The diaspora lives in a rural and pre-industrial host country and/or one with	c. The diaspora lives within an urban, industrialized society and/or one with wide-

widespread, pluralis-   spread   chauvinistic
tic traditions.   views in linguistic
(and cultural) matters.

Lebanese diaspora-groups in several West African countries, mainly in Sierra Leone, have experienced no difficulty in adapting to a rural, pre-industrial society and pursuing there their business, continuing to use their Arabic and French, gradually settling there and abandoning plans to return to Lebanon. On the other hand, Algerians in France, mostly crowding together in large urban centers such as Paris or Marseilles, continue to follow their own customs and use their particular Arabic dialects (although they frequently know French too), which in time has caused a certain animosity towards them amongst some French groups who have come into frequent contact with them.

d. The host coun-   d. The host country's
try's language is a   language is a minor
major language of   language, while that of
world stature, while   the diaspora's home
that of the dias-   country is a major one
pora's home country of world stature.
is a minor one; or,
at, least, both are
world languages.

The Dutch diaspora had an added incentive in assimilating in the United States in that English was a major language of world stature, so they gradually abandoned their original language, thus weakening ties with their home country. On the other hand, the Sudeten Germans in Czechoslovakia between the two World Wars loudly fought for increasing the public status of their major language. This struggle, in education and other areas, increased the friction of this diaspora with its host country until finally it was annexed, temporarily, to what the Sudeten considered their home country.

e. The diaspora's   e. The diaspora's
language (as well as language (and culture)
culture) has many af- is highly disparate
finities with that of from that of the host
the host country.   country.

The fact that Portuguese is a Latin language no doubt assisted the Portuguese diaspora in France in being accepted and in integrating so smoothly that few French realize that there are more Portuguese in France than Algerians. In contrast, the disparate character of both the Turkish and Greek languages, respectively, very probably created additional difficulties in the integration of these two diasporas in the Federal Republic of Germany and strengthened their own ties with their home countries.

f. The diaspora's language problems (in a milieu ready for cultural compromises and a conscious official policy supporting, for example, consent to redistributive taxation) do not combine with other factors (religion, political culture, social strife, economic interests), thus defusing conflicts with the majority in the host country and hindering the compounding of multi-level kinship with the home country.

f. The diaspora's language problems (particularly in a milieu where official pressures are consciously applied), when converging with other factors (religion, political culture, social strife, economic interests), aggravate conflict with the majority in the host country and compound multi-level kinship with the home country.

The Swedes in Finland provide a good example of how a diaspora has integrated in practically every area of life, not renouncing their own language but considering themselves Finns, while the latter have striven hard to allow the Swedes full equality in a pluralist society. The same applies, to a great extent, to the German diaspora in Denmark. By contrast, the Turkish diaspora in Cyprus, which differs from the Greek majority in language, culture, religion, political culture and economy, considers itself a persecuted minority in culture, political power and economic interests; this view was shared by some political circles in their home country, which were influential in fostering public attitudes leading to the 1974 Turkish military intervention in Cyprus and the partitioning of the island.

g. The home country, and the diaspora, abstain from initiating or encouraging a language policy, suggesting the likelihood of adversely influencing the host country's political, economic or other interests (as the host country's majority sees them).

g. The home country initiates and fosters what appears to be a planned language campaign for its diaspora, suggesting the likelihood of adversely influencing the host country's political, economic or other interests (as the host country's majority sees them); if this campaign has an irredentist basis, it tends to further alienate relations between host country and diaspora.

The Republic of Turkey has officially and consistently abstained from initiating a language policy for the Turkic groups in the Soviet Union, or encouraging them in any other visible way, thus minimizing the possibility of conflict on this level. Blatantly different was the effort invested by Mussolini's Italy in the promotion of the Italian language and culture as a political tool within the Italian diasporas (chiefly those in Libya and Ethiopia). More recently, this has been the case of the Albanian diaspora in Yugoslavia which, dissatisfied with what it considered discrimination against its language and culture, increasingly inclined towards irredentist claims, officially supported (and possibly inspired) by Albania.

Our right-hand column comprises many, possibly most of the variables which may have an impact on conflict between the diaspora and the host country, and/or between the host country and the home country. Keeping in mind that language nationalism is our constant, one can only surmise which variables have the greater impact. Until more research on a global scale is carried out, any statement on the matter remains of necessity tentative and open to discussion. The only hypothesis which appears provable is that when language and culture combine with other factors, they have a much greater impact on the relations of a diaspora with its host country and home country (as the cases of the Turkish diaspora in Cyprus and the Albanian one in Yugoslavia, among others, demonstrate).

The Language Factor and the Diaspora:
Some Political Comments

Evidently, not all language differences lead to political conflict. But they can be a potent symbol of cultural or ethnic differences. When combined with other factors, language can play a contributory role (Rothschild 1981, pp. 89 ff.) in the rise and fall of ethnic movements. It certainly has a part in determining the diaspora's relations with both host country and home country.

Determining the diaspora's impact on accommodation and disruption is another matter, of course. In 1972, a Round Table of the International Political Science Association met at Laval University in Montreal to discuss "Multilingual Political Systems: Problems and Solutions." The lectures, published three years later under the same title (Savard & Vigneault 1975) reflect some of the difficulties in definition and interpretation. Several of the papers presented, discussing Canada and other countries, considered education as a prime factor in predetermining the knowledge of, and attitudes to, languages of diasporas. It is largely instrumental, doubtlessly, in also establishing the political relations of diasporas towards home countries and host countries. Indeed, the education of diasporas and its impact merit exhaustive research (some of which has already been carried out, e.g., Verdoodt 1977). The difficulties of Algerian children in France in integrating into French schools--20 percent are said to drop out without learning to read and write French (Bergheaud 1983)--are indicative of the problems this diaspora has had to face in relating to its host country. The relatively small but articulate Turkish diaspora in Western Thrace has been struggling continuously for the right to educate its children in Turkish and use this language in the administration of its own public affairs. The obstacles which the Greek authorities are said to raise add yet another source of friction between Turkey and Greece. On the other hand, the much larger and stronger diaspora groups in Singapore have the privilege, which they zealously guard, to use their respective languages at their place of work in what amounts to a very mixed environment. This readiness for accommodation, so different from that of Western Thrace, reflects accurately the generally amicable relations between the states whose diasporas reside in Singapore; conversely, it also has

a direct impact on the comparatively cordial relations among the home countries of these diasporas.

Similarly I would like to venture (by revert-
ing for a moment to an earlier period) the suggestion that one of the most important causes for the
foundering and dismemberment of the Austro-
Hungarian Empire was its blatant inability to
solve the difficulties involved in the issues of
multilingualism among the Empire's eleven larger
communities (not to mention several smaller ones)
in the domains of education and public administration. Needless to say, several of those communities openly regarded themselves as diasporas of
other nations in countries outside the Empire. The
well-known example of the railway station that was
designated merely by 'G' is explained by the fact
that no agreement could be reached which sign
should come first: German GOERTZ, Italian GORICIA
or Slovenian GORICE. Demands by minority groups,
including diasporas, for special recognition--in
more extreme cases, equal recognition--of their
respective languages were part and parcel of the
nationalist movements among those groups in the
Austro-Hungarian Empire. The failure to settle
linguistic differences and comply with language
demands continued into the successor states of this
Empire, even in a model pluralistic democracy like
Czechoslovakia, where the Sudeten Germans raised
linguistic and cultural demands with a definite
chauvinistic flavor, which later contributed to the
physical annexation of this diaspora into the Third
Reich and to the precipitation of World War II.

Our categorizations, salient but by no means exhaustive, do not enable us to reply definitively
to the question whether language drives diasporas
to link together or to separate states and peoples.
Nevertheless, they do indicate that, at least with
regard to linguistic matters, the relations between
diaspora, host country and home country are largely
predetermined by several conditions in any given
situation. Experience has shown that, in the long
run, relations between the diaspora and the host
country have less of an impact upon the first
generation (although much depends on the diaspora's
linguistic tenacity and its readiness to tax itself
for the instruction of its own language) but more
on the second one as it tends to linguistic acculturation and adaptation (e.g., it becomes bilingual), while later generations tend to assimilate
to varying degrees (frequently becoming mono-
lingual--in the language of the host country's

majority). As a general rule, the impact of the host country on the diasporas's language increases with time. The opposite appears true of the home country's impact upon the diaspora's language, which decreases with time. Any reversal of these trends may well kindle the concern of the host country's or home country's majority spokesmen in the matter. Reactions and counterreactions have often caused tension, and sometimes bitter conflict, in more than one host country. However, history has demonstrated that even when such tensions preserve the latency of language conflicts, they are unlikely to cause serious international trouble, even if they affect inter-state relations. Generally, accommodation of a diaspora defuses language nationalism and smoothes relations between home country and host country, as the cases of the United States, Finland and Singapore demonstrate. The converse may lead either to extra caution in international politics, as the foreign relations of both Turkey and Federal Germany with the Soviet Union indicate, or to increased tension, as in the case of Turco-Greek relations. However, wherever diasporas are involved, a serious disruption of international relations is more likely to be brought about by political, military and economic interests than by linguistic and cultural considerations, which contribute but one ingredient, albeit a forceful one.

References

Abadan-Unat, N., ed. 1976. **Turkish Workers in Europe 1960-1975: A Reappraisal.** Leiden: Brill.

Akiner, Sh. 1983. **Islamic Peoples of the Soviet Union.** London: Kegan Paul International.

Anderson, T. and M. Boyer. 1970. **Bilingual Schooling in the United States,** 2 vols. Washington, D.C.: U.S. Government Printing Office.

Bergheaud, Ed. 1983. Algériens: la deuxième génération. La déchirure des 'enfants perdus'. **Le Figaro** (Paris), 12 October 1983.

Fishman, J. A. 1973. **Language and Nationalism: Two Integrative Essays.** Rowley, MA: Newbury House.

Füssel, U. 1982. Accusations Fly in Row Over Greek Schools. **The German Tribune** (Hamburg), 26 December 1982, pp. 12-13, (translated from **Frankfurter Rundschau,** 9 December 1982).

Harris, G. S. 1977. Ethnic Conflict and the Kurds. **The Annals of the American Academy of Politi-**

cal and Social Science 423 (July): 112-24.
Himmelfard, G. S. and S. Dellapergola. 1982. Enrollment in Jewish Schools in the Diaspora. Jerusalem: The Institute of Contemporary Jewry.
Khanazarov, K. Kh. 1982. Resheniye natsional'noyazikovoy problemi v SSSR [The Solution of the National-Language Problem in the Soviet Union]. In Russian. Moscow: Political Literature Press.
Krane, R. E., ed. 1975. Manpower Mobility Across Cultural Boundaries: Social, Economic and Legal Aspects: The Case of Turkey and West Germany. Leiden:Brill.
Landau, J. M. 1979. Johnson's 1964 Letter to Inönü and Greek Lobbying of the White House. Jerusalem Papers on Peace Problems, no. 28. Jerusalem: The Leonard Davis Institute for International Relations.
-----. 1980. Politics, Economics and Religion: Turkey and the European Common Market. Oriente Moderno (Rome) 60: 1-6 (June): 163-71.
-----. 1981. Panturkism in Turkey: A Study of Irredentism. London: Christopher Hurst.
-----. 1982. The Nationalist Action Party in Turkey. Journal of Contemporary History (London) 17, no. 4 (October): 587-606.
Le Page, R. B. 1964. The Native Language Question. London: Oxford University Press.
Lewis, E. G. 1972. Multilingualism in the Soviet Union: Aspects of Language Policy and Its Implementation. The Hague & Paris: Mouton.
Lyons, J. 1981. Language and Linguistics. Cambridge: Cambridge University Press.
Merlier, O. 1972. Nouvelles grecques. Paris: Klincsieck.
Mughan, A. 1983. Accomodation or Defusion in the Management of Linguistic Conflict in Belgium. Political Studies 31, no. 3 (September): 434-51.
al-Na'uri, I. 1967. Adab al-Mahjar [The Literature of the Diaspora]. In Arabic. Cairo: Dar al-Ma'arif.
Oppenheimer, J. 1977. Culture and Politics in Druze Ethnicity. Ethnic Groups 1, no. 3: 221-40.
Renner, H. 1976. The National Minorities in Czechoslovakia After the Second World War. Plural Societies (The Hague) 7, no. 1 (Spring).
Reuter, J. 1982. Die Albaner in Jugoslawien.

Oldenburg: Sudost-Institut.
Rogers, K. H. 1981. Selected Recent Studies in Linguistic Nationalism in the Romance Languages. **Canadian Review of Studies in Nationalism** 8, no. 2 (Autumn): 267-83.
Rothschild, J. 1981. **Ethnopolitics: A Conceptual Framework.** NY: Columbia University Press.
Savard, J. G. and R. Vigneault, eds. 1975. **Multilingual Political Systems: Problems and Solutions.** Quebec: Les Presses de l'Université Laval.
Simon, W. B. 1969. Multilingualism: A Comparative Study. In **Studies in Multilingualism,** ed. Nels Anderson. Leiden: Brill.
Svalastoga, K. and P. Wolf. 1969. A Town in Danish Borderland. In **Studies in Multilingualism,** ed. Nils Anderson. Leiden: Brill.
Trudgill, P. and G. A. Tzavaras. 1977. Why Albanian-Greeks are not Albanians: Language Shift in Attica and Biotia. In **Language, Ethnicity and Intergroup Relations,** ed. Howard Giles. London: Academic Press.
Tudjman: F. 1981. **Nationalism in Contemporary Europe.** Boulder: East European Monographs.
Verdoot, A. 1977. Educational Policies in Languages: The Case of the Children of Migrant Workers. In **Language, Ethnicity and Intergroup Relations,** ed. Howard Giles. London: Academic Press.
Vlachos, E. C. 1968. **The Assimilating of Greeks in the United States.** Athens: National Centre of Social Researches.
Waddams, A. 1975. The Kurds Have No Friends. **New Statesman** 89 (11 April): 477.
Weinstein, B. 1979. Language Strategists: Redefining Political Frontiers on the Basis of Linguistic Choices. **World Politics** 31, no. 3 (April): 345-64.
Wheeler, G. 1974. Modernization in the Muslim East: The Role of Script and Language Reform. **Asian Affairs** 61 (June): 157-64.
Wood, R. E. 1981. Selected Recent Studies in Linguistic Nationalism in the Germanic Languages. **Canadian Review of Studies in Nationalism** 8, no. 1 (Spring): 55-84.
Wurm, S. 1954. **Turkic Peoples of the USSR.** London: Central Asian Research Centre.
Zeiss, M. 1982. Abitur auf Griechisch: Warum Ausländer in Deutschland ein eigenes Schulsystem unterhalten. **Die Zeit,** 11 June 1982, p. 33.

THE INDIAN DIASPORA: INFLUENCE ON INTERNATIONAL RELATIONS

Arthur W. Helweg

There are over 11 million people of Indian origin scattered throughout 136 countries (see appendix A for major countries). Sizable populations exist in Africa, South East Asia, the Middle East and the West (Government of India 1980). Their numbers may not seem significant compared to India's population of 730 million, but they continue to have an impact on the foreign policies of their homeland and countries of residence. The development of India's diaspora can be broadly classified into three phases: ancient, colonial, and modern. During the ancient period, the goals for emigration were to promote trade, conquer, and spread the teachings of Buddha. During the colonial period India provided cheap labor for the development of Britain's holdings. The modern phase began after the Second World War when India gained independence and her diaspora began to advance from servitude to participation in the modern mercantile and industrial world.

Ancient Emigration

The movement of Indians to far-off lands dates back to earliest times. Being located on the trade routes between East and West, the Indus Valley civilization had world-wide contacts as evidenced by archaeological finds in the area (Wheeler 1966, pp. 37-53). It is likely that merchants of the region visited other lands as information was provided by traders. After the death of Buddah (563-483 B.C.), prominent eastward movements were begun by his disciples, who traveled to remote areas of central and eastern Asia to propagate Buddhism--a process that expanded under the reign of Emperor

103

Ashoka (265-237 B.C.). Later, from the sixth to
eleventh centuries, kingdoms along India's eastern
seaboard developed networks and sent expeditions
into Southeast Asia--some with considerable military success. In general, however, "the role of
the Indian overseas in ancient times was that of
peacemaker" (Tinker 1974, p. xi), as they took
Buddah's message to people who had worshiped devils
and demons.
    The effect of these ancient forays is visible
in the art, mythology and beliefs of Asia today.
Buddhist precepts are prominent in Central and East
Asia, especially in China, Korea and Japan, and
have strongly influenced social, economic and political life in these areas. The stories of the
Ramayana and Mahabharata dominate parts of Southeast Asia, especially Cambodia, Indonesia and Thailand, where these epics are reflected in art,
mythology, dance and theater. In spite of the
strong influence Indian culture had on the East, a
distinctive overseas Indian population did not
develop there--the emigrants married local women
and soon became indistinguishable from the indigenous people (Basham 1965 pp. 261-66, Kondapi 1951,
pp. 1,2, Thapur 1966, pp. 194-222 and Tinker 1977,
pp. 1,2).
    Ancient movements to Africa from western India
focused mainly on trade; consequently their cultural influence was less prominent than in Asia.
In Africa, Indians competed with Persians and Arabs
for the Indian Ocean trade, and though South Asian
settlements were established, they did not dominate
the region. Superficial data indicate activity as
early as the second century A.D., and continuing
through Portuguese and British rule. Indian merchants were generally suppliers of cotton cloth,
beads and various manufactured articles. They were
importers of ivory, gold, iron, gum, coral, amber-
gris, incense and slaves--possibly supplying the
Muslims as they advanced and consolidated their
position in India after the fourteenth century.
While the Portuguese, Arabs and, later, the British
vied for dominance in Africa, the Indians continued
their merchandising while maintaining communities
that remained separate from the local populace.
Some lived as "commuters", periodically returning
home to their wives and families in India. Others
regarded India as their home and were termed "pas-
senger Indians," the implication being that they
were sojourners and not permanent settlers (Mangat
1969, pp. 1-26 and Tinker 1977, pp. 1-3).

In general, the mercantile groups of western India operated in East Africa, Aden and the Persian Gulf with an emphasis on trade. Indians of the eastern sector focused on Southeast Asia, from Burma to Indonesia and Mauritius. Many ethnic and regional Indian communities emphasized emigration and international trade as a livelihood, and this emphasis developed into an ideology which is still strong today, particularly in Gujarat, Kerala and Punjab. It helped lay the foundation for international kinship and economic networks which are still very important to the Indian diaspora.

Colonial Period

The nineteenth century brought radical change to the development of India's diaspora. Under the British, the previously small-scale movement turned into mass migration. England established her Empire with control over the South Asian continent. Slavery was becoming uneconomical and, with its abolition, various colonies needed cheap labor for plantations, construction and middle-level bureaucratic positions in the colonial administration. In places like East Africa, the local population was either unwilling to work for white rulers or lacked sufficient education in Western bureaucratic methods to be of help to the colonial masters. The exploitative tradition was to be carried on under the guise of indenture, a scheme Hugh Tinker rightly termed "a new system of slavery."

The indentured-worker system operated from 1830 to 1916 to recruit workers for Britain's colonies, primarily those with plantation economies such as Fiji, Mauritius, Trinidad, British Guyana, and Malaysia, as well as other holdings such as Dutch Guiana (Surinam). Administrators, plantation owners and entrepreneurs found the Indians efficient and obedient workers who functioned well in hot, humid climates. According to this system, and to the nature of their contract and whether the contractor honored it), individuals were recruited to work abroad for the stated period and then return to India.

Initially, itinerant laborers came from the urban centers of Calcutta, Bombay and Madras, but as these sources became inadequate, systematic recruitment focused on tribals, especially from the Chota Nagpur area. As the tribals moved to work on the plantations of Assam and Bengal, the rural districts of Bihar and eastern United Provinces (now Uttar Pradesh) became recruitment areas. This latter contingent was evenly balanced between high and low castes, spoke a Hindu dialect, adhered to Hindu religious precepts, and generally comprised male agriculturalists. Emigration was highest during times of poor economic conditions and most workers left with the expectation of returning to India with enhanced assets. Wives and families were left behind, and the regulation that 40 women were to be enlisted with every hundred men was often evaded, ignored or fulfilled with widows and prostitutes.

There were many abuses of the system. Men were sometimes kidnapped or lured by prostitutes, many came from villages and knew nothing of the wider world or what their future was likely to be. The mortality rate was sometimes as high as twenty percent because ships were overcrowded and filthy, and medical care was inadequate. On the plantations similar problems of congestion, poor medical facilities and neglect of rights and freedoms were common. The situation bore the legacy of slavery; workers were in essence their employers' property. They were managed by overseers who drove them and used flogging and stocks as punishments, and the laws coerced Indians into accepting the system. It is interesting to note that suicide, which is foreign to the Hindu tradition, was prevalent on plantations and during voyages, and alcoholism became common.

The effect of indenture on the emigrants was similar to that of slavery. Sexual abnormalities and irregular marriage patterns debilitated their societies for years to come. Many workers had left with the intention of temporary residence abroad, and this contributed to the development of a transient, normless society without direction or purpose. Eventually, many would continue to claim Indian identity, although they had lost their ties to India to the extent of forgetting their area of origin, caste and cultural dictates that guide the practicing Hindu (Tinker 1974, pp. 116-235).

With the end of the indenture system in 1916, the people of the Gangetic Plane ceased following the route of their forebears, but those originating from South India (the region surrounding Madras continued going abroad to gain a livelihood. In the Madras area there was congestion and a clear social gulf between high and low castes. Therefore, in the 1840s, Tamil-speaking Indians responded to Ceylon's labor shortage and emigrated, later moving to Burma, South Africa and Fiji. When the indenture process stopped, the outward movement of Indians continued because emigration was essential in dealing with poverty. The outflow and return fluctuated with economic and political conditions at home and abroad and the end result was a sizable Tamil Indian population in Ceylon, Burma and Malaya.

Migration to East Africa was different. The labor force employed there by the British rulers consisted predominantly of artisans and clerks who were used to build public works (such as the Ugandan Railway), and run the bureaucracy and development of agriculture, business and industry. These were not plantation coolies. They came from the northwestern sector of India, primarily Punjab, where they had developed the Canal Colonies of the Northwest Frontier, and from the State of Gujarat. Although there were Muslims and Hindus, the majority were Sikhs, a religious community that stressed militaristic pride and assertiveness. Most were Jat agriculturalists, but there were also Ramgardiahs who had artisan and mercantile skills. Initially, Sikhs were prominent in Africa but as they learned of opportunities elsewhere, often due to their service in the armed forces, they migrated and developed communities on the west coast of Canada and the United States, as well as in Bangkok, Hong Kong, Singapore, Manilla and other areas. Unlike their coolie counterparts, the Punjabis maintained their culture abroad and promoted ties with their home villages. They remitted money which contributed to Punjab's prosperity, and brought spouses from India. Their kinship and social networks were no longer bound by village or national barriers but extended across oceans.

Another group of adventurers were the Patidars, more commonly known as the Patels of Gujarat. They originated from the Kheda District near Ahmedabad. The Patidars, who also claimed Jat origins (Dahiya 1980 p. 74), were farmers and the other Gujaratis were astute businessmen. A famine in Gujarat at the turn of the century had forced them to return to an old pattern for survival--trade and emigration. The British administrators encouraged them towards Africa since many Gujaratis had experience on the Indian railroads and were skilled in growing cotton and grains that would be useful in the development of East Africa's economy. Like the Punjabis, the Patidars fostered close

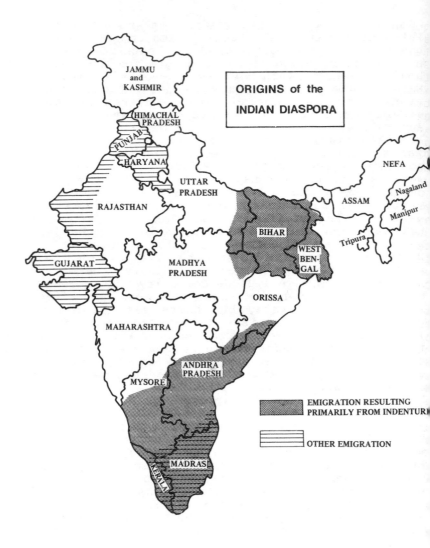

ORIGINS of the
INDIAN DIASPORA

JAMMU and KASHMIR

HIMACHAL PRADESH

PUNJAB

HARYANA

NEFA

UTTAR PRADESH

ASSAM

Nagaland

Manipur

RAJASTHAN

BIHAR

WEST BEN-GAL

Tripura

GUJARAT

MADHYA PRADESH

ORISSA

MAHARASHTRA

ANDHRA PRADESH

MYSORE

EMIGRATION RESULTING PRIMARILY FROM INDENTURE

OTHER EMIGRATION

MADRAS

KERALA

contact with their homeland and guarded their
strong Hindu traditions (Kondapi 1951, Tinker 1974,
1976 and 1977, pp. 5-9). Similar to the Punjabis,
Gujaratis remitted money, married spouses from
India and returned to retire in their home area.
While traveling through Kheda and Jullundur districts today, one can see communities of wealthy
ex-emigrants with prosperous farms and nice houses,
and also hospitals, schools, and libraries that
have been built with capital from Africa and Fiji.
The social networks span oceans and continue to
make emigration and international trade a viable
way to gain a livelihood.

During this period of India's emigration, a
professional element, mainly from Bengal, to some
extent adopted foreign fashions and behavior, emphasized higher education, ate English food, and
read British newspapers and books. They emigrated
to all countries where Indians had settled, but
usually set up a community apart from their uneducated, rural counterparts.

During the three decades following the indenture system (1920-1950), the Indian diaspora shifted from positions of servitude to participation in
the economic activities and urban societies of
their adopted lands. Certain groups, such as the
Sikhs, Patels and Ismailis, conspicuously adhered
to their culture and internal solidarity, often
drawing their strength from mother India. However, the vast majority who had been coolies in the
indentured system were "creolized, bastardised in
some respects and almost everywhere fragmented and
weak in leadership" (Tinker 1976, p. 8). In Africa,
Malaya, Burma and Ceylon, the Indian was perceived
as an exploiter because he had exerted authority as
a middle-level bureaucrat for the British. The
Indian clerk, not the British manager, had dealt
with the local people. He was further criticized
in Africa for not assimilating or inter-marrying
with the indigenous population.

The influence and far-reaching implications of
India's diaspora on international relations during
the colonial period are felt even today. Not only
did nonresident Indians influence the foreign policies of India and their host societies, but they
had a great impact on Britain's relations with her
colonies and other countries. In fact, the Indian
diaspora played a definite role in the decline of
colonialism itself.

The diaspora community was concerned with fair
treatment. It was not a volatile society and there

were few outbreaks of hostility. Although the
South Asians suffered and were exploited, they
seldom resorted to violence. If there was a protest, it was usually not to demand an increase, but
because a right or remuneration had been taken
away. They tended to look to magistrates and administrators for protection and justice, which were
seldom forthcoming.

The host society, and, particularly, plantation owners were mainly concerned with obtaining
cheap labor. They pressured the central authorities in Britain and India to relax regulations so
they could obtain more workers with few or no
regulations--especially without those strictures
concerning wages, conditions and rights of the
indentured. In cases such as Indian-South African
relations, the problems of the colonial period
still affect relations today (India and South Africa still do not have diplomatic relations because
of the treatment ethnic Indians receive in that
country). Although this interaction was primarily
with members of the British Commonwealth, there
were also other colonial powers involved. Britain
India's colonial master, wanted to develop the
economy of her colonies, but also wanted to promote
good relations with the Dutch and French, who also
used Indian labor on their plantations.

The British government wanted to be sensitive
to the planters, entrepreneurs and colonial administrators who wanted cheap labor, but also wished
to maintain harmony in the Commonwealth--an increasingly difficult task as members gained autonomy. White racist doctrines in countries such as
Australia and South Africa discriminated against
those with darker skins. Ideally, England wanted
free movement of Commonwealth members from one
nation to another, a goal which was not universally
accepted, and thus resulted in animosities between
the ruling country and the affected societies.

India herself had two concerns: preventing
exploitation of her citizens abroad and alleviating
poverty at home. Emigration helped economically
destitute regions and added to India's wealth. But
the mistreatment of expatriates abroad became an
issue in India because it symbolized, for educated
and uneducated alike, the inferior social position
that others ascribed to them. Therefore it was the
sensitivity of the caste conscious and proud people
of Hindu heritage which put an "end to the system
(indenture)," with public opinion in India contributing to its demise (Tinker 1974, p. xv). This

significantly fueled the fire of the independence movement. In fact, Hugh Tinker argues that Britain lost India largely due to the way her overseas community was treated; the result was that India became a pioneer in protesting Western domination (Tinker 1974, p. xv).

The plight of the overseas community and the independence movement were closely related. Mahatma Gandhi had made Indians conscious of the plight of nonresident Indians. In South Africa he developed the tactic of **satyagraha**, a mode of passive resistance used throughout the freedom struggle. Other nationalist leaders, such as Gokhale and Nehru, took up the cause along with activists C. F. Andrews and Rabindranath Tagore. They investigated, pressured and promoted public sentiment in India, and to a degree in England, to limit and finally eliminate the indenture system.

Initially, Nehru's message was that "Our countrymen abroad must realize that the key to their problems lies in India. They rise or fall with the rise and fall of India..." (Tinker 1974, p. 178). For a time, public opinion in India was the primary force advocating rights for the South Asian diaspora. But, as the struggle for independence became more intense within India and the indenture system was abolished, the plight of nonresidents became less important and the expatriates had to rely more on their own devices. Even Gandhi, who had initially made Indias's diaspora a major issue, shifted his energy towards gaining freedom from British rule. Expatriates also made a contribution to the movement for independence. The Indian community published papers and generated political and public opinion in America to favor a foreign policy that would pressure Britain into supporting India's freedom movement (Kamath 1976 and Jensen 1980). The notable Ghadr Party which was based in California aimed at liberating Punjab from British rule. There was a great deal of activity and British agents maneuvered in the United States and in India to end this movement. Although the cause was aborted it had international implications. It was a matter for the colonist and the colonized, and for the US. The British government wanted the US to help quell the insurrection--a factor which affected Anglo-American relations (Singh 1966, pp. 185-193). The Indian diaspora in Canada and Britain further promoted their motherland's quest for freedom from colonialism and became an extension of the Indian Congress Party.

The Indian diaspora had international significance during the colonial period. The diaspora
helped India alleviate the problem of scarce resources in areas of poverty by leaving and remit-
ting money. In the receiving societies, Indians
were crucial for production; for the colonizers,
they were instrumental in developing the wealth of
colonies, trade with other countries and enhancing
the assets of the Empire. Thus, all four sectors
(diaspora, receiving, sending and colonizing societies) interacted out of mutual self-interest.

Modern Phase

Emigration from India has continued, but it is not
limited to British colonies. As opportunities in
colonies dwindled and the Empire was dismantled,
South Asians looked to England itself, as well as
Canada, the United States, Australia and later the
Middle East, for opportunities. During the recovery period after the Second World War, England
needed unskilled labor and Punjabis and Gujaratis
migrated to the homeland of their former colonial
ruler. The movement was dominated by Sikh Jats and
Patels, many of whom had established an affinity
with their white rulers. Later, people from Bengal
(part of which is now Bangladesh) and other groups
followed. In 1954-1955 and 1958, presumably under
pressure from the British government, India attempted to restrict emigration by limiting the
issuance of passports to those going to England.
This led to a large trade in forged documents which
made an appreciable impact on the numbers migrating. In Britain, the Commonwealth Immigrants Act
of 1962 implemented a voucher system regulating
immigration from 1963 to 1965 and changing the
balance of Britain's South Asian population from
unskilled to educated and skilled immigrants (Desai
1963, pp. 3,4 and John 1968, pp. 24,25,91,92).
Various other measures since the 1962 legislation
have virtually halted the Asian influx to England.
A rise in immigration to the United States,
Canada and Australia is due to revision in their
immigration legislation. In 1965, the US government set forth a priority system based on educational level and technical competence, with equal
numbers being admitted from the eastern and western
hemispheres. This allowed a larger number of pro-
fessionally skilled Asians to enter. Canada altered its rules for entrance in 1963, thus removing

the distinction between white and nonwhite Commonwealth immigrants; and, in 1966, Australia adopted a policy giving preference to highly-trained people who could fulfill the needs of the country. India's large educated population took full advantage of these rule changes and seized the opportunities being offered overseas. As a result, the West has gained a fine cadre of competent immigrants who are contributing greatly to their new country of residence.

But, the migration was not all from the Indian subcontinent. Economic discrimination in Burma and Kenya, and the 1972 expulsion of South Asians from Uganda, led to Afro-Asian emigration to England, India, Canada, Australia and the United States. India's 1964 treaty with Ceylon to repatriate laborers resulted in 90,000 families, or 360,000 people, returning to their homeland.

Since the mid-1970s the oil-rich Middle East has become a focus for South Asians, especially artisans. The movement of over half-a-million South Asians to Arab states is considered temporary, with artisan castes and traders given initial preference followed by professionals and managers. Whether moving east or west, for hundreds of years emigrants have cherished one dream: to obtain wealth quickly and return to a life of ease and prestige.

A survey of India's diaspora today reveals six types of status for expatriates and their host countries: (1) second-class citizenship; (2) independent but still colonized; (3) auxiliary minority; (4) likely to be deported; (5) entertaining hopes of integration (Tinker 1977); and (6) temporary laborers (Weiner 1982). The first category describes those in South Africa (3% Indian), Sri Lanka (18% Tamil) and Zimbabwe (2% Indian). Each of these countries is highly authoritarian, and generally the rights of Indians there have either been reduced or frozen. In fact, Sri Lanka practices a type of apartheid. These societies regard Indians as outsiders and would like to "resolve their 'Indian problem' by repatriating them to their ancestral motherland...The Indians remain: unwanted, unregarded but still around" (Tinker 1977, p. 20). These host communities, however, have not yet resorted to forced repatriation.

Those countries that are categorized as independent but still colonized are Trinidad (40% Indian), Guyana (50% Indian), Mauritius (51% Indian) and Fiji (50% Indian). Although these

countries are politically independent, they still
have a plantation-type economy in which those in
control either live in the cities or come from
other countries. Though independent, these countries are economically subservient to outsiders.
Their economies are geared to cheap labor, which
continues to be supplied by Indians and blacks. The
position of Asians in these regions is a result of
the indenture system--workers could not create a
community of their own because their society was an
extension of the estate. They did, however, maintain a degree of separateness and preserved their
identity to some extent, creating a semblance of
rural India. Although the distinction between
rural and urban is ever present, and urbanite and
educated Indians have remained separate from their
lowly brethren, racist pressures have forced all
Indians to identify with each other to some extent.
    The Indians in Malaysia (11%, mostly Tamils)
and East Africa (less than 1%) constitute an auxiliary minority in that they are distinct and separate communities but their limited numbers force
them to conform to the majority. They are not outsiders like the Indians in Sri Lanka and South
Africa, yet their numbers are insufficient to allow
them to compete actively in the political process.
In both countries the South Asians find themselves
caught within a majority community that has a
strong sense of nationalism.
    They miscalculated during the crucial period
just before independence, and were reluctant to i-
dentify with the new states and become citizens.
They were not part of the nation-building process,
and by their actions excluded themselves, thereby
becoming suspect.
    The category comprising Indians likely to be
deported applies to those in Burma and Uganda who
have now become refugees. They were forced to
leave these countries either because of danger or
government order. In both countries they were
visible, periodic victims of national sentiment,
especially during economic hard times, as they were
perceived as exploiters and pariahs (Benedict 1965,
Gillion 1962, Mayer 1961, 1963 and Tinker 1976,
1977).
    Indians in the United Kingdom, North America
and Australia hope to integrate. These communities
have developed since World War II, although each
nation has had an Indian contingent since the turn
of the century (Hiro 1979 and Helweg 1979).
    Lastly, the temporary workers' category com-

prises those who work in the oil-rich states of the Gulf. Beginning in the early 1970s, this migration has taken place on the understanding that it would be provisional, with migrants returning to India at the discretion of the host society (Weiner 1982). Initially, South Asians dominated the flow, but more recently Korean and Taiwanese companies have been awarded contracts so that they are obtaining an increasing share of opportunities.

Influence on International Networks

Although the composition and status of India's diaspora today is varied, generalization can be extrapolated from the way Indians impinge on transnational networks. For nonresidents, India is their cultural homeland, but the meaning of India as an ethnic home varies for different groups. For those in East Africa, India is the place to return to for retirement, the home of their kinsmen, the location of their ancestral land, the source of their culture and the reason for their extensive, present-day networks. For others, such as those of indenture origins in Trinidad, India evokes in them an emotional feeling and nothing more. Politically, the Indian diaspora had high expectations that after independence, India would intercede to counter injustices against them. Instead, Prime Minister Nehru and Indian ambassadors such as Apa Pant urged the overseas Indian community to give primary loyalty to the countries in which they were permanently residing (Tinker 1976, 1977). The communities realized that they would have to rely on their own devices within their new countries.

There have been momentary signs of hope for improved relations in places like Kenya, where a student exchange program was instituted with India. However, this program turned out to be disastrous. As a result of the racist attitudes against African blacks exhibited in India, Kenyans who studied in India, such as the Kikuyu Politician Gatugata, returned with such extreme anti-Asian hostility that the program had negative repercussions on the African-Asian community. Nevertheless, India's diaspora has continued to develop cultural, economic and social networks with their ethnic homeland.

Culturally, since 1970, the Indian overseas entertainment industry has boomed. Classical and popular performers and movie stars are invited by wealthy Indians in Britain, Canada, Kenya and the

United States. In fact, movies are often released abroad via video before they are screened in India. Some families have established a network whereby those flying from Fiji to Australia and New Zealand carry video cassettes of Indian movies for friends and relatives who watch the shows and then tape Western television programs and movies to be returned for Indians there.

Similar arrangements exist with religious leaders, who regularly tour Britain, East Africa, the United States and Canada. Gurdwaras and temples around the world frequently receive India's Sants and religious musicians to provide spiritual enhancement.

Economic networks initiated by the diaspora are considerable, both in the form of business and benevolences. For example, Indians in the clothing trade in New York look to relatives or friends in India to be reliable suppliers of shirts, blouses, dresses and shoes. Among the Gujaratis especially, family businesses extend to multinational dimensions. One example is Mohinder Patel, a doctor in Australia. His brother farms his land in India, his sister is part-owner and manager of his motel in Los Angeles and his wife's family administers his stores in Fiji. Generally such networks expand only as far as kinship ties allow, for blood relations, according to Gujarati beliefs, are the only ones to be trusted. Thus kinsmen scattered around the globe can provide economic and social security to a people who have learned well that fortunes can change quickly.

Indians in the West, Australia and East Africa return to India for visits approximately once every three years, thus perpetuating the travel business, which has become a lucrative but competitive industry. With travel come gifts--the nonresident returning home feels compelled to demonstrate his success abroad by bringing thousands of dollars worth of presents to family and friends. Gifts are a matter of concern for the overseas South Asian, for he fears that if his presents are not sufficiently appreciated, he and his family will lose respect and esteem. This business has become so voluminous that in most major cities like London, New York and Chicago, Indians have opened special stores which carry items geared to India's 220 volt electrical system.

Benevolence is another economic consideration. Those abroad send money back to needy parents and relatives. Some also invest in India because they hope to return. India has set up schemes whereby if products, such as scooters, are paid for in foreign currency, they are delivered immediately instead of after the usual years of waiting. Welfare-type organizations have been established in India, and money is raised abroad for charities in India. For example, the India Development Service, working from Chicago, has a twenty-one village economic development project going in Karnataka. Traveling through the Kheda District of Gujarat one sees numerous hospitals, libraries and prosperous farms which have been financed by Gujaratis in Africa, Britain and the United States. Universities like the Sardar Patel Institute in Gujarat and Indian Institute of Management in Ahmedabad have fostered contacts with their alumni overseas and use them effectively in developing projects. India bestows on the non-resident who has retained social ties greater recognition and esteem for his assets than does his country of residence.

Socially, India is a source of spouses for emigrants. Some countries, such as Great Britain, do not automatically allow spouses to immigrate. But among many Indians, a spouse from India is perceived as culturally pure, living up to Hindu precepts, and likely to be of higher character. Thus contacts are maintained not only because of consanguine relationships but also to fulfill matrimonial requirements.

India's diaspora benefits the receiving society by enhancing its economy, while simultaneously alleviating undesirable social situations in India. But now, at the insistence of the receiving country, India is helping to deal with the resultant social problems of its diaspora--specifically with repatriation schemes or by limiting emigration. Britain most likely influenced the Indian government to limit emigration in the 1950s. Burma, Sri Lanka and Uganda worked with India to develop repatriation schemes to lessen and eliminate ethnic tensions within their borders. In the case of ex-colonies, issues concerning the diaspora have involved Britain when citizenship and responsibility were not clear. In the case of Uganda, many of the Afro-Asians held British passports, although ethnically Indians. India initially disclaimed responsibility for those who had opted for British citizenship although she was ultimately pressured into accepting some.

Indians living in countries with unstable economic and political situations often send their money abroad, mostly to British banks. This has caused concern leading to resentment in countries like Uganda and Kenya, but has not affected the economically and politically more stable countries of the West or the Middle East.

The greatest effect of India's diaspora is on India herself. The issues have become more numerous and more serious since independence, and now, unlike during the colonial period, India alone has to deal with them. India has no specific policy towards nonresidents except that officially it is her concern to protect the rights and interests of her citizens. The protection of citizens is not always a clear issue with countries that, like Australia, recognize dual citizenship, as India does not recognize nonresidents as citizens if they owe allegiance to a foreign power. Other international matters to be taken into consideration are: diplomatic relations, economic exchanges and non-resident involvement in internal affairs.

Diplomatically, India has strained relations with Burma, Sri Lanka and Uganda over the issue of repatriation. The overseas communities in Sri Lanka and Britain have been of much concern because of public opinion within India among the Tamils--who want to intercede, some even advocating military intervention, when their ethnic counterparts are persecuted in Ceylon. This became an election issue for Mrs. Gandhi, for the South was a strong area of support for her and crucial to her political future (Narayan 1981). During the riots against Asians and blacks in England in the summer of 1981, the Indian government expressed grave concern to the British High Commissioner. The seemingly small matter of a Sikh boy being humiliated by white boys who forcibly cut his unshorn hair became a parliamentary issue in India.

The Indian government is sensitive to public opinion within India. If the people identify with their brothers abroad, then the government will often respond. But self-interest is also at work for when the government attempted to limit emigration to the Gulf as a result of the plight of Indians there, public pressure forced the authorities to reverse their stand (Weiner 1982).

The development of trade involving non-residents has generally been initiated by the diaspora not by India. Remittances are of increasing importance to the government of India. The growth rate of money being submitted by expatriates increased annually by an average of 20 percent from 1967 to

1977, and is now worth about five billion dollars annually (see table 1).

Table 1

Remittances from Overseas Indians[3]

Year	Dollars in Billions
1977	1.90
1978	2.21
1979	2.72
1980	4.46

This capital from abroad has considerably decreased India's international balance of payment deficit. The potential contribution of overseas workers to national and local development in India is recognized by the central, state and village governments, for all three levels are developing programs to encourage investments by Indians overseas. Nonresident Indians certainly have the means to bring foreign capital into India--their wealth is estimated at 60-90 billion dollars (Mandawat 1984). According to Dr. Badri Madan, vice president of The Foundation for Critical Choices for India, overseas Indians in 1982 invested 12 million dollars in India, as opposed to five billion outside India (Chawla 1983). Generally, it is the uneducated, unskilled Indian laborers of rural origins who send earnings back to India, while educated professionals and business people invest where they can obtain better returns (Bhatt 1981). Since there continues to be a need for Indian labor in the Middle East, the capital from nonresident sources will most likely remain at its present levels, but may eventually decrease (Government of India Planning Commission 1981, p. 72).

In the 1950s and 1960s most of India's expatriate money came from Africa and England. But by 1978, the proportion from the oil-producing countries, the US, and Canada grew rapidly. A 1978 Bombay Chamber of Commerce study indicated that for Gujarat, 33 percent came from the Middle East, 26 percent from the UK, and 21 percent from the other countries. For Punjab, the percentage from the UK is probably higher because of the larger Punjabi population in the UK, whereas in Kerala, the percentage from the Middle East dominates.

At present, one of the goals of the Indian government is to obtain foreign currency to aid in decreasing her international debt. In the past year India has changed her currency regulation to entice ethnic Indians to invest in and remit to their motherland, giving even those Indians with foreign passports preference over foreigners of non-Indian origins. These economic policies are too recent to allow full evaluation of their results, but they face some opposition by resident Indians. The expatriate generally has much more money and greater investment options than the resident Indian, who cannot maintain his economic position and operate within India's currency restrictions. An editorial in **India Today** (1983a) claims that this new policy creates nonresident gods, and opposes the policy because: (1) it creates further divisions in what is already a very hierarchical society; (2) it enables and encourages those in the black market to launder their money through nonresidents; (3) it creates a category of privileged foreigners; and (4) wealthy nonresidents owe their homeland a debt for the education they received in India. The policy has thus encouraged resentment towards India's diaspora by resident Indians.

In India there is also grave concern over the country's loss of talent, the "brain drain" (Glaser 1978, 1980). A UN Council on Trade and Development (UNCTAD) study estimates that a qualified doctor who leaves to settle elsewhere represents a $40,000 loss to India and a scientist a $20,000 loss. The United States, however, gains $648,000 for each foreign-trained doctor and $236,000 for each scientist. It is estimated that between 1961 and 1972 India lost $144 million because of emigrating physicians alone. In the 1960s an estimated one-quarter of all engineers and one-third of all doctors trained in India left the country (**India Today** 1983a). Currently, India loses between 24-30 percent of its graduate doctors and engineers (Agency for International Development 1979; Newland 1979).

Statistics do not tell the whole story. Emigration is a selective process in which initially the most innovative and daring leave. Therefore, a receiving country gains capable, highly motivated individuals who may or not have the formal qualifications to be considered part of the "brain drain." They generally work hard, have initiative and usually make a strong contribution to their country. To counter this situation, India has proposed: restrictive emigration policies, deposits placed by those traveling abroad, and taxation of emigrants, but none of these policies have yet been legislated. Taxation of expatriates would be almost impossible since it would be difficult to define who should be targeted, and the consent of the host country would be required to extract money from its residents.

The Development Program of the United Nations entitled "Transfer of Know-How Through Expatriate Nationals (TOKTEN)" was set up to help nations tap the expertise of their skilled professionals working abroad and encourage them to return to help their country of origin. From the United States, 250 Indian professionals responded; the effects on India, however, have not yet been determined (**India** Abroad 1980).

To further understand the reason for this brain drain, one has to look at India's employment picture. The World Health Organization (WHO) estimates that 80,000 doctors in India are underemployed, that is they are over-qualified for the jobs they are doing. Yet the doctor-population ratio is only 2.2 physicians per 100,000 (**India Abroad** 1980, 1983a, 1983b; Tinker 1977). In 1980, 7,662,000 educated job-seekers were unemployed and it has been projected for 1982-1983 that nearly 300,000 science graduates and post-graduates will be jobless (Mathew 1982, p. 540).

Statistics indicate that India's educational system is so productive that the nation cannot absorb the highly skilled personnel it is training. If that is the case, it would seem that the concept of the brain drain for India may be a moot point, as it is for other underdeveloped countries. Dr. Manoranjan Dutta, Professor of Economics at Rutgers University and ex-president of the Association of Indians in America (AIA), made a crucial point when he said that "a brain that cannot be used is a dead brain. Therefore, what good does it do to have an emigrant return if his brain will be killed" (Dutta 1980).

On the other hand, the educated emigrant does benefit the home country in many ways. Emigrants send new technological ideas back to India; in Jandiali this took the form of farming publications and new seeding varieties. Most Indians want to be recognized for their achievements in their home country, so they willingly act as experts and consultants to the Indian government and to Indian universities. Some formal schemes to capitalize on this talent have been set up. For for example, the Council for Scientific and Industrial Research (CSIR) encourages Indian scientists to return by promising them aid in finding jobs and granting a stipend until they are gainfully employed. States such as Gujarat have also established bureaus like the Industrial Extension Bureau (INDEXTB) which have schemes which grant preference to returning Indians for services such as telephone, gas, loans, land, and even school entrance for children. Indians abroad can also help India to a great extent by lobbying to promote her national policies. For example, in 1980, the Federation of Indian Associations in America began to exert pressure on the Carter administration to supply fuel to India's Tarapur nuclear power plant. The goal was successfully achieved under the Reagan administration. The Indian community in the United States is not large, but it has obtained influence, chiefly through financial contributions to American politicians. The wealth and social prominence of this minority make it a useful pressure group for India's interests.

On paper, programs for repatriation and nonresident investment look good, but their poor administration is one reason why they are not more successful. And, as one bureaucrat stated, "the only people we want to have return are those with money or specialized skills such as microelectronics." Those residing or trained abroad find it difficult to have their children considered in quotas for Indian universities because they do not come under state residency. Nonresidents are also at a disadvantage in joining the Indian National Service, and private companies prefer to hire the Indian-trained rather than foreign-educated staff. Expatriates are categorized as argumentative, prone to dissatisfaction and "square pegs in round holes" (Kabra 1976, p. 12; Helweg 1984, pp. 53-55). Public opinion in India is becoming antagonistic toward the overseas experience, which was not the case a decade ago. Prime Minister Gandhi made it clear that returnees will not block the way of those who have remained in India (**India Abroad** 1983b). In general, those who have large amounts of capital or needed skills are encouraged to return, but the skills needed are limited and those with money can maintain a better quality of life elsewhere. Therefore, it is only people who have been unsuccessful abroad or who have personal reasons for returning (such as aging parents or the desire to raise children the Indian way) who actually return.

Expatriates' influence on internal matters is another issue. The present Sikh agitation in Punjab has been partially blamed on their emigrant community in Canada. Many of those in England and the United States left with a dream of returning to India as politicians or members of parliament--a dream which has not materialized. When traveling abroad, Indian politicians visit expatriates (this was not always the case with Mrs. Gandhi, possibly due to national considerations), and some rich businessmen from the United States return to India to campaign during elections, act as headmen for villages, and use their resources to gain a following and to develop local programs. Recently India passed legislation making it possible for expatriates to vote in elections (**India Abroad** 1984). Thus the ties between overseas Indians and India become closer.

Periodically, rhetoric indicates that India feels itself responsible for the cultural enhancement of her diaspora. But, other than the efforts of the various consulates to promote Indian culture abroad, little has been done--except in Mauritius, where the Government of India supported the establishment of a Mahatma Gandhi Institute. There have been other contributions by individual states. The Andhra Pradesh government has helped finance the building of Indian temples in the United States and even supplied well-trained stone masons.

Conclusions

The Indian diaspora has an ongoing influence on the international networks of many countries and communities. Not only does it have an impact on the policies of host societies, but it influences Indian domestic and international programs. The manner in which Indians overseas influence transnational networks for both the host and home nations varies according to the period of emigration, type of community involved, nature of ties with India, situation of the expatriate community, needs of the countries involved, and perceptions of the local people.

The Indian diaspora continues to be an exploited community. The host societies want the labor and skills of the Indians, but do not want to provide the services necessary to alleviate social

tensions. The contribution of the immigrants to
the economy is usually forgotten by the host country. India, on the other hand, wants to attract
their money and skills back to the homeland. To
achieve this, a great deal depends on how the
indigenous population perceives the diaspora and
interprets repatriation, and whether or not it
remembers the diaspora's helpful remittances and
work abroad.

Notes

1 Research for this project was funded as
follows: A Fulbright Hays Faculty Research Grant,
1977-1978 and 1982, Smithsonian Foreign Currency
Program, 1981-1982, and Western Michigan University
Faculty Research Grants and Fellowships, 1979, 1980
and 1983.
2 To illustrate the wealth of Indians in
America and Canada, **India Abroad** (1979a), the largest newspaper in the United States for overseas
Indians, did a random survey of its 16,000 readers,
in which 212 out of 600 questionnaires were completed. The survey showed that 76.1 percent hold
professional or managerial positions, 89 percent
earn over $15,000 a year, 58.5 percent earn over
$25,000, 31 percent earn over $35,000, and 15 percent earn over $50,000 annually. (It must be kept
in mind that these responses were made by heads of
households).
A similar survey of 603 families, or 2,509
persons, was made in the Vancouver area by the
National Association of Canadians of Indian Origin.
It disclosed that five percent had an income of
$3,000 to $25,000, while 38 percent earned $25,000
to $35,000, and 22 percent earned over $35,000.
Seventy-five percent owned their own home. Their
educational and professional levels were not as
high as the American South Asians, but if the
survey had been made in Toronto or Ottawa, it would
probably would have revealed different results
(Jain 1981).
3 Although these are the official figures
used by the Government of India in accounting for
emigrant remittances, they are determined as part
of the Balance of Payments data compiled by the
Reserve Bank of India, and represent gross non-
export receipts such as shipping receipts, insur-
ance receipts, dividend receipts, tourism receipts,
etc. Besides, there are four kinds of receipts

relevant to the term "Inward Remittances," namely: (1) family maintenance; (2) savings of nonresidents; (3) migrant transfers; and (4) money order receipts (Government of India 1981). For a more detailed report, see the current Reserve Bank of India Bulletin, Annual Report, and Government of India Five Year Plan.

References

Agency for International Development. 1979. Business Brief: Migrating to Work. Washington, D. C.

Basham, A. L. 1954. **The Wonder That Was India.** New York: Grover Press, Inc.

Benedict, Burton, 1954. **Mauritius: Problems of a Plural Society.** London: Pall Mall Press for the Institute of Race Relations.

Bhatt, Tararath. 1981. Foreign Remittances--Need for Rationalisation and Channelisation. **India Quarterly** 37, no. 4.

Chawla, Prabhu. 1983. Non-Residents Talking Terms. **India Today** 8, no. 12 (30 June): 62-3.

Dahiya, B. S. 1980. **Jats: The Ancient Rulers.** New Delhi, Bangalor, Jullundur: Sterling Publisher Pyt., Ltd.

Desai, Rashmi. 1962. **Indian Immigrants in Britain.** London: Oxford University Press for the Institute of Race Relations.

Dutta, Monoranjan. 1980. Interview.

Gillion, K. L. **Fiji's Indian Migrants.** Melbourne: Oxford University Press.

Glaser, William. 1978. **The Brain Drain: Emigration and Return.** Oxford and New York: Pergamon Press.

-----. 1980. International Flows of Talent. In **Sourcebook on the New Immigration: Implications for the United States and the International Community,** ed. Roy Simon Bryce-Laporte. New Brunswick: Transaction Books.

Government of India. 1980. Statement of Indians Pending in Various Countries. In **Parliamentary Record,** Enclosure to L. S. USQ No. 5460, 24 July.

-----. 1981. Remittances from Abroad. In **Parliamentary Record,** Unanswered questions Nos. 2535, 15 September, and 4522, 20 March.

Government of India Planning Commission. 1981. **Sixth Five Year Plan 1980-85.** New Delhi: Government of India.

Helweg, Arthur. 1983. Emigrant Remittances: Their Nature and Impact on a Punjabi Village. **New Community** 10, no. 3.

-----. 1984. Emigration and Return--Ramifications for India. **Population Review** 28, nos. 1, 2.

Helweg, Arthur, and Usha M. Helweg. 1982. Indians in America: Doing Well. **Span** 23, no. 2 (February).

Helweg, Usha M. 1982. Studying in America: Then and Now. **Span** 23, no. 8 (August).

Hiro, Dilip. 1979. Indians in Britain. **India International Centre Quarterly** 6: 217-24.

India Abroad. 1980. 250 Indians Respond to TOKTEN. **India Abroad** 14, no. 7: 18.

-----. 1983a. Unemployed Doctors. **India Abroad** 14, no. 7: 18.

-----. 1983b. India Welcomes Scientists' Return. **India Abroad** 14, no. 13: 6.

-----. 1984. MP's Bill Would Allow Expatriate Candidacy. **India Abroad** 14, no. 14: 1.

India Today. 1983a. The Non-resident Gods. **India Today** 8, no. 18: 4.

-----. 1983b. The Talent Trap. **India Today** 8, no. 21: 5.

Jain, Suresh. 1981. Canadian Study Finds High Indian Income. **India Abroad** 9, no. 37.

Jensen, Joan M. 1980. East Indians. In **Harvard Encyclopedia of American Ethnic Groups,** ed. Stephan Thernstrom. Cambridge, MA: The Belknap Press of Harvard University Press.

John, DeWitt. 1969. **Indian Workers' Association in Britiain.** London: Oxford University Press for the Institute of Race Relations.

Kabra, K. N. 1976. **Political Economy of Brain Drain.** New Delhi: Arnold-Heinemann.

Kamath, M. V. 1976. **The United States and India 1776-1976.** Washington, D.C.: The Embassy of India.

Kondapi, C. 1951. **Indians Overseas: 1838-1949.** New Delhi: Indian Council of World Affairs; London: Oxford University Press.

Mandawat, S. L. 1984. How Remittances Help Boost Indian Economy. **India Abroad** 14, no. 23: 2.

Mangat, J. S. 1969. **A History of the Asians in East Africa.** Oxford: Clarendon Press.

Mathew, K. M. 1982. **Manorma Yearbook '82.** Lottayam: Manoram Publishing House.

Mayer, Adrian C. 1961. **Peasants in the Pacific: A Study of Fiji Indian Rural Society.** London: Routledge & Kegan Paul.

-----. 1963. **Indians in Fiji.** London: Oxford

University Press for the Institute of Race
Relations.
Narayan, S. Venkat. 1981. Trouble in Paradise.
India Today (1-15 September).
Newland, Kathleen. 1979. International Migration:
The Search for Work. Worldwatch Paper 33.
Washington, D.C.: Worldwatch Institute.
Singh, Khushwant. 1966. A History of the Sikhs
Volume 2 1839-1964. Princeton: Princeton
University Press.
Thapar, Romila. 1966. A History of India. Balti-
more: Penguinn Books.
Tinker, Hugh. 1974. A New System of Slavery.
London: Oxford University Press.
------. 1977. The Banyan Tree. New York: Oxford
University Press.
Weiner, Myron. 1982. International Migration and
Development: Indians in the Persian Gulf.
Population and Development Review 8, no. 1.
Wheeler, Sir Mortimer. 1966. Civilizations of the
Indus Valley and Beyond. New York: McGraw-
Hill.

Appendix A

Count of Indians Abroad as of 15 July 1980

Ser. No.	Country	No. of persons of Indian origin residing abroad	No. of Indians who accepted foreign citizenship
1.	Afghanistan	30,000	25,000
2.	Algeria	1,500	40
3	Australia	42,100*	15,982
4.	Bahrain	40,000	200
5.	Bhutan	40,000	20
6.	Botswana	820	500
7	Brazil	2,000	8
8.	Burma	3-4 Lakhs	7,300
9.	Canada	17,000	95,000
10.	Denmark	637	65
11.	Egypt	600	1
12.	Ethiopia	2,350	450
13.	Fiji	300,697	300,650
14.	France	500	6
15.	Germany(FRG)	13,082	1,521
16.	Ghana	1,250	44
17.	Grenada	3,900	3,700
18.	Guyana	424,400	424,100

APPENDIX A (Continued)

19.	Hong Kong	12,600	4,000
20.	Indonesia	20,000	5,000
21.	Iran	20,800	920
22.	Iraq	20,250	10,000
23.	Italy	900	–
24.	Jamaica	50,318	50,000
25.	Japan	1,858	110
26.	Jordan	3,515	–
27.	Kenya	79,000	72,500
28.	Kuwait	65,000	100
29.	Lebanon	600	7
30.	Lesotho	1,020	800
31.	Liberia	1,000	–
32.	Libya	10,000	–
33.	Malgasy	20,000	15,500
34.	Malawi	4,900	3,640
35.	Malaysia	1,208,500	1,009,500
36.	Mauritius	623,500	612,527
37.	Morocco	500	125
38.	Mozambique	22,043	21,792
39.	Nepal	3,800,000	2,387,973
40.	Netherlands	101,500	100,000
41.	New Zealand	10,000	9,200
42.	Nigeria	15,000	3
43.	Norway	1,450	75
44.	Oman	60,000	5
45.	Pakistan	unavailable	unavailable
46.	Panama	1,500	250
47.	Philippines	3,000	500
48.	Portugal	6,000	5,939
49.	Qatar	30,000	125
50.	Saudi Arabia	120,000	2,000
51.	Seychelles	500	350
52.	Sierra Leone	612	12
53.	Singapore	159,500**	122,000
54.	Somalia	1,072	172
55.	Spain	4,000	37
56.	Sri Lanka	1,350,000	432,986
57.	Sudan	1,800	98
58.	Surinam	124,900	124,750
59.	Sweden	1,889	1,172
60.	Switzerland	2,434	449
61.	Tanzania	59,000	55,000
62.	Thailand	20,000	10,000
63.	Trinidad & Tobago	421,000	420,000
64.	Uganda	430	300
65.	United Arab Emirates	152,000	2,000

APPENDIX A (Continued)

66.	United Kingdom	500,000	250,000
67.	U.S.A.	365,000***	35,000
68.	USSR	750	2
69.	Yemen Arab Republic	3,500	300
70.	Yemen(PDR)	100,000	99,500
71.	Zaire	700	200
72.	Zambia	22,600	9,000

*   Based on recent census.
** Also include nationals of peripheral countries of India.
*** Based on recent census.

Source: Government of India, 1980

THE CHINESE DIASPORA IN SOUTHEAST ASIA

Milton J. Esman

Political elites, intellectuals, and opinion
makers in Southeast Asia are nationalists, jealous
of their independence, fearful of China, and suspi-
cious of resident ethnic Chinese. [1]. The 15-16
million Nanyang (South Seas) Chinese comprise about
5 percent of the total population of Southeast
Asia. As table 1 indicates, the proportions vary
from about 35 percent in Malaysia, 9 percent in
Thailand, 2.7 percent in Indonesia, to a low 1.4
percent in Burma.

Chinese traders and trading communities have
been active in Southeast Asia for centuries. Most
of the overseas Chinese, however, migrated during
the century between 1840 and 1940 in order to
escape the grinding poverty of South China and
take advantage of the growing demand for labor
associated with colonial economic development.
Like most labor diasporas, the great majority considered themselves "sojourners," intending to return eventually to China, as millions did. [2] Gradually, however, many formed families, established
businesses, acquired assets, and settled down permanently in Southeast Asia. More than a generation
after the cessation of immigration, a growing majority are now locally born and educated, have no
expectation of ever returning to China, and are
increasingly acculturated to their surrounding
societies.

Their circumstances, however, differ considerably from country to country. They are by no means
a homogeneous community. They are fragmented by
dialect group, for despite a common written language and a common cultural inheritance, residents
of different areas in China communicate in mutually
incomprehensible dialects. Despite close family
ties and lineage obligations they are, like most

130

ethnic groups, stratified by class. The majority
have few economic assets except for their labor,
but a substantial number are middle class traders,
shopkeepers, skilled workers, or professionals, and
a small but conspicuous minority are very wealthy
and economically powerful capitalists. This capitalist minority is highly influential in the economic life of Southeast Asia; because of their
wealth, they have access to local elites and are
accepted as the interlocutors between these elites
and the Chinese communities.

Overall, the material standards of living of
the overseas Chinese are much higher, usually more
than double those of the native majority.³ The
native image of their economic superiority is exacerbated by the Chinese prominence in middleman
roles and in urban areas, the Chinese having moved
into and quickly dominated small commerce, which
was denigrated by native peasant societies. Because of their highly visible economic success and
their "foreign" identity they are widely resented
and politically vulnerable to demagogic politicians, populist intellectuals, native business
competitors and venal officials. During the past
three centuries Southeast Asia has periodically
witnessed violent attacks on Chinese persons and
property. Like the Jews, another entrepreneurial
diaspora with whom they are frequently compared,
"perhaps no minority has been more chronically
harassed than these twelve million people scattered
throughout the region originally conceived of as
the 'new promised land'" (Viraphol 1972, p. 3).

A number of ethnic Chinese have assimilated
into native societies, but the majority, even of
those who speak local languages and adopt local
names, maintain their separate identity as Chinese.
The Nanyang Chinese have demonstrated impressive
organizational skills for mutual assistance and for
the promotion and defense of group rights and in-
terests.⁴ These dense organizational networks
reinforce their separateness from native society
and sustain their economic and especially their
sentimental links with China. The more local
societies harass and discriminate against them, the
more they must depend on their own organizations,
solidarity and identity as Chinese.

This continuing solidarity and links with
China confirm widespread indigenous suspicions that
the resident Chinese, whether citizens or aliens,
represent an exploiting foreign minority which can
be manipulated by the government of China, a great

power suspected of hegemonic designs over Southeast
Asia. That the Peoples Republic of China (PRC)
continues to exert influence in the affairs of
Southeast Asian countries and has never agreed
categorically to cast the Nanyang Chinese adrift
lends credence to native suspicions about their
unreliability and dangerous dual loyalties. These
fears and suspicions combined with the continuing
interest of the Chinese Communist Party (CCP) in
Southeast Asia generate major tensions between the
PRC and the independent states of Southeast Asia.
A cause of frustration, resentment and guilt among
many of the Southeast Asian elites is their dependence on the financial resources and business skills
of Chinese entrepreneurs, from which local elites
often extract substantial financial benefits. Many
of the Chinese entrepreneurs operate through secretive transnational economic networks of Byzantine
complexity beyond the control of the individual
states, but with close links to Singapore, Hong
Kong, and Taiwan, and shadowy connections with the
PRC.

The development, expression, trends and significance of these relationships for international
affairs in southeast Asia are the subject of this
paper. The data are drawn from a rich and extensive literature, from which the references at the
end of the paper have been selected.

FOUR PERSPECTIVES

Diaspora politics involve tri-lateral relationships
between: (a) a home government, in this case China;
(b) a host government in countries where the diasporas reside; and (c) the diaspora communities. We
shall organize our analysis along these three perspectives, but must add a fourth to incorporate the
transnational economic networks which are a vital
component of the contemporary overseas Chinese
phenomenon.

The Home Government: China

The Manchu (Ch'ing) rulers of China (1644-1911)
were uninterested in commerce with foreign bar-
barians and specifically forbade emigration, for
which the penalty was death by beheading. The
Ch'ing government regarded emigrants as pirates,
bandits or rebels. This was a reasonable assess-

ment during the first century of their rule, since
many of the emigrants were Southerners who could
not reconcile themselves to what they considered a
usurping foreign dynasty. In their declining years
late in the nineteenth century, the Manchu were
forced to abandon this policy under pressure from
the European powers who wrote into the "unequal
treaties" they imposed on the Ch'ing government
provisions that recognized the reciprocal rights of
the parties to protect their subjects residing
abroad. The 1893 repeal of the law forbidding
emigration accepted, de jure, the established fact
that hundreds of thousands of Chinese had emigrated, mostly to Southeast Asia, that they controlled considerable wealth which could be useful
to the impecunious regime in Peking, and that overseas Chinese communities had become centers of
intrigue against an unpopular regime whose failures
had brought humiliation to a once proud people.
Two years before its overthrow in 1911, the Ch'ing
court adopted a nationality law which incorporated
the principle of **ius sanguinis,** that any person of
Chinese ethnic origin remained a Chinese subject
regardless of his or her place of birth or residence.

The successor nationalist regimes, especially
the Kuomintang (KMT), attached high priority to the
overseas Chinese, the 1911 Revolution having been
financed primarily by overseas Chinese contributions. The KMT, which maintained special agencies
dealing with overseas Chinese affairs both in the
KMT party and in the government, emphasized Chinese
national solidarity and the continuing links between China and its ethnic compatriots abroad. Its
consulates assumed the role of protector of the
interests of local Chinese. This was acceptable to
the colonial regimes, which preferred to regard
resident Chinese as aliens who would channel their
political energies toward China, rather than toward
local nationalist movements.

The KMT facilitated the emigration of hundreds
of teachers to organize, staff and supervise
schools for overseas Chinese; in these schools
kuoyu (Mandarin) became the common medium of instruction. The content emphasized Chinese culture
and Chinese political nationalism, thus separating
the Chinese further from the indigenous nationalism
that was beginning to take root in most of Southeast Asia (Fitzgerald 1972, p. 8). Overseas Chinese were encouraged to send their children to China
for secondary and higher education. Xiamen Univer-

sity was established in 1921 in Amoy to educate overseas Chinese and train cadres to work among them. As the Communists began to compete with the KMT for the support of overseas Chinese, the KMT became even more insistent on promoting its version of Chinese nationalism. A major interest of the KMT was to encourage remittances from overseas Chinese to relatives and to communities on the mainland, and especially investment in government securities and in industrial ventures. Remittance agencies and special messenger services were established throughout Southeast Asia to facilitate the flow of funds to the financially hard-pressed governments, first in Canton then Nanking. The brutal encroachments of Japan on Chinese territory in the 1930s provided the occasion for urgent appeals for financial assistance for relief and military equipment, thus strengthening the links between China and its blood brothers abroad. To symbolize this link, representation was provided for overseas Chinese in the organs both of the KMT and the Nanking government. The KMT nationality law of 1929, which reaffirmed the doctrine of **ius sanguinis,** is still in force in Taiwan.

The victory of the Communists in 1949 and the establishment of the PRC inaugurated a new era in the outreach of the home government toward Chinese overseas. There was some continuity, including special units to supervise overseas Chinese affairs, Peking's role as protector, and especially the cultivation of Nanyang Chinese as economic assets for the development and modernization of China.[5] There were two major changes, however: (1) the commitment of the Chinese Communist Party (CCP) to class struggle and to proletarian revolutions in ex-colonial countries; and (2) the need for the PRC to come to terms with the nationalism of the elites of the newly-independent Southeast Asian governments. These two problems, which sometimes generated internal conflicts in PRC policy, required fresh initiatives. The PRC's policies and behavior toward the Nanyang Chinese can be divided into four periods.

During the first period, 1949 to 1955, the new government was groping for a position on a topic to which, as a revolutionary movement, its leaders had devoted little thought. Since it was compelled to compete with the KMT for the sympathy and support of overseas Chinese, the PRC could not allow itself to be outbidden in its demands for their favorable treatment and for equal rights for them. The 1953 census listed overseas Chinese as part of the population of China, and the 1954 Constitution provided representation for them in the National People's Congress. To facilitate remittances and investments, special inducements were introduced and overseas Chinese who chose to reside in China were granted preferential treatment, including the right to live in relative comfort on interest and profits from funds remitted and invested by them or their overseas relatives.

The PRC was forced to confront not only the implacable competition of the KMT government in Taiwan, but also the "containment" policy of the US, which sought to isolate the PRC from the newly-independent states of Southeast Asia. If Peking was to establish its legitimacy in diplomatic competition with Taiwan and to break out of the US-sponsored ring of encirclement, certain changes would be required, notably in its claim to represent, protect and speak for all overseas Chinese. The doctrine of **ius sanguinis** would have to yield to the demands of the Southeast Asian governments to control the national status of its permanent residents, to their unwillingness to tolerate dual citizenship, and to their insistence that China abandon its "colonial" claims on the allegiance of ethnic Chinese in their midst. It would also be necessary to soft-pedal the CCP's appeal to overseas Chinese to participate in revolutionary and anti-imperialist struggles.

The second phase, 1955-1966, was initiated by China's participation in the Bandung Afro-Asian conference in 1955, where Chou En Lai seized the occasion to proclaim China's new policy of "peaceful coexistence" and its willingness to conclude agreements with Southeast Asian countries regulating the nationality and citizenship status of overseas Chinese. Subsequently, the overseas Chinese were advised to choose local nationality.[6]

The principle which was incorporated into the Sino-Indonesian Dual Nationality Treaty of 1955 provides that overseas Chinese should be free to choose local or Chinese citizenship. Those voluntarily selecting Indonesian citizenship would no longer fall under Chinese jurisdiction; thus the PRC abandoned the Ch'ing and KMT doctrine of **ius sanguinis**. Those who chose Chinese citizenship could be repatriated to China or, if they remained aliens, would be expected to abide by the laws of the host country, contribute to its development, and refrain from political activity. The PRC would feel free to encourage cultural and especially economic links with the homeland, including travel, family remittances and investments. The irritant of dual nationality would, however, be exorcised.[7]

The PRC's understanding of the implementation of this treaty failed to account for the powerful indigenous suspicions of China and of overseas Chinese, whether citizens or aliens, and the rising currents of economic nationalism in Indonesia as in every other country in Southeast Asia. A bitter dispute erupted between the PRC and the government of Indonesia over economic measures in the late 1950s which discriminated blatantly against ethnic Chinese. The practice of circumscribing the economic activities of ethnic Chinese regardless of citizenship status and of preferential treatment for indigenous businessmen was galling to the PRC and appeared to violate the letter and the spirit of the treaty. It compromised the PRC and its relations with overseas Chinese, especially when Taiwan denounced the treaty as well as its implementation. After bitter but fruitless attacks on these measures, however, the PRC quietly abandoned its protest, considering it more important to maintain friendly relations with President Sukarno, who was moving toward a foreign policy alignment with Peking, than to defend the interests of overseas Chinese.

This decision established the dominant pattern of future PRC behavior; when Peking's foreign policy interests clashed with the defense of overseas Chinese, the former would have to prevail.[8] A corollary policy adopted during this period was that the interest of the PRC as a state would have to prevail over the CCP as an agent of proletarian revolution. Thus, the PRC accommodated to the "bourgeois" regime of General Ne Win in Burma, allowing the Burmese Communist Party to shift for itself.

This policy of pragmatic accommodation was set aside during the third phase from 1966-1972 when brief efforts were made to export the Great Proletarian Cultural Revolution which Mao had unleashed in 1965. The most dramatic triumph of revolutionary ideology over diplomacy occurred in Rangoon, where in June 1967 the Chinese embassy, in defiance of the Burmese government, issued Mao buttons to students of ethnic Chinese origin. When Chinese students persisted, despite a government order forbidding the wearing of these badges, the Burmese government closed schools. The Chinese embassy then organized a mass demonstration of students which precipitated a violent reaction among Burmese youth in which 50 to 60 local Chinese met their death and hundreds suffered serious property damage (Taylor 1974, pp. 208-33). The response of the PRC was to launch a propaganda barrage against the "fascist" Ne Win government which it had previously befriended and provided with technical and economic assistance, and to renew overtly its support of an insurrection led by the Burmese Communist Party. During this brief period of Red Guard diplomacy the PRC attempted to activate the overseas Chinese on behalf of the Cultural Revolution, straining relations even with relatively friendly governments such as a communist North Vietman.[9] The "lesson," however, was not lost on the indigenous elites of Southeast Asia: Peking, despite protestations to the contrary, was prepared to use the overseas Chinese as instruments of its policy when this seemed expedient. Lest these memories lapse, the Soviet Union continues to remind the Southeast Asian elites of this possibility (Andreyev 1975).

The Cultural Revolution exhausted itself in 1970, and after 1972 a degree of normalcy returned to China. This was symbolized by the visit of President Nixon in 1972 demonstrating that the PRC considered the US, which was about to withdraw from Vietnam, a lesser danger than the Soviet Union. The declining presence of the US, and the threat of a unified and expansionist Vietnam, persuaded ASEAN states, including Malaysia, Thailand and the Philippines, to recognize and normalize relations with the PRC. The PRC was eager to reciprocate in order to avert what it perceived as a Soviet effort to encircle China with hostile neighbors. During the fourth and current period conventional diplomacy prevails. Local Chinese are once again advised to be loyal citizens of their adopted Southeast Asian country in the event they voluntarily accept local citizenship, or to abide by the laws of their country of residence and live in harmony with local people if they decide to remain PRC nationals. Nevertheless, such declarations promising noninterference continue to raise hackles in Southeast Asia because they are accompanied by the statement that ethnic Chinese citizens of Southeast Asian countries are "still our kinsfolk and friends" and that the PRC "has the duty to protect the legitimate

The Chinese Diaspora in Southeast Asia

rights and interests" of overseas Chinese resident
aliens[10] (Suryadinata 1978b, pp. 39-40).

Since 1980 Peking has successfully liquidated
the decade-long guerrilla movement in northern and
northeastern Thailand conducted by the Communist
Party of Thailand, many of whose cadres and fighters are Thai Chinese. Peking apparently determined
that the insurgency was weakening the ability of
the Thai Government to withstand pressure from the
Vietnamese forces on Thailand's long eastern border
with occupied Cambodia and Laos. From the PRC
perspective, revolutionary activity in Thailand is
less important than resisting the Vietnamese
threat, which they regard as a Soviet surrogate.
To most Southeast Asian elites this development
meant that the PRC is willing and able to manipulate local Communist parties and especially their
Chinese cadres to promote the foreign policy objectives of China, even when these conflict with
the interests of the local Commumnist parties. If
revolutionary activity could be suspended at Peking's behest, could it not also be reinstituted at
a later date with the help of locally-resident
Chinese? The PRC, according to this view, will
continue to intervene in Southeast Asian affairs
through Communist parties and ethnic Chinese whenever it suits its purposes.

During the current phase, the PRC has stepped
up its interest in economic relations with Nanyang
Chinese. It actively fosters and encourages tourism, remittances and investments. Peking hopes to
increase these financial flows substantially from
the mid-1970s level of $400 million to an annual $1
billion. While the estimated 12 million overseas
Chinese residents in China were vilified as bourgeois counter-revolutionaries during the Red Guard
period, and many were harassed and forced to leave,
the PRC now goes out of its way to attract both
money and technical and business skills from the
Nanyang in support of its modernization goals. It
is willing to provide domestic overseas Chinese
with preferences, privileges, comforts and even
special institutions not available to ordinary
Chinese (Fitzgerald 1972, p. 4). It maintains an
elaborate system of banking facilities, investment
corporations, tourist services, special shops,
resettlement agencies and schools to cater to their
needs (Fitzgerald 1972, pp. 12-34).

The PRC has innovated a doctrine that distinguishes state-to-state from party-to-party relations (Taylor 1972, p. 234-40). This permits the

PRC elites to follow diplomatically correct practices of coexistence and noninterference in state-
to-state relations, while continuing to support the
subversive activities of local communist parties.
To most Southeast Asian elites this is sheer hypoc-
risy, since the same people who control the CCP
also control the PRC government. The anti-commun-
ust Suharto government in Indonesia believes that the
embassy of the PRC, supported by funds extorted
from local Chinese businessmen, conspired with the
Communist Party of Indonesia (KPI) in the gestapu
coup of October, 1965, to seize control of the
government.[11] Since 1948 the Communist Party of
Malaya, manned entirely by ethnic Chinese, has
conducted an insurrection, first against the British colonial government, then against the indigenous Malayan and Malaysian regimes. While no
longer a serious threat, this Chinese-led insurgency is a nagging preoccupation for Kuala Lumpur. It
is perceived as an effort by a section of the
Chinese diaspora to take over the Malaysian state.
As the price of recognition, the Malaysians asked
Peking to discontinue its support to the Malayan
Communist Party, including the regular radio broadcasts (the "Voice of the Malayan Revolution") from
transmitters located in southwest China. The PRC
at first refused to honor this request, despite the
continuing suspicion that it breeds, invoking the
aforementioned distinction between state-state and
party-party relations. It later removed the trans-
mitter from Yunna, after which similar broadcasts
began from guerrilla bases in south Thailand. The
PRC elites suggest that if the CCP were to abandon
such overt support for Southeast Asian communist
movements, the latter would soon be embraced by the
Soviet Union, which would be contrary to the interests both of China and of the Southeast Asian
governments.

To summarize, the practices of the PRC towards
the overseas Chinese are tailored to particular
situations and opportunities in the various countries in Southeast Asia. The following policies
have evolved during the past three decades:

1. The foreign policy requirements of the PRC
   take precedence over the protection of overseas Chinese. Except for the interlude of the
   Cultural Revolution this policy has been
   maintained. The recent contrast between
   Vietnam and Cambodia illustrates this point.

After the unification of Vietnam in 1975 the Hanoi government tightened its military and economic links with the Soviet Union, much to the discomfiture of Peking. In January 1979 it moved its armies into Cambodia, displacing the Khmer Rouge regime which was and still remains a client of Peking both at state and party levels. Fearing a fifth column, Hanoi began to move ethnic Chinese from strategic areas and then implanted a program of liquidating petit bourgeois enterprises. The great majority of victims happened to be ethnic Chinese whose nationality status was in dispute between the two governments. This harassment and pillaging resulted in the overland flow of tens of thousands of refugees to China and the pathetic odyssey of the "boat people" in the South China Sea. The PRC protested vigorously and launched a propaganda campaign against Hanoi for willfully persecuting resident Chinese. Its military invasion of Vietnam in 1979 to "teach the Vietnamese a lesson" was prompted by the PRC's many grievances against the Hanoi government, including its mistreatment of ethnic Chinese.[12] Prior to these events, the Khmer Rouge in Cambodia had slaughtered thousands of innocent Sino-Cambodians in its genocidal attack on urban residents of all races, but Peking failed to utter a single word of protest. Its foreign policy required it to support a friendly client regime in Cambodia, while the persecution of Chinese in Vietnam provided an additional reason to attack an unfriendly government. In each case, Peking's foreign policy interests dictated its responses to the mistreatment of overseas Chinese.

2. Peking intends to maintain its links with "kinsfolk and friends" among the Nanyang Chinese, whether local citizens or alien nationals. The PRC is not prepared to cast them adrift. It believes it needs their economic support for the modernization of China and this support the PRC will continue to cultivate. It would be a mistake, however, to underestimate the sentimental ties and ethnocentric obligations that continue to bind the responsible leaders of any regime in China to its co-ethnics abroad, especially when they are victimized or in distress. As a great

power and the guardians of the culture of the "Middle Kingdom," China's elites must be sensitive to the needs of overseas Chinese though they may not, in every case, be willing or able to intervene, even verbally, on their behalf. These continuing links may, as the leaders of Southeast Asian countries fear, be available as instruments of the PRC's foreign policy, for intelligence collection, for propaganda, for market penetration, and for exercising influence in political and economic decision making in host countries.

3. The PRC finds it useful to persist in the distinction between state and party relations. Where the local communist party is primarily Chinese, as in Malaysia, or is suspected of close relations with local Chinese and the PRC, as in Indonesia and Burma, this inevitably compromises the PRC policy of normalizing relations. The PRC seems prepared to pay this price in order to protect its position in competition with the Soviet Union for influence in international communist circles.

Host Government Elites

During the colonial period the authorities in the various Southeast Asian countries tolerated Chinese immigrants as laborers and traders who performed necessary economic functions and contributed to the economic development of the colonies. As alien communities they were largely self-governing, obedient, and required few public services. Such political energies as they expended were primarily oriented toward China--a state that had been so weakened by the end of the nineteenth century that it represented no threat to the colonial regimes. They had little interest in indigenous independent movements. Only after World War I, when the KMT succeeded in politicizing many overseas Chinese communities and when the communist movement began to recruit among overseas Chinese, did the colonial governments begin to concern themselves with political activity among resident Chinese. The British dissolved the KMT in Malaya in 1925 as a threat to security. Following World War II, the British authorities were forced to deal with the Chinese-dominated Malayan Communist Party, which in 1948 launched a dangerous and costly insurrection.

While the insurrection was defeated, it contributed to the termination of British rule in 1957. The indigenous nationalists who succeeded the European colonialists shared none of their predecessors' benign tolerance towards the Chinese in their midst. They resented their determination to maintain separate identity and institutions and their sense of cultural superiority which the Chinese made little effort to conceal. The Chinese were suspect not only as an alien presence, but as economic exploiters and parasites who had been compliant beneficiaries of the colonial policy of suppressing indigenous entrepreneurship. Their relatively high living standards and conspicuous wealth were believed to have been accumulated at the expense of local people and as clients of the colonial policy of divide and rule. With few exceptions the Chinese failed to contribute to the independence struggle. Moreover, they continued to maintain sentimental and economic links with China, many rejecting local citizenship even when it was offered. Many Indonesians, for example, were shocked at what appeared to them to be the hesitant and opportunistic approach of the majority of Chinese to the citizenship provisions of the 1955 treaty.[13] Where, local nationalists ask, do their true loyalties lie? With minor variations, economic exploitation and dual loyalty have been and remain the underlying suspicions of indigenous Southeast Asians of all classes toward the Nanyang Chinese. The city-state of Singapore, with its 75 percent Chinese minority, is an understandable exception. Suspected by its neighbors of being a "third China" in their midst, Singapore trades actively with the mainland but maintains a discreet political distance.

What accentuates the hostility of indigenous elites to their overseas Chinese residents is their pervasive fear of China. With its vast population, growing military power, and its revolutionary mission, China is suspected of harboring hegemonic designs over the nations of Southeast Asia. Despite Peking's protestations about its peaceful intentions and its doctrine of coexistence, Southeast Asians are aware of its invasion of Vietnam in 1979, its continuing military and diplomatic support for the Khmer Rouge in Cambodia, its continuing propaganda support for the Malayan Communist Party's insurgency and, until very recently, for the Communist Party of Thailand, the activation of Chinese students in Burma in 1967--all of which imply the ability and the intention of the Asian "colossus of the North" to interfere in the affairs of these smaller countries in an unfriendly way (Taylor 1974, p. viii). Are the resident ethnic Chinese a "fifth column" that can be activated on behalf of China when its foreign policy or the exigencies of international communist competition dictate? Do the economic links between China and local Chinese businessmen provide leverage for Peking to distort the economic development of their countries? Soviet spokesmen continue to remind Southeast Asians that the overseas Chinese bourgeoisie operate as "tools of Peking" bleeding their local economies, often through illegal channels, which benefit China to the detriment of Southeast Asia's domestic economies (Andreyev 1975).

In response to these fears and suspicions every Southeast Asian government has taken steps to promote the cultural indigenization of its resident Chinese. Education in the Chinese medium has been strictly circumscribed and curricula, even in the remaining Chinese schools, are closely supervised to emphasize national rather than Chinese information and orientation. The Chinese are encouraged to adopt local names and to intermarry, a process that has progressed much further in Buddhist Thailand and Cambodia and in the Christian Philipines than in Islamic Malaysia and Indonesia. All Southeast Asian governments, Singapore excepted, have instituted economic measures that grant preferences to native businessmen and frequently discriminate against Chinese, both citizen and alien, in order to break the Chinese "stranglehold" on their economies. Public sector enterprises serve the policy of economic nationalism by excluding or severely limiting Chinese employment and direct financial participation; attempts have even been made in Thailand and Malaysia to give indigenous businessmen or state enterprises control of trade with China.[14]

Communist governments in Indochina have attacked and gravely weakened the economic bases of their overseas Chinese communities by expropriation, combined with genocide in the case of Cambodia, and expulsions from Laos and Vietnam. The ASEAN countries that are developing along capitalist lines follow a dual policy: to limit the economic role of local Chinese, especially in the highly visible small business and trading sectors through preferential treatment for indigenous entrepreneurs plus discrimination and occasional harassment of Chinese; and to capitalize, at least for the time being, on the business skills, international contacts and financial strength of the large Chinese firms to facilitate their national economic development. One pattern has emerged in Thailand and in Indonesia where senior politicians, military officers and officials participate with Chinese financiers and industrialists in what amount to joint ventures: the Chinese contribute managerial skills and much of the capital, while the local elites provide protection and access to government licenses, credit and sometimes monopoly privileges. Both parties participate in the profits of these often substantial enterprises in this symbiotic partnership between men of power and men of wealth. Some of the benefits trickle down to rank and file Chinese through subcontracts and patronage networks. To the Chinese capitalists these arrangements represent a tax, a cost of doing business. But they also buy a measure of protection for them and for their Chinese communities, since they commit local elites to pragmatic policies that benefit private enterprise and limit the permissible harassment of Chinese. For the local elites these arrangements combine personal profit with participation in the economic development of their country.

These practices of "pragmatic" national elites have drawn fire in all the ASEAN countries from leftist and populist intellectuals, students and nationalists who charge that they sanction the exploitation of the native majority. The Chinese extract high profits at the expense of native businessmen who are shut out of these lucrative enterprises while their national leaders allow themselves to be suborned and corrupted by the wily Chinese. Through their control of the economy, the nationalists argue, the Chinese can and do exert undue political influence. This is the language of native opposition groups in all the Southeast Asian countries, Singapore excepted. Offended that indigenous elites are growing wealthy as partners and patrons of exploiting, unscrupulous and potentially subversive foreigners, they reject the argument that the wealth and skills of the local Chinese are necessary to the economic development of their countries. They fail to distinguish between alien Chinese and citizens of Chinese extraction, or between local Chinese and China, which they believe are bound by indissoluble ties of consanguinity, cultural affinity and economic interest. They distrust their Chinese compatriots and deplore their economic power as threats to national security and to the development of an indigenous business community. Like the Jews in the West, the overseas Chinese are regarded with suspicion and turned into scapegoats for being simultaneously capitalists and communists.

The pragmatic elites who tolerate and work with local Chinese capitalists take account of these populist stereotypes by enforcing real or symbolic economic restrictions against the Chinese. The Chinese are able to circumvent some of these restrictions through convenient marriages, Ali-Baba arrangements or bribery.[15] Malaysia found it impossible to accept Chinese boat people in 1979-1980 as permanent residents, though Muslim refugees from Cambodia were readily admitted. In response to student rioting during a visit by the Japanese prime minister in 1974, which resulted in the burning and looting of Chinese businesses, Jakarta decided that henceforth foreign (Japanese) investors must choose native (**primbumi**) Indonesians rather than ethnic Chinese as their local business associates (Suryadinata 1978, p. 143).

Southeast Asian countries differ somewhat in their degree of hostility and suspicion of the PRC. At one extreme is the government of Vietnam, which now ascribes all of its acute economic woes to a conspiracy between the government in Peking and unscrupulous resident Chinese (**New York Times,** 15 June 1982, p. A-3). Among the ASEAN countries which attempt to concert their foreign policies, Malaysia and Indonesia continue to regard Chinese hegemonial ambitions as a greater long-term danger to Southeast Asia then Vietnamese expansionism. Singapore, with its Chinese majority, the Philippines, with a very small Chinese minority, and Thailand, facing Vietnamese armies on its long eastern borders, all consider Vietnam the greater immediate threat and welcome Chinese pressure on the Soviet's Indochinese client. The Malaysian-Indonesian position is motivated by their concern that Peking may interfere in their affairs by using local Chinese as proxies. After the Chinese invasion of Vietnam in 1979, the Indonesians decided to slow down the process of normalizing diplomatic relations with China, which had been suspended since 1967. Their expressed concern was that a PRC embassy in Jakarta might attempt to mobilize local Chinese for activities inimical to Indonesia's national interest (Suryadinata 1978b, p. 33).

Given their version of the embassy's complicity in the 1965 coup, their memory of the 1967 funeral protest, and the close links the embassy maintained with local Chinese and with the Indonesian Communist Party, Jakarta regards any diplomatic link with Peking as potentially troublesome. Dual nationality has been a sensitive problem affecting relations between the PRC and Southeast Asian states. Peking has formally renounced the policy of **ius sanguinis** and proposed to regulate the status of overseas Chinese by bilateral agreements, as previously described. The implementation of the 1955 Treaty with Indonesia, however, produced disagreements and tensions which, after 25 years, were still not resolved.[16] Severe disputes have also arisen with Burma and with Vietnam. Peking rejects the claims of these governments to the power to confer citizenship unilaterally on resident Chinese in the absence of voluntary choice and formal agreement with Peking (Suryadinata 1978, p. 24). This implies that Peking will not give up jurisdiction over overseas Chinese except by international agreement. Yet there is evidence to the contrary (Fitzgerald 1974, p. 110-15).

The PRC has not challenged Malaysia's "Merdeka Compact," which conferred citizenship on locally born ethnic Chinese after its independence in 1957, and established procedures for the naturalization of others (Amyot 1972, pp. 12-13). Peking's surrender of jurisdiction over Nanyang Chinese who opt for local citizenship and its advice to them to choose local nationality have left many Southeast Asians unconvinced that Peking really means to let go, especially when it clearly intends to contineue to appeal to ethnic Chinese citizens of Southeast Asian countries for financial transfers and to regard them as "kinsfolk and friends."

The Diaspora Communities

By the late nineteenth century some Nanyang communities had been established for centuries. These included the "Baba" Chinese in the British Straits Settlements and the "Peranakan" in Java. Some were absorbed into local societies; many leading families have some Chinese blood, including the Thai royal family (Skinner 1957, p. 26). Though they acculturated to indigenous languages and customs, were educated in the colonial language, and achieved responsible positions in business and in the professions, descendants of the early settlers for the most part retained their group identy as Chinese. They never managed to achieve social equality with Westerners.

The great majority of the Chinese who streamed into Southeast Asia from the turn of the century until the outbreak of World War II considered themselves "sojourners" who had come to the Nanyang as guest workers and intended to return to China. Many did earn their fortunes and returned, but the majority who survived the hardships of labor in the tin mines, plantations, and frontier settlements and moved on to small business and urban occupations chose to remain in Southeast Asia, as did their children.

They retained their Chinese identity, however. Their propensity to organize into secret societies, kinship and dialect associations, and occupational guilds helped to maintain their solidarity. They provided education for their children in the Chinese medium. They developed their own newspapers and social welfare insititutions. They remitted substantial funds to their families and contributed to community institutions, such as schools, clinics and temples in their home communities in China. The Colonial authorities left them alone, except when competition among the secret societies disturbed public order. Under colonial protection and economic laissez faire the overseas Chinese communities prospered and pursued a vigorous community life.

At the turn of the century, fresh currents of nationalism swept through the Chinese communities, nourished by a recognition of their common status as Chinese in alien environments, rather than as men from a particular village or dialect community.[17] From colonial sources their writers and teachers became acquainted with the concept of nationalism and this was dramatized by the humiliation of China by Japan in the war of 1895. Nationalist sentiment was spread by such missionaries as Dr. Sun Yat-sen, whose 1911 revolution was financed in large measure by overseas Chinese. Chinese nationalism, which preceded indigenous nataionalism in most of Southeast Asia, enhanced the solidarity of the overseas Chinese. It reinforced their not inconsiderable cultural pride and their contempt for local cultures and lifestyles, thereby retarding what tendencies had existed for identification with local societies. With few exceptions they felt secure and satisfied under colonial rule. They

secretly feared the consequences of indigenous
nationalism, which gradually took root during the
1920s and flourished during the Japanese occupation
of 1942-1945, while the Japanese bore down heavily
on the Chinese as enemy nationals. With few exceptions they failed to participate in the indigenous
independence movements, for which the victorious
nationalists have not forgiven them. In the independent regimes of Southeast Asia which are legitimated by indigenous nationalism, the Chinese emerged as a vulnerable minority, economically powerful
and conspicuous, unwilling to assimilate, suspected
of foreign loyalties and even of subversive intentions regardless of their formal status as citizens or aliens.

The Chinese diasporas are cross pressured.
Since immigration has declined to a trickle since
1940, an annually increasing majority is locally
born with no direct knowledge of China and no
intention of ever returning. They are under strong
pressure from their host governmnents to assimilate. Except in Malaysia, they cannot engage in
communal politics. Links with China are frowned
upon, even for registered aliens who enjoy the
formal protection of Peking's diplomatic establishment. The majority would like to be respected and
accepted by local society and escape the stigma of
dual loyalty, but without abandoning their Chinese
cultural heritage or identity.[18] Some have returned to China. Others have chosen to assimilate
as individuals.

The main trend, however, is the acceptance of
local citizenship, claims for equal rights and
nondiscriminatory treatment as individuals in public affairs, education and economic life, combined
with the right to cultural maintenance, including
community institutions and Chinese schools. Their
aspirations for cultural pluralism invite suspicion
from all the Southeast Asian governments. The Thai
reject it categorically and promote cultural assimilation. Indonesia will not grant the Chinese the
status of an indigenous ethnic group. Despite the
national slogan "Unity in Diversity," Indonesia's
elites are unwilling to legitimize a permanent
Chinese presence which could be manipulated by the
PRC. Malaysia alone, with its 34% percent Chinese
minority, is willing to accept the logic of communal pluralism, but only within the framework of a
vigorous Malay language policy and "national unity"
doctrine, combined with government sponsored
preferences for Malays in higher education, govern-

ment employment, and ownership and management roles in the private sector. While they acquiesce in economic transactions, the Southeast Asian governments discourage cultural contacts with China. Why do the majority of overseas Chinese, now mostly locally born and educated, persist in maintaining their ethnic identity and solidarity in the face of strong contrary pressures from governments and indigenous majorities which brand them as foreigners suspected of dual loyalty? One reason clearly is cultural pride, to which they are socialized by family and community, combined with a low evaluation of indigenous societies and cultures. These cultural loyalties are reinforced by the Herzl syndrome, the fear that even if they conscientiously attempt to identify with native society they will remain marginal and never fully accepted.[19] Thus, the highly respected Chinese-Indonesian nationalist and communist, Lien Koen Hian, who devoted his life to the struggle for an integrated Indonesian society, decided to end his career as a Chinese nationalist and citizen of the PRC (Suryadinata 1978a, pp. 80-112). A number of Malaysian Chinese high school students have reacted against alleged educational discrimination by militant assertion of their Chinese identity. This fear of rejection and marginalization is especially true among ethnic Chinese in the Muslim societies of Malaysia and Indonesia.[20]

Equally important is the economic price that many Chinese would have to pay if they were to assimilate to the point where they lost their links with Chinese business enterprises. These economic links afford overseas Chinese greater economic opportunities, more economic security and much higher living standards than they could expect elsewhere under prevailing conditions in Southeast Asia. Chinese firms, financial networks, and distribution systems are not merely economic enterprises. They are social systems as well. Those who leave the community lose their claim to participate in these enterprises as suppliers, employees and distributors, once the essential bonds of trust and obligation are severed. So long as Chinese firms maintain this social character it is dangerous for the individual Chinese to defect from the community, especially when he is unsure of his options and can expect to be discriminated against in government, the parastatals, and foreign enterprises, which are the only alternative employers. Unless Chinese enterprises and economic networks are eliminated, while other employers, including governments, accept Chinese on a nondiscriminatory basis, there is little likelihood that many Chinese will accept assimilation as a feasible life strategy. Thus, the inclination toward cultural maintenance is reinforced by the economic opportunity structure which disciplines most overseas Chinese in the direction of community solidarity.[26]

Except in Malaysia, where it must be with discretion, the Nanyang communities cannot mobilize publicly on behalf of any international interest they may feel, and certainly not on behalf of the Peoples' Republic of China. The political systems of these countries are simply not open to this form of public pressure or lobbying, least of all for Chinese advocating support of the PRC by their government. The very suspicion of such activity would confirm the worst fears of indigenous intellectuals about the dual loyalty of the resident Chinese and their vulnerability to manipulation by the PRC. In these systems, the Chinese diasporas can exercise influence by discreet petitioning, by informal negotiation with elites, and by judicious bribery and gift giving, but usually only on domestic matters of interest to Chinese groups or to the Chinese as a community, not on matters of foreign relations. The interlocutors for the Chinese are usually successful business leaders who are respected by, and enjoy access to, local elites. Chinese intellectuals who challenge the dominance of the business leaders over their community are usually unsuccessful because the native elites will not deal with them.[22] This has been the experience of the Democratic Action Party in Malaysia, which is led by intellectuals; it is losing out in competition with the capitalist-dominated Malayan Chinese Association.[23]

Transnational Economic Networks

It is estimated that in Indonesia the Chinese control 70 percent of the wholesale and retail trade. In Thailand 23 of the 25 leading private businessmen are Chinese (**Far Eastern Economic Review,** 16 June 1978, pp. 22-23). They control 80 percent of the country's rice, tin, rubber and timber exports, and virtually all retail and wholesale trade (Viraphol 1972). In Malaysia, 1971 government figures estimated that foreign interests controlled 63

percent of the modern corporate sector of the economy, Chinese 27.4 percent and Malays a mere 2.4
percent. After ten years of the New Economic Policy designed explicitly to increase Malay partipa-
tion, the foreign share had fallen to 47.5 percent;
the Malay share, most of it held by government
agencies in trust for the Malay people, had increased to 12.4 percent, while the Chinese share
had grown to 40.1 percent. These figures under-
state Chinese economic power in Malaysia, where
they hold a near monopoly in small industry, distributive businesses, and rural money lending.

The value of overseas Chinese investments and
other holdings in Southeast Asia in 1975 has been
estimated at US $16.6 billion (Wu and Wu 1980,
p. 34). It would be a mistake however, to believe
that this impressive accumulation of wealth and
economic power is confined within the national
borders of these countries. As every knowlegeable
offical and journalist in Southeast Asia knows, the
Nanyang Chinese financiers and traders operate on a
transnational basis through networks that are
founded through networks that are founded on extended kinship and other nonformal relationships.[24]
Based in Hong Kong or Singapore, these networks
control vast financial resources which can be moved
quickly and efficiently to support profitable investment opportunities--hotels and flour mills in
Bangkok, housing estates and shopping centers in
Malaysia, logging operations and shipping lines in
Indonesia.[25] The success of national development
plans in capitalist Southeast Asian countries depends far more on maintaining a favorable investment climate for the overseas Chinese transnationals than on flows of foreign aid. For this reason
Southeast Asian elites must consult the leaders of
these financial networks when considering large
investment projects. Like most businessmen, their
operations are mainly apolitical. Many are known
to have connections both in Taiwan and in Peking.
Since family remittances appear to be declining as
more and more overseas Chinese are locally born and
as several countries enforce foreign currency con-
trols, Peking must rely on these firms to meet its
annual target of one billion dollars in foreign
exchange flows from overseas Chinese. In the
Southeast Asian countries their operations must be
legitimated and fortified by working arrangements
with government elites. Government agencies and
sometimes senior politicians and officials participate as their local partners in most large under-

takings (Skinner 1957, p. 360). These arrangements create a moderate environment, which tends to protect security and maintain economic opportunities for overseas Chinese and keep the populist demogogues under wraps.[26] Because they operate informally and secretively, there is little systematic information or published data about these economically powerful networks. A few examples will, however, suffice to indicate the scale, scope and style of their activities. In May 1978 seven hundred businessmen of Chinese backround from all the ASEAN countries held a symposium at the Philippine Plaza Hotel in Manila. The medium of communication was Mandarin. The theme was "the role of the businessman in promoting prosperity and stability in the ASEAN region." President Marcos and three of his cabinet ministers attended sessions of this symposium, suggesting the importance that native elites attach to goodwill of the Chinese transnational financiers (Adicondro 1979). The collapse in 1982 of the speculative property boom in Hong Kong had ramifications throughout the Chinese business communities in Southeast Asia. Many of the promoters of property speculation were overseas Chinese "godfathers" and some of the money that was lost in these ventures came from overseas Chinese investors attracted by the prospect of high speculative returns (Bowring 1982, pp. 64-66).

On 27 March 1982, Chang Ming Thien of Penang was found dead in his room in the Merlin Hotel in Kuala Lumpur. Through the Overseas Trust Bank (OTB) in Hong Kong and a holding company, International Consolidated Investments, Ltd. he controlled a vast economic network which extended throughout the region:

> In addition to OTB and its rapid growth and expansion in the 1970s, Chang has wide interests in hotels, property, resources, finance and investment, particularly in Thailand and, though to a lesser extent after recent sales, in Malaysia. The total size of his holding may have been known only to himself, though his children have acted as his regional proxies for some time--Patrick Chang in Hong Kong, Miss Chang (his daughter) in Malaysia, Singapore and Thailand and another son, Eric Chang, in Taiwan and Thailand. But the family has not always been united. In the early 1970s Eric was jailed in Singapore for in-

volvement in an unsuccessful plot to kill his
father's mistress (**Far Eastern Economic
Review**, 11 June 1982, pp. 105-8).

Chang's close business associates included persons
from Indonesia, Thailand, the Philippines and
Malaysia. His syndicate had growing relations with
Middle East oil tycoons and at various times attempted to gain control of US banking institutions,
including the American Express International Bank
for which he unsuccessfully offered $250 million in
1981. Some of the larger Chinese transnationals now
operate worldwide.[27]
What is most significant about the late Mr.
Chang's financial empire is not its intricacy or
its scale, but its ability to operate over all of
non-communist Southeast Asia, as well as in Taiwan,
Hong Kong, and probably the PRC. Most of his
operations required not only the acquiescence of
host governments, but negotiated partnership participation by government agencies or local influen-
tials. At times Chang was compelled by governments
to relinquish major holdings, such as divestiture
at the insistence of the government of Malaysia of
his majority holding in the United Malayan Banking
Corporation, Malaysia's second largest.
Rumors abound in Southeast Asia that the overseas Chinese networks attempt to exert political
influence on behalf of resident Chinese interests,
for example, by withholding investments in protest
against Malaysia's Industrial Coordination Act of
1975 which allegedly imposed unfair and discriminatory burdens on Chinese-controlled enterprises.
These suspicions, along with similar charges that
these networks operate as economic and political
tools of Peking, have never been verified, but they
tend to be believed by large numbers of Southeast
Asians of all classes who regard all Chinese as
part of a grand conspiracy to dominate their countries. For the time being, these transnationals
are valued, if not fully trusted, by national
elites who depend on them for their skills, their
contacts, and the funds they can mobilize. If the
pragmatic capitalist-oriented elites of the Southeast Asian countries should be forced to yield to
more populist and ideologically nationalist competitors, the transnationals might have a more
difficult time operating in these countries and
would be less able to defend the interests of the
oversea Chinese communities.

The Chinese Diaspora in Southeast Asia

The Persistence of the Overseas Chinese "Problem"

International relations in Southeast Asia during this century cannot be understood without reference to the position of overseas Chinese. Every expression of diaspora politics is reflected in the rich history and the current circumstances of the Nanyang Chinese:

1. The home government, China, has intervened and continues to exert influence on the affairs of the Southeast Asian states. The nature of these interventions is conditioned by the foreign policy priorities of the home government. The present regime in China must weigh its interest in normalizing and maintaining correct relations with Southeast Asian states against its need to contend with Taiwan for the support of overseas Chinese and with Moscow for leadership of the Asian communist movements. The fear that China may interfere in their affairs or use the interests of ethnic Chinese as pretexts to intervene remains a source of tension between China and Southeast Asian governments.

2. The diaspora communities have acted, though not necessarily in unison, to influence events in the home country. They have raised funds to finance a revolution, supported competing factions bidding for control of the motherland, and boycotted the Japanese enemy. While their ability to intervene directly is now quite limited, the current effect of the overseas Chinese transnationals is to encourage those groups among the competing PRC elites who favor pragmatic strategies of economic growth and modernization.

3. The home government seeks to capitalize on the overseas diaspora as economic and foreign policy assets. It unashamedly attracts funds from the diaspora for its economic growth which represent unrequited financial transfers from Southeast Asian countries. It maintains an elaborate set of institutions and services to foster and maintain financial flows. It has used diaspora groups to advance the interests of the PRC and of the communist movement at the cost of incurring deep suspicions among Southeast Asian elites and compromising the

position of the diaspora communities. Peking is not willing to forego these assets entirely but may expediently withold their use in the interests of better relations with individual Southeast Asian states. The PRC's foreign policy needs have taken, and are likely to continue to take, precedence over the protection of overseas Chinese or the interests of local communist parties when these come into conflict.

4. There is little evidence that host governments have attempted to use the diasporas to promote their own foreign policy goals. A close examination would probably indicate that Southeast Asian governments have drawn on information available to local Chinese and may have used them as interlocutors in dealing with Peking and Taiwan. They do, however, draw on the Chinese transnationals to promote their economic development goals as well as the personal financial interests of members of the political and administrative elites.

The end of immigration, restrictions on Chinese-medium education, and intense local nationalism bring heavy pressures on individuals in the diaspora to acculturate and eventually assimilate, but the degree and pace of acculturation depend in considerable measure on the willingness of local societies to accept them. This willingness varies from country to country and appears to be greater in Thailand and the Philippines than in Indonesia or Malaysia.[28] In addition to cultural pride, most overseas Chinese are reluctant to sacrifice or put at risk the protection and the substantial economic benefits they derive from membership in the Chinese communities in exchange for the uncertain economic prospects and social rejection they might encounter if they should attempt to assimilate. Nor is it in China's interest that these communities wither away. Ironically, it is much more likely that they would wither away under communist governments which would destroy their ecomomic base than under regimes that foster capitalist enterprise and maintain links with transnational Chinese enterprises.

The intense native suspicion of overseas Chinese is exacerbated by the exigencies of domestic politics. The political "outs," regardless of their ideological orientation, are likely to charge government elites with excessively indulging the universally unpopular Chinese. There are, however, special circumstances which breed continuing suspicion and distrust. First, China is a large, powerful and threatening presence to most Southeast Asians. The PRC's propensity to interfere in Southeast Asian affairs continues to nourish these fears, despite the PRC's current doctrine of normalization and coexistence. Second, China is suspected not only as a great power seeking hegemony, but also as a subversive force willing to deploy the overseas Chinese to promote its revolutionary mission (Taylor 1974, p. 390). Of the great powers interested in Southeast Asia, only China has both a revolutionary mission and resident ethnic communities that could act as a fifth column.

Finally, by their conspicuous wealth and their cultural pride, the diaspora communities are a provocation to local nationalists. As Milne (1974, p. 100) observes, "the Chinese in Southeast Asia affect foreign policy not by bringing their influence to bear on it but rather by the mere fact of their conspicuous and disturbing existence." Admired for their industry, they are distrusted as ruthless and unscrupulous economic exploiters who dominate the local economies, corrupt national leadership, but resist incorporation into native society while retaining cultural and economic links with a potentially hostile country. This is a classical expression of the vulnerability of diasporas to being the scapegoats and to charges of dual loyalty.

Combined, these conditions are certain to perpetuate native distrust of the Chinese diasporas, both in their domestic and international roles. Many indigenous nationalists think in ethnic categories and thus are unable to distinguish between China and local residents of Chinese origin, nor does formal citizenship status matter much to them.[29] The PRC is not willing to oblige by severing its links with overseas Chinese in a categorical and convincing way. Nor are the Chinese overseas transnationals, with their links to domestic Chinese businessmen, to Peking and Taiwan, and to Southeast Asia's political elites likely to vanish from the scene. So long as these factors persist--a home government that will not let go, host governments and local publics that distrust and fear both the home government and the resident diasporas, and economically powerful diaspora communities that intend or feel constrained to maintain their separate identity and institutions--the overseas Chinese "problem" in Southeast Asia's regional politics will not go away.

Notes

1   The exception to many of these general statements is the city-state of Singapore, with its large Chinese majority.

2   Skinner (1957, p. 61) estimated that the rate of return from Thailand to China between 1882 and 1917 ranged from 56 to 78 percent of annual immigration. There are an estimated 10-12 million overseas Chinese returnees now residing in China (Fitzgerald 1972).

3   For a careful analysis of the Malaysian data on income distribution see Snodgrass (1974). Since the ethnic division of labor is similar, the 2-to-1 ratio probably applies to all the Southeast Asian countries.

4   A recent estimate for Malaysia is that more than 4000 occupational, social, and mutual assistance organizations serve the Chinese communities in that country, many of them federated into powerful interest groups.

5   There were reports that the PRC, like earlier regimes, extorted funds from overseas Chinese by threatening their relatives in China (Skinner 1957, p. 363). There were similar reports of reprisals against relatives in China for anti-regime activities by overseas Chinese (Glick 1980, pp. 224 ff.).

6   Fitzgerald (1972, p. 142) quotes the following statement made in 1957 by leading members of the Overseas Chinese Affairs Bureau: "The broad masses of overseas Chinese resident abroad must now put aside any reservations, and, on the principle of free choice, choose local nationality. They must live and work in peace in the countries of residence, actively cooperate and coexist with the local people, and strive for the peace, happiness, and prosperity of the countries in which they live. This will be of assistance in promoting friendly relations between China and the countries of residence."

7   Those who chose neither Indonesian nor Chinese citizenship would be considered stateless persons whose allegiance would be to the KMT government in Taiwan.

157

8 "Underlying the CCP's approach to all these matters was an uncompromising principle...that overseas Chinese policy should be subordinate to foreign policy....This did not mean necessarily that overseas Chinese policy always had to serve policy; it could also pursue its own objectives so long as these did not conflict with or disrupt the pursuit of foreign policy objectives" (Fitzgerald 1972, p. 91).

9 In Jakarta in April 1967, the Chinese Embassy mobilized local Chinese in a large funeral procession protesting the death of a Chinese in police custody. Serious rioting erupted in Jakarta, followed by attacks by Red Guards on the Indonesian Embassy in Peking. This led to the suspension of diplomatic relations which have not yet been restored (Suryadinata 1978b, pp. 182-84).

10 From an editorial of 4 January 1978 in Jin-min Jih-pao, reproduced in Suryadinata (1978b, p. 37). Similar language can be found in an address by former Chairman Hua Kuo-feng on 21 February 1978 (Suryadinata 1978b, p. 41).

11 There is a continuing dispute about the events of 30 September 1965 and their aftermath. For a position contrary to that held by the current Indonesian government, see Anderson and McBey (1966).

12 For a detailed treatment of these events, see essays by Benoit and Sutter in Elliott (1981).

13 Robert Elegant (1959) quotes a Chinese in Indonesia: "It really doesn't matter at all what we say on the (citizenship) documents. When the Chinese come we'll be Chinese again."

14 According to Andreyev (1975, pp. 172-73), this policy is brazenly disregarded by Peking in collusion with Chinese businessmen in these countries.

15 Ali the indigenous front man, Baba the Chinese who finances and manages the enterprise.

16 For a detailed treatment of this subject see Suryadinata (1978, pp. 113-27). Indonesia renounced the dual nationality treaty in 1969.

17 For an account of the spread of nationalist sentiments in an overseas Chinese community, see Glick (1980, pp. 269-309).

18 Nanyang Chinese are sensitive to events in China both for their intrinsic interest and because of possible effects on their status and security. Many were appalled and embarrassed by the "insanity" of the Cultural Revolution, though

the Cultural Revolution did inspire some Chinese-educated youth.

19 Theodore Herzl, the founder of modern Jewish nationalism (Zionism), was an assimilated Austrian Jew who became convinced that Jews would never be accepted into European societies. The nationalist reponse to rejection in Southeast Asia is discussed by Williams (1960b, p. 201)

20 Malaysian Chinese who embrace Islam are not considered Malays and are not eligible for the educational and employment preferences reserved for Malays.

21 Benoit argues that most of the "boat people" left Vietnam because they were unwilling to accept the reduced economic opportunities and lower living standards that the Vietnamese government policy would have imposed on them, though these would not have been lower than average living standards among ethnic Vietnamese (Elliott 1981, pp. 139 ff.).

22 Skinner (1958) found that the highest ranking members of the Chinese Community in Bangkok are Thai born, Thai speaking, wealthy businessmen.

23 Prime Minister Mahatir Mohammed during the 1982 Parliamentary election campaign reportedly said: "If Datuk Lee whispers in my ear, I can hear him very well. If the DAP screams, I cannot hear anything." Datuk Lee is the head of the business-dominated MCA, associated with the government; the DAP is an opposition party led by intellectuals. **Far Eastern Economic Review**, 3 Sept. 1982, p. 46.

24 "An interesting recent development is the emergence of syndicates formed by Chinese capitalists and entrepreneurs in different countries who sometimes in association with Western investors invest funds in enterprises in Southeast Asia....In the new multinational groupings both racial and national boundaries have become increasingly blurred....Further extension of regional and multinational investment and joint ventures has already become a principal objective of ethno-Chinese business activities in Southeast Asia. For this reason operations are frequently based in Hong Kong where syndication and cooperation with Western or Japanese financial interests can take place relatively easily" (Wu and Wu 1980, pp. 100-103).

25 Wu and Wu (1980) report no fewer than 143 Chinese controlled banks, many with foreign branches, operating in Southeast Asia. Most of them have connections with Hong Kong banks where funds can be moved for placement anywhere in South-

east Asia and beyond. The Chinese are the dominant force in the large Asia dollar market.

26 Implications of the increasing dependence of Indonesia's Chinese on right-wing politicians is discussed in Mackie (1976, pp. 137-38).

27 A good example is the First Pacific group, a Hong Kong-based holding company controlled by the Liem family of Jakarta. Associated with the Liem family are close relatives of President Suharto. Liem's multinational, which is active in trading, manufacturing, real estate and financial services in Indonesia, has recently acquired the Hibernia Bank in California and a large, well-established Dutch trading firm, Hagemeyer NW. The growth of this overseas Chinese-controlled Indonesian multinational and the help it has received from the Indonesian government are detailed in the **Far Eastern Economic Review,** 7 April 1983, pp. 44-56.

28 From her study of Japanese Americans in the US, Edna Bonacich has developed a general theory of middleman minorities. It maintains that entrepreneurship and ethnic solidarity are functions of social discrimination, not of culture, and that the disappearance of social discrimination presages the decline in group solidarity and in entrepreneurship among middleman minorities (Bonacich and Modell 1980). According to this theory, entrepreneurial drive and ethnic solidarity among the overseas Chinese are maintained primarily by the hostility of native societies. Assuming the validity of this theory, there is little evidence that hostility toward Chinese minorities is diminishing in Southeast Asia. Modernization might indeed exacerbate economic competition as indigenous entrepreneurs seek to displace the Chinese.

29 "...it was often impossible for Southeast Asian governments to disentangle three factors: China, Communism (including communist subversion being carried on in the country), and the local Chinese minority" (Milne 1974, p. 119). He argues that recently these governments have begun to perceive these three dimensions separately and to "balance" them accordingly.

References

Adicondro, C. Y. 1979. From Chinatown to Nanyang: An Introcution to Chinese Entrepreneurship in Indonesia. **Prisma,** no. 13 (June).

Amyot, Jacques. 1972. **The Chinese and the National Integration in Southeast Asia.** Bangkok: Institute of Asian Studies, Chulalongkorn University.

Anderson, Benedict and Ruth McVey. 1966. A Preliminary Analysis of the October 1, 1965 Coup in Indonesia. Interim Report, CMIP, Southeast Asia Program, Cornell University, January.

Andreyev, M. A. 1974. **Overseas Chinese Bourgeoisie--A Peking Tool in Southeast Asia.** Moscow: Progress Publishers.

Armstrong, John A. 1976. Mobilized and Proletarian Diasporas. **American Political Science Review** 70, no. 2 (June): 393-408.

Bonacich, Edna and John Modell. 1980. **The Economic Basis of Ethnic Solidarity: Small Business in the Japanese-American Community.** Berkeley, CA: University of California Press.

Bonavia, David. 1978. The Overseas Chinese. **Far Eastern Economic Review,** 16 June: 17-24.

Bowring, Phillip. 1982. Myth, Mystery and Mitty: In the Concrete Jungle. **Far Eastern Economic Review,** 26 Nov.: 64-66.

Corell, Gary. 1982. A Giant Spiderless Web: The Complex Financial Empire of Chang Ming Thien. **Far Eastern Economic Review,** 11 June: 105-8.

Elegant, Robert. 1959. **The Dragon Seed.** New York: St. Martin Press.

Elliott, David W. P., ed. 1981. **The Third Indo-China Conflict.** Boulder, CO: Westview Press.

Esman, Milton J. 1975. Communal Conflict in Southeast Asia. In **Ethnicity: Theory and Experience,** eds. Nathan Glazer and Daniel P. Moynihan. Cambridge: Harvard University Press.

Fitzgerald, C. P. 1965. **The Third China: The Chinese Communities in Southeast Asia.** London: Angus and Robertson.

Fitzgerald, Stephen. 1972. **China and the Overseas Chinese: A Study of Peking's Changing Policy, 1949-1970.** Cambridge University Press.

Glick, Clarence E. 1980. **Sojourners and Settlers: Chinese Migrants in Hawaii.** Honolulu: University Press of Hawaii.

Godley, Michael K. 1981. **The Mandarin Capitalists**

from Nanyang: Overseas Chinese Enterprise in the Modernization of China, 1893-1911. Cambridge University Press.

Journal of Southeast Asian Studies. 1981. Special issue on "Ethnic Chinese in Southeast Asia", edited by C. F. Yong, 12, no. 1 (March).

Mackie, J. A. C. 1976. The Chinese in Indonesia. Honolulu: The University Press of Hawaii.

Milne, R. S. 1974. The Influence on Foreign Policy of Ethnic Minorities with External Ties. In Conflict and Stability in Southeast Asia, eds. Mark W. Zacher and R. S. Milne. Garden City, NY: Anchor Books.

Mozingo, David. 1976. Chinese Policy Toward Indonesia (1949-1967). Ithaca: Cornell University Press.

Nevadomski, Joseph-John and Alice Li. 1973. The Chinese in Southeast Asia: A Selected and Annotated Bibliography of Publications in Western Languages, 1960-70. Berkeley: Center for South and Southeast Asia Studies, University of California.

Purcell, Victor. 1960. The Chinese in Modern Malaya. Singapore: Eastern Universities Press.

-----. 1965. The Chinese in Southeast Asia, 2d ed. London: Oxford University Press.

Skinner, G. William. 1957. Chinese Society in Thailand: An Analytical History. Ithaca: Cornell University Press.

-----. 1958. Leadership and Power in the Chinese Community of Thailand. Ithaca: Cornell University Press.

Snodgrass, Donald. 1974. Trends and Patterns in Malaysian Income Distribution, 1957-70. Cambridge: Harvard University, Insititute for International Development.

Somers, Mary F. 1964. Peranakan Chinese Politics in Indonesia. Ithaca: Southeast Asia Program, Cornell University.

Steinberg, David, ed. 1971. In Search of Southeast Asia: A Modern History. New York: Praeger Publishers.

Suryadinata, Leo. 1978. Pribumi Indonesians, the Chinese Minority and China: A Study of Perceptions and Policies. Kuala Lumpur: Heinemann Educational Books (Asia).

-----. 1978a. The Chinese Minority in Indonesia: Seven Papers. Singapore: Chopman Enterprises.

-----. 1978b. "Overseas Chinese" in Southeast Asia and China's Foreign Policy, and Inter-

pretive Essay. Singapore: Institute of South-
east Asian Studies.
Taylor, Jay. 1976. China and Southeast Asia:
Peking's Relations with Revolutionary Move-
ments, 2d ed. New York: Praeger Publishers.
Viraphol, Sarasin. 1972. The Nanyang Chinese.
Bangkok: Institute of Asian Studies, Chula-
longkorn University.
Wang, Gungwu. 1959. A Short History of the
Nanyang Chinese. Singapore: Eastern Univer-
sities Press.
Williams, Lea E. 1960. Overseas Chinese National-
ism: The Genesis of the Pan-Chinese Movement
in Indonesia, 1900-1916. Glencoe, IL: The
Free Press.
Wu, Yuan-li and Chun-shi Wu. 1980. Economic
Development in Southeast Asia, The Chinese
Dimension. Stanford, CA: Hoover Institution
Press.

BLACK AMERICA AS A MOBILIZING DIASPORA: SOME INTERNATIONAL IMPLICATIONS

Locksley Edmondson

Africa's emergence on the world stage and her scattered descendants' growing consciousness of their racial identity (and hence of their ancestral links and interests) have sparked a burgeoning scholarly interest in the African Diaspora. A significant manifestation of this phenomenon has recently emerged from Black American academia in the form of a publication--the most comprehensive on the subject--entitled **Global Dimensions of the African Diaspora** (Harris 1982). This volume, based on the proceedings of the First African Diaspora Studies Institute convened at Howard University, Washington, D.C., in 1979, is indicative of scholarly trends elsewhere in the Black World.

To cite one example from the Caribbean segment of the African diaspora, in Barbados in 1980 at a UNESCO meeting of experts on "The African Cultural Presence in the Caribbean and in North and South America," much attention was devoted to "the concept of the African diaspora, its characteristics and significance" and the dynamics of the links between the diaspora and Africa. More recently, a symposium on the "Dynamics of the African/Afro-American Connection: From Dependency to Self-Reliance", which was convened in Liberia in 1983, concluded "that the time has come to institutionalize more effectively the quest for a deeper reunion between Africa and her Diaspora in time for the new dawn of year 2000," and to that end agreed eventually to establish on the African continent a permanent organization for Inter-African and Diaspora Relations.

164

Burgeoning Afro-American Diasporic Identity

As shall be illustrated, the critical presence and impact of Black America in the African diasporic setting is a matter of historical record. More significant to domestic American politics and wider international relations is the sense of Black American self-consciousness as an African diaspora, which has burgeoned over the past two decades. With Black American political mobilization now growing apace--and in 1984 having been catalyzed further by Jesse Jackson's Presidential aspirations--the subject of diasporic mobilization becomes all the more salient (Edmondson 1984). This contemporary phenomenon may be assessed first in a historical perspective. The extent to which Black Americans historically "rejected" identification with Africa has long been subject to debate, with profound variations on the acceptance/rejection theme influenced by time, place and circumstances. By the 1950s, the oversimplified view that Black Americans overwhelmingly rejected identification with Africa became popular in certain circles.

This was in strong contrast to the Africa-conscious epoch of Garveyism (Cronon 1955; Martin 1976) and the Harlem Renaissance (Huggins 1971) in the decade up to the mid-1920s, and to the subsequent revival of Black consciousness beginning in the 1960s. And yet, in that interim period, Black American identification with African causes continued to be manifested in various ways, though on a less sustained basis--for example in the powerful expressions of support for Ethiopia when subjected to Italian aggression in 1935 or in the involvement of various Black organizations in seeking to advance African interests during the post-World War II settlement.

Some might argue that there is a real difference between being politically supportive of African advancement and being psychologically attuned to identification with Africa. But apart from the difficulty of separating manifestations of the former with relevant psychological predispositions, the main issue being raised here is that the patterns of Black American "acceptance" or "rejection" of Africa have historically been much too complex, varied and at times contradictory to be pinned down to simplistic formulae.

As a measure of the transformed sense of diasporic self-consciousness of Black America, it is of interest to recall Harold Isaacs' controversial generalization in 1959 (p. 232) that "in almost every Negro environment, the word 'black' became the key word of rejection," and more so to reiterate his valid observation that the association of the words "Black" and "African" are of profound significance in shedding light on the semantics of the psychology of "acceptance" or "rejection" of the African connection.

In this light, it is significant that "Black" has now become the most acceptable language of self-description. For example, of a list of 390 relevant groups listed in a 1978 national directory of minority organizations consulted for this purpose, 289, or 74 percent, were discovered to include the word "Black" in their title; another 17 percent had either "African" or "Afro" as part of their name; 8 percent were labelled "Negro"; and only six such organizations (about 1.5 percent) were called "Colored," (Cole 1978). This conforms to the evident impression of a widespread embrace of Black and Afro-related themes which underpin a heightened sense of diasporic consciousness in Black America.

It is essentially in this context that this paper perceives Black America as a "mobilizing diaspora," in the literal sense of its developing recognition and deployment of its diasporic resources for the benefit of the "homeland." This approach is not to be confused in any way with John Armstrong's conceptualization (1976) of "proletarian" and "mobilized" diasporas--the former being "essentially a disadvantaged product of modernized politics" and the latter perceived as "an ethnic group which does not have a general status advantage yet which enjoys many material and cultural advantages compared to other groups in the multiethnic polity."

In most respects, Black America can appropriately be characterized as a "proletarian diaspora." But this essay's concern with the projection of Afro-American interests into the international system is better captured under the rubric of diasporic mobilization as an underlying and now intensifying urge in Black America.

Analytical Issues and Perspectives

It is important at the outset to emphasize that whenever we posit the idea of a "diaspora" as a unit of analysis, this involves not simply matters of internal relevance to a given diasporic group but also necessarily embraces the dynamics of that group's external relationships, especially with its "homeland." In other words, the condition of Black America as an African diaspora is but a starting point for comprehending ultimately Black American orientations toward and interactions with the African continental homeland. But while essentially concerned with the network of relationships established directly by the diaspora with the homeland, as well as with the capacity of the diaspora to influence host country policies toward the homeland, the enquiry is obliged to proceed beyond these frontiers to encompass other international orientations of the diaspora especially when relevant to the issues of African advancement and racial uplift in the wider sphere of international relations.

The focus is thus on advances by the diaspora toward the homeland and the wider world, stimulated by domestic and/or external factors. In the latter connection it is essential to recognize the impact on the evolution of the Black American outlook of external/international forces, not least those originating from the homeland. For example, of pertinence in recent times have been the impact of World War II (Wynn 1976); the Cold War and East-West tensions (Roark 1971; Solomon 1971); the African independence movement (Emerson and Kilson 1965); the Vietnam War (Taylor 1973); the rise of the Third World (Barnett 1977); general transformations in the international environment (Isaacs 1963; Edmondson 1973); and a variety of Africa-related issues in the current epoch concerning in particular southern African liberation struggles. But considerations of this type will not be developed systematically in their own right, being instead subsumed within the context of Black American diasporic drives.

Such an enquiry should ideally address a variety of motivating forces and functional areas, such as political, ideological, economic, cultural, religious, educational and psychological/attitudinal. It should also encompass a range of actor activity variables including the idiosyncratic (that is those individuals prominently involved in Africa-related causes); organizational (including specialized and non-specialized groups and movements seeking to influence the course of events pertaining to Africa); and institutional (referring in this context to relevant established Black religious, educational, business and communication institutions and, as in the case of the Congressional Black Caucus, including Black American interests formally institutionalized within the broader policy-making process).

Such forces and variables are best comprehended within three interrelated levels of international relations analysis, foreign policy, transnational and international systemic levels. At the foreign policy level we would, for example, be concerned with the kind of interest Blacks have displayed toward the formalities of the US decision-making process, especially as these bear on the position of states in the outer Black world. Transnational (non-governmental) activities by contrast involve direct Afro-American outreach to, or linkages with, the African continent in a variety of political, cultural and other areas. At the international systemic level it is germane to recall attempts made by Black Americans to influence directly international organizational and legal processes, whether for their own interests at home or in the interests of Blacks elsewhere.

Two particularly important analytical considerations arise from this discussion of motivating forces, actor variables and levels of analysis. The first is that to confine attention only to the essentially political aspects of Black America's relations with the African homeland would limit and indeed distort understanding. Intellectual and educational, religious and other cultural ties have been historically significant in the relationship, the more so as Africa's international status and image especially in the colonial era were long governed unfavorably by such considerations. Second, to focus on governmental or foreign policy-related transactions in this context would limit unnecessarily and misrepresent comprehension of Black America's interest in or impact on African affairs, especially in a historical context, where conventional interstate channels of domestic and international politics were effectively closed to Black diaspora and homeland alike.

In the contemporary era of the "politicization of black ethnicity" in America and since the late 1950s (Kilson 1976, p. 471), some observers have wondered why Black Americans have not had a significant impact on US foreign policy toward Africa and why America's largest minority group has not displayed the organization and clout manifested by other racial/ethnic minorities in such matters.

To seek answers to this question it is important to take account of intervening variables such as: (1) the comparative situation of other resident ethnic/racial diasporas in terms of advantages enjoyed or disadvantages experienced; (2) the orientations of the "host country" (in this instance the United States) toward its various resident diasporas on the one hand and toward the interests of their respective homelands on the other; (3) wider international systemic inducements or constraints--for example, the composition of the interstate system and the salience of respective international issue-areas--affecting the articulation and promotion of a given diaspora's interests.

The pertinence of such variables is well demonstrated by drawing on the analogy of Jewish American influence on US foreign policy in matters concerning Israel. Not only has this analogy been the subject of academic discourse (e.g., Weil 1974), but it is also worthwhile recalling that long before the establishment of the state of Israel, early twentieth century pan-Africanists such as the Afro-American political activist, W.E.B. DuBois, perceived the Zionism of that time as a model worthy of emulation for the mobilization and consolidation of Black support for the African continental homeland.[1]

The effectiveness of Jewish American influence on matters concerning Israel in contrast to the relatively uninfluential role of Black Americans in African affairs arises from a number of inter-related factors. The most obvious and usually cited explanation lies in the different political capabilities of these groups in terms of economic clout and of influence on the media and other moulders of public opinion.

But these are often reinforcing factors embedded in the US foreign policy process. For one thing, the fact is that groups having an objective interest in transforming policy directions start off at an automatic disadvantage in comparison with those wishing to sustain the status quo, the consequence being that Blacks necessarily encounter difficulties in shifting American policy in favor of African interests which Jews hardly experience in maintaining traditional US support for Israel. What is more, the priority accorded the Israeli connection in US foreign policy is a function of its congruence with US global interests in the East-West confrontation, while African concerns in the context of the North-South cleavage (not to mention in the racial/colonial crises in southern Africa) tend objectively towards less compatibility with US interests.

Yet another factor underlying the unequal influence exerted on foreign policy by Black and Jewish Americans derives from an international structural consideration. The existence of an African "homeland" of over fifty countries with varying ethno-social and political conditions and international relations interests, complicated by relatively less settled states of nationhood in this early post-colonial era, poses real complexities to Blacks in terms of developing specialized foci and concrete goals and priorities. This problem is facilitated in the more typical case of a diaspora being linked to a single and specific ethno-national territorial homeland. The latter is the position of Israel which thus becomes an easier focus of Jewish diasporic support, especially in the perceived priority of national survival in a hostile environment. The infinitely more complex and challenging diasporic "responsibilities" of Black Americans are further complicated by an increasingly felt need to relate to another target area besides the African homeland, namely the Caribbean with its numerous states, peoples and interests.

Thus it should not be automatically assumed that a lack of effective foreign policy clout--the official governmental dimension--necessarily connotes a lack of interest or activity concerning Africa, since conventionally Blacks have developed their own networks of foreign relations--the non-governmental/transnational dimension--with the homeland in political and non-political areas.

The lack of Black influence in foreign policy is less due to Black inertia than to systemic barriers, the latter indeed having a conditioning impact on the former. To legitimize scholarly "recognition" of a diaspora essentially in terms of a demonstrated capacity to influence host country policy toward the homeland would be to stack the cards in favor of examining the politics of influence and of introducing advance biases against the study of the systematization of powerlessness. For the latter has characterized the dominant orientation of the American system toward Blacks for the better part of the nation's history.

Despite such constraints, superimposed on conditions of rupture and racial degradation cementing the origins of Black America, the search for building mutually beneficial ties with the homeland has been a constant feature of the diasporic experience. The enthusiasm and intensity accompanying that search has naturally varied over time, place and issue, but even at its lowest ebb the challenge has always existed. The heightened and widespread contemporary sense of diasporic consciousness cannot be properly understood in isolation from certain historical foundations.

Scholarly Recognition of Diasporic Identity and Challenge

It is not now surprising, as illustrated by the elaborate bibliography submitted herewith, that there is a burgeoning scholarly literature recognizing African diasporic identity and the Black American interest, role, and potential in seeking, over time, to affect the course of US relations with Africa as well as Africa's position in the world.

In introducing a volume by Kilson and Rotberg entitled **The African Diaspora,** George Shepperson (1976, p. 2), a distinguished scholarly pioneer of this subject, submitted that while the "parallels and links between Jewish and Black American experiences of uprooting from their homelands had been noticed at least from the early nineteenth century" by Africans, New World Blacks and some Europeans, it is difficult to say when the expression 'the African diaspora' was first used. "Probably the 1960s could be claimed as its gestation period," he opines.

The dominant emphasis on the African diaspora in the New World has, Shepperson continues, "served largely to veil from the sight of scholars the significance of the African presence in Asia" and has "concealed the presence of Africans and people of African descent in European countries" (p. 5).

The Caribbean and Black America remain the two most significant focal points of such diasporic concern. But there is relatively greater salience in the latter environment than in the former of Black racial consciousness and hence of Black identity strivings (Edmondson 1979). This is dictated partly by the minority status which in every respect characterizes the Black American condition. And with the exception of unliberated southern Africa, the relatively greater entrenchment of

White racism in the United States than elsewhere attaches special racial significance and mission to the African diaspora in the United States. The expanding literature being discussed is thus symptomatic of that condition and need. Referring to the bibliographical entries, we first began to witness theories and conceptualization about the Black diaspora in J. Harris (1968), Shepperson (1976, 1978), Walters (ca. 1979) and in various essays in J. Harris' edited volume (1982). There is also the long-awaited major work by the veteran Black American scholar, St. Clair Drake, on the Black Diaspora, one advance chapter of which appeared on its own (Drake 1970). What trends can one detect in the study of Black American relationships with Africa in the context of direct transnational ties and influences, on the one hand, and in terms of US foreign policy as it affects Africa, on the other?

Referring for illustrative purposes to the bibliographical entries, the first thing to note is the growth of a number of both comprehensive and specialized studies addressed to the conventionally significant and often controversial theme of Black American identification or dissaffection with Africa. In probing the issues of images, attitudes, interests and linkages, these more recent contributions are for the most part shorn of the negativism which pervaded earlier studies of this kind. Some of these--e.g., Edmondson (1973), Emerson and Kilson (1965) and Isaacs (1963)--have as their point of departure transformations in the international system (especially as it pertains to the rise of Africa from colonial status) conditioning a more sustained Afro-American involvement in Africa. Other studies have as their starting point the evolutionary dynamics of Afro-American nationalism, cases in point being Akpan (1980), Anosike (1982), Davis (1958), Drachler (1975), Drake (1963, 1966), Edmondson (1968), Essien-Udom (1971), Hill and Kilson (1969), Magubane (1967), Moikobu (1981), Nagenda (1967), Reid (1976), Shepperson (1960), Skinner (1973), Uya (1971), Weisbord (1973). One interesting aspect of the latter group is a strong representation of African-born scholars.

If interest in promoting these kinds of studies seemed to have waned somewhat by the mid-1970s, what has now begun to pick up are analyses of Black American interests or involvement in American foreign policy toward Africa. Significantly, of the relevant studies cited all but two (those by

Hero and Davis published in 1969) were written in
the 1970s and 1980s, for example works by
Challenor, Garrett, Henry Jackson, The Joint Center
for Political Studies, LeMelle, McHenry, Jake
Miller, Morris, Moss, Obatala, Smythe and Skinner,
Philip White (1981b). This is symptomatic of recent Black American efforts to develop a systematic
capacity to influence US foreign policy, best manifested in the creation in the 1970s of a permanent
professional lobby in the form of TransAfrica.

A variety of more specialized studies of past
and present Black American interests in Africa have
been steadily appearing. The southern African
situation has naturally arisen as a continuing
source of concern (Keto 1973; Kornegay 1979; Philip
White 1981a), while stimulating a scholarly search
for historical manifestations of Black interests in
that region (Gatewood 1976; Keto 1972).

An interesting array of historical studies has
emerged addressing other topics such as Black attitudes to the late nineteenth century partitioning
of Africa (Jacobs 1981) and to US imperialistic
expansion of that era (Gatewood 1975; Marks 1971);
Black interests in Ethiopia (Asante 1973; Scott
1978; Shack 1974; Weisbord 1972); the theme of
black emigration (Redkey 1969) and its most concrete expression in the founding of Liberia (Shick
1980).

The attitudes of the Black press to Africa
have been explored by Clarke (1961), Hooker (1967),
Marks (1971) and Williams (1973). Illustrative of
the historical role of Black American educational
institutions in aiding African advancement is the
study of Kenneth King (1971), perhaps the most
comprehensive of its kind. The role of the Black
church and missionaries in Africa has attracted
attention, for example in Drake (1980), Jacobs
(1980-81), Shepperson (1953) and Williams (1982).

Black mass attitudes to foreign policy and
international affairs based on public opinion surveys have been examined, all too infrequently, as
in studies by Hero (1969) and Hoodley (1972). Another infrequent area of study--dictated however by
concrete realities and limitations in this area--
has been the forging of economic ties between Black
America and Africa, the potential for which has
been broached by Willard Johnson (1983) and Donald
Warden (1977).

A very promising area of inquiry involving
systematic comparison of Black America with other
African diasporas has been opened up by Van den

Berghe (1976). As noted in a previous section, the impact of various international forces and developments on Black Americans has been explored in a variety of areas. Given less attention have been Afro-American interests and involvement in the wider parameters of the international system (Edmondson 1969, 1971; R. Harris 1982), an area of study which will surely be developed the more the Black diasporic mobilization grows.

This bibliographical exercise, which has not even touched on studies of various Afro-American individuals and organizations involved in pan-African and related international activities, has been designed to indicate that if there was any doubt about recognizing the importance of Black America in the field of diaspora studies the volume of relevant literature alone should prove otherwise.

Black America: Uniqueness and Significance

At this stage in the analysis it would be well for us to raise some salient characteristics of Black America involving certain critical demographic, historical, political, socio-economic, cultural and racial factors which are basic to an understanding of the group's conditions and outlook as a diaspora. The more significant of these characteristics will be highlighted, with attention being drawn to those which are unique in comparison with other diasporas resident in the host country. Additionally, some factors of systemic relevance, seen from the standpoint of the basic character of host system relationships with the homeland, will be broached as essential to an understanding of the diasporic dilemma and challenge. For present convenience the main factors and issues will be enumerated.

Five preliminary significant demographic factors can be noted:

1. With a 1980 census population of 26.5 million, accounting for close to 12 percent of the nation's population, Black Americans are the largest racial/ethnic minority group in the United States. This fact highlights the theoretical political potential of this group but also draws attention to its actual relative powerlessness.

2. The group is at least the fourth largest national concentration of Blacks in the world
after Nigeria, Brazil and Ethiopia.[2]
3. Additionally, as pointed out in the **Harvard
Encyclopedia of American Ethnic Groups** (1980,
pp. 5-6), Afro-Americans are "larger than any
ethnic subgroup in Africa."
4. The previous point draws attention to the
relative socio-cultural homogeneity of this
group which developed relevant characteristics
mostly through shared experiences in America.
With migration from the neighboring African
diasporas in the Caribbean on the increase,
and especially with a larger proportion than
previously originating from the non-Anglophone
Caribbean, this internal socio-cultural homogeneity is being somewhat eroded but not sufficiently to undermine the fundamental socio-
cultural cohesion of the group.
5. Now the most urbanized subgroup of the American
population and heavily concentrated in the
major inner cities, Blacks are being aroused to
their political strength resulting from this
strategic concentration, while nonetheless continuing to suffer from the socio-economic
traumas of their environment.

Proceeding with this pattern of enumeration,
another five basic considerations pertaining to the
conditions and consequences of this diaspora's
creation emerge for discussion, as not merely
significant but unique in comparison with the
experiences of other resident diasporas:

6. This diaspora was enforced through involuntary
migration caused by the tran-Atlantic slave
trade, to which must be added that organized
servitude represented the original condition
of Afro-Americans (the few escaping its direct
burden never escaped its socio-racial consequences). Systematized prejudice, discrimination, exploitation and oppression explain and
characterize this diaspora's creation and
perpetuation throughout most of the nation's
history.
7. If the above sum up some of the traumas of
adjustment to the host country, the traumas
associated with enforced rupture from the
homeland are also of import. Cultural uprooting and loss of direct ties with particular
homeland cultural groups and political systems

resulted, complicating the diaspora's capacity to cement concrete ties with a "homeland" existing in a more general continental than specific ethno-national sense.

8. One option explored historically as a way of overcoming the dilemmas of host country persecution and loss of specific homeland was the re-creation of a homeland on African soil through emigration; this is how Liberia came into existence. This example, unique from an American perspective, but perhaps not altogether unique at a wider comparative level, of a new homeland being in effect the original diaspora's "diaspora,"[3] is less important as a method of resolution to the problem of a diaspora's adjustment to the host country since relatively few Blacks took up the option to emigrate. The significance of this case is that it serves as a reminder of some strongly-felt views in the host country that dispersed Africans were doubtful prospects for full citizenship in the American polity.

9. Not merely the facts but more so the historical conditions of rupture and servitude have been of continuing significance to Black diaspora and homeland alike. The persistent devaluation by White authority of the Black heritage and potential, and the entrenchment of international White supremacist notions accompanying first the establishment of racial slavery and eventually colonialism in Africa and elsewhere have traditionally given an urgency to racial uplift and African/Black rehabilitation as factors underpinning diaspora-homeland exchanges. It is in this sense of politico-cultural reaffirmation and challenge that in the arena of folkways and mores the cultural dimension of such interactions are better understood.

10. If Black Americans have lost their specific ethno-national origins they have in turn sought to "reclaim" a continental homeland. The observations of the late veteran pan-Africanist, W.E.B. DuBois (1965, p. 7) are of moment:

> The idea of one Africa to unite the thought and ideals of all native peoples of the dark continent belongs to the twentieth century and stems naturally from the West Indies and the United

> States. Here various groups of Africans,
> quite separate in origin, became so
> united in experience and so exposed to
> the impact of new cultures that they
> began to think of Africa as one idea and
> one land.

The suggestion has been re-confirmed by George
Shepperson (1976, p. 8) who maintains that "it
is no exaggeration to call pan-Africanism the
latter-day ideology of the African diaspora."
Here lies one of the persistent undercurrents
of the urges and directions of Black diasporic
links to a continental homeland. On the other
hand, as previously mentioned, a "homeland" of
over fifty countries is of an order quite
different and inherently more complex than the
more typical case of a diaspora linked to a
single, specific ethno-national territorial
homeland.

A further four significant characteristics
regarding pertinent aspects of the Black American
condition can now be broached:

11. Blacks--who at one stage in the early nine-
    teenth century comprised close to 20 percent
    of the nation's population--arrived in America
    before most other migrant groups. Yet they
    constitute the most disadvantaged diaspora of
    all.[4] The facts of racial origin are objec-
    tively of less significance than are the con-
    ditions of racial powerlessness.
12. And yet the facts of racial origin, the badge
    of color, have made the physical visibility of
    this diaspora (unlike most others) an easier
    and more convenient target of discrimination.
13. Since the late 1960s Blacks have made some
    relatively significant gains in and through
    the political system. For example, there has
    been a proliferation of Black office-holders
    at most levels of the system.[5] With the elec-
    tion in 1983 of Black mayors in Chicago and
    Philadelphia, Blacks now occupy that office in
    four of America's six largest cities--Los
    Angeles and Detroit being the other two--in
    addition to other major cities like Atlanta,
    Birmingham, Gary, Newark, New Orleans and
    Washington, D.C. This phenomenon, together
    with Jesse Jackson's unexpectedly impressive
    performance in pursuit of the Democratic Par-

ty's Presidential nomination in 1984, simultaneously generated by and having an impact on
a heightened sense of Black political mobilization, should not, however, be overestimated
in terms of the effectiveness of Blacks in
substantively influencing policy. For there
still is a pattern of significant under-repre-
sentation of Blacks in political offices,
especially in the higher echelons.[6] Black
underrepresentation in the critical administrative levels is even more clearcut, and more
so in foreign policy decision-making ranks
(Miller 1978; Smythe and Skinner 1976; White
1981b, pp. 47-48).[7] Interestingly, there is
an overrepresentation of Blacks in the armed
forces, though here again one is sure to find
a highly disproportionate Black presence in
the lower ranks. Data from late 1981 released
by the Armed Forces Information Service reveal
that Blacks make up 29.8 percent of the Army,
20.3 percent of the Marine Corps; 14.4 percent
of the Air Force; and 10.8 percent of the
Navy.[8]

14. The political cohesion displayed by Blacks at
the polls is regarded by many as one of the
group's most important political resources.
But given the non-salience of Africa-related
issues in electoral politics, that potential
is as yet unexploited.

Two final considerations, now pertaining to
systemic US orientations, need to be mentioned:

15. Except for the special case of Liberia, official US ties with the African continent were
historically very weak. For example, "it was
not until 1957 that the US State Department
actually established a Bureau of African
Affairs" and "in that same year there were
still more Foreign Service personnel stationed
in West Germany alone than in the entire continent of Africa" (Dellums 1983, p. 16). Thus,
to understand the late arrival of a Black
American "foreign policy" interest in the
homeland is partly to understand the relatively recent official American attention to that
continent. The rise of African nations on the
international stage, now influenced profoundly
by US global interests, has introduced a new
situation challenging the attention and concern of the African diaspora in America.

16. In no two areas of the world has the structuring of patterns of White domination and Black subordination been as historically perfected as in the United States and southern Africa. The challenges surrounding United States relations with South Africa will continue to be haunted by this factor, thanks to the presence of a substantial African diaspora in America.

Diaspora-Homeland Interaction and Afro-American Internationalism

The time is now ripe to review and assess the developing interaction between the diaspora and its African continental homeland from the standpoint of the interests and exertions of the former. As noted earlier, there exists a variety of specialized studies on this subject, some of a comprehensive nature. Among the briefer, yet incisive, overviews of this relationship are studies by Herschelle Challenor (1981), St. Clair Drake (1966), Henry Jackson (1982) and Inez Smith Reid (1976), cast in the kind of historical/evolutionary framework which facilitate the present analysis.

For example, Reid's essay on "Black Americans and Africa" is helpful as a guide to describing and categorizing the variety of relevant interests and activities. In dealing first with the period up to 1957, she identifies six main Afro-American approaches to the African connection: missionary and religious endeavors; colonization and emigration (better known as back-to-Africa) schemes; educational projects (involving not only the training of Africans at or through Black institutions, but also intellectual activity to correct distortions of the African heritage and potential); special interest in the Belgian Congo, Ethiopia and Liberia;[9] support for African self-determination efforts (promoted especially through various pan-African movements); and organizational interests (a catch-all category including a variety of philanthropic, academic, cultural and political groups displaying either specialized or ad hoc involvement).

Referring to a "noticeable shift in black American attitudes to Africa" beginning to occur by the late 1950s (attending the rise of the Civil Rights movement at home and the African independence movement abroad) and developing momentum through the 60s (with the resurgence of Afro-Ameri-

179

can nationalism in the form of the Black Power movement and the heightening intensity of African liberation struggles), Reid, like the other analysts mentioned, identifies a broadened and more sustained range of pro-African interests, manifested in a proliferation of new organizations, movements and activities.

It is not possible here to enter a detailed description and analysis of such trends in a historical/evolutionary context. Instead, the three levels of analysis--the transnational, foreign policy and international systemic--posed at the outset will be employed as frameworks for interpreting and assessing the political and ideological aspects of Black-American individual, organizational/movement and institutional efforts to project their interests toward the homeland and other relevant external arenas.

These three levels of analysis (or arenas of activity) and three categories of actors cannot, of course, be sharply demarcated from each other. Indeed the relevant actors and operational arenas often overlap, as was the case during the 1935-1936 Italian invasion of Ethiopia which evoked a range of protest reactions and pro-Ethiopian supportive endeavors at all three levels among a variety of Black individuals, organizations/movements and institutions.

No single event before or since was as instrumental in catalyzing and demonstrating the sense of Afro-American identification with Africa which could erupt under certain conditions. As noted by Scott (1978), whose documentation is supported by Asante (1973), Shack (1974), and Weisbord (1972), support for Ethiopia, manifested in all sections of the United States with substantial Black populations, came from Black intellectuals, churches, Black newspapers "universally", protest and civil rights organizations including the NAACP (National Association for the Advancement of Colored People) and the Urban League, and especially from a variety of Black nationalist organizations and movements, some expressly created for that purpose.

The focus of these actors ranged across the three levels. Transnational activities were demonstrated, for example, in the recruitment of Black volunteers to provide direct military assistance to Ethiopia;[10] in the raising of funds,[11] and the formation of various relief organizations; and the creation of political support groups linked to similar continental African and Afro-Caribbean movements. Attempted influence of foreign policy, which came to no avail, was characterized by lobbying of or protests to the US State Department, spearheaded by the NAACP, in its search for protecting Ethiopian sovereignty and isolating the Italian aggressor. Cables from a mass rally in Harlem to various nations around the world for aid to Ethiopia and petitions by various Afro-American organizations to the League of Nations were symptomatic of an international systemic focus, complementing the other types of activities.

Similarly, when we come to consider Black American involvement in southern African liberation struggles--currently the most salient and, from a historical perspective, the most sustained of their external concerns (see for example, Philip White 1981a; Kornegay, 1979)--all three levels of analysis and activity need to be addressed in comprehending the subject.

An important reason for identifying these three levels of analysis/activities is that by examining their interrelation we can arrive at a more balanced picture of Black American internationalist orientations. Thus the fact that until recently Blacks seemed not to be overly involved with foreign policy concerns does not necessarily imply a lack of interest in other alternatives. Indeed it can be argued that for a long time, the search for transnational linkages especially under the rubric of pan-Africanism became a necessary substitute for Black inability to gain access to, let alone seek effectively to influence, the United States decision-making system.

Transnational Linkages

The prominent historical contribution of Black Americans to the initiation and development of pan-African endeavors remains the most characteristic expression of transnational outreach to Africa and the wider Black world.

By way of selective illustration, we may profitably begin with the cases of W.E.B. DuBois (1868-1963) and Marcus Garvey (1887-1940), the two most illustrious examples of these tendencies in terms of their individual impact, organizational initiatives and institutional affiliations.

After participating prominently in the First Pan-African Conference in 1900, convened in London by a Trinidadian, Henry Sylvester Williams, DuBois, the scholar-activist, thereafter initiated a Pan-

African Congress series beginning with the First Congress in Paris in 1919, convened to coincide with the post-war deliberations at Versailles. Such organizational initiatives directed by DuBois extended to the Fourth Pan-African Congress of 1927 in New York--the Second and Third Congresses of 1921 and 1923 having been convened in various European cities--and laid the groundwork for the Fifth Pan-African Congress of 1945 in Manchester, England, at which, in his capacity as honorary chairman, he was hailed by a younger generation of African nationalists, now taking command of the movement, as the "father of Pan-Africanism" (DuBois, 1965, pp. 7-15, 235-245; Geiss 1974, **passim;** Logan 1965). Other related organizational activities on DuBois' part included his constant effort to link the NAACP--of which he was a founding member in 1909 and for a time a major official--to African causes (Watson 1977) and in his later years he was involved in the Council on African Affairs which from 1937-1955 emerged as "the most important American organization specifically concerned with Africa" (Lynch 1978).

The Jamaican-born Marcus Garvey, the universally recognized twentieth century mentor of Black nationalism, arose to political prominence in the 1915-1925 period from a Black American base with his "back-to-Africa" message promoted through the UNIA (Universal Negro Improvement Association) which he founded and whose organizational presence he extended throughout all parts of the Black world (Cronon 1955; Langley 1969; Martin 1976). While Garvey's approach contained notions of repatriation of Blacks in the Americas to the African continent, it was more one of psycho-political identification with Africa as a means of mounting Black nationalist challenges to the racial status quo in the United States and elsewhere.

DuBois' and Garvey's outlooks were indicative of persisting pan-Africanist tendencies in Afro-American life. For example, DuBois' political approach was presaged in David Walker's 1829 **Appeal...to the Colored Citizens of the World But in Particular and very Expressly to those of the United States,** characterized by Harding (1980, p. 31) as "the first Pan-African-oriented call to struggle published in America." In the contemporary era, Black American activity in the convening of the Sixth Pan-African Congress in Tanzania in 1974 were consistent with an organizational tradition established by DuBois.

Garvey's nineteenth century Black nationalist predecessors included Martin Delaney and Henry Highland Garnet who, in the pre-Civil War period, were active exponents of Black emigration to Africa, as well as Henry McNeil Turner who, as shown by Redkey (1969), was among the more prominent of those identified with a later wave of back-to-Africa movements emerging in the 1890s. Among Garvey's more notable successors must be numbered Malcolm X, whose short-lived Organization for Afro-American Unity expressly created in 1964--a year before his assassination--to "include all people of African descent in the Western Hemisphere, as well as brothers and sisters of the African continent" was inspired by the UNIA example and legacy, and whose strident nationalist posture of the early 1960s helped to sow the seeds of the Black Power movement emerging later in that decade. The Congress of African Peoples which was active from 1970-1972 under the leadership of Imamu Baraka (previously known as Le Roi Jones) of Newark, New Jersey, with its predominant cultural nationalist and Black separatist underpinnings was reminiscent of the ideological style of Garvey's UNIA.[12]

The Black Power movement emerging in the late 1960s in its international thrust signified not only a merger of the DuBosian and Garveyite pan-Africanist political traditions, it also represented a coalescence of various functional strands of pan-Africanism including cultural, educational, economic and religious aspects. Thus, a good part of the international outlook of Black Power constituted an updating of concerns and approaches which had emerged at previous junctures of Afro-American history (Edmondson 1968). The point thus needs to be reemphasized that the contemporary manifestations of diasporic mobilization in Black America are better understood in the light of historical foundations as well as transitions.

For example, the more widespread sense of Black cultural nationalism in recent times has some equivalents in the literary and artistic outburst of the 1920s which came to be known as the Harlem Renaissance (Huggins 1971), while having much deeper roots now in all segments of the Black community.[13]

There is a connection across time between the "Negro History Movement" initiated by Carter G. Woodson in 1915 and the current Black Studies movement, both concerned with the rehabilitation and projection of the Black World heritage, which is symptomatic of a pan-Africanist tradition among certain Afro-American educational institutions. In this connection the historical role of DuBois as a scholar is significant, not only because he was a pioneer of the revisionist study of African history and culture but also because he handed down the legacy of the scholar-activist since emulated by organizations such as the African Heritage Studies Association (AHSA) and the African-American Scholars Council (AASC) created in 1968 and 1971 respectively.[14]

The pan-Africanist vision consciously nurtured and promoted in recent times by certain religious Afro-American institutions has some historical parallels with the contribution of Black missionaries to the spread of African nationalism. Indeed, the pan-African political implications of Afro-American religion have been given renewed meaning in Burkett's study, **Garveyism as a Religious Movement,** (1978), indicating that much of the success of Garveyism in Afro-American political mobilization was a function of Garvey's central theme of African redemption being rooted in the Black religious tradition.

Less frequent have been efforts to institutionalize economic and philanthropic links with Africa. That challenge is being increasingly recognized, however, now that the development problems of the newly independent African nations have become a more salient international relations issue. One example is Africare, a private Black aid program established with US governmental assistance in 1971. Another case in point is RAINS (Relief for Africans in Need in the Sahel) created in 1973 for the specific short-term purpose of coordinating relief assistance among twenty Black organizations for the drought-stricken Sahel region,[15] serving as a lobby toward that end. As noted by Walters (1980), financial and other donations (like clothes and medical supplies) have been transmitted from time to time by groups supportive of southern African liberation struggles. Not least is the case of Operation Crossroads Africa--which came to provide a model for the US Peace Corps established by President Kennedy in 1961--founded in 1957 by James Robinson, a Black clergyman, through which volunteers are recruited to assist African development projects. Such endeavors, it should be noted, can find some historical parallels in the technical assistance missions from Booker T. Washington's Tuskegee Institute to the Anglo-Egyptian Sudan and

German Togoland during the first decade of the twentieth century. These glimpses of comparative history help portray the recurrence of transnational outreach from this diaspora to the Black World beyond. The forging of such linkages with racial interests abroad not only served historically as compensation for political ineffectiveness at home, but was based on assumptions that Afro-Americans were objectively well positioned to seek to influence the international racial situation, which in turn might have positive effects on the situation in America. It was in activities such as these that Black Americans were able to have a meaningful historical impact on the political course of events in colonial Africa, as has been pointed out by Shepperson (1960). Indeed, certain pan-African movements developed by Blacks in the Americas performed the roles of political recruitment and political socialization with respect to future African leaders whose opportunities for engaging in meaningful political activity were inhibited by the colonial system (Edmondson 1975). A host of African nationalists have paid tribute to this political assistance emanating from African diasporas in the New World. That much was admitted at the All-African Peoples Conference held in Accra in 1958 when Ghana's then Prime Minister Kwame Nkrumah--whose verdict is all the more authoritative considering that he was the first to dismantle colonial rule in Sub-Saharan Africa the previous year--welcomed the presence of American and Caribbean Blacks in the following way:

> These sons and daughters of Africa were taken away from our shores and despite all centuries which have separated us they have not forgotten their ancestral links....Many of them have made no small contribution to the cause of African freedom. Names which spring immediately to mind in this connection are those of Marcus Garvey and Dr. W.E.B. DuBois....Long before many of us were conscious of our own degradation these men fought for African national and racial equality.

What is more, in a White-dominated interstate system with limited Black World representation and access due to the pervasiveness of colonialism, these earlier pan-African political groupings constituted a Black World diplomatic presence so to speak. W.E.B. DuBois' proclamation in 1923 that he was the "ambassador of pan-Africa" was, in that sense, no idle boast. Such political functions of pan-Africanism are now no longer relevant in the era of African independence. But pan-Africanist sentiments in Black America have indeed heightened in the contemporary era as manifested in the expanding range of transnational linkages to which we have alluded. Such sentiments serve additionally to underpin the recently escalating Afro-American focus on US foreign policy.

Foreign Policy Input

Historically, the more Black Americans shifted their activity from the transnational/nongovernmental level to foreign policy the less of an impact they were able to have. Part of the problem lay in the relative inaccessibility and insensitivity of the US policy-making system at large to Black demands and needs. Another factor was the limited and intermittent level of official contact between the United States and Africa until fairly recently.

The NAACP's vigorous protest against American intervention in Haiti in 1915 and its subsequent pressure to terminate as well as ameliorate the effects of the military occupation which lasted until 1934 is perhaps the earliest example on record of a methodical and sustained Afro-American attempt to influence foreign policy (Plummer 1982). But as indicated by Challenor (1981, pp. 146-158), from time to time up to the end of World War II there emerged a number of Black efforts to influence foreign policy. One such concern was to assist the political integrity and economic viability of Liberia which occupied the attention of Booker T. Washington around 1909 and of the NAACP and other interested organizations in the 1930s. Another focus of Black lobbying in the 1930s was the Italian occupation of Ethiopia, as already discussed. At the end of World War I and more so at the end of World War II, there were various Black attempts to influence US input into the post-war settlement, especially relating to Africa's future. But with the exception of "the radical, black-led and interracial" Council on African Affairs, which existed from 1935-1937, its goal being "to en-

lighten the public about Africa and to promote the
liberation of the continent" through appropriate
petition and protest, and whose Marxist orientation
caused it to become a victim of McCarthyism, no
other Black (indeed American-based) organization
sought to focus consistently and specifically on
Africa as a policy concern (Lynch 1978).

Prior to the 1960s a general assessment of
Black orientations to the foreign policy process
would lead to the conclusion that such concerns
were more often than not diffuse in nature, and
were only expressed sporadically, usually in the
form of verbal protest rather than organized pressure. It was difficult enough for Blacks to seek
to influence the domestic policy process, let alone
foreign policy.

The intensification of Afro-American political
activism and militancy over the past two decades
has been accompanied by an escalation of interest
and involvement in foreign policy concerns, particularly those relevant to African affairs. The
founding in 1962 of the American Negro Leadership
Conference on Africa (ANLCA), mainly by Black
elites in the then dynamic Civil Rights Movement
signalled the institutionalization of such Afro-
American pressure to protect and enhance African
interests. Comprised of 28 organizations, including the major Civil Rights organizations and various labor unions, religious groups and voluntary
associations, the ANLCA had disintegrated by 1967
having achieved only limited success, mainly in
pressing for the recruitment of more Blacks to the
foreign policy establishment and in alerting US
officialdom to certain critical Africa-related
concerns of the Black community.[16] Yet its vision
and function have not disappeared, having been
revived in some quarters and transformed in others.

Illustrative of the first is the fact that
ANLCA's leading organizational participant, the
NAACP, subsequently set up its own task force on
Africa in 1976 to study and develop "a meaningful
policy" on Africa "for the guidance of its members
and the nation." The resulting **NAACP Task Force on
Africa Report of 1978** reiterated many of the original ANLCA aims while extending others to include,
for example, a call for full (instead of partial)
economic sanctions against the South African racist
minority regime.

Illustrative of a second tendency, namely the
transformation of ANLCA's approach, was the more
activist and grassroots-based African Liberation

Support Committee (ALSC) which emerged in the early 1970s. After a very dramatic start in staging a massive demonstration in 1972--estimates ranged between 10,000 and 50,000 participants--in Washington, D.C., protesting colonial and racist rule in southern Africa and US involvement there, as well as demonstrating uncompromising support for the liberation movements, by the late 1970s ALSC had split into various factions divided over ideological and tactical differences. But despite their lack of organizational unity, the proliferation and persistence of such African liberation support groups is significant in its own right.

Within the arenas of pressure group, bureaucratic, and Congressional politics, we find reinforcements to the phenomenon of burgeoning Afro-American efforts to influence the foreign policy decision-making process.

Easily the most significant development with respect to Black pressure group activity has been the emergence of TransAfrica, established in 1977 at the instigation of a Black Leadership Conference on Southern Africa in 1976--convened by the Congressional Black Caucus--which entered a commitment to mobilizing a Black constituency for Africa and catalyzing within the wider American community an interest in a more forward looking policy toward Africa (see Black Leadership Conference on Southern Africa, 1976). In TransAfrica's presence we see an interest in enhancing professionalism (as an organized lobby with its research staff and the recent addition of a research and educational affiliate called TransAfrica Forum); in developing specialized talents (as a full-time lobby with full-time concern with the outer Black World); and in extending vision beyond a purely African to include a Caribbean focus. Regarded by one analyst (Challenor 1981, p. 172) as "the key institutional voice in the Black community on foreign affairs," Trans-Africa achieved some success especially under the Carter administration but has necessarily had a more difficult time in the Reagan era. The fact that TransAfrica has not yet seemed able to affect the foreign policy process substantively is perhaps less important than the fact that the task of serious foreign policy mobilization is under way in Black America.[17]

The more the Afro-American political mobilization has grown apace, the more insistent have been accompanying demands for a larger and more diversified representation of Blacks in the foreign policy bureaucracy (Henry Jackson 1982, pp. 150-53; Jake Miller 1978, **passim;** Smythe and Skinner 1976; Philip White 1981b, **passim).** Thus was explained the emergence in 1969 of the "Thursday Group," comprising the handful of Blacks in major foreign affairs agencies collectively seeking an expanded Black recruitment and demanding an end to (what the group's leader characterized as) the "ghetto-ization" of Black ambassadors (meaning their tradi-tional assignment to Black World countries only). More recently similar concerns have again surfaced institutionally in the form of an Organization of Black Ambassadors created in February 1983 for the long term purpose of heightening an interest in foreign affairs within the Black community and encouraging younger Blacks to consider foreign service careers. "We must not be spectators but participators," declared one of the founding mem-bers, a former ambassador to Uganda, "we can have an impact," he concluded.[18]

But comments of the latter type raise an un-resolved issue. To what extent, it may be asked, are Black bureaucrats and diplomats able to wield meaningful influence in the sense of being archi-tects, as opposed to being instruments, of the foreign policy process? Certainly the kind of foreign policy visibility and influence which an Andrew Young was able to attain, during his twenty month tenure (1977-79) as the Carter Administra-tion's Permament Representative to the United Na-tions was unique. And it is all the more instruc-tive that he was removed prematurely after a career constantly plagued with controversy within the foreign policy establishment because of his innova-tive tendencies.[19]

More room for independent and innovative Black political initiatives exists in the legislative arena, thus helping to explain why the Congression-al Black Caucus (CBC), although ultimately con-strained by wider institutional and national sys-temic realities, has appeared to be more in the forefront of seeking a transformative foreign poli-cy. In the activities of the CBC lie a significant measure of the escalating Afro-American concern with US policy toward Africa and the Caribbean and, indeed, toward the wider American role in the global system.[20]

Currently comprised of 20 members, the CBC first emerged under another name (the Democratic Select Committee) in 1969 among 9 Blacks in the House of Representatives and was formally organized two years later with 13 such participants. Its appearance was symptomatic of a shifting emphasis in the Black community "from protests to politics" (Barker and McCorry 1980, p. 275) or more accurately from "movement-style politics to...electoral politics" (Barnett 1982, p. 28). Indeed, this decision to institutionalize a Black Congressional presence could hardly have arisen before the late 1960s, given the significantly lower and even more marginal level of Black representation existing previously--an apt reminder of the conventional systemic restrictions and constraints on Black political activity.[21]

Of particular significance to the present study is the fact that from the outset the Congressional Black Caucus had a clear conception of the integral links between the domestic needs and the international interests of the Black community, and has accordingly sought consistently to bring appropriate pressure to bear on the foreign policy process. Thus, in its first major policy pronouncement, a statement to President Nixon made in March 1971, almost one-sixth of its 64 demands bore directly on African policy including proposals for an increase in foreign aid, for facilitating Africa's access to development funds, and for "a major overhaul" of US policies in southern Africa.[22]

One of the CBC's strategies is to bring greater Congressional visibility and salience to African issues which, from the outset, was facilitated and indeed pioneered by the then Congressman Charles Diggs, who in addition to being the CBC's first chairman simultaneously chaired the House Sub-Committee on Africa. Another strategy has been to take the lead in mobilizing Black political input on foreign policy matters, for example in hosting "think tanks," convening Black leadership forums, or being instrumental in the creation of the Trans-Africa lobby.

A significant index of the CBC's firm commitment to active critical involvement in foreign relations lies in the creation of a CBC Foreign Affairs Braintrust comprised of six task forces, each chaired by different Black Congressmen, addressing these specialized concerns: Africa, the Caribbean, Latin America and Cuba, Foreign Assistance and Economic Development, Defense Policy, and Refugees/Migration. What is more, this spread of interest beyond a narrow focus on Africa is symptomatic of an emerging international systemic perspective on the part of certain Afro-American interests, which is the focus of our third level of analysis.

The International Systemic Arena

The international systemic (globally related) setting has predictably not been as significant a focus of Afro-American attention as the other two (transnational and foreign policy) arenas previously analyzed. One fundamental consideration is that non-state interests are necessarily more limited in the roles they can play in international systemic processes. Despite that, this has not inhibited Black American efforts in times past to seek to influence interstate organizations operating at the global level, as I have documented elsewhere (Edmondson 1971).

For example, there were various Afro-American attempts in 1919 to influence the shaping of the League of Nations Covenant so as to protect and enhance African interests. This was followed up over the next decade by various petitions to the League in furtherance of such goals. Although such initiatives did not bear fruit in an unreceptive international environment of entrenched White dominance, their meaning was not lost on an emerging generation of African nationalists such as Senegal's Alioune Diop who subsequently testified that:

> In the twentieth century and especially during and after World War I it was the American Negro who spoke forcefully for African Negro rights during the making of the treaty of Versailles when we were not in a position to speak for ourselves.[23]

So too, in the drafting of the United Nations Charter in 1945, concerned Black Americans sought a strengthening of the anti-colonial and racial equality provisions.

But Afro-American international systemic outreach has been dictated not only by a concern with the African homeland but also for reasons of domestic self-interest in the host country. For one thing, such outreach was often premised on the assumption that improvements in the wider international politico-racial order might have advantageous spill-over effects on the American racial scene. Some Afro-Americans have indeed sought directly to engage international systemic processes on behalf of their domestic struggle for racial equality.

With respect to the latter, it is relevant to recall occasions when Blacks sought or threatened to petition international organizations for a redress of their domestic grievances. The petitions to the United Nations in 1946 by the National Negro Congress, in 1947 by the NAACP and in 1950 by the Civil Rights Congress are cases in point. Malcolm X's frequent exhortations to Blacks to lodge American racism within the ambit of international human rights as opposed to domestic civil rights represents another such perspective.

As implied earlier, there have been recent suggestions of a widening of Afro-American international concerns, beyond a natural Africa focus to embrace other regions, other issues, and, indeed, fundamental aspects of global politics. In support of this line of argument, it is revealing to allude to the Black Caucus' statement of March 1981, "the first major Congressional critique of any aspect of the Reagan Administration's foreign policy" according to Kornegay (1982, p. 18):

> The Congressional Black Caucus believes that the most realistic perspective for a global policy during the latter half of the twentieth century is one that recognizes a North-South as well as an East-West dimension to foreign policy. Therefore, we reject as unrealistic and potentially disastrous to American global interests, the Reagan Administration's notion that foreign policy issues, especially in the developing world, must be seen primarily in the context of a purely East-West confrontation.

The CBC statement thereupon proceeded to elaborate on the need for promoting a North-South dialogue to facilitate economic interdependence, and further said that "it rejects and will oppose any policies toward developing countries that emphasize either overt or covert military intervention aimed at destabilizing established governments or blocking progressive reform."

Similarly instructive is the "Defense, Foreign Policy and Nuclear Disarmament" plank appearing in **The People's Platform,** a manifesto developed by the National Black Coalition for 1984 in cooperation with the National Black Leadership Roundtable representing more than 150 national Black organizations (civil rights, religious, labor, social, fraternal, business, youth, media and political). In addition to specific positions articulated on Africa (mainly with respect to South Africa), Central America and the Caribbean, the Middle East, and Nuclear Freeze and Disarmament, the global interest of **The People's Platform** is clearly established in its introductory "statement of principles," calling among other things for a reduction in East-West tensions; encouragement of a North-South dialogue; and "the mutual elimination of weapons of mass destruction and cessation of the world-wide arms trade."

Jesse Jackson's frequent, and often controversial, interventions on US foreign policy and wider international issues, during his search in 1984 for the Democratic Presidential nomination, cannot thus be viewed simply as either a function of his idiosyncracies or a dictate of the exigencies of the Presidential campaign. For they seem to reflect, and to flow logically out of, the emerging concerns of the Black community, Jackson's primary support base.

But Jackson's candidacy also raises another challenge pertaining to the Afro-American capacity for participating meaningfully in the shaping of US policy and by extension of wider international relations processes. On this score **The People's Platform** is very clear in urging greater participation by minorities and women "at all levels in US foreign policymaking," in order "to secure the best talent and to guarantee that sensitivity to and interest in **all parts of the world** are brought to bear...on the making of US foreign policy" (emphasis added).

We may thus conclude that the more significant implication of Black American political mobilization on international systemic processes lies in its potential to influence meaningful transformations in the style and content of US foreign policy decision-making. Since Afro-American interests in many essentials remain opposed to the perpetuation of the US foreign policy status quo, any such correctives to the present state of imbalanced domestic input would in turn convey wider global connotations, given the realities of American power and influence in the international system.

Conclusion

In conclusion, the deepening of Afro-American interest and involvement in Africa since the 1960s is being accompanied by a widening of concern with American foreign policy and developments in the international system. At least three significant features of the contemporary phase of the connection with Africa should be noted. First, **conscious** pro-Africanism has now spread from the avowedly Black nationalist groups to organizations of an integrationist tendency. Related to this is a second consideration broached by Challenor (1981, p. 160) to the effect that "unlike the earlier period when primarily the poor and the leadership class acted upon an interest in Africa, members of the Black middle class now demonstrate concern about Africa." Third, these more widespread interests in Africa have come to be linked more clearly than ever before to the immediacy of the freedom struggle in Black America itself.

Thus African and various other international issues are being more and more routinely incorporated in the agendas of Afro-American politics. Such homeland/international outreach is being integrally linked to and enmeshed with a heightening search for domestic empowerment. But this is not only a matter of outreach to Africa flowing out of burgeoning Black political mobilization on domestic issues. It is also the case that the Africa connection serves to boost racial solidarity which underpins Afro-American political mobilization efforts.

The focus of this analysis has been on historical/evolutionary trends and tendencies, ultimately with a view to examining the style and content of Afro-American diasporic mobilization since the 1960s. It has not systematically sought to assess the impact of such developments, which is an issue deserving of treatment in its own right.

To facilitate a balanced assessment of the impact of Black diasporic mobilization--which will not be attempted here--our focus of attention and measure of effectiveness should be clearly established at the outset. While such diasporic mobilization has been largely ineffective in substantively influencing relevant directions in US foreign policy, it has had some clearer positive impact on stimulating a race conscious political activism in Black America. Additionally the historical record, as we have seen, has unearthed some positive Black diasporic contributions to the development of African nationalism. What is being witnessed, however, is a burgeoning but unfulfilled Black diasporic thrust whose potential is largely circumscribed by constraints long embedded in the host country's politico-racial order. Thus this analysis has focused on mobilizing tendencies, leaving for future determination an assessment of mobilized impact.

In a sense these developing expressions of a linking of interests with the African homeland may be perceived of as another stage in the fulfillment of a historic American pattern of ethnic groups mobilizing their influence to bear on matters affecting their ancestral lands. And such developments are consistent with what may be formulated as a general rule, namely that **the more heightened a sense of racial or ethnic identity, the greater the propensity for such expressions to transcend national boundaries.**
But there is a particularly sharp edge to the rising Afro-American identification with African causes. There is, so to speak, a dual racially-significant attachment. For here we have a developing relationship not only conditioned by the facts of common racial origin, but also impregnated with the realities of common racial traumas.

Influences associated with the rise of Africa in world politics have thus intruded externally and internally on United States foreign policy and international relations processes. To put it another way, with respect to Africa, United States decision making is simultaneously challenged by racial developments from within and by racial considerations from without. The United States foreign policy process is enmeshed in this dialectical interplay between the inner and outer worlds of race.

In the final analysis perhaps here lies the ultimate test, making the African presence in America a continuing challenge to the creation of a more viable international racial order.

White-controlled South Africa raises the most significant threat to the realization of that goal, which provokes yet another concluding thought. It would be the greatest irony if that mobilization against South African racism came to be the instrument through which links between Black America and Africa were most effectively consolidated.[24]

Notes

1 As DuBois wrote in the February 1919 issue of **The Crisis,** the official organ of the National Association for the Advancement of Colored People: "The African movement means to us what the Zionist movement must mean to the Jews, the centralization of race effort and the recognition of a racial fount. To help bear the burden of Africa does not mean any lessening of effort in our own problem at home. Rather it means increased interest. For any ebullition of action and feeling that results in an amelioration of the lot of Africa tends to ameliorate the condition of colored peoples throughout the world" (p. 166).

2 Nigeria's 1980 population was 86 million. The actual size of the "Black" Brazilian population is unknown but there is no question that Brazilian Blacks outnumber their American counterparts. Ethiopia, with a 1980 population of 31.2 million, is clearly more sizeable than Black America, but for a reason I have yet to determine, some observers have classified Black America as the third largest concentration. Perhaps, they do not regard Ethiopia as being overwhelmingly Black, as I do. Were one to speak here strictly of African as opposed to a Black population base, Egypt with its 42 million (1980 data) would qualify for inclusion here.

3 There seems to be some comparability here with the creation of the state of Israel as being largely the handiwork of European Jews. This analogy of a disapora's diaspora requires further examination.

4 Perhaps the greater disadvantages experienced by native Americans do not arise for present consideration, paradoxically due to the fact that this is the only ethnic group in the United States having no status as a diaspora, the United States being their original homeland.

5 As of 1982, there were 5,160 elected Black officials in the US (compared with 1,469 in 1970). Of these, 18 (increased to 21 by mid-1984) sit in the 435-member House of Representatives; there are no Black Senators at the national level (only one having been elected in the twentieth century); 330 Blacks comprise 4.4 percent of State legislators nation-wide; there are 223 Mayors, overwhelmingly located in medium to small size cities, with a few located in critical major cities. See Joint Center for Political Studies (1982).

6   Despite a considerable increase in the number of Black officeholders, an estimate from the late 1970s by the Joint Center for Political Studies was that at the rate of increase Black officeholders would comprise only 3 percent of all officeholders by the year 2000. Much more recently Jesse Jackson had this to say: "There are 512,000 elected officials in America, 512,000, and 5,200 Black. We're about 1 percent of the elected officials and we're slightly over 12 percent of the population. So at the rate of 1 percent every 18 years it will take us 198 years to achieve parity." ("Jesse Jackson Speaks: 'I Could Have Work,'" **Ebony** 34 (August 1984): 174).

7   Professor Henry Jackson (1982, p. 152) observes that "In policy implementation, whether in missions abroad or in the State Department bureaucracy at home, Black input has been marginal." He notes that in 1978 Blacks accounted for 1.5 percent of senior foreign service officers and 4.0 percent of middle-level officers and that "even in Africa Blacks held only 6.6 percent of the foreign service posts." This was the situation in the Jimmy Carter administration which was less insensitive than previous ones to Black input and which saw a few key positions being filled by Blacks, in particular Goler Butcher (head of the Africa Division of AID), John Reinhardt (chief administration of the International Communication Agency), Andrew Young (Ambassador to the United Nations) and his deputy and eventual successor, Donald McHenry.

Blacks have been better represented in the Ambassadorial ranks than elsewhere in the foreign policy establishment. Beginning in 1949, forty-four Black ambassadors have been appointed to date. But there are now only 6 Blacks serving in the Reagan administration out of 133 ambassadorial positions while there were 15 during the Carter administration, indicative of the fact that Black officeholding and influence in the federal bureaucracy has suffered significant setbacks under Reagan.

8   The military was the first governmental institution to be desegregated by Harry Truman's Presidential Order in 1948, but charges and incidents of racism still persist. The main reason for the high Black intake lies in the lack of economic opportunities available to them, thus leading some observers to refer to the existence of a "Poverty Draft." According to a recent news report the "loyalty" of an increasing proportion of Blacks

(and Hispanics) in situations of armed involvement in Black or certain Third World environments is becoming worrisome to the military establishment; see "Blacks Cut From Strike Forces," **Jackson Advocate** (Jackson, Mississippi), 10-16 May 1984.

9   This special interest in the Belgian Congo in the late nineteenth and early twentieth century was sparked off mainly by reactions to King Leopold's atrocities. The greater interest in Ethiopia and Liberia as symbols of Black sovereignty during the colonial era--which was also manifested toward Haiti in the neighbouring Caribbean segment of the African diaspora--was reinforced by pride in Ethiopia's ancient glories and its solidarity with the Afro-American outpost of Liberia. In the contemporary era of African independence only southern African colonialism or racial liberation situations qualify clearly as "special interest" areas in this sense.

10   Scott (1978, pp. 128-129) mentions one estimate of over 17,000 such volunteers being recruited within one week who were, however, curbed by federal statute from enlisting in a foreign army. But at least two of these--John Robinson of Chicago and The Trinidadian-born Hubert Julian with long-established residence in Harlem, New York-- reached the warfront and served as pilots in the Ethiopian Air Force.

11   Scott (1978, p. 127) in quoting the observation made in December 1935 by the Black educator Carter G. Woodson that "the Negroes of the United States, now in the bread line, have nothing to give," points out that little material assistance of this kind was forthcoming. This example points to a wider analytic issue, namely that students of diaspora-homeland relations should be wary of utilizing the extent of fund-raising activities as a reliable index of the commitments of the former to the latter. The relative economic deprivation of the Afro-American condition superimposed on the variety of potentially competing target areas of assistance in multiple homeland situations serve as constraints on effective fund-raising activities.

12   See Baraka (1972). The Congress of African Peoples eventually disintegrated largely due to Baraka's ideological conversion to Marxism.

13   In addition to a host of grassroots Black cultural nationalist organizations which have developed since the 1960s, the interest of the Black intelligentsia in institutionalizing cultural linkages with Africa in the form of AMSAC (the American

Society of African Culture) should be noted. Created in 1957, AMSAC's aim was "to promote greater knowledge of the African heritage through art exhibitions, conferences, publications and cultural exchange programs." By the late 1960s AMSAC had disintegrated after it transpired that unknown to its membership some of its funding was indirectly channeled by the US Central Intelligence Agency (Reid 1976, pp. 668-72).

14   The AHSA broke away from the White-dominated African Studies Association in order to promote a more Afrocentric line and not to remain aloof from the pressing issues of African development and liberation. While including African and Caribbean scholars it consists mainly of Afro-Americans. The AASC was created to support research on African development problems.

15   Complementing the activities of the RAINS coalition were separate fund-raising ventures by Africare and a food collection program by Jesse Jackson's organization PUSH (People United To Save Humanity).

16   Challenor (1981, pp. 163-64) and St. Clair Drake in his "Introduction" to Lynch (1978, pp. 11-12) offer some reasons for ANLCA's demise, including its low visibility and failure to mobilize mass support; its inhibited capacity to lobby partly due to the need to reconcile opposition to US policies with a search for more Black representation within the system; a reluctance to cope with radical African liberationist options; and, as Challenor submits, "an effort by the White House to undermine it."

17   Challenor (1981, pp. 170-72) and Henry Jackson (1982, pp. 123-26) discuss TransAfrica's successes and promise; Beaubien (1982) describes its deteriorating relations with the Reagan Administration; Kornegay (1982, pp. 22-26) analyses some of TransAfrica's tactical shortcomings.

18   Another ex-ambassador who had served in Africa emphasized that it is "particularly important that Blacks represent the US abroad because they not only represent a significant portion of the American population but also tend to serve Third World nations more effectively [with greater sensitivity] than their white counterparts." For contemporary reports on the creation of the Organization of Black Ambassadors announced during a weekend tribute to current and former Black US ambassadors organized by the Boston (Massachusetts) Support Group of TransAfrica, see the **Boston Globe**

(6 February 1983), the **Bay Street Banner** (10 February 1983) and **Jet Magazine** (28 February 1983).

19   Young was forced to resign as a result of a diplomatic blunder on Middle East policy, involving an apparently unauthorized meeting with the UN representative of the Palestine Liberation Organization which contravened the United States policy of non-recognition of the PLO. But his previous unconventional pro-Africa positions had made him so controversial as to pave the way to his isolation. See further the revealing discussion by Henry Jackson (1982, pp. 153-60) on "The Rise and Fall of Andrew Young."

20   On the Congressional Black Caucus generally, see Barker and McCorry (1980, pp. 267-77) and Barnett (1982). Specifically on its orientations toward US foreign policy, see Diggs (1976); Kornegay (1982, pp. 17-21).

21   Between 1929--when Oscar DePriest, a Republican from Illinois, became the first Black to win a House of Representatives seat in the twentieth century and the first ever to be elected from a Northern state--and 1944, Blacks occupied only one seat in Congress (DePriest having by then been succeeded successively by two Black Democrats). Blacks captured a second seat in 1944, a third in 1954, a fourth in 1957, a fifth in 1962 and a sixth in 1964. The election of three more Blacks in 1968, bringing the overall total to nine (all Democrats), signalled the opportunity to institutionalize the caucus idea. The lone Black Senator, serving from 1966-1978, opted not to join the CBC, most likely due to his Republican affiliations.

22   "Congressional Black Caucus' Recommendations to President Nixon," **Congressional Record**, 92nd Congress, 1st Session, 30 March 1971.

23   Taken from Diop's introductory comments "Our AMSAC Brothers" in Davis (1958), p. xii. Diop, a distinguished figure in pan-African literary and cultural circles, was instrumental in the founding of the Societe Africaine du Culture which publishes the journal **Presence Africaine.**

24   This concluding observation is especially pertinent in the light of an unexpected wave of demonstrations--sparked off by Blacks with later support from White allies--beginning in late November 1984, involving picketing the South African Embassy and various consulates in the United States in protest over increasing political repression by the apartheid regime. Spearheaded by TransAfrica, and involving "direct action" strategies, these

protests (which at the time of writing in late
December are still escalating) have placed Presi-
dent Reagan on the defensive in terms of his policy
of "constructive engagement" with South Africa.
See for example, "Black Leaders Form Group on South
Africa," **The Washington Post,** 24 November 1984;
"South Africa's Image in U.S. Shatters," **The Chris-
tian Science Monitor,** 10 December 1984.

Bibliography and Further Readings

Akpan, Emmanuel. 1980. Africa in the Development
of Black-American Nationalism. In **Contem-
porary Black Thought: Alternative Analyses in
Social and Behavioral Science,** eds. M.K.
Asante and A.S. Vandi. Beverly Hills: Sage
Publications.
American Society of African Culture, ed. 1962.
Pan-Africanism Reconsidered. Berkeley and Los
Angeles: University of California Press.
Armstrong, John. 1976. Mobilized and Proletarian
Diasporas. **American Political Science Review**
70 (June): 393-408.
Asante, S.K.B. 1973. The Afro-American and the
Italo-Ethiopian Crisis, 1934-1936. **Race** 15
(No. 2): 168-81.
Baraka, Imamu Amiri (Leroi Jones), ed. 1972. **Af-
rican Congress: A Documentary of the First
Modern Pan-African Congress.** New York:
William Morrow.
Barker, Lucius J. and Jesse McCorry, Jr. 1980.
Black Americans and the Political System, 2d
ed. Cambridge, MA: Winthrop Publishers.
Barnett, Marguerite Ross. 1977. Introduction to
Part 5, Non-Alignment and the Afro-American
People. In **The Non-Aligned Movement in World
Politics,** ed. A.W. Singham. Westport, CT:
Lawrence Hill and Co.
-----. 1982. The Congressional Black Caucus:
Illusions and Realities of Power. In **The New
Black Politics: The Search for Political
Power,** eds. Michael Preston, Lenneal Henderson
Jr. and Paul Puryear. New York: Longman.
Beaubien, Michael. 1982. Making Waves in Foreign
Policy. **Black Enterprise** 12 (April): 37-42.
Bertelsen, Judy, ed. 1977. **Non-State Nations in
International Policies: Comparative Systems
Analysis.** New York: Prager.
Black Leadership Conference on Southern Africa.

1976. The African-American Manifesto on Southern Africa. **Freedomways** 16 (No. 4): 216-21.

Bond, Horace Mann. 1961. Howe and Isaacs in the Bush: The Ram in the Thicket. **Negro History Bulletin** 25 (December): 67-72.

Browne, Robert S. 1961. **Race Relations in International Affairs.** Washington, D.C.: Public Affairs Press.

Bunche, Ralph. [1936] 1968. **A World View of Race.** Washington, NY: Kennikat Press.

Burkett, Randall. 1978. **Garveyism as a Religious Movement: The Institutionalization of a Black Civil Religion.** Metuchen, NJ and London: The Scarecrow Press and the American Theological Library Association.

Challenor, Herschelle. 1981. The Influence of Black Americans on U.S. Foreign Policy Toward Africa. In **Ethnicity and American Foreign Policy,** rev. ed., ed. Abdul Said. New York: Praeger.

Chick, C.A. 1962. The American Negroes' Changing Attitude Toward Africa. **Journal of Negro Education** 31 (Fall): 531-5.

Chidozie, Ogene Francis. 1974. Group Interests and United States Foreign Policy on African Issues. Ph.D. dissertation, Case Western Reserve University, Cleveland.

Chrisman, Robert. 1977. History of Black Involvement in International Politics. In **The Non-Aligned Movement in World Politics,** ed. A. W. Singham. Westport: Lawrence, Hill and Co.

Clarke, John Henrik. 1961. Africa and the American Negro Press. **Journal of Negro Education** 30 (Winter): 64-8.

Cole, Katherine W., ed. 1978. **Minority Organizations: A National Directory.** Garrett Park, MD: Garrett Park Press.

Cronon, Edmund. 1955. **Black Moses: The Story of Marcus Garvey and the Universal Negro Improvement Association.** Madison: University of Wisconsin Press.

Davis, John A. ed. 1958. **Africa From the Point of View of American Negro Scholars.** Dijon: Presence Africaine.

------. 1969. Black Americans and United States Policy Toward Black Africa. **Journal of International Affairs** 23 (No. 1): 236-49.

Dellums, Ronald. 1983. U.S. Military Aid to the Third World. **TransAfrica Forum** 1 (Winter): 9-22.

Diggs, Charles C. Jr. 1976. The Black American Stake in U.S. Policy Toward Africa. **Ebony** (August): 76-82.

Drachler, Jacobs. ed. 1975. **Black Homeland/Black Diaspora: Cross Currents of the African Relationship.** Port Washington: Kennikat Press.

Drake, St. Clair. 1963. Hide my Face?: On Pan-Africanism and Negritude. In **Soon One Morning: New Writing by American Negroes, 1940-1962,** ed. Herbert Hill. New York: A.A. Knopf.

-----. 1966. Negro Americans and the Africa Interest. In **The American Negro Reference Book,** ed. John Davis. Englewood Cliffs: Prentice-Hall.

-----. 1970. **The Redemption of Africa and Black Religion.** Chicago: Third World Press.

DuBois, W.E.B. 1935. Interracial Implications of the Ethiopian Crisis: A Negro View. **Foreign Affairs** 14 (October): 88-92.

-----. 1965. **The World and Africa,** enlarged ed. New York: International Publishers.

Edmondson, Locksley. 1968. The Internalization of Black Power: Historical and Contemporary Perspectives. **Mawazo** 1 (December): 16-30; reprinted in **Is Massa Day Dead? Black Moods in the Caribbean,** ed. O. Coombs. New York: Doubleday, 1974; also reprinted in **Black Separatism and Social Reality,** ed. R. Hall. Elmsford, NY: Pergamon Press, 1976.

-----. 1969. The Challenges of Race: From Entrenched White Power to Rising Black Power. **International Journal** 24 (Autumn): 693-716.

-----. 1971. Race and Human Rights in International Organization and International Law and Afro-American Interests: Analysis and Documentation. **Afro-American Studies** 2 (December): 205-24.

-----. 1973. Africa and the African Diaspora: Interactions, Linkages and Racial Challenges in the Future World Order. In **Africa and World Affairs: The Next Thirty Years,** eds. Ali Mazrvi and Hasu Patel. New York: Third Press.

-----. 1975. Pan-Africanism and the International System Past and Present: Challenges and Opportunities. Paper read at the Symposium on Pan-Africanism: New Directions in Strategy, Queen's College, City University of New York, May.

-----. 1979. Black Roots and Identity: Compara-

tive and International Perspectives. **International Journal** 24 (Summer): 408-429.
-----. 1981. Pan-Africanist Prospectus. In **Blacks in the Year 2000**, ed. J. Washington. Philadelphia: Afro-American Studies Program, University of Pennsylvania.
-----. 1984. Black American Political and Diasporic Mobilization: Toward the Heightening of a Linkage. **CAAS Newsletter** 8 (No. 1): 1, 10-12.
Emerson, Rupert and Martin Kilson. 1965. The American Dilemma in a Changing World: The Rise of Africa and the Negro American. **Daedalus** 94 (Fall): 1055-84.
-----. 1967. **Africa and United States Policy.** Englewood Cliffs: Prentice Hall.
Erskine, Hazel. 1968. The Polls: World Opinion of U.S. Racial Problems. **Public Opinion Quarterly** 32 (Summer): 299-312.
Essien-Udom, E.U. 1962. The Relationship of Afro-Americans to African Nationalism. **Freedomways** 2 (Fall): 391-407.
-----. 1971. Black Identity in the International Context. In **Key Issues in the Afro-American Experience**, vol. 2, ed. Nathan Huggins, Martin Kilson and Daniel Fox. New York: Harcourt Brace Jovanovich.
Fierce, Milfred. 1976. African-American Interest in Africa and the Interaction with West Africa: The Origins of the Pan-African Idea in the United States. Ph.D. dissertation, Columbia University.
Foster, Badi. 1972. United States Foreign Policy Toward Africa. **Issue** 2 (Summer): 45-51.
Garrett, James. 1977. Afro-Americans and American Foreign Policy. In **The Non-Aligned Movement in World Politics**, ed. A.W. Singham. Westport: Lawrence Hill and Co.
Gatewood, Willard B. Jr. 1975. **Black Americans and the White Man's Burden, 1898-1903.** Urbana: University of Illinois Press.
-----. 1976. Black Americans and the Boer War, 1899-1902. **South Atlantic Quarterly** 75 (Spring): 226-44.
Geiss, Immanuel. 1974. **The Pan-African Movement.** London: Methuen.
Gerson, Louis. 1964. **The Hyphenate in Recent American Politics and Diplomacy.** Lawrence: University of Kansas Press.
Glicksberg, Charles. 1947. Negro Americans and the African Dream. **Phylon** 8 (No. 4): 323-29.
Harding, Vincent. 1980. **The Other American Revo-**

lution. Los Angeles: Center for Afro-American Studies, University of California.

Harlan, Louis. 1966. Booker T. Washington and the White Man's Burden. **American Historical Review** 71 (January): 441-67.

Harris, Joseph. 1968. Introduction to the African Diaspora. **Emerging Themes in African History,** ed. J.O. Ranger. Nairobi: East African Publishing House.

-----, ed. 1982. **Global Dimensions of the African Diaspora.** Washington, D.C.: Howard University Press.

Harris, Robert L. Jr. 1982. In Search of International Support for Afro-American Rights During the 20th Century. Paper presented at the 1982 Annual Convention of the Association for the Study of Afro-American Life and History.

Harvard Encyclopedia of American Ethnic Groups. 1980. Cambridge, MA: Harvard University Press.

Helmreich, William B., comp. 1977. **Afro-Americans and Africa, Black Nationalism at the Crossroads.** Westport: Greenwood Press.

Hero, Alfred O. Jr. 1959. **Americans in World Affairs.** Boston: World Peace Foundation.

-----. 1969. American Negroes and U.S. Foreign Policy: 1937-67. **Journal of Conflict Resolution** 13 (June): 220-51.

----- and John Barrat, ed. 1981. **The American People and South Africa: Publics, Elites and Policy-Making.** Lexington: D.C. Heath.

Hill, Adelaide Cromwell and Martin Kislon, comps. 1969. **Apropos of Africa: Sentiments of American Negro Leaders on Africa from the 1800s to the 1950s.** London: Frank Cass.

Hill, Sylvia. 1977. Pan-Africanism and Non-Alignment. **The Non-Aligned Movement in World Politics,** ed. A.W. Singham. Westport: Lawrence, Hill & Co.

Hoadley, J. Stephen. 1972. Black Americans and U.S. Policy Toward Africa: An Empirical Note. **Journal of Black Studies** 2 (June): 489-503.

Hooker, J.R. 1967. The Negro-American Press and Africa in the 1930s. **Canadian Journal of African Studies** 1 (March): 43-50.

Huggins, Nathan. 1971. **Harlem Renaissance.** New York: Oxford University Press.

Issacs, Harold. 1959. The American Negro and Africa: Some Notes. **Phylon** 20 (Fall): 219-33.

-----. 1962. American Race Relations and the

United States Image in World Affairs. **Journal of Human Relations** (Winter-Spring): 266-80.
-----. 1963. **The New World of Negro Americans.** New York: Viking Press.
Jackson, Henry. 1982. Afro-Americans and Africa: The Unbroken Link. In **From Congo to Soweto: U.S. Foreign Policy Toward Africa Since 1960.** New York: William Morrow.
Jackson, Larry. 1971. The Mutual Reciprocity Between the African and Afro-American Revolutions. **Afro-American Studies** 2 (June): 1-13.
Jacobs, Sylvia. 1980-81. Black American Missionaries in Africa: A Selected Bibliography. **A Current Bibliography on African Affairs** 13 (No. 2): 166-172.
-----. 1981. **The African Nexus: Black American Perspectives on the European Partitioning of Africa, 1880-1920.** Westport: Greenwood Press.
Johnson, Sterling. 1979. Nation States and Non-State Nations: The International Relations and Foreign Policies of Black America. Ph.D. dissertation, Ohio State University.
Johnson, Willard. 1983. Afro-American and African Links: Cooperation for Our Long-Term Economic Empowerment. **TransAfrica Forum** 1 (Spring): 81-92.
Joint Center for Political Studies 1981a. **Black Americans and the Shaping of U.S. Foreign Policy: Proceedings of a Roundtable, May 1980.** Washington, D.C.
-----. (1981b). **Foreign Trade Policy and Black Economic Advancement: Proceedings of a Roundtable, May 1980.** Washington, D.C.
-----. 1982. **National Roster of Black Elected Officials** vol. 12. Washington, D.C.
Katz, William. 1971. The Afro-American Response to U.S. Imperialism (1898-1900). **Freedomways** 11 (No. 3): 284-91.
Keto, Clement. 1972. Black Americans and South Africa, 1890-1910. **A Current Bibliography on African Affairs** 5 (July): 383-406.
-----. 1973. Black American Involvement in South Africa's Race Issue. **Issue** 3 (Spring): 6-12.
Kilson, Martin. 1976. Political Status of American Negroes in the Twentieth Century. In **The African Diaspora: Interpretive Essays,** eds. Martin Kilson and Robert Rotberg. Cambridge: Harvard University Press.
King, Kenneth James. 1971. **Pan-Africanism and Education: A Study of Race Philanthropy and**

Education in the Southern States of America and East Africa. Oxford: Clarendon Press.

King, Martin Luther, Jr. 1968. Where Do We Go From Here: Chaos or Community? New York: Bantam Books.

Kornegay, Francis A. Jr. 1972. Southern Africa and the Emerging Constituency for Africa in the United States: A Selected Survey of Periodical Literature. A Current Bibliography on African Affairs 5 (January): 29-39.

------. 1979. Black America and U.S.-Southern African Relations: An Essay Bibliographical Survey of Developments During the 1950s, 1960s and early 1970s. In American-South Africa Relations: Bibliographic Essays, ed. Mohamed El-Khawas. Westport: Greenwood Press.

------. 1982. Washington and Africa: Reagan, Congress and an African Affairs Constituency in Transition Washington, D.C.: The African Bibliographic Center--Habari Special Report.

Langley, J. Ayo. 1969. Garveyism and African Nationalism. Race 11 (October): 157-72.

LeMelle, Tilden. 1970. Race and the United States Foreign Policy: The Case of U.S.-African Relations. Social Action 37 (October): 7-21.

------. 1971. Black Americans and Foreign Policy. Africa Today 18 (October): 18-22.

------. 1972. Race, International Relations, U.S. Foreign Policy and African Liberation Struggle. 3 (September), 95-109.

Lincoln, Eric. 1966. The Race Problem and International Relations. New South 21 (Fall): 2-14.

Logan, Rayford. 1945. The Negro and the Post-War World: A Primer. Washington, D.C.: Minorities Press.

------. 1965. The Historical Aspects of Pan-Africanism: A Personal Chronicle. African Forum 1 (Summer): 90-104.

Lynch, Hollis. 1966. Pan-Negro Nationalism in the New World Before 1862. In Boston University Papers on Africa 2, ed. Jeffrey Butler. Boston: Boston University Press.

------. 1978. Black American Radicals and the Liberation of Africa: The Council on African Affairs, 1937-1955. Monograph Series No. 5. Ithaca: Africana Studies and Research Center, Cornell University.

------. 1982. Pan-African Responses in the United States to British Colonial Rule in Africa in the 1940s. In The Transfer of Power in

Africa: Decolonization, 1940-1960, eds. Prosser Gifford and Wm. Roger Louis. New Haven: Yale University Press.

Magubane, Bernard. 1967. The American Negro's Conception of Africa: A Study in the Ideology of Pride and Prejudice. Ph.D. dissertation, University of California at Los Angeles.

Marks, George, comp. 1971. The Black Press Views American Imperialism, 1898-1900. New York: Arno Press.

Martin, Tony. 1976. Race First: The ideological and Organizational Struggles of Marcus Garvey and the Universal Negro Improvement Association. Westport: Greenwood Press.

Mathias, Charles Mc. Jr. 1981. Ethnic Groups and Foreign Policy. Foreign Affairs 59 (Summer): 975-98.

McHenry, Donald. 1974. Captive of No Group. Foreign Policy No. 15 (Summer): 142-49.

Miller, Jake. 1978. The Black Presence in Foreign Affairs. Washington, D.C.: University Press of America.

Moikobu, Josephine. 1981. Blood and Flesh: Black Americans and African Identifications. Westport: Greenwood Press.

Moore, Richard B. 1963. Africa Conscious Harlem. Freedomways 3 (Summer).

------. 1965. DuBois and Pan-Africa. Freedomways 5 (Winter): 166-87.

Morris, Milton. 1972. Black Americans and the Foreign Policy Process: The Case of Africa. Western Political Quarterly 25 (September): 451-63.

Moss, James. 1970. The Civil Rights Movement and American Foreign Policy. In Racial Influences on American Foreign Policy, ed. George Shepherd, Jr. New York: Basic Books.

Nagenda, John. 1967. Pride or Prejudice? Relationships Between African and American Negroes. Race 9 (October): 159-72.

Obatala, J.K. 1976. Black Consciousness and American Policy in Africa. In Ethnicity in an International Context, eds. Abdul Said and Luiz Simmons. New Brunswick, N.J.: Transaction Books.

Obichere, Boniface. 1975. Afro-Americans in Africa: Recent Experiences. In Black Homeland/Black Diaspora, ed. Jacob Drachler. Port Washington: Kennikat Press.

Plummer, Brenda. 1982. The Afro-American Response

to the Occupation of Haiti, 1915-1934. **Phylon** 43 (June): 125-43.

Redkey, Edwin. 1969. **Black Exodus: Black Nationalists and Back to Africa Movements, 1890-1910.** New Haven: Yale University Press.

Reid, Inez Smith. 1976. Black Americans and Africa. In **The Black American Reference Book,** ed. Mabel Smythe. Englewood Cliffs: Prentice-Hall.

Roark, James. 1971. American Black Leaders: The Response to Colonialism and the Cold War. **African Historical Studies** 4 (No. 2): 253-70.

Rodgers, Barbara. 1974. Congress and Southern Africa. **A Current Bibliography on African Affairs** 7 (Winter): 22-37.

Said, Abdul and Luis Simmons, eds. 1976. **Ethnicity in an International Context.** New Brunswick: Transaction Books.

------ed. 1977. **Ethnicity and American Foreign Policy.** New York: Praeger.

Scott, William. 1978. Black Nationalism and the Italo-Ethiopian Conflict, 1934-1936. **Journal of Negro History** 63 (April): 118-34.

Senghor, Leopold. 1966. Address at Howard University, Washington, D.C., September. Text in Mercer Cook, President Senghor's Visit: A Tale of Five Cities. **African Forum** 2 (Winter 1967): 74-86.

Shack, William. 1974. Ethiopia and Afro-Americans: Some Historical Notes, 1920-1970. **Phylon** 35 (June): 142-55.

Shankman, Arnold. 1975. Brothers Across the Sea: Afro-Americans on the Persecution of Russian Jews, 1881-1917. **Jewish Social Studies** 37 (Spring): 114-21.

Shepherd, George, ed. 1970. **Racial Influences on American Foreign Policy.** New York: Basic Books.

Shepperson, George. 1953. Ethiopianism and African Nationalism. **Phylon** 14 (Spring): 9-18.

------. 1960. Notes on Negro American Influences on the Emergence of African Nationalism. **Journal of African History** 1 (No. 2): 299-312.

------. 1968. The African Abroad or the African Diaspora. In **Emerging Themes in African History,** ed. T.O. Ranger. Nairobi: East African Publishing House.

------. 1976. Introduction to **The African Diaspora: Interpretive Essays,** eds. Martin Kilson and Robert Rothberg. Cambridge: Harvard University Press.

Shick, Tom. 1980. **Behold the Promised Land: A History of Afro-American Settlers in 19th Century Liberia.** Baltimore: Johns Hopkins University Press.

Skinner, Elliot. 1973. **Afro-Americans and Africa: The Continuing Dialect.** New York: Columbia University Urban Center.

Smythe, Hugh and Elliot Skinner. 1976. Black Participation in U.S. Foreign Relations. In **The Black American Reference Book,** ed. Mabel Smythe. Englewood Cliffs: Prentice-Hall.

Solomon, Mark. 1971. Black Critics of Colonialism and the Cold War. In **Cold War Critics: Alternatives to American Foreign Policy in the Truman Years,** ed. Thomas Paterson. Chicago: Quadrangle Books.

Stack, John, ed. 1981. **Ethnic Identities in a Transnational World.** Westport: Greenwood Press.

Stillman, Richard J., II. Black Participation in the Armed Forces. In **The Black American Reference Book,** ed. Mabel Smythe. Englewood Cliffs.

Suhrke, Astri and Lela Noble. eds. 1977. **Ethnic Conflict in International Relations.** New York: Praeger.

Taylor, Clyde, comp. 1973. **Vietnam and Black America: An Anthology of Protest and Resistance.** Garden City: Anchor Press.

Turner, James. 1970. Afro-American Perspectives. In **The African Experience,** vol. 1 Essays, eds. John Paden and Edward Soja. Evanston: Northwestern University Press.

Uya, Okon Edet, ed. 1971. **Black Brotherhood: Afro-Americans and Africa.** Lexington: D.C. Heath.

Van Den Berghe, Pierre. 1976. The African Diaspora in Mexico, Brazil and the United States. **Social Forces** 54 (March): 530-45.

Walters, Ronald. ca. 1979. A Theory of the Black Diaspora. Department of Political Science, Howard University, Washington, D.C. Mines.

------. 1980. Pan-Africanism: From National Liberation to National Reconstruction. Paper read at the Conference on The Next Decade: Consolidating Africana Studies and Bonding African Linkages, Africana Studies and Research Center, Cornell University, September.

Warden, Donald. 1977. Can Black Americans Play a Major Role in the Development of Africa? **Black Law Journal** 5 (No. 2): 257 ff.

Watson, Denton. 1977. The NAACP and Africa: An Historical Profile. **The Crisis** (April): 131-38.

Weil, Martin. 1974. Can the Blacks Do For Africa What the Jews Did for Israel? **Foreign Policy** No. 15 (Summer): 109-30.

Weisbord, Robert. 1972. Black America and the Italian-Ethiopian Crisis: An Episode in Pan-Negroism. **The Historian** 34 (No. 2): 230-41.

-----. 1973. **Ebony Kinship: Africa, Africans and the Afro-American.** Westport: Greenwood Press.

Weston, Rubin. 1972. **Racism in U.S. Imperialism: The Influence of Racial Assumption on American Foreign Policy, 1893-1946.** Columbia: University of South Carolina Press.

White, Philip. 1981a. The Black American Constituency for Southern Africa, 1940-1980. **The American People and South Africa: Publics, Elites and Policymaking Processes,** eds. Alfred Hero Jr. and John Barratt. Lexington: D.C. Heath.

-----. 1981b. Blacks and U.S. Foreign Policy. In **Black Americans and the Shaping of U.S. Foreign Policy: Proceedings of a Roundtable May 1980.** Washington, D.C.: Joint Center for Political Studies.

White, Walter. 1945. **A Rising Wind.** Garden City: Doubleday, Doran & Co.

Wilkins, Roger. 1974. What Africa Means to Blacks. **Foreign Policy** No. 15 (Summer): 130-42.

Williams, Walter. 1973. Black Journalism's Opinion About Africa During the Late Nineteenth Century. **Phylon** 34 (September): 224-35.

-----. 1982. **Black Americans and the Evangelization of Africa 1877-1900.** Madison: University of Wisconsin Press.

Wynn, Neil. 1976. **The Afro-American and the Second World War.** New York: Holmes and Meier.

THE JEWISH PEOPLE AS THE CLASSIC DIASPORA: A POLITICAL ANALYSIS

Daniel J. Elazar

There is little doubt that the Jewish people represents the classic diaspora phenomenon of all time. Indeed, it seems that the term diaspora itself originated to describe the Jewish condition.[1] The Jewish diaspora has existed for at least 2,600 years and, if certain local traditions are accurate, perhaps even longer. It has existed alongside a functioning Jewish state and, for almost precisely 2,000 years, without any state recognized as politically independent. Moreover, for 1,500 years the Jewish people existed without an effective political center in their national territory, that is to say, exclusively as a diaspora community, so much so that the institutions of the Jewish community in Eretz Israel were themselves modeled after those of the diaspora and the Jews functioned as a diaspora community within their own land (Baron 1973; Kaufman 1961; Lestschinsky 1958; Patail 1971; Tartakower 1959). Nevertheless, the Jewish people not only preserved their integrity as an ethno-religious community, but continued to function as a polity throughout their long history through the various conditions of state and diaspora.

Approaching the Jewish Diaspora

Most analyses of diaspora phenomena focus on the diaspora group as a sociological category, whether it is considered an ethnic group, a religious group, or both. Political analyses of this sociological phenomenon will go a step further to examine the impact of this sociological category on the host societies in which the diaspora group finds itself. These are certainly important dimensions of the diaspora experience for Jews as well as for every other group. Jewish self-preservation through religious and cultural differentiation and endogamy are without doubt worthy of examination from a sociological perspective. For example, the way in which the Jews as a diaspora community created a way of life of their own, involving a calendar of daily specificity which established a separate rhythm of Jewish life, setting them apart from their neighbors, is worthy of the closest study. In a parallel way, it is possible to study the nature of Jewish exclusion from Christian and Muslim societies through a combination of anti-Jewish attitudes and measures on the one hand, and the mutually acceptable principle that the Jews were a nation in exile and hence deserving of corporate autonomy, on the other.

A focus on either of these, however, would be essentially historical, since both have undergone great changes in the modern epoch and to the extent that they survive at all, survive only as remnants in the postmodern epoch. Thus, while **halakhah** (Jewish law) still specifies a completely separate rhythm of life for Jews, no more than five percent of Jews in the diaspora today live so fully in accordance with that rhythm that they separate themselves from the society around them, and perhaps another 10 percent live sufficiently according to that rhythm to be considered fully part of it. Other Jews are touched by that rhythm to varying degrees depending on the extent of their connection to Jewish life. In every case it is a voluntary matter since with the rise of the modern nation-state, the notion of the Jews as a separate nation in exile was abandoned, first by the state builders and then by most diaspora Jews as they accepted the terms of emancipation (Elazar 1976, forthcoming).

Similarly, the anti-Jewish attitudes of Christians and Muslims which developed in an age when religion was at the center of life, were transformed into modern anti-Semitism (Parkes 1969, 1930). The latter remains a factor in shaping the Jewish diaspora, certainly one that is high in the consciousness of Jews everywhere. It substantially diminished as an active force in the aftermath of the Holocaust and is only now beginning to reappear in certain circles as a legitimate form of expression.

It would be more useful to examine the role of the Jews as an ethnoreligious community within the societies of which they are a part. In most of these societies they play the role of a catalytic minority, making a contribution far in excess of their percentage of the total population, in a variety of fields, especially those at the cutting edge of social activity (Baron 1973, vol. 12; Zener 1975).

One strong characteristic of the Jews as a group in their relationship with the rest of the world is their strong tendency to gravitate to the center of whatever universal communications network exists at any particular time and place. According to the best opinion of the historians of the ancient world the first Jews, symbolized by Abraham, Isaac, and Jacob, were already involved as nomads in the trading patterns of the Fertile Crescent. Their settlement in Canaan put them at the very center of that network with its two anchors in Egypt and Mesopotamia (Albright 1963; Bright 1981; Orlinski 1967). Subsequent generations of Jews have continued that tradition. Thus Jews have always gravitated to the capital cities of the world, and have been able to make their influence, as individuals and as a group, felt disproportionately. Not only that, Jews have always been involved in communication-related enterprises; whether communicating religious ideas, as in their earliest history--ultimately to half of mankind--or in radio, motion pictures, and television in the twentieth century, communicating new lifestyles worldwide.

This phenomenon has left the Jews exposed as well as influential, and Jews have paid the price for that exposure. In other words, Jews have played a very dangerous game as a small group of extraordinary importance and centrality in world affairs. As such, they have generated both strong positive and negative images and expectations, which have led to periodic efforts to cultivate them and equally frequent attacks upon them--outbreaks of persecution which have at the very least culminated in expulsion and at the worst, in massacre and Holocaust.

As a result of these pushes and pulls, the Jewish diaspora is different from other diasporas except, perhaps, the Gypsies, because it has been a diaspora in constant movement. The conventional view of Jewish history is that of shifting centers of Jewish life, so that the Jews themselves have the self-image of a people on the move. These constant migrations were, on the one hand, disrupting, but, on the other, they offered the Jews as a group opportunities to renew life and to adapt to

new conditions. In other words, they served the
same purpose as Frederick Jackson Turner and his
school have suggested that the land frontier served
in the history of the United States--enabling life
repeatedly to begin anew, willy-nilly if not by
choice (and it was a mixture of both, since Jews
often chose to migrate to new areas and were not
simply forced to do so), which offered new opportunities for adaptation and change (Turner 1920;
Billington 1949; Webb 1953).

At the same time, the constant migrations
generated a religious culture based upon time
rather than space, upon the shared expressions of a
common temporal rhythm rather than rootedness in a
common land (Heschel 1969). Every civilization
must somehow combine the spatial and the temporal
--it must be located geohistorically. Particularly
in premodern times, most emphasized the spatial
over the temporal, existing and functioning because
of deeprootedness to a particular land and relatively unaware of the changes wrought by time. The
accelerated pace of change since the opening of the
modern epoch, and even somewhat before, has made
people aware of time and its passage in ways that
were not true earlier (Elazar 1970; Goody). For
most, however, the emphasis on space over time has
remained, transformed by the rise of the modern
state with its emphasis on territoriality and sovereignty within particular territories as the guiding principle in the organization of civilization.

The Jews remained the anomaly in all this.
Not having a functioning territorial state of their
own and not even being concentrated in a particular
territory, the Jews emphasized the temporal and
organized time in the service of Jewish survival
and self-expression. **Halakhah** (literally, the way)
emphasizes the organization of time, the rhythm of
its passage and the obligations of Jews to sanctify
those rhythms--in daily prayers and study, the
weekly Sabbath, and through holy days, festivals,
and celebrations at representative seasons.

On the other hand, the Jews were not uncon-
cerned about space--that would have made them uni-
dimensional. The Land of Israel remained a vitally
important space for them, one to which they expected to be restored at the right time and in which
they sought to maintain organized Jewish life at
all times, through regular reinforcements from the
diaspora even in the worst times (Epstein 1974;
Halpern 1969; Parkes 1949). Ultimately, modern
Jews took matters into their own hands rather than

wait for the restoration only in messianic times. Through the Zionist movement they reestablished first an autonomous Jewish community and then a Jewish state in the land (Laquer 1976; Vital 1975). Despite the success of Zionism, for three-quarters of world Jewry the State of Israel still remains "over there." They are devoted to it, but do not seek to make it the state of their citizenship or residence. So, just as moderns transformed the premodern commitment to space over time into a more modern commitment through the modern state system so did modern Jews or, more accurately, postmodern Jews, transform the particular Jewish relationship between time and space formed in premodern times into a more contemporary expression of the same.

This new relationship is at the heart of the new forms of Jewish diaspora political expression vis-à-vis the external world. Working on behalf of Israel has become a principal expression of Jewishness in the postmodern epoch whose secular character has served to diminish further the religious dimension of Jewish identification (Cohen 1983; Elazar 1981b; Medding 1981). The existence of Israel has stimulated a sense of political efficacy among diaspora Jews as well as among those in the Jewish state, which not only manifests itself in Jewish lobbies for Israel, but also in Jewish political self-assertion in other matters which Jews perceive as affecting the Jewish people as a group.

The definition of what Jews see as affecting them as a group can also be examined extensively. In the latter half of the modern epoch, Jewish self-interest came to be considered almost totally coincident with liberalism and even left-liberalism, since the liberals and the left were the principal advocates of Jewish emancipation while the conservatives and the right, in their support for the **ancien regime,** implicitly if not explicitly denied Jews full entry into the larger society (Fuchs 1956; Himmelfarb 1973; Stephen 1974; Liebman 1973; Medding 1981a; Sklare 1974; Weyl 1968). Certainly by the latter half of the nineteenth century the vast majority of all Jews, traditional or modern, accepted the liberal outlook if only because they had no other choice. This convergence of interest was so great that Jews came to believe that it had always been so, whereas, in fact, in premodern times the interests of diaspora Jews converged at least as frequently--and usually more--with the conservatives and guardians of the status quo as with those seeking change, often at Jewish expense. This overwhelming Jewish identification with liberalism had a latent functional utility in providing a unifying ideology for Jews at a time when traditional Jewish society was breaking down and Jews were losing the traditional bonds which had united them. The reestablishment of the Jewish state and the shifting goals of left-liberalism have led to the gradual breakdown of that automatic convergence, at the same time as the Jews found another rallying point around which to coalesce. Today, faithfulness to liberalism is no longer a requisite for the maintenance of common Jewish ties in the diaspora. Israel now serves that purpose, even for those who may be critical of the policies of a particular Israeli government.

Viewing the Jewish People as a Polity

These lines of analysis can be pursued and deserve to be. The remainder of this article, however, will focus upon the Jewish people as a polity, especially as seen from the inside. The suggestion that it is possible to talk about a world Jewish polity is based upon a combination of factors. In part, it rests upon the persistence of the sense of common fate among Jews all over the world, the sense of which was reactivated as a result of the events of this century. This sense has led to concrete efforts to work together to influence the shape of that fate wherever Jews have settled, particularly whenever they have required the assistance of their brethren. This, in turn, has led to the development of institutionalized frameworks for cooperation in a variety of contexts, in our times increasingly revolving around the State of Israel for self-evident reasons.

Finally, the entire effort has acquired a certain legitimacy in the eyes of Jews and non-Jews alike as a result of the emerging redefinition of what constitutes the proper context for political linkage and action, namely, the recognition--in the Western world, at least--that there are other forms of political relationship than those embraced within the nation-state, that polity is a far more complex condition than statehood, and that it can involve multiple relationships, not all of which are ter itorially based. In many respects, this represe..ts a rediscovery of what had been an ac-

The Jewish People as the Classic Diaspora

cepted phenomenon in the Western world until the
modern era.
    In short, we are beginning to recognize that
all polities are not states. The Greeks, as usual,
had a word for it. The Hellenistic world coined
the term **politeuma** to describe phenomena such as
the worldwide Jewish polity of that age in which
Jews simultaneously maintained strong political
links, including citizenship, with their respective
territorial polities, the Hellenistic cities, and
with one another across lands and seas.

An Historical Survey

Jewish tradition has it that the Jews were born as
a diaspora people, although a central aspect of
their birth was identification with the land which
became known to them as Eretz Israel--the Land of
Israel. According to the Bible, the first Jew was
Abraham, son of Terah, who was born in Ur of the
Chaldeans, located in southern Mesopotamia near the
Persian Gulf, who migrated with his family to Har-
an, now in northern Syria. On God's instructions,
Abraham migrated to the land of Canaan (now Israel)
which he subsequently left briefly because of a
famine, but to which he soon returned.
    Of Abraham's immediate descendants, only his
son Isaac never left Canaan. His grandson Jacob
(renamed Israel) sojourned for 20 years in Aram
(now Syria) as a young man, returned to the land,
and then spent his final days in Egypt. Abraham's
great-grandson, Joseph, was forcibly taken to Egypt
but remained there, later bringing his whole family
which expanded from an extended family into a
league of tribes while in Egypt.
    The B'nai Israel (Children of Israel or Jacob)
left Egypt as a people in a dramatic exodus led by
a charismatic figure, Moses. In the course of the
immediate exodus, Moses, as God's spokesman, established the basis for citizenship, promulgated a
common law for the tribes immediately following the
passage through the waters, and organized a full-
blown polity at the foot of Sinai within seven
weeks, through a national covenant and the introduction of a more regularized judicial structure
and political organization (Albright 1963; Elazar
and Cohen 1984).
    Whether the traditional account is historical-
ly accurate is far less important than what that
account teaches us about the origins of the Jewish

218

people and how it has shaped the Jews' self-perception over at least three and perhaps closer to four
millenia. As a people who perceives itself to have
been born in exile, as it were, diaspora is not an
abnormal condition even if it is not a desired one.
The people's political, social, and religious institutions were, from the first, organized so that
they were portable and did not need to be attached
to the national soil in order to function.

No doubt as a consequence of these experiences, the basic form of Jewish organization was
designed to accommodate migration as well as concentration in a national state. Since the beginning of political science, all political theory has
converged on one or another of three basic forms of
political founding, organization, and development:
hierarchical, organic, and convenantal (Elazar
1981a). Hierarchical forms, which usually are the
result of some initial conquest leading to the
establishment of a political order, require a high
concentration of power within a power pyramid, a
more or less orderly structure, with a clear chain
of command. Hierarchical forms are particularly
useful for the governance of peoples concentrated
within a single structure and clearly subject to
the authority of those who dominate it. This kind
of government went against the grain of Jewish
political culture from earliest times, even when
the Jews were concentrated in one land. Once they
were scattered, and without any state whatsoever,
this form of political organization was utterly
impractical.

The organic form presumes a gradual and continuous development of political institutions serving a population rooted in one place, into a political system which can continue to function as long
as the population is so rooted, but which once
detached no longer has the wherewithal to survive.
Obviously for the Jews this was equally impractical.

The covenantal form of political organization
emerges out of agreements among equals, or at least
equals for the purposes of the agreement, to form
partnerships for purposes of political organization. It does not presuppose a territory, a clear
chain of command, or organic development in a particular place. On the contrary, it is flexible in
form, it can be territorial or aterritorial as the
case may be, and it is capable of binding people
who cannot be bound by force or by custom because
they are not bound to a particular territory.

219

The Jewish people opted for the covenantal form no later than the exodus from Egypt and so organized themselves during their formative generation in the desert. Granted, the tribes themselves had an organic dimension in the sense that the members of each claimed to be descended from a common ancestor. In that sense, the Jewish people has always tried to combine kinship and consent, the organic with the covenantal dimension, to secure its unity (Elazar 1978; Freeman 1969; Hiller 1969). As a result, the Jews have been able to function as an ethnic group based upon primordial ties of kinship, a religious group based upon acceptance of the responsibilities of the Jewish religion, and a polity which rests upon the combination of both kinship and consent.

Over the centuries the Jews have refined this form of polity building. After the founding covenant at Sinai, the Israelite tribes renewed that covenant in the plains of Moab just before entering the land and then renewed it again at Shekhem under Joshua at the time of the conquest of Canaan (Deut. 34:1-4; Josh. 24:1-25). When Israel changed its regime to add a king to the tribal federation, the first strictly national-political covenant was made between the tribes and David (2 Sam. 5:1). Much later, after David's kingdom had been divided and the northern kingdom conquered by Assyria, the regime was reconstituted under King Hezekiah through another covenant (2 Kings 18). When the exiles returned from Babylonia after the first diaspora, they covenanted once again to reestablish the state of Judea within the framework of the Persian Empire (Ezra 1:2; Neh 8:1-8). Finally, in the last reconstitution of the Jewish polity within the Land of Israel until our own times, Simon the Hasmonean reconstituted an independent Jewish state through a covenant with the representatives of the people and the other institutions of the community (1 Macc. 8:1-9).

Subsequent to the exile, when it was no longer possible to use covenants in state building, they were transformed into instruments for community building with any ten men able to constitute themselves as a community and as a court of law within the context of the Torah through an appropriate covenant (Blidstein 1975; Elon 1975). Finally, in our own times the reestablishment of the State of Israel rested on a series of covenants, culminating in the Declaration of Independence, referred to in Hebrew as the "Scroll of Independence," which was

accepted, witnessed, and signed by a wall-to-wall
coalition of the Jewish community in Eretz Israel
at the time, as at least a quasi-covenantal
document, and has been so treated by the courts
(Aricha n.d.; Kallen 1958; Rubinstein, 1979).

Beyond the fact of communal survival, consent
has remained the essential basis for the shaping of
the Jewish polity. Jews in different localities
consented (and consent) together to form congregations and communities--the terms are often used
synonymously (Baeck 1965; Elazar 1967). They did
(and do) this formally through articles of agreement, charters, covenants, and constitutions. The
traditional Sephardi term for such articles of
congregational-communal agreement, **askamot** (articles of agreement), conveys this meaning exactly.
The local communities were (and are) then bound by
further consensual arrangements, ranging from formal federations to the tacit recognition of a particular **halakhic** authority, **shtadlan,** or supralocal
body as authoritative (Finkelstein 1964; Ben-Sasson
1969). When conditions were propitious, the de
facto confederation of Jewish communities extended
to wherever Jews lived. When this level of political existence was impossible, the binding force of
Jewish law served to keep the federal bonds from
being severed.

Thus, over the course of many centuries a very
distinctive kind of polity has developed as the
organized expression of Jewish communal life.
While it has undergone many permutations and adap-
tations, an unbroken thread of institutions and
ideas has run through the entire course of Jewish
political life to give the Jewish people meaningful
continuity.

It is important to emphasize this covenantal
device, because of the way in which it made possible organized Jewish life in the diaspora beyond
the merely religious sphere. Covenanting was only
one of a range of complementary devices developed
by the Jewish people to maintain their collective
integrity even in the diaspora, with or without a
center in the Land of Israel. In premodern times,
when the Jewish community was all-embracing, whether in the state or the diaspora, these devices
formed a framework within which all or virtually
all Jews functioned. After the autonomous Jewish
community had given way to the integration of individual Jews into the states in which they lived,
this framework had to be readapted to a voluntaris-
tic situation in which it provided a core, or

magnet, around which those Jews who wished to could coalesce--rather than a framework embracing Jews whether they wanted to be included or not (Elazar 1976; Himmelfarb 1973; Liebman 1973; Sachar 1958). But the basic instruments have survived the transition and continue to offer the opportunity to do so under these new circumstances.

In sum, the Jewish people has the distinction of being the longest-lasting and most widespread 'organization' in the history of the world. Its closest rival to that title is the Catholic Church. Curiously--and perhaps significantly--the two are organized on radically opposed principles. The Catholic Church is built on hierarchical principles from first to last and gains its survival power by their careful and intelligent manipulation (Samuel 1967). The Jewish people is organized on covenantal or federal (from the Latin **foedus**, i.e., covenant) principles from first to last and enhances its survival power by applying them almost instinctively in changing situations. The contrasting characteristics of these two modes of organization are intrinsically worthy of political and social investigation. So, too, is the role of the Jewish polity in the development and extension of federal principles, institutions, and processes.[2]

Heterogeneity of the Jewish Diaspora

Sometime in the thirteenth century B.C.E. the Israelite tribes crossed the Jordan into Canaan and began an unbroken period in what was renamed Eretz Israel. For seven and a half centuries the Jews remained concentrated in their land under independent governments of their own. This is the classic period of Jewish history as described in the Bible. During that period there may have been temporary settlements of Jews outside of the country and there are traditions of permanent Jewish settlements in such places as Yemen, although there is no corroborative evidence of this. But, in fact, ninety-nine percent of the Jewish people were located in the Land of Israel.

In 721-22 B.C.E. the northern kingdom, comprising 10 of the 12 original tribes, was conquered by Assyria and a major if undetermined portion of its population exiled to other parts of the Assyrian Empire, apparently in northern Mesopotamia. Popular legend has it that these exiles disappeared by assimilating into the local populations but there are traditions among the Jews of northern Iraq, Iran, and Afghanistan that they are descended from those exiles. Some historians hypothesize that at least a segment later merged with the subsequent exiles of the Jews from Judea who were exiled from their country after the conquest of the southern kingdom by the neo-Babylonians in the first decades of the sixth century B.C.E. (Malamat; Ephal 1979, Ben-Sasson n.d.).

Whether this was the first diaspora or not, it is clear that the recognized Jewish diaspora begins with the Babylonian captivity. It was then that organized communities of Jewish exiles were established in Babylonia and Egypt. They quickly developed institutions to accommodate their corporate needs in the diaspora, including the **Bet Knesset** which has come to be known to us in its Greek translation as the synagogue and which, in fact, means house of assembly, a kind of town hall, where Jews could undertake all their public functions, especially governance, study, and worship. Indeed the Hebrew term **knesset** (assembly) is from the Aramaic **kanishta** which is a translation of **edah**, the original Hebrew term describing the Jewish polity, the assembly or congregation of the entire people. Thus, the **bet knesset** was a miniature version of that larger assembly--one which could be established anywhere (Baeck 1965; Baron 1972; Levy 1963). Thus the framework established over 2,500 years ago has remained the basic framework for diaspora Jewish organization ever since.

It should be noted that the **bet knesset** is a product of the Babylonian exile; Jews who left Eretz Israel for Egypt tried to develop another framework around a temple constructed as a surrogate for that in Jerusalem, a system which required territorial permanence and did not gain acceptance outside of Egypt (Porten 1968, chap. 4). Even there it was replaced by the Babylonian system some 400 years later, precisely because of the portability of the **bet knesset** and the possibility of establishing synagogues wherever ten Jewish men gathered.

Seventy years after the destruction of Jerusalem in 537 B.C.E., Cyrus the Great conquered the neo-Babylonian Empire and, following his policy of the conciliation of minority peoples through the granting of cultural autonomy, allowed the Jews to return to Judea to rebuild their Temple. In fact, only a relatively small number of Jews chose to do

so and while they and subsequent migrations, culminating in the great reconstitution of Ezra and
Nehemiah approximately a century later, did succeed
in reestablishing Eretz Israel as the center of
Jewish life, a large diaspora community remained in
Babylonia and, indeed, under Persian rule, spread
throughout the Persian Empire. It was paralleled
by a somewhat smaller but still significant diaspora in Egypt which spread into other parts of
northern Africa, Cyprus, and Asia Minor.

For the next millenium the Jewish people were
organized in a point-counterpoint arrangement. The
Jewish concentration in their land claimed and
usually exercised hegemony within the Jewish polity, but with a substantial population, perhaps
consistently a majority, scattered in diaspora
communities throughout the civilized world at that
time. Until its destruction in 70 C.E., the Temple
in Jerusalem served as the focal point for both,
with the Temple tax uniting Jews in the land and
outside of it.

The principal institutions of the **edah**--the
Jewish people as a whole--were located on the Temple Mount. New institutional arrangements were
developed to provide representation for diaspora
Jewry in those institutions, the first of which was
known as the **Anshei haKnesset haGedolah** (men of the
great assembly) which later gave way to a successor
institution, the Sanhedrin, which is a corruption
of the Hebrew corruption of the Greek term for
assembly. But given the problems of transportation
and communication in that period, there were difficulties in providing diaspora Jews continuous access and representation in those common institutions (Hoenig 1953, Mantel 1961).

In the diaspora itself two patterns developed,
each a response to the particular host civilization
in which Jews found themselves. In most of western
Asia, where the Persians and their successors
ruled, the Jews tended to be concentrated in particular areas and could organize their public life on
a quasi-territorial basis, with regional as well as
local institutions. Out of this evolved the "Babylonian" Jewish community which was concentrated in
what is today the heartland of Mesopotamia. By the
second century C.E. it had an extensive political
structure headed by a **resh galuta** (exilarch) whose
powers were those of a protected king--for Jews a
constitutional monarch who was recognized as being
a descendant of the House of David. The **resh
galuta** shared his powers with two great **yeshivot**

(another Hebrew term for assembly) which had custody of the teaching and interpretation of the
Torah. Together these institutions governed the
collectivity of local Jewish communities within the
empire (Baer 1967; Neusner 1978). This framework
persisted until the eleventh century, even after
the seventh century Arab conquest which transformed
the language, culture, and religion of western
Asia. Until the fifth century C.E., it was at
least formally subordinate to the equivalent polity
in Eretz Israel which had a similar structure, but
after the elimination of that polity the **resh
galuta** and the **yeshivot** extended their control over
virtually the entire Jewish world.

This was facilitated by the Arab conquests of
the seventh and eighth centuries that brought over
ninety-five percent of all Jews under the rule of
the Muslim caliphate, which empowered the **resh
galuta** and the **yeshivot** to represent the Jewish
community as their predecessors had. It was only
with the breakup of the original Muslim empire and
the development of independent successor states,
that the Jews lost this common well-nigh worldwide
diaspora structure (Elazar and Cohen 1984).

Meanwhile, in the Mediterranean world, where
Hellenistic civilization held sway and first the
Greek and then the Roman empires provided a common
political structure, the Jews were concentrated in
cities. (The exception here was Egypt, which also
had a wider territorial concentration for several
centuries). There they formed a part of the **polis**
organization developed for each city as part of its
Hellenization after the Alexandrian conquests of
the fourth century B.C.E.

It was in those cities that Jews formed autonomous communities within each **polis,** for which the
Greek term **politeuma** was invented. Each of the
politeumata represented a separate structure with
connections to Jerusalem but with no formal linkages between one another. Thus the Jewish communities in the Hellenistic and Roman worlds were far
more fragmented. The institutions within each
politeuma were based on Jewish models influenced by
Greek practices and often bearing Greek names, but
each was autonomous even when the Jews had citizenship within the **polis** itself (Baron 1972). Most of
these **politeumata** were destroyed during the up-
rising of the Hellenistic diaspora against the
Romans in the years 115-117 C.E. The communities
reconstituted subsequent to that event had more
limited rights. It was only after the Arab con-

quest that regional organizations of communities were established in those countries linked to the **resh galuta** and **yeshivot** in Babylonia, which was also the seat of the caliphate. Both forms of diaspora organization were linked to Jerusalem when an independent Jewish state was reborn in the middle of the second century B.C.E. That state survived for less than a century, then went through a period of upheavals for the next 200 years until the failure of the Bar Kokhba rebellion (132-135 C.E.) led the Jews to abandon major efforts to rebel against Rome and rather reconstitute themselves along the model of the diaspora communities within their own land. The **nesiut** (patriarchate) and Sanhedrin which formed the new structure of the community of Eretz Israel, also functioned as **prima inter parus** in the governance and religious leadership of the Jewish people, until those institutions were abolished in the middle of the century, after which Jewish communal organization in Eretz Israel became even more diaspora-like in character, undergoing changes under different rulers from then until the reestablishment of the Jewish state in 1948, some 1,500 years later (Albeck 1963, n.d.; Alon 1980; Avi-Yonah 1976; Baumgarten 1974; Goldenberg 1959).

Thus the diaspora became the moving force in Jewish life. For 600 years the Babylonian center predominated. In the eleventh century there was increased Jewish migration to both southern and northern Europe which led to the transfer of power to the Jewish centers in Spain and, to a lesser extent, northern France and the Rhineland. The Iberian Peninsula and west central Europe remained the centers of Jewish life until the fifteenth century, when expulsions, on the one hand, and attractive offers of refuge, on the other, led the Jews from both centers to move back eastward: Iberian Jewry forming new concentrations in the Ottoman Empire, particularly in the Balkans, and central European Jewry concentrating in Poland. These two regions remained the principal centers of Jewish life until the nineteenth century (Baron 1973, vol. 10, chap. 45, and vol. 16; Elon 1975; Agus 1965).

At first, Spanish Jewry--the Sephardim--followed the Babylonian pattern of regional organization, with local communities subordinate to the regional leadership. Under Christian rule, the local communities rose to predominance and the regional organization was limited to confederal arrangements. That pattern was later preserved in the Ottoman Empire where every congregation was autonomous and even within the same city congregations were often no more than confederated. The Jews of west central Europe--the Ashkenazim--developed local autonomy from the first, with loose leagues or confederations of communities providing whatever unification there was. But once they moved eastward to Poland they formed regional structures culminating in the **Vaad Arba Aratzot** (Council of the Four Lands), a fully-articulated federation of the Jewish communities of Poland, and its parallels in Lithuania, Bohemia, and Moravia.

Worldwide, the Jewish people lost any common political structure after the middle of the eleventh century but remained tied together by a common constitutional-legal system (the **halakhah**), which was kept dynamic by a system of rabbinic decision-making which was communicated to Jews wherever they happened to be through an elaborate network of **responsa**--formal written questions posed to leading Jewish legal authorities which produced formal written responses that came to form a body of case law. This was possible because 1,500 years earlier, at the time of Ezra and Nehemiah, the Jews had developed a legal system parallel to their political structure which translated the original constitutional materials of the Torah into an elaborate structure designed to enable every Jew to conduct his entire life within the framework of Jewish law, no matter where he happened to reside (Assaf 1955; Cohen 1957, 1969; Elon 1975; Freehof 1973; Ginsberg 1970; Tchernowitz 1953).

The legal system that emerged became, in effect, a portable state. The **halakhah's** avowed purpose was to transform each individual Jew into a person concerned with holiness. Hence, it was not designed with a political purpose in the usual sense, but this very concern for individual and collective holiness in a larger sense became a political end which served to provide a basis for the unity of Jewry, even in exile, as long as there was a general commitment to this end or at the very least to living under Jewish law as distinct from any other law.

While it is clear that not every Jew had the same commitment to holiness as an ultimate end, or to the particular path to holiness developed by the **halakhah**, in the centuries immediately following the destruction of the Temple this legal system gained normative status among Jews so that even those who were not highly motivated by its ultimate goals but who wanted to stay within the framework of the Jewish community felt the necessity to conform. Because of its attention to minute detail, every aspect of life, public and private, civil and criminal, religious and "secular" (a category which did not exist within the Jewish vocabulary), the **halakhah** was able to become all-embracing. The political structures developed by the Jews to conduct their public affairs were authorized by the **halakhah** and rooted in it, and a major task of Jewish communities was to enforce **halakhic** regulations.

The opening of the modern epoch in the middle of the seventeenth century slowly eroded this comprehensive framework, in waves rolling from west to east. Jewish autonomy was the first casualty in western Europe as the new nation-states dismantled medieval corporatism, a system which had protected Jewish communal separatism. At first, Jews became people without civic status in the new states and without the possibility of maintaining their own states within the state. This led them to demand emancipation and citizenship as individuals, which they ultimately gained after a struggle sometimes taking two centuries (Baron 1973; Sachar 1958). Finally, in the nineteenth century, the elimination of Jewish autonomy and then emancipation moved eastward to engulf the major concentrations of Jews in eastern Europe and the eastern Mediterranean, although it was not until the twentieth century that emancipation was completed in either region (Friedenreich 1979; Katz 1974, 1976; Katzburg 1981; Levitats 1943; Mendelsohn 1983; Weinreb 1972; Wilenski 1970).

While these changes were taking shape, a two-pronged demographic shift of great importance began. In the first place, the live birth and survival rate among Jews rose rapidly, causing the number of Jews in the world to soar. In the second, the Jews began to migrate at an accelerating pace to the lands on the Western world's great frontier: the Western hemisphere, southern Africa, and Australia in particular, but also in smaller numbers to East Asia, thus initiating a shift in the balance of Jewish settlement in the world (Altman n.d.; Baron 1973, vol. 15; Ettinger 1976; Hertzberg 1968; Reinharz 1975; Roth 1964).

Medieval corporatism never gained a foothold in the New World and the Jews who migrated to those lands entered into their host societies as individuals (Elazar 1976, forthcoming; Elazar and Medding 1983). Hence all Jewish life was voluntary in character from the first.

While the majority of Jews readily abandoned communal separatism for the advantages of modern society, only a minority were ready to give up fully their Jewish ties in return. Most wanted to find some way to remain within the Jewish fold even while participating as individuals in the civil societies in which they found themselves or to which they migrated. Hence they were faced with the task of adapting Jewish institutions to a new kind of diaspora existence.

Once again the great flexibility of covenantal institutions proved itself. The Jews transformed their **kehillot** (communities) into voluntary structures. In the Western world, where pluralism was tolerated principally in the religious sphere, the Jews transformed the **bet knesset** into the synagogue as we know it, whose manifest purposes were avowedly religious and whose central functions revolved around public worship, but which was able to embrace within it the various ethnic, social, educational, and welfare functions which the Jewish community sought to preserve, principally on a supplementary basis.

In eastern Europe, where modernization frequently meant secularization, new forms of Jewish association developed, principally cultural and political, utilizing similar principles and, with the exception of the public worship dimension which was absent from them, were devoted to the same ethnic, social, educational, and welfare purposes, only on a more extensive basis because Jews remained nationally separate in that part of the world. By and large, Jews in the Arab world followed the Western pattern when they began to modernize, but within a framework in which their separate ethnic identity was clearly recognized by one and all, and in which they preserved a certain legal authority over the community members by virtue of their continued control of personal status laws involving marriage, divorce, and inheritance (Elazar 1969).

Nevertheless, the new voluntarism did make it very difficult, if not impossible, to provide a comprehensive framework for the maintenance of Jewish culture and civilization. It rapidly became clear that the open society would lead to the assimilation of many of the most talented members of the Jewish community who saw greater opportunities outside of the Jewish fold. It was in response to this as well as to anti-Semitism that the Jewish national movement developed, which made as its goal the restoration of Jewish statehood in Eretz Israel. This movement, known as Zionism, was initially organized on the same convenantal principles as every other such Jewish endeavor, developing first through local societies and then, in a massive leap forward represented by the First Zionist Congress in 1897, through the World Zionist Organization established at that congress. In 50 years the WZO succeeded in bringing about the establishment of a Jewish state (Laqueur 1976; Vital 1975).

Zionism from the first embodied two conflicting goals. There were those who were Zionists because, while they wanted the Jewish people to survive, they wanted them to become normalized like other nations. They believed that if the Jewish people or some substantial segment of them were to return to their own land, they could live like the French, the Italians, the Czechs, the Poles, etc. The other trend in the Zionist movement was to see Zionism as a means of restoring the vitality of Jewish civilization, which would retain its uniqueness but be better able to survive under modern conditions by being rooted in a land and state where Jews formed a majority.

The first approach more or less negated the continued existence of a diaspora once a Jewish state was established. According to it, those Jews who wanted to remain Jews would settle in the state where they would live increasingly normalized lives, interacting with the rest of the world as nationals of any state interact with nationals of any other. The rest of the Jews would assimilate as individuals into their countries of residence, no longer needing to preserve their Jewishness. Many of those who embraced the second view also wished to negate the diaspora in the sense that they wanted all Jews to settle in Israel. But they did not see diaspora existence as impossible per se. Rather, the Jewish state could become the focal point of the renewed Jewish people, whether living in the state or in the diaspora (Herzberg 1975).

Reality forced the issue. The state was established. Even after an initial mass migration of Jews from Europe, North Africa, and Western Asia, only about twenty percent of the Jewish people were concentrated within it (the figure is

230

now twenty-five percent). Moreover, despite assimilatory tendencies, the great bulk of the Jews outside the state showed every inclination of wanting to remain Jews. Consequently, a new interplay between state and diaspora began to emerge. In this, the second generation since the establishment of the state, it is still evolving (HaChug L'Ydiyat Rotenreich, Abramov and Bauer 1977-78).

The Contemporary Situation

World War II marked the culmination of all the trends and tendencies of the modern era and the end of the era itself for all mankind. (The dates 1945-1948 encompass the benchmark of the transition from the modern to the postmodern eras). For the Jewish people, the Holocaust and the establishment of the State of Israel provided the decisive events that marked the crossing into the postmodern world. In the process, the focus of Jewish life shifted and virtually every organized Jewish community was reconstituted in some way.

Central to the reconstitution was the reestablishment of a Jewish commonwealth in Israel. The restoration of a politically independent Jewish state created a new focus of Jewish energy and concern precisely at the moment when the older foci had almost ceased to attract a majority of Jews. As the 1967 and subsequent crises demonstrated decisively, Israel was not simply another Jewish community in the constellation but the center of the world for Jews.

The Jewry that greeted the new state was no longer an expanding one which was gaining population even in the face of the attrition of intermarriage and assimilation. On the contrary, it was a decimated one (even worse, for decimated means the loss of one in ten; the Jews lost one in three); a Jewry whose very physical survival had been in grave jeopardy and whose rate of loss from defections came close to equaling its birth-rate. Moreover, the traditional strongholds of Jewish communal life in Europe (which were also areas with a high Jewish reproduction rate) were those that had been wiped out.

At the end of the 1940s, the centers of Jewish life had shifted decisively away from Europe to Israel and North America. By then, continental Europe as a whole ranked behind Latin America, North Africa, and Great Britain as a force in

Jewish life. In fact, its Jews were almost entirely dependent upon financial and technical assistance from the United States and Israel. Except
for those in the Muslim countries that were soon
virtually to disappear, the major functioning Jewish communities had all become sufficiently large
to be significant factors on the Jewish scene only
within the previous two generations. In effect,
the shapers of those communities were still alive,
and in many cases were still the actual community
leaders. The Jewish world had been thrown back
willy-nilly to a pioneering stage.

This new epoch is still in its early years,
hardly more than a single generation has passed,
hence its character is still in its formative
stages. Nevertheless, with the establishment of
the State of Israel in 1948 the Jewish polity began
a constitutional change of revolutionary proportions, inaugurating a new epoch in Jewish constitutional history. For the first time in almost two
millenia, the majority of the Jewish people were
presented with the opportunity to attain citizenship in their own state. Indeed, Israel's very
first law (**Hok haShevut**)--the Law of Return) specified that citizenship would be granted to any Jew-
per-Jew wishing to live within the country. The
reestablishment of a Jewish state has restored a
sense of political involvement among Jews and
shaped a new institutional framework within which
the business of the Jewish people is conducted.

The virtual disappearance of the remaining
legal or even social or cultural barriers to individual free choice in all but a handful of countries has made free association the dominant characteristic of Jewish life in the postmodern era.
Consequently, the first task of each Jewish community has been to learn to deal with the particular
local manifestation of this freedom.

The new voluntarism extends itself into the
internal life of the Jewish community as well,
generating pluralism even in previously free but
relatively homogeneous community structures. This
pluralism is increased by the breakdown of the
traditional reasons for being Jewish and the rise
of new incentives for Jewish association. At the
same time, the possibilities for organizing a pluralistic Jewish community have also been enhanced by
these new incentives. What has emerged is a matrix
of institutions and individuals linked through a
unique communications network; a set of interacting
institutions which, while preserving their own

structural integrity and filling their own
functional roles, are informed by shared patterns
of culture, activated by a shared system of organization, and governed by shared leadership cadres.
The character of the matrix which has emerged
and its communications network varies from community to community. In some communities, the network
is connected through a common center which serves
as the major (but rarely, if ever, the exclusive)
channel for communication. In others, the network
forms a matrix without any center, with the lines
of communication crisscrossing in all directions.
In all cases, the boundaries of the community are
revealed only when the pattern of the network is
uncovered and this in turn happens only when both
of its components are revealed--namely, its institutions and organizations with their respective
roles and the way in which communications are
passed between them.

The pattern itself is inevitably a dynamic
one. That is to say, there is rarely a fixed
division of authority and influence but, rather,
one that varies from time to time and usually from
issue to issue, with different elements in the
matrix taking on different "loads" at different
times and relative to different issues. Since the
community is a voluntary one, persuasion rather
than compulsion, influence rather than power, are
the only tools available for making and executing
policies. This, too, works to strengthen its character as a communications network since the character, quality, and relevance of what is communicated
and the way in which it is communicated frequently
determine the extent of the authority and influence
of the parties.

The structure of the contemporary Jewish polity is that of a network of single and multipurpose
functional authorities, no single one of which
encompasses the entire gamut of Jewish political
interests, although several have attempted to do so
in specific areas: (1) "National Institutions"--
e.g., Jewish Agency, World Zionist Organization,
Jewish National Fund; (2) multicountry associ-
ations--e.g., ORT, World Jewish Congress; (3) educational institutions defined as under the auspices
of the entire Jewish people--e.g., the universities
in Israel; (4) organizations under more specific
local sponsorship whose defined sphere of activity
is multicountry--e.g., the Joint Distribution Committee.

Another way of grouping the multicountry asso-

ciations is by their principal goals. Here are the
broad categories, with prominent examples for each.

Political-general purpose:
World Zionist Organization (WZO)
World Jewish Congress (WJC)
Political-special purpose:
World Conference of Soviet Jewry
Distributive:
Conference on Jewish Material Claims Again
Germany
Memorial Foundation for Jewish Culture
Services-operational:
World Ort Union
Services-coordinating:
European Council of Jewish Communities
Religious:
World Union for Progressive Judaism
World Council of Synagogues
Agudat Israel World Organization
Association-fraternal:
B'nai B'rith International Council
Association-special interest:
World Sephardi Federation
World Union of Jewish Students

The political associations listed here as "general"
are those concerned with the status of the Jewish
people as a whole; in this they are both outer-
directed to the non-Jewish world and inner-directed
to the Jewish community. Although the Israeli
government has largely preempted political activity
on the world scene, it has not explicitly claimed
to act as the diplomatic agent for the Jewish
people beyond its borders. This leaves some room
for diplomatic activity by the Jewish nongovernmen-
tal organizations, especially where Israel is not
represented or is particularly limited in its access (Elazar and Dortort 1984; Stock 1974-75).
Figure 1 summarizes the situation in diagram-
matic form. Each side of the triangle expresses a
particular facet of Jewish life as it is manifest
today.

Jewish Communities in the New Epoch

Jews are known to reside in 121 countries, 82 of
which have been permanent organized communities
(Elazar 1969; Elazar and Cohen 1984). At least
three and perhaps as many as twelve others are

FIGURE 1

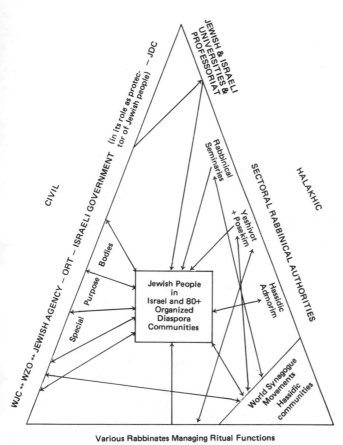

RITUALISTIC

remnant communities where a handful of Jews have custody of the few institutions that have survived in the wake of the emigration of the majority of the Jewish population. Fourteen more are transient communities where American or Israeli Jews temporarily stationed in some Asian or African country create such basic Jewish institutions (e.g., religious services, schools) as they need. Only 21 countries with known Jewish residents have no organized Jewish life.

The largest communities are:

1.	United States	5.9 million
2.	Israel	3.5 million
3.	USSR	2.1 million
4.	France	650,000
5.	United Kingdom	410,000
6.	Argentina	350,000
7.	Canada	310,000
8.	Brazil	150,000
9.	South Africa	120,000
10.	Hungary	80,000
11.	Australia	70,000

In the late 1940s and the 1950s the reconstruction and the reconstitution of existing communities, and the founding of new ones, were the order of the day throughout the Jewish world. The Jewish communities of continental Europe all underwent periods of reconstruction or reconstitution in the wake of wartime losses, changes in the formal status of religious communities in their host countries, immigration to Israel, internal European migrations, and the introduction of new, especially Communist regimes. Those communities in Muslim countries were transformed in response to the convergence of two factors: the establishment of Israel and the anticolonial revolutions in Asia and Africa. The greater portion of the Jewish population in those countries was transferred to Israel, and organized Jewish life, beyond the maintenance of local congregations, virtually came to an end in all of these countries except Iran, Morocco, and Tunisia.

English-speaking Jewry and, to a somewhat lesser extent, those Jews of Latin America, were faced with the more complex task of adapting their organizational structures to three new purposes: to assume the responsibility passed to them as a result of the destruction of European Jewry, to play a major role in supporting Israel, and to accommodate the internal changes of communities still in the process of acculturation. Many of the transient Jewish communities in Asia and Africa were actually founded or shaped in this period, while others, consisting in the main of transient merchants or refugees, were abandoned.

At first, the pattern of Jewish communal organization followed that of the modern epoch with some modifications, but as the postmodern epoch leaves its own imprint, the differences in status and structure are diminishing. A common pattern of organizations is emerging, consisting of certain basic elements, including:

1. Government-like institutions, whether umbrella organizations or separate institutions serving discrete functions, that play roles and provide services at all levels (countrywide, local, and, where used, intermediate) which, under other conditions, would be played, provided, or controlled, whether predominantly or exclusively, by governmental authorities--(for instance, services such as external relations, defense, education, social welfare, and public, that is, communal, finance), specifically: a more or less comprehensive fundraising and social planning body; a representative body for external relations; a Jewish education service agency; a vehicle or vehicles for assisting Israel and other Jewish communities; various health and welfare institutions.

2. Local institutions and organizations that provide a means for attracting people to Jewish life on the basis of their most immediate and personal interests and needs, specifically: congregations organized into one or more synagogue unions, federations, or confederations; local cultural and recreational centers, often federated or confederated with one another.

3. General purpose mass-based organizations, operating countrywide at all levels, that function to: (a) articulate community values, attitudes, and policies; (b) provide the energy and motive force for crystallizing the communal consensus that grows out of those values, attitudes, and policies; and (c) maintain institutionalized channels of communication between the community's leaders and "actives" ("cosmopolitans") and the broad base of the affiliated Jewish population ("locals") for dealing with the

problems facing the community, specifically: a Zionist federation and its constituent organizations; fraternal organizations.

4. Special interest organizations which, by serving specialized interests in the community on all planes, function to mobilize concern and support for the various programs conducted by the community and to apply pressure for their expansion, modification, and improvement. The resultant model is presented in schematic form in figure 2.

UNITED STATES: The United States, with over half of all the Jews in the diaspora, stands in a class by itself. The combination of a very large, fully modern society, established from the first on individualistic principles, pluralistic in the full sense of the word, settled by several significantly different waves of very adventurous Jewish immigrants who shared a common commitment in seeking new lives as individuals, was not conductive to the development of sufficient homogeneity to permit the formation of a neat communal structure (Cohen 1983; Elazar 1976; Feingold 1981; Handh 1945; Sklare 1971; Waxman 1983).

The organized American Jewish community is entirely built upon an associated base. That is to say, not only is there no inescapable compulsion, external or internal, to affiliate with organized Jewry, but all connections with organized Jewish life are based on voluntary association with some particular organization or institution, whether in the form of synagogue membership, contribution to the local Jewish Welfare Fund (which is considered to be an act of joining as well as contributing), or affiliation with a B'nai B'rith lodge or Hadassah chapter. Indeed, the usual pattern for affiliated Jews is one of multiple association with memberships in different kinds of associations reinforcing one another and creating an interlocking network of Jewish ties that bind the individual more firmly to the community. Without the associational base, there would be no organized Jewish community at all; with it, the Jewish community attains social, and even a certain legal, status that enables it to fit well into the larger society of which it is a part.

The associated basis of American Jewish life is manifested in a wide variety of local and countrywide organizations designed to suit every Jewish taste. While these organizations may be confined

FIGURE 2

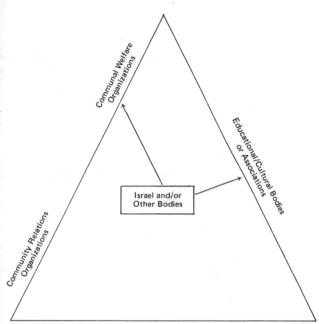

to specific localities or may reflect specific interests, classes, or types on a strictly supralocal basis, the most successful ones develop both countrywide and local facets. It is no accident that B'nai B'rith, a countrywide (even worldwide) federation of multistate districts and local lodges, and Hadassah, a countrywide organization that emphasizes the role of its local chapters (which are further divided almost into neighborhood groups) are the two most successful mass Jewish organizations in the United States. The key to their success is that they provide both an overall purpose attuned to the highest aims of Jewish life and local attachment based on the immediate social needs of the individual Jew in such a way as to allow people to be members for either reason. Sooner or later, all large countrywide Jewish organizations have found that their survival is contingent upon developing some sort of serious local dimension to accommodate the very powerful combination of American and Jewish penchant for organizational arrangements on federal principles.

While certain of its organizations sometimes succeeded in developing from the top down, the institutions of the American Jewish community are essentially local and, at most, loosely federated with one another for very limited purposes. The three great synagogue movements, for example, are essentially confederations of highly independent local congregations, linked by relatively vague persuasional ties and a need for certain technical services. The confederations function to provide the requisite emotional reinforcement of those ties and the services desired by their member units. As in the case of the other countrywide organizations, they combine countrywide identification with essentially local attachments. With the exception of a few institutions of higher education (and, once upon a time, a few specialized hospitals, now nonsectarian), all Jewish social, welfare, and educational institutions are local in name and, in fact, some loosely confederated on a supralocal basis.

The demands placed upon the American Jewish community beginning in the late 1930s led to a growing recognition of the need to reconstitute the community's organizational structure at least to the extent of rationalizing the major interinstitutional relationships and generally tightening the matrix. These efforts at reconstitution received added impetus from the changes in American society as a whole (and the Jews' position in it) after

1945. They signaled the abandonment of earlier chimeral efforts to create a more orthodox organizational structure in imitation of foreign patterns which, given the character of American society as a whole, would have been quite out of place.

What has emerged to unite all these highly independent associations is a number of overlapping local and supralocal federations designed for different purposes. The most powerful among them are the local federations of Jewish agencies and their countrywide confederation, the Council of Jewish Federations (CJF), which have become the framing institutions of American Jewry and its local communities. They are the only ones able to claim near-universal membership and all-embracing purposes, though not even the CJF has the formal status of an overall countrywide umbrella organization. Other federal arrangements tend to be limited to single functions and their general organizations rarely have more than a consultative role or power of accreditation.

This unity on a confederative basis, which characterizes American Jewry, is very different from unity on a hierarchical one; what emerges is not a single pyramidal structure, nor even one in which the "bottom" rules the "top" (as in the case of most of the communities with representative boards), but a matrix consisting of many institutions and organizations tied together by a crisscrossing of memberships, shared purposes, and common interests, whose roles and powers vary according to situation and issue.

JEWRIES OF THE BRITISH COMMONWEALTH: While there are variations among them, characteristic of all of the Jewish communities whose origin is in the British Commonwealth is an ambivalence in defining their Jewishness. On the one hand, there is the sense on the part of both the community and the larger society of which it is a part that Jewish attachment is a form of "religious affiliation" and that every individual has free choice in the matter. On the other, there is an equally strong feeling that somehow Jews stand apart from the majority "Anglo-Saxon" population and can never bridge that gap. Regardless of the intensity of their Jewish attachments, the overwhelming majority of Jews in these countries have culturally assimilated into the wider society's way of life. Thus the associational aspects of Jewish affiliation are far more important than the organic ones, however real the latter may be, and the community structure is built around associational premises from top to bottom (Cohen 1982; Elazar 1976; Medding 1968, 1973; Shimoni 1980).

The communities themselves have no special status in public law. At most, there is an umbrella organization which is formally or tacitly accepted as the "address" of the Jewish community for certain limited purposes, and subsidiary institutions which are occasionally accorded government support (along with similar non-Jewish institutions) for specific functions. Nor do the communities have any strong tradition of communal self-government to call upon. All are entirely products of the modern era, hence their founders were either post-emancipation Jews or Jews seeking the benefits of emancipation and desirous of throwing off the burdens of an all-encompassing corporate Jewish life.

The larger communities in this category, at least, were created by successive waves of immigration, the greatest of which arrived in the past 100 years; hence the history of their present communal patterns does not go back more than three or four generations, if that. Most of their present leaders are sons of immigrants, if not immigrants themselves.

Boards of Deputies: Eleven of these communities have representative boards, usually called "Boards of Deputies," as their principal spokesmen. These representative boards in most cases formally embrace virtually all the other Jewish institutions and organizations in the community. Those other organizations, however, while nominally associated with the Board are, for all practical purposes, independent of and even equal to it in stature and influence. Fundraising, religious life, and social services tend to be under other auspices. The Board tends to be pushed in the direction of becoming the ambassador of the Jewish community to the outside world rather than its governing body. This tendency has been accelerated since World War II by the "coming of age" of the last great wave of immigrants and the consequent diminution of the monolithic character of most of the communities. The increase in competing interests, the decline in religious interest, and the growth of assimilatory tendencies have all contributed to this change.

Communities with representative boards are also constructed on federal lines. ·At the very least, the Boards become federations of institutions and organizations. In federal or quasi-federal countries, they become territorial federations as well.

LATIN AMERICA: The Eastern European Jews who migrated to Latin America in the twentieth century established replicas of the European **kehillah**, without official status but tacitly recognized by Jews and non-Jews alike as the organized Jewish community. The central institutions of these communities have a distinct public character but no special recognition in public law. Founded in the main by secularists, these communities were built in the mold of secular diaspora nationalism as it developed in Eastern Europe and emphasize the secular side of Jewish life. Since they function in an environment that provides neither the cultural nor the legal framework for a European-model **kehillah**, they must rely on the voluntary attachment of their members. The Latin American communities were relatively successful in maintaining this corporate pattern until recently because the great social and cultural gap between Jews and their neighbors aided in giving the Jews the self-image of a special and distinct group, but it has become increasingly difficult to do so as the gap disappears.

Ashkenazim and Sephardim organized their separate communities, in some cases by country or city of origin. Just as Jewish immigrants did not assimilate into their host countries, so, too, they did not assimilate among themselves. In the course of time, these communities loosely confederated with one another to deal with common problems that emerged in their relations with their external environment, essentially problems of immigration, anti-Semitism and Israel. At the same time, each country-of-origin community retains substantial, if not complete, autonomy in internal matters and control over its own institutions.

In three of the larger Latin American countries (Argentina, Brazil and Colombia) the indigenous federal or quasi-federal structure of the countries themselves influenced the Jews to create countrywide confederations based on territorial divisions (officially uniting state or provincial communities which are, in fact, local communities concentrated in the state or provincial capitals). In the other countries, the local community containing the overwhelming majority of the Jewish population itself became the countrywide unit, usually by designating its federation as the "council of communities". The community councils of the

243

six Central American countries (total Jewish population 7,250) have organized the Federation of
Central American Jewish Communities to pool resources and provide common services.

None of these tacitly recognized communal
structures has been in existence for more than
three generations, and the communities themselves
originated no more than four generations ago. Most
of the smaller ones are just now entering their
third generation, since they were created by the
refugees of the 1930s and 1940s. Consequently,
many, if not most, are still in the process of
developing an appropriate and accepted communal
character.

The great postwar adjustment that has faced
the Latin American communities centers on the emergence of a native-born majority. This new generation has far less attachment to the "old country"
way of life with its emphasis on ideological and
country-of-origin ties, hence the whole community
structure is less relevant to them.

Moreover, most of the 625,000 Jews living in
Latin America are located in unstable environments
that do not necessarily encourage pluralism. Many
of them are already beginning to assimilate into
their countries, or at least into the local radical
movements, in familiar Jewish ways. For an increasing number of Jews, the **deportivo,** or Jewish
community recreation center, often seems the most
relevant form of Jewish association and the building block for Jewish organizational life. The rise
of these new institutions may foreshadow a new
communal structure, based on local territorial
divisions, that is emerging in these communities,
with its accompanying substructure of associational
activities whose participants are drawn in on the
basis of common interest rather than of common
descent (Avni 1971-72, vol. 13-14; Davis 1963;
Liebman 1978; Weissbrot 1979).

FREE EUROPE: In the wake of the destruction
in World War II and subsequent communal reconstruction, the Jews in this region have developed new
forms of communal association while at the same
time retaining the formal structures of governance
of the previous epoch. This is most obvious in the
case of those communities which in the modern epoch
had exhibited either the characteristics of a
Kultusgemeinde (comprehensive state-recognized communal structure) or a **consistoire** (state-recognized
or semiofficial religious structure.

Kehillot, or state-recognized communal structures, were to be found in Central Europe, or areas influenced by Central European culture, before World War I. In recent years these communities have, by and large, lost their power to compel all Jews to be members and must now build their membership on a consensual basis. This usually means that all known Jews are automatically listed on the community's rolls but have the right to opt out if they choose to do so.

Structurally, the **kehillah** communities remain all-embracing. All legitimate institutions or organizations function within their overall framework, except where the state has allowed secessionist groups to exist. As countrywide communities, they are generally organized along conventional federal lines with either "national" and "local," or "national," "provincial," and "local," bodies, each chosen through formal elections and linked constitutionally to one another with a relatively clear division of power. In some cases, authority remains in the local community, perhaps with some loose confederal relationships uniting the various localities. The greatest source of strength of the state-recognized communities lies in their power to tax or to receive automatically a portion of their member's regular taxes from the authorities.

The state-recognized community, once the basis of Jewish life, is losing ground in size and importance in the Jewish world at the same time as it is losing its compulsory character. Most are declining communities, decimated by war, emigration, and assimilation. Moreover, an increasing number of Jews within those communities may be opting out of community membership (and the taxes that go with it). In 1980, 150,000 Jews lived in such communities (Elazar, forthcoming; Elazar et al. 1984a, 1984b).

Despite its importance during the nineteenth century, only a remnant of the **consistoire** pattern still exists in France. Somewhat more faithful models are to be found in those countries within the orbit of French culture in Europe and Africa. In some, the **consistoire** has a certain legal status as a religious body and its officials are usually supported by government funds, but affiliation with it is entirely voluntary. It is distinguished by its emphasis on the exclusively religious nature of Judaism and its centralized character.

The **consistoire** is a casualty of the growing pluralism within the Jewish community. The refugees from Eastern Europe and, later, North Africa,

245

who became major, if not the dominant, forces in many of the **consistoire** communities after World War II rejected its exclusively sacerdotal emphasis while the growth of secularism made Jewish identification via a state-recognized religious structure increasingly incongruous. The new ultra-Orthodox congregations created by certain of the refugees rejected the laxity of the official "orthodoxy" of the **consistoire**, and the tasks of communal reconstruction in the aftermath of the war proved too much for the consistorial bodies to handle alone. Above all, the rise of Israel generated demands for mobilization of diaspora resources that went beyond the capabilities of the **consistoire** structure, necessitating more appropriate organizational arrangements. In a broader sense, the times themselves conspired against the old system, as committed Jews the world over rediscovered the national-political aspects of Jewish existence.

New, entirely voluntary organizations began to emerge with a civil orientation to reach those elements which were otherwise not part of the official community. In the process, they began to assume the functions of umbrella organizations to the extent that their local situation encouraged such organizations within the context of an emerging pluralism in Jewish communal life. Consistorial bodies survive but without the centrality they once had in Jewish life (Grielsammer 1978, 1979; Salzburg 1971).

COMMUNIST EUROPE: The communities located in the Communist countries of Eastern Europe are basically remnant communities, most of whose earlier residents either died in the Holocaust or emigrated to Israel. They, too, are subjugated in the way all potential rivals for citizens' interests are curbed in totalitarian societies. The communities in Czechoslovakia, Hungary and Rumania have actually a formal status similar to that of their sister communities in other continental European countries and, within the severe limits imposed upon them, function through state-recognized communal or religious structures. The communities of Bulgaria and Poland are organized under Communist-imposed structures. In the USSR, Jews are forbidden any organization beyond occasional synagogues and a few "showcase" institutions. In any case, whatever organized Jewish life there is, exists on sufferance of the authorities, and the authorities are fully willing to intervene in Jewish affairs in every way as a matter of ideology and policy.

With the exception of the USSR, all these communities became subjugated after World War II. Russian Jewry, subjugated since World War I, lost the last remnants of its organized communal life in the Stalin purges in the aftermath of World War II. Some 2.3 million Jews live in these subjugated countries (Fain and Verbit 1984; Friedenreich 1979).

THE MUSLIM WORLD: The communities located in the Islamic countries of the Middle East are the remnants of what were, until the rise of Israel, flourishing traditional **kehillot**. Their present state of subjugation or dissolution dates from their host countries' attainment of independence or from the establishment of Israel, and therefore reflects another kind of postwar reconstitution. The character of the subjugation varies from virtually complete suppression of all communal and private Jewish activities (Iraq) to government appointment of pliable leadership to manage the community's limited affairs (Tunisia). Only Morocco and Turkey have allowed their Jewish communities to continue to function with a minimum of distrubance, albeit under close government supervision.

In every case, the situation has deteriorated after each Israeli victory and the number of Jews remaining in the communities has decreased. Since emigration from the larger ones is not impossible, it seems clear that they, too, are fated to disappear or to become no more than very small remnant communities in the near future. In the meantime, communal life continues, as much as possible. This usually means some form of religious life, increasingly limited opportunities to provide children with a Jewish education, and a few limited social services (Fried 1962; Zenner 1968).

Considerations

What can be learned about diaspora existence from the Jewish experience which is new and unique? Four points can be made in particular.

First, long-term diasporas seem to be an Asian phenomenon, in that the peoples who seem to be able to produce and sustain diasporas are overwhelmingly Asian or emerged from Asia. European emigres to new territories break off into fragments of their original cultures, as Louis Hartz has pointed out in **The Founding of New Societies,** and then become

247

separate peoples in their own right (Hartz 1964). Traditional African cultures remained tribal, even in the case of the great tribal empires, and handled migration within Africa through the break-off of families or clans and their reconstitution as new tribes. Africans who migrated outside of Africa did so on a forced basis as slaves and hence were given no chance to establish a diaspora. Although in recent times there has been some effort to impose a diaspora-style context on American Blacks, it has not succeeded.[3] It seems that the nature of peoplehood in Asia and its relationship to statehood--whereby peoples are far more enduring than states--is an essential condition for the creation of diasporas. The Jews are a prime example of an Asian people who carried their diaspora first into North Africa, then Europe, and then into the New World, but they never lost this Asian dimension of their being.

A second point is that the Jewish experience is the quintessential example of how diasporas can be state-initiators. The history of the reestablishment of the State of Israel may be the classic of its kind, but it is not the only such example. It was the Norwegian diaspora in the United States which initiated the separation of Norway from Sweden, which led to Norwegian independence in 1905, and the Czech diaspora which initiated the establishment of Czechoslovakia after World War I. At any given time there may be a number of diasporas that are actively trying to establish states, such as the Armenians, for example. This is an important dimension in the reciprocal state-diaspora relationship (Akzim 1964).

A third point is that the nature of interflows between state and diaspora and segments of the diaspora need to be more fully examined. This article has suggested some of those interflows in the contemporary Jewish world. Elsewhere, I have mapped the shifting nature of such flows and the different institutional frameworks for them in different epochs of Jewish history (Elazar and Cohen 1984). One would expect that this would be useful to do in connection with other diasporas as well.

What has been characteristic of the Jews is that at times they have had highly visible frameworks for such interflows. We have already noted how, in the days of the Second Temple, Jews throughout the world made pilgrimage and paid an annual Temple tax as well as accepted the authority of the Sanhedrin, which sat in the Temple. Several hundred years later, the **resh galuta** and **yeshivot** in Babylonia exercised authority over ninety-seven percent of the Jews of the world who happened to be within the Arab caliphate.

At other times, the institutional structure was articulated but not quite as apparent to most Jews, even if they were influenced by it. That is the condition today with the various authorities which link Israel and the diaspora and the various diaspora communities with one another. What is becoming clear to those involved is that the reconstituted Jewish Agency for Israel and its constituent organizations are beginning to play a similar role on a voluntary basis.

Finally, there were situations in which external conditions prevented any visible institutional framework other than the institutions of local decision-making, whereby **halakhic** authorities from all parts of the Jewish world were in correspondence with one another and turned to one another for decisions binding on the entire Jewish people. The communications among these authorities helped maintain the formal constitutional structure of the Jewish people, which halped keep the Jewish constitutional framework intact even when Jews had no political institutions to unite them. This formal legal framework was supplemented by the continuing movement of travelers and migrants among most, if not all, of the communities of the Jewish world at any given time, which served to preserve the ethnic as well as the constitutional ties uniting the Jewish people.

Finally, any proper study of diaspora should consider the role of technology in making possible the maintenance of links between diaspora and state or one diaspora community and another. At the beginning of the Jewish diaspora, 2,500 years ago or more, it is very likely that Jews who spread beyond the limits of continued communication with their brethren (such as the Jews who settled in China), given the technologies of the time, disappeared as Jews. No doubt, the fact that first the Persians and then the Romans emphasized road-building to facilitate communication among the farflung reaches of their respective empires had a vital impact on the Jews' efforts in maintaining their links.

Later, in medieval times, the relative ease of water communication in the Mediterranean world held the Jewish communities of the Mediterranean Basin together while Jews who moved north of the Alps, while not out of communication with the rest of the Jewish world, developed a subculture of their own. The two subcultures persist to this day in the form of Sephardim and Ashkenazim. In our own times, it is clear that the possibility of reviving common institutions for the Jewish people has been strengthened by the availability of such instruments as the telephone and the jet plane. Certainly, technology has served to heighten diaspora consciousness among other peoples. It would be worth investigating whether this has also helped foster links between other groups in the way it has with the Jews.

Notes

1 According to the Oxford English Dictionary, the term diaspora originates from the Septuagint, Deut. 27:25, "thou shalt be a diaspora in all kingdoms of the earth."
2 A few historians and social scientists have taken note of the convenant community as a distinct socio-political phenomenon from this perspective. Mead (1952), for example, suggests that the Jewish polity and other covenant communities deserve special exploration. For an eloquent evocation of the spirit and character of the covenant community, see Smith 1967.
3 For a contrasting opinion see Locksley Edmondson's article in this volume.

REFERENCES

Agus, I. A. 1965. **Urban Civilization in Pre-Crusade Europe.** New York: Yeshiva University Press.
Akzin, B. 1964. **State and Nation.** London: Hutchin son University Library.
Albeck, C. 1963. Hasanhedrin U'Nesieiha [The Sanhedrin and its President]. **Zion** 8: 165-78.
Albeck, S. L. n.d. **Batei Hadin Bimei HaTalmud** [Courts of the Talmudic Period].
Albright, W. F. 1963. **The Biblical Period from Abraham to Ezra.** New York: Harper and Row.
Alon, G. 1980. **The Jews in the Land in the Talmudic Age,** vol. 1. Trans. and ed. G. Levi. Jerusalem.

Altman, A.   n.d. **Moses Mendelssohn: A Biographical Study.**
Aricha, Y.   n.d. **Megilat Haazmaut--Cazon Vemetsiut.** [Israel's Declaration of Independence--Vision and Reality]. Faculty of Political Science, Bar Ilan University. Unpublished.
Assaf, S. 1955. **Tekufat Hagaonim Vesifruta** [The Period of the Sages and its Literature]. Jerusalem: Mosad Harav Kook.
Avni, H. 1971-72. Argentine Jewry: Its Socio-Political Status and Organizational Patterns. **Dispersion and Unity,** vol. 13-14.
Avi-Yonah, M. 1976. **The Jews of Palestine--A Political History from the Bar Kochba War to the Arab Conquest.** Oxford.
Baeck, Leo. 1965. **This People Israel: The Meaning of Jewish Existence.** Philadelphia: Jewish Publication Society.
Baer, M. 1967. **Rashut Hagolah B'Bavel Bimei Ha-Mishna VhaTalmud** [Leadership and Authority in the times of the Mishna and the Talmud]. Tel Aviv.
Baron, S. W. 1972. **The Jewish Community: Its History and Structure to the American Revolution.** Westport, Conn.: Greenwood.
------. 1973. **A Social and Religious History of the Jews.** New York: Columbia University Press.
Baumgarten, A. I. 1974. The Akiban Opposition. **Hebrew Union College Annual** 50: 179-97.
Ben-Sasson, H. H. 1969. **Perakim Betoldot Hayehudim Beyamei Habaynayim** [Chapters in the History of Jews in the Middle Ages]. Tel Aviv.
Ben-Sasson, H. H., ed. n.d. **A History of the Jewish People.** London: Wiedenfield and Nicolson.
Billington, R. A. 1949. **Westward Expansion--A History of the American Frontier.** New York: Macmillan.
Blidstein, G. 1981. Individual and Community in the Middle Ages. In **Kinship and Consent--The Jewish Political Tradition and its Contemporary Uses,** ed. Daniel J. Elazar. Ramat Gan, Israel: Turtledove. Bright, J. 1981. **A History of Israel.** 3d ed. Philadelphia: Westminster Press.
Cohen, Boaz. 1957. **Law and Ethics in the Light of the Jewish Tradition.** New York: Ktav.
------. 1969. **Law & Tradition in Judaism.** New York: Ktav.
Cohen, Steven M. 1983. **American Modernity and Jewish Identity.** New York: Tavistock.

Cohen, Stuart A. 1982. **English Zionists and British Jews.** Princeton, New Jersey.
Davis, M. 1963. Centers of Jewry in the Western Hemisphere: A Comparative Approach. **Jewish Journal of Sociology** 5, no. 1 (June).
Elazar, Daniel J. 1967. The Quest for Community: Selections from the Literature of Jewish Public Affairs, 1965-1966. **American Jewish Yearbook,** vol. 68. New York and Philadelphia: American Jewish Committee and Jewish Publication Society.
------. 1969. The Reconstruction of Jewish Communities in the Post-War Period. **Jewish Journal of Sociology** 11, no. 2 (December).
------. 1970. **Cities of the Prairie.** New York and London: Basic Books.
------. 1976. **Community and Polity--The Organizational Dynamics of American Jewry.** Philadelphia: Jewish Publication Society of America.
------. 1978. Covenant as the Basis of the Jewish Political Tradition. **Jewish Journal of Sociology,** no. 20 (June): 5-37.
------. 1981a. Covenant and Freedom in the Jewish Political Tradition. Annual Sol Feinstone Lecture, Gratz College, March 15.
------. 1981b. Renewable Identity. **Midstream** (January).
------. Forthcoming. **People and Polity--The Organizational Dynamics of Post-Modern Jewry.**
Elazar, Daniel J. and Stuart A. Cohen. 1984. **The Jewish Polity.** Bloomington: Indiana Press.
Elazar, Daniel J. and A. M. Dortort, eds. 1984. **Understanding the Jewish Agency--A Handbook.** Jerusalem: Jerusalem Center for Public Affairs.
Elazar, Daniel J., et al. 1984a. **The Balkan Jewish Communities--Yugoslavia, Bulgaria, Greece and Turkey.** Lanham, London and New York: University Press of America and Center for Jewish Community Studies, Jerusalem Center for Public Affairs.
------. 1984b. **The Jewish Communities of Scandinavia--Sweden, Denmark, Norway and Finland.** Lanham, London and New York: University Press of America and Center for Jewish Community Studies, Jerusalem Center for Public Affairs.
Elazar, Daniel J. and P. Medding. 1983. **Jewish Communities in Frontier Societies.** London, New York: Holmes and Meir.

Elon, M., ed. 1975. **The Principles of Jewish Law.** Jerusalem: Institute for Research in Jewish Law Publications.

-----. 1981. On Power and Authority: Halachic Stance of the Traditional Community and its Contemporary Implications. In **Kinship and Consent,** see Blidstein.

Ephal, I. 1979. Israel: Fall and Exile. In **The World History of the Jewish People,** eds. A. Malamat and I. Ephal. Vol. 4, chap. 8. Jerusalem: Massada Press.

Epstein, Isidore. 1974. **Judaism--A Historical Presentation.** Middlesex, England: Penguin.

Ettinger, S. 1976. The Modern Age. In **A History of the Jewish People,** part 3, ed. H. H. Ben-Sasson. Cambridge, Mass.

Fain, B. and M. F. Verbit. 1984. **Jewishness in the Soviet Union.** Jerusalem: Jerusalem Center for Public Affairs and Association for Jewish Self-Education/Tarbuth Foundation.

Feingold, H. 1981. **Zion in America: The Jewish Experience form Colonial Times to the Present,** rev. ed. New York: Hippocrene.

Finkelstein, C. 1964. **Jewish Self-Government in the Middle Ages,** 2d ed. New York.

Freehof, S. B. 1973. **The Responsa Literature.** New York: Ktav.

Freemen, G. 1981. Rabbinic Conceptions of Covenant. In **Kinship and Consent,** see Blidstein.

Fried, J. ed. 1984. **Jews in the Modern World.** New York: Twayne.

Friedenreich, S. W. 1979. **The Jews of Yugoslavia.** Philadelphia: Jewish Publication Society of America.

Fuchs, L. H. 1956. **The Political Behaviour of American Jews.** Illinois: Free Press.

Ginsberg, L. 1970. **On Jewish Law and Lore.** New York: Atheneum.

Goldenberg, E. n.d. Darko shel R. Yehuda Hanasi Besidur Hamishna [THe Methods of Rabbi Yehuda Hanasi in the Arrangement of the Mishna]. **Tarbitz** 28: 160-69.

Goody, J. Time. In **International Encyclopedia of the Social Sciences,** vol. 16.

Greilsammer, I. 1978. Jews of France: From Neutrality to Involvement. **Forum,** no. 28-29 (Winter).

-----. 1979. **Les Processus de Democratisation d'Une Communaute--Le Cas du Judaisme Francais.** Jerusalem: Center for Jewish Community Studies, Jerusalem Center for Public Affairs.

Halpern, B. 1969. **The Idea of a Jewish State.** 2d

ed. Dambridge, Mass.: Harvard University Press.

Halpern, B. and I. Kolatt. 1970-71. Amadot Mistanot B'Yehesai Medinat Yisrael VeHatefutsot [Changing Relations Between Israel and the Diaspora]. **HaChug L'Ydiyat Am Yisrael B'Tfutzot B'Beit Nasi Hamedina** [Study Circle on World Jewry in the Home of the President of Israel]. 3d series, no. 6-7. Shagar Library, Institute of Contemporary Jewry, Hebrew University of Jerusalem.

Handhn, O. 1945. **Adventure in Freedom: Three Hundred Years of Jewish Life in America.** New York.

Hartz, L. 1964. **The Founding of New Societies: Studies in the History of the United States, Latin AMerica, South Africa, Canada and Australia.** New York: Harcourt, Bruce and World.

Hertzberg, A. 1968. **The French Enlightenment and the Jews.** New York.

------. 1975. **The Zionist Idea.** Westport, Conn.: Greenwood.

Heschel, A. J. 1969. **Israel: An Echo of Eternity.** New York: Farrar, Strauss and Giroux.

Hiller, D. R. 1969. **Covenant, the History of a Biblical Idea.** Baltimore: Johns Hopkins.

Himmelfarb, M. 1973. **The Jews of Modernity.** New York: Basic Books.

Hoenig, S. 1953. **The Great Sanhedrin.** Philadelphia: Dropsie College.

Isaacs, Stephen. 1974. **Jews and American Politics.** New York: Doubleday.

Kallen, H. M. 1958. **Utopieans at Bay.** New York: Theodor Herzl Foundation.

Katz, J. 1974. **Tradition and Crisis.** Harvard.

------. 1976. **Out of the Ghetto.** Harvard.

Katzburg, N. 1981. **Hungary and the Jews.** Ramat Gan.

Kaufman, Yehezkel. 1961. **Gola V'Nechar** [Diaspora and Exile]. Tel Aviv: Dvir.

Laqueur, W. Z. 1976. **A History of Zionism.** New York: Schocken Books.

Lestschinsky, J. 1958. **Tfutzot Yisrael Ahar Hamilhama** [The Dispersions of Israel after the War]. Tel Aviv.

Levitats, J. 1943. **The Jewish Community in Russia, 1772-1844.** New York.

Levy, Isaac. 1963. **The Synagogue: Its History and Function.** London: Valentine Mitchell.

Liebman, S. B. 1978. **The Jewish Community of**

Mexico. Jerusalem: Center for Jewish Community Studies, Jerusalem Center for Public Affairs.
Liebman, C. S. 1973. **The Ambivalent American Jew.** Philadelphia: Jewish Publication Society of America.
Malamat, A. Assyrian Exile. **Encylopedia Judaica,** vol. 6.
Mantel, H. 1961. **Studies in the Historyof the Great Sanhedrin.** Cambridge, Mass.: Harvard University Press.
Mead, Margaret. 1952. Introduction. In **Life is with People,** M. Zborowski and E. Herzog. New York.
Medding, P. Y. 1968. **From Assimilation to Group Survival--A Political Study of an Australian Jewish Community.** Melbourne: Chesire.
-----. 1973. **Jews in Australian Society.** Melbourne: Macmillan.
-----. 1981a. Patterns of Political Organization and Leadership in Contemporary Jewish Communities. In **Kinship and Consent,** see Blidstein.
-----. 1981b. Toward A General Theory of Jewish Political Interests and Behaviour in the Contemporary World. In **Kinship and Consent,** see Blidstein.
Mendelsohn, E. 1983. **The Jews of East Central Europe between the World Wars.** Bloomington, Indiana.
Neusner, J. 1978. **There We Sat Down: Talmudic Judaism in the Making.** New York: Ktav.
Orlinski, Harry M. 1967. **Ancient Israel.** 2d ed. Ithaca: Cornell University Press.
Parkes, James William. 1930. **The Jew and His Neighbour.** London: Student Christian Movement.
-----. 1949. **A History of Palestine from 135 A.D. to Modern Times.** New York: Oxford University Press.
-----. 1969. **The Conflict of the Church and the Synagogue.** New York: Atheneum.
Patai, Raphael. 1971. **The Tents of Jacob: The Diaspora Yesterday and Today.** New Jersey: Prentice Hall.
Porten, B. 1968. **Archives from Elephantine.** Berkeley and Los Angeles: University of California Press.
Reinharz, J. 1975. **Fatherland or Promised: The Dilemma of the German Jews, 1893-1914.** Ann Arbor.
Rotentreich, N., Z. Abramov, and Y. Bauer. 1977-78. Achrayuta Shel Medinat Yisrael Latfutzot [Israel's Responsibility to the Diaspora]. 9th

series, no. 7. Study circle, see Halpern and Kolatt 1972-73.

Roth, C. 1964. **History of the Jews in England,** 3d ed. Oxford.

Rubenstein, Amnon. 1979. **Hamishpat Hakonstitutzioni shel Medinat Yisrael** [The Constitutional Law of the State of Israel]. Jerusalem: Shocken Books.

Sachar, H. M. 1958. **The Course of Modern Jewish History.** New York: Dell Publishing Co.

Salzburg, M. 1971. **French Jewry and American Jewry.** Jerusalem: Center for Jewish Community Studies, Jerusalem Center for Public Affairs.

Samuel, E. 1967. The Administrator of the Catholic Church. **Public Administration in Israel and Abroad, 1966.** Jerusalem.

Schweid, E. 1972-73. HaKarat HaAm HaYehudi B'Hinuch B'Yisrael [Identification with the Jewish People in Israeli Education]. 6th series, no. 6. Study circle, see Halpern and Kolatt 1972-73.

Shimoni, Gideon. 1980. **Jews and Zionism: The South African Experience 1910-1967.** Cape Town: Oxford University Press.

Sklare, M. 1971. **America's Jews.** New York.

------. 1974. **The Jew in American Society.** New York: Behrman House.

Smith, Page. 1967. **As a City Upon a Hill.** New York.

Stock, E. 1974-75. Jewish Multi-Country Associations. In **American Jewish Yearbook.** New York and Philadelphia: American Jewish Committee and Jewish Publication Society of America.

Tartakower, A. 1959. **Hahevra Hayehudit** [Jewish Society]. Tel Aviv.

Tchernowitz, Ch. 1953. **Toledoth Hahalacha** [The History of Halacha]. New York: Vaad Hayovel.

Turner, F. J. 1920. **The Frontier in American History.** New York: Holt.

Vital, D. 1975. **The Origins of Zionism.** Oxford: Clarendon Press.

Waxman, Ch. I. 1983. **America's Jews in Transition.** Philadelphia: Temple University Press.

Weyl, J. 1968. **The Jew in American Politics.** New Rochelle: Arlington House.

Weinreib, B. D. 1972. **The Jews of Poland.** Philadelphia.

Weissbrot, R. 1979. **The Jews of Argentina.** Philadelphia: Jewish Publication Society of America.

Webb, W. P. 1953. **The Great Frontier.** London: Secker and Warburg.

Wilenski, M. 1970. **Hasidim Umitnagdim.** Jerusalem.

Zenner, W. P. 1968. Syrian Jews in Three Social Settings. **Jewish Journal of Sociology** 10, no. 1 (June): 101.

-----. 1975. **Jewish Retainers as Power Brokers in Traditional Societies.** Paper presented as 74th meeting of the American Anthropological Association, San Francisco.

POLITICAL ASPECTS OF JEWISH FUNDRAISING FOR ISRAEL

Gabriel Sheffer

Fundraising by modern ethnic diasporas is not an innocent and purely philanthropic activity. Even intuitively it can be grasped that these diasporas have many purposes in initiating and implementing fundraising. The IRA and the PLO, on the one hand, and the Lebanese, Greek and Jewish diasporas, on the other, are engaged in an activity which is more than just collecting money for marginal communal needs in their host countries, or for altruistic unilateral transfers to their respective parent organizations or homelands. The motivation for contributing and the maze of organized activities surrounding fundraising also have wider political ramifications for the ethnic diaspora, its homeland and host country. And if the triadic relationships involving diasporas, homelands and host countries do form meaningful trans-state networks, then fundraising is one of their most essential ingredients. Fundraising supplies the most vital material resources which sustain these networks.

This issue, however, has only been researched marginally. Fundraising by specific ethnic minorities has been studied either as a **sui generis** phenomenon, or as an example of personal and group voluntary philanthropic activity. Except for sporadic articles in the media, and extensive efforts by various intelligence agencies in the West, there are very few studies in this field. Fundraising by the United Jewish Appeal (UJA) in the United States is an outstanding exception in this regard. Although the UJA leaders are reluctant to encourage critical studies of their organization, or to supply detailed information about its activities and performance, a number of studies have already been conducted about it, and others are under way now (Goldin 1978; Manor and Sheffer 1975, 1977, 1979;

Bloom 1982). At the same time very little is known about the large campaigns of the United Israel Appeal (UIA)-Keren Hayesod in Jewish communities outside the USA.

Fundraising within various European and Latin American Jewish communities, however, has a long tradition, is highly organized, and as a result of its endeavors large sums of money are transferred to Israel. Even though fundraising is becoming a controversial issue within the Jewish diaspora communities and in Israel, Jewish fundraising serves as a model for other ethnic diasporas, especially the Palestinian and Lebanese. The governments of certain host countries have tried to use the threat of the denial of fundraising as a potential source of pressure on their Jewish communities as well as on Israel. Therefore, a comparative study of Jewish fundraising in the US and in other Jewish communities can be a valuable step toward a better understanding of the political questions involved in the existence of modern diasporas.

As a first step into the complex and secretive world of fundraising and its channeling of funds to homelands, two main questions will be discussed here. The first pertains to the structure of the trans-state networks created by diasporas, homelands and host countries. More specifically, what is fundraising's contribution to the creation of formalized links between these three participants. The second question pertains to the nature of these networks, namely to the extent of Jewish communities' autonomy in pursuing their own goals in this sphere, and thus becoming a relatively independent trans-state factor. In other words, to what extent are the organizational and procedural patterns of fundraising, and its channeling, influenced either by the political structures and traditions of the ethnic diasporas themselves, or by constraints created by host countries, or by the host countries' policies regarding the respective homelands. The other side of the coin is the degree of the diasporas' autonomy in determining their own activities without undue intervention by their homelands.

When considering these two questions a number of related subjects emerge: (1) the capability of the diasporas and their influence on the levels of fundraising: do the diasporas' permanence; levels of organization, mobilization, education and income; and degree of acculturation and conformity to accepted norms within their host countries impinge on their performance? (2) the readiness of host countries to tolerate the political, social and financial activities of these diasporas; (3) the state of the host countries' relations with the homelands; (4) the specific characteristics of the United Jewish Appeal in the US, and Keren Hayesod in other Jewish communities, as manifestations of the broader and more general organizations and activities of the communities; (5) the reasons for fluctuations in the levels of fundraising in various societies.

For the purpose of comparison, fundraising endeavors in five Jewish communities will be discussed here, namely, the American, French, British, Argentinian and South African Jewish communities. These are among the largest, most fully developed, highly organized and mobilized in World Jewry. These communities exist and function within five social and political systems sufficiently different from each other to allow interesting and meaningful insights into the complexities of the subject.

Demographic, Educational, and Occupational Characteristics

The five above mentioned communities are among the nine largest Jewish communities in the world. Table 1 illustrates the ranking of the nine communities; table 2 focuses on the five communities chosen for the purpose of comparison.

All these communities are characterized by low fertility (zero growth is the regular rate in these communities), a considerable rate of mixed marriages involving loss of children to the communities, further losses caused by other assimilatory trends, and aging. The combination of assimilation and aging in turn reduces the birth rate and raises the death rate. Therefore, in these communities the combined balance of natural and affiliative changes is now negative. Moreover, there are many Jews who have not formally embraced another religion, but are very estranged (they are known as "marginal Jews"), or have become alienated from Judaism and the Jewish communities. All these trends reduce the potential membership of Jewish communal organizations, as well as the potential for pro-Israeli segments and contributors to Jewish fundraising organizations (Schmeltz and Della Pergola 1982).

Table 1

Countries with Largest Jewish Population, 1980

Rank/ Country	Jewish Population	Percent of the Total Jewish Population In the Jewish Diaspora	In the World
1. US	5,690,000	58.4	43.7
2. Israel	3,282,700	--	25.2
3. Sov. Union	1,700,000	17.4	13.1
4. France	535,000	5.5	4.1
5. GB	390,000	4.0	3.0
6. Canada	308,000	3.2	2.4
7. Argentina	242,000	2.5	1.9
8. Brazil	110,000	1.1	0.8
9. So. Africa	108,000	1.1	0.8
Total 8 Largest Diasporas	9,083,000	93.2	69.7
Total 9 Largest Communities	12,365,700	--	94.9

Source: **American Jewish Yearbook,** 1982

Table 2

Estimated Jewish Population, 1980

Country	Total Population	Jewish Population	Jews per 1,000 Population
US	220,584,000	5,690,000	25.8
France	53,478,000	535,000	10.0
GB	55,883,000	390,000	7.0
Argentina	26,729,000	242,000	9.1
So. Africa	28,483,000	108,000	3.7

Source: **American Jewish Yearbook,** 1982

As a result of precarious political and social conditions prevailing in two countries--Argentina and South Africa--Jews are leaving, usually moving to the US and Canada. In the past, immigration to Israel had been regarded as a fundamental aspect of Zionism, but since 1973, immigration to Israel from these communities has become minimal. For complex political, economic and cultural reasons, Israel has ceased to attract even dedicated Zionists. Hence, an additional open question has emerged focusing on the impact of these trends on the affiliation in pro-Israeli organizations, and on the donations to Israeli fundraising. Otherwise stated, there are grave doubts whether Zionist ideology is a good predictor of personal donations and involvement in fundraising organizations.

Yet, despite the increased rates of assimilation, conversion, lower birth rates and migration, there is no doubt about the permanency of the Jewish communities in these five countries. The hard core of each of these communities will maintain its special identity and character, and barring major political catastrophes, no fundamental changes should be predicted in their basic social composition and political organization.

Table 3

Age and Income of Jewish Families in the US, 1975

Age of Head of Family	Average Income	Percent of All Families
65 and above	$ 5,000	21.4
60-64	$14,770	8.9
30-59	$18,525	57.1
18-30	$10,415	11.5
All families	$12,630	

Source: "National Jewish Population Survey", published by the Council of Jewish Federations and Welfare Funds (CJFWF), 1975

In each of these countries the Jews are concentrated in metropolitan areas or in the suburbs of large cities. The major local American Jewish communities are located in New York (2,000,000), Los Angeles (503,000), Philadelphia (295,000), Miami (225,000), and Boston (170,000). Thus, more than 3,000,000 American Jews live in five large cities. In France more than half of the Jewish community is located in Paris and its suburbs, with the rest concentrated in Marseille, Lyon, Toulouse, Nice and Strasbourg. In Britain the Jewish communities are concentrated in London, Manchester, Leeds and Glasgow. Regarding mobilization, organization and fundraising, there are technical advantages in the high concentration in urban areas. But, the other social and demographic trends mentioned above counterbalance these advantages. More surprising is the greater effectiveness of fundraising in small communties, which will be discussed below.

These five Jewish communities in the US are relatively affluent and the majority of Jews are middle class. Both the aging of the American Jewish community, and its high level of income are demonstrated in table 3. The situation in the Jewish communities in the other countries discussed here is basically similar.

During the last two or three decades a marked change has also occurred in the nature and level of education in the communities, and subsequently in their occupational structure. While Jewish education has lost its attraction, and the Jewish educational systems established by the communities are deteriorating quite rapidly now, the attainment of general higher education has become the accepted norm among second and third generation Jews in these communities. According to the CJFWF survey, 54 percent of adult Jews (25 years and older) have obtained college education and 78 percent of Jewish males in the 24-29 age group have obtained higher education. A similar trend can be observed in France: in Paris 26 percent of the total adult Jewish population (15 years and older) have obtained higher education, while the percentage for the same group living in other parts of France is 24 percent. Consequently, there are now more Jews in the professions and in white collar occupations than ever before. According to recent estimates, 10 percent of the Jewish manpower force in Argentina belong to the upper middle class, 80 percent are white collar and professionals, and only 10 percent are in manual jobs or in services. These trends are further reflected in Tables 4 and 5 relating to the Jewish communities in France and the US.

These profound changes in education and occupation have created significant adverse consequences in the attitudes of second and third generation Jews. A greater percentage of educated Jews and of those in professions tend to negate the old Jewish establishment and refrain from either becoming volunteers or contributors to Jewish fundraising (Cohen 1980, pp. 272-90).

Table 4

Socio-Occupational Patterns of the Jews in Paris
(15 years and above)

Socio-Occupational Category	Percent
Senior positions in the professions	22%
Industrialists and merchants	21%
Managerial and skilled workers in middle echelons	46%
Manual workers and services	11%

Source: Doris Bensimon, "La Communaute Juive de France" in **Handbook of European Jewish Communities**, Tel Aviv: Turtledove, 1982.

Table 5

Occupations of Jewish Males in the US, 1975

Age	20-25	30-39	40-49	50-64	All Ages	All Amer. Males
Occupation						
The Professions	41.2	46.0	29.1	20.1	29.3	14.3
Directors and Manpower Directors	32.3	35.0	41.8	48.2	40.7	15.1
Managerial	5.7	1.8	2.2	3.6	3.2	6.3
Commerical	15.0	9.8	14.8	15.5	14.2	6.2
Services, Manual	5.7	7.5	12.1	12.6	12.7	58.2

Source: **NJPS,** 1975

The Organization of the Jewish Communities

There is much truth in the description of the Jews as an "archetypal diaspora" (Armstrong 1976). Among other features, the Jewish diaspora can be

characterized by its high degree of communal organization. This is the case especially in Western
democracies where a great deal of similarity in the
main patterns of organization in the various communities can be discerned. In the US the community
has established hundreds of organizations that
cover many aspects of the lives of individuals,
households and local communities. These organizations vary in regard to their own age, the age of
their members, their size and demographic characteristics. They also vary in their goals, mission,
degree of professionalization, policy-making patterns, and performance. The older organizations on
the national level were established in the 19th
century (e.g., B'nai Brith, 1843, the Union of
American Hebrew Congregations, 1875) and the younger organizations founded in the 1960s and 1970s
(e.g., the International Council on Jewish Social
and Welfare Services, 1961). Their membership
varies from a few hundred, to many thousands (e.g.,
donors to the UJA, or members of Hadassah). There
are single-purpose specialized organizations, and
multipurpose and multinational organizations, such
as those dealing with the welfare of overseas Jewish communities (e.g., the Joint Distribution Com-
mittee--JDC). There are democratic organizations
(e.g., several student organizations) and highly
elitist organizations (such as the American Jewish
Committee--AJC). There are unitary, federative or
front organizations. In short, the American Jewish
community has created a maze of various organizations. The UJA and other pro-Israeli organizations
must compete with other organizations in order to
draw attention and membership. Table 6 demon-
strates the number of Jewish organizations in the
US and the various aspects they cover (Maslow 1975;
Elazar 1976).

The larger Jewish organizations in the US now
show certain structural and procedural similarities. The UJA, American Jewish Committee, American Jewish Congress and Hadassah, for example, have
all acquired a common profile which deviates from
their traditional classification. Their profiles
are similar in regard to their multipurpose missions, federative structure, efforts to broaden
their basis for recruitment of members and resources, major patterns of policy-making which are
very heavily influenced by professionalization and
professionals, and in the diversified targets of
their outputs.

Table 6

American-Jewish National Organizations, 1974

Sphere	Number
Religious and Educational	110
Zionist and Israeli-Related	53
Cultural	31
Welfare	27
Community Relations	24
Youth and Students	24
Professional Associations	19
Women	19
Overseas Aid	18
Social	15
Total	340

Source: **The American Jewish Yearbook,** 1974

Usually analysts and leaders of the French community make a threefold distinction between the Jewish organizations: religious, social-communal and Zionist (Bensimon 1978). It seems that this threefold classification is applicable to all Jewish communities other than those in the US. In any case, all the religious aspects of Jewish communal life in France are under the jurisdiction of the veteran Consistory which was established during the Napoleonic era. The group which supports this Consistory is the Ashkenazi Orthodox congregation. While in the past the Consistory dealt with and represented all Jewish interests, now it is confined to the religious-educational sphere. In the social-communal sphere the most important organization is the Fond Social Juif Unifie (FSJU), which was established only in 1950. Its purpose was to plan and coordinate non-religious cultural, educational and social activities. However, since the French government has undertaken the financing of more communal activities, and since after 1967 the FSJU has lost its independent financial basis, it is becoming less influential and has been replaced by the local Keren Hayesod. The Zionist organization in France (MFS) is dominated by the Zionist parties, which are in fact only external branches of the respective Israeli parties. Keren Hayesod activities are extremely important in this context. More recently the newly-established Sephardic segment within the community has begun to establish its own social, financial and educational organizations which are already competing with the older organizations.

Similar divisions also exist in the British Jewish community. The main political representative body of Jewish interests is the Board of Deputies. Recently it has lost some of its luster and power. Its counterpart in the social sphere is the Jewish Welfare Board which is desperately trying to raise adequate funds for its various activities. Two other foci of power in the British Jewish community are the religious congregations, and the Zionist movement and its local fundraising organization (Cohen 1982, pp. 272-90; Frankel 1981).

More than in any other community in World Jewry, the Argentinian community has been organized along political lines. This mainly secular and politicized community has adopted a strong Zionist inclination, hence a high percentage of adult Jews have developed a strong Zionist affiliation. The central organization here is the socially-inclined Associacion Mutual Israelita Argentina (AMIA). It deals with the large Jewish educational system, as well as with other communal services and their financing. The Delegacion de Asociaciones Israelita Argentina (DAIA) is responsible for the struggle against anti-Semitism and anti-Zionism, and for the representation of Jewish interests to the authorities. In Argentina Sephardic Jews have established their own parallel organizations. The Organisacion Sionista Argentina (OSA) is the central Zionist body whose tasks were to encourage immigration to Israel and to strengthen contact with Israel. AMIA, DAIA and OSA are controlled by the Jewish parties.

And finally, the same divisions exist in the South African Jewish community and determine the pattern of the community's action. By virtue of its origin and of the country's connections with Britain, the nature and structure of the Jewish organizations were heavily influenced by those in Britain. In the political sphere the Board of Deputies is the main representative body, in the social sphere the United Communal Fund (UCF) strives to establish a predominant position. Within the Zionist organization the Herut party is very popular and enjoys considerable support and membership (Shimoni 1980).

The fundraising organizations are regarded as the strongest in these communities not least be-

cause their leaders perform important political
functions within the community and the general
political system. Their strength stems also from
the fact that they control both the finances for
communal activities and another most vital
commodity--continuous ties with the Israeli political elite.

The Social and Political Openness
of Host Societies

The social and political openness and tolerance
which are shown by host societies toward ethnic
diasporas determine the latter's practical access
to senior policy-makers, as well as the degree of
legitimacy of their organizations and action.
Needless to say, these five communities differ
greatly in these areas. Access is determined by
the different traditions as well as the divergent
social and political norms prevailing in each of
the host societies. In the US the basis for the
legitimation of Jewish mobilization, organization
and action is ethnic; in Britian it stems from a
combination of religious and political tolerance;
in France it is formally still religious; in South
Africa it is political; and in Argentina it depends
on the benevolence, tolerance and short-range interests of the rulers and juntas in government.
      Among the five communities, those in the US
and Britain enjoy the highest degree of freedom of
action. Neither British nor American society poses
formal political barriers to the mobilization of
the Jewish communities there, or to their political
activation. Similarly they do not produce insur-
mountable social obstacles for individuals who wish
to defect from the Jewish community through assimilation or conversion. Despite this freedom and a
general political acceptance, both blatant and
subtle examples of anti-Semitism can be detected in
both countries. Anti-Semitism in general, and
particularly in these two countries, provokes contradictory reactions among Jews. On the one hand,
anti-Semitism pushes Jews to adhere more strongly
to their leaders and community, but on the other
hand, it encourages assimilation and conversion,
which result in net population losses to the community. In both countries one can also detect
subtle discrimination in career opportunities and
in social integration.

Nevertheless, in the US there are a number of
forceful political and social factors which encourage Jewish communal organization and fundraising. Among other factors, the federal structure of
the US and the basically liberal capitalist economic subsystem create vast needs, together with
opportunities and incentives for voluntary action
and financing. Ethnic communal needs are not met
by any state agencies and their fulfillment is left
to the initiative and action of the ethnic groups
themselves. Other factors include a long tradition
of absorption of ethnic minorities in the US. Once
again the absorption of compatriots is left to the
ethnic groups themselves. All these factors determine the breadth, number and diversity of Jewish
organizations. And finally, the well-established,
almost sacred, norms connected to the freedom of
political lobbying, and fundraising for political
purposes, encourage politically-oriented Jews to
broaden their means of concerted action. Since the
American Jewish community has always demonstrated
its interest in politics, and its generosity in
contributing to political campaigns, its access to
American politicians has been relatively easy, with
local and national leaders considering their demands and accepting their contributions.

In Great Britain the main source for the political legitimacy of Jewish communal representation,
and the basis for the relatively easy access to
senior policy-makers, is the traditional tolerance
toward religious and political groups. It is interesting to note that during the period in which
Britain held the mandate for Palestine, successive
British cabinets carefully refrained from dealing
with the Jewish question as an ethnic problem.
British politicians were apprehensive of the possibility that due to Britain's particular responsibilities as the mandatory power in Palestine, it
would also be burdened with the responsibility of
solving the entire Jewish problem. From this point
of view the British withdrawal from Palestine in
1948, and the establishment of the State of Israel,
simplified matters. Indeed, since then the British
Jewish community has had no further need to justify
either its internal social and political organization, or its pro-Israeli positions. However, while
British Jewry obtained considerable political power
during the pre-state period, since 1948 a marked
decrease has occurred in its achievements. The
potential for political action still exists, but
because of social and cultural stagnation the like-

lihood of a massive mobilization of British Jewry is relatively small. The future of the South African Jewish community is closely related to the durability and stability of the white government there. Hence, far-reaching changes in the basic political arrangements of the country may lead to a massive exodus of Jews. Within white society Jewish existence is also problematic and shrouded with ambiguities. While there is a degree of hostility and mistrust in their relations with the Afrikaners, the Jews have been more fully accepted, or tolerated, by the Anglo-Saxons. The fact that large Jewish groups hold liberal political attitudes further contributes to their problematic position and to the difficulties that they encounter in their dealings with the government. These difficulties, however, are counterbalanced by current friendly relations between the South African and Israeli governments, which will be discussed later.

In Argentina neither individual nor communal existence is secure. The dominant Catholic culture and tradition and the authoritarian nature of the regime do not encourage the proliferation of free voluntary associations and produce restrictions on organizations which represent the interests of Jews and other ethnic groups. Recently Jewish access to the Argentinian government has been rendered more difficult. It is not surprising, therefore, that the community's attempts to act on behalf of the Jews who had disappeared or been arrested have failed. Nevertheless, since 1948 successive rulers and juntas have tolerated the pro-Israeli organizations, such as the local Zionist movement and the various Zionist parties. The politicized nature of the Jewish community should be partly attributed to the innate nature of Argentinian society despite the recent emergence of a democratic government. In addition to the hostile cultural traditions, recent anti-Semitic outbursts have made organized Jewish life extremely unpleasant. These outbursts and the general political instability, push Jews to emigrate and to seek refuge in the US and Canada. This trend contributes to the dwindling of the Jewish community in Argentina and reduces its capacity for mobilized action. This phenomenon is very clearly reflected in the performance of the local branch of Keren Hayesod.

Finally, a general observation about the attitude of the media in these countries toward Jewish fundraising: on the whole the media has not referred to this activity. It seems that this is not a theme which attracts wide coverage, particularly since these organizations try to keep their activities out of the public eye. Only in extreme rightist anti-Semitic newspapers has the issue been dealt with occasionally. Thus, respective governments make their decisions about Jewish fundraising free from both media influence and public pressure.

The Impact on Fundraising of Host Governments' Relations with Israel

The more problematic and precarious the position of Jewish communities within their host countries, the greater the importance of the status of formal and informal relations between the host governments and Israel, for regular fundraising and for the transfer of funds. In discussing this issue the distinction between raising the money and its transfer to Israel is essential.

As it has been observed in the relatively stable Jewish communities of the US and Britain, raising money and its transfer depend almost exclusively on the Jewish communities' capabilities. The likelihood that the American or British governments would stop fundraising itself is very small. The fact that in these two countries voluntary action is highly respected and sustained by tradition, coupled with the fact that the Jewish communities have maintained relatively easy access to their respective governments and the media, serve as a deterrence against any serious attempt to limit fundraising.

Transferring the money to Israel is a different matter. The British have shown the greatest restraint in this respect. In the US there were at least two serious attempts to use the threat of denial of UJA money as a source of pressure on the Israeli government in regard to its Middle Eastern policies. On both occasions the Americans retreated from their intention as a result of prompt Jewish and Israeli response.

In France the situation is somewhat more complicated. Although there are no recorded indications that the government has ever contemplated limiting Jewish fundraising, the tranfers to Israel could have suffered within the framework of general limitations occasionally imposed on unilateral transfers to foreign countries, or within foreign exchange regulations. The most recent instance is

the regulations imposed by the Mitterrand administration on foreign exchange and unilateral transfers. In fact, the transfers to Israel have not
been hampered. This can be explained by the French
government's desire to improve its relations with
Israel, and to play a more active and decisive role
in the solution of the Middle Eastern conflict.

In Argentina and South Africa fundraising and
its transfer depend entirely on the good will of
the host governments. In the early 1970s the South
African government imposed severe restrictions on
fundraising for Israel. The government then issued
an open warning to this effect. Since the mid-
1970s, however, and as a result of the marked
improvement in Israeli-South African relations,
this embargo was cancelled. Currently there are no
limitations either on fundraising or its transfer.
A similar development has occurred in Argentina.
Both raising money and its transfer were formally
prohibited until the early 1980s. Nevertheless, it
is no secret that even during that period the
Argentinian government had informally permitted
these activities. In the early 1980s the local
Keren Hayesod campaign (CUJA) was once again formally permitted. This change in the Argentinian
government's attitude should also be attributed to
closer relations with Israel.

Keren Hayesod and the UJA:
Organization and Political Activities

Keren Hayesod was established by the World Zionist
Organization in 1920 as the main organization to
promote donations for building the Jewish National
Home in Palestine. Two principles served as the
basis for the fund's activities: it should direct
its efforts at every Jew, and donations should be
regarded as an annual tax levied on every Jew at
the rate of 10% of their income. In 1929, the
Enlarged Jewish Agency was established. It was
aimed at attracting non-Zionist Jews to the creation of the National home in Palestine. This step
did not lead to a unification of fundraising campaigns within Jewry even for overseas needs. This
was especially true in the US, where other major
organizations functioned in this sphere. Several
attempts were made at joint campaigns in the US (in
1930, 1934, 1935); but the meager results of these
campaigns were not encouraging and they were abandoned (although combined campaigns were conducted

on a local level in several communities). It was
only after Kristallnacht that a national agreement
was reached between the various Jewish organizations in the US resulting in joint campaigns and
the formation of the United Jewish Appeal (UJA).
Thus, as of 1938, Zionist fundraising was conducted
within the framework of fundraising for overseas
needs by the UJA which was a body of the American
Jewish community, in which American Zionists were
only a part. These developments in the US contributed to the decision to concentrate Keren Hayesod
fundraising efforts outside the US.

The establishment of the State of Israel
marked the beginning of a new era in fundraising,
creating a number of fundamental questions about
the roles of the Jewish Agency and Keren Hayesod in
financing the new state's needs. The World Zionist
Organization (WZO) Action Committee decided in 1948
that the Jewish Agency and Keren Hayesod would
continue to function as the main financial instruments of the Zionist movement, concentrating on the
financing of immigration and immigrant absorption
in Israel, education, and the promotion of Israel-
Diaspora relations. These arrangements had been
formalized in the Israeli law concerning the status
of the Jewish Agency in Israel and in an agreement
which was consequently signed between the Agency
and the Israeli government. The WZO also decided
to create a "United Israel Appeal" which would
serve as the main channel for the transfer of funds
raised in the Diaspora.

In the wake of the waves of mass immigration
to Israel of the early 1950s, the Jewish Agency and
Keren Hayesod indeed directed their activities
mainly at settlement of new immigrants, their education and employment. Since then there has been a
growing realization that it would not be feasible
to base the fundraising campaigns only on immediate
political issues. Consequently, the campaigns have
been conducted with a view to more permanent problems. In 1956, Keren Hayesod adopted a new constitution which included avowed intentions of promoting goals beyond the sheer mobilization of financial aid for Israel.

Keren Hayesod is directed by bodies elected by
the WZO: (1) the Board of Trustees, elected by the
General Assembly of the World Zionist Organization;
(2) the President, who heads the Board of Trustees
and is elected by the Zionist Executive Committee.
Ex officio, he is a member of that committee; (3)
the Board of Directors, which is the main executive

body of the organization and comprises the President, members of the Zionist Executive, and the Jewish Agency Assembly; (4) the Director General, nominated by the Board of Trustees.

Thus, activities are controlled jointly by the Zionist Executive and the World Zionist Congress. Keren Hayesod's budget is approved by the Standing Financial Committee of the Zionist Executive.

Keren Hayesod is directly subordinate to the Zionist institutions and, indirectly, to the Jewish Agency. Since 1972, however, a clear change has been introduced into the status of the organization's relations with the WZO, which followed general reforms of the Jewish Agency. An assembly which was gathered to establish the new Enlarged Jewish Agency consisted of 142 representatives of the WZO and 108 representatives of other signatory bodies, the latter mainly Jewish fundraising organizations (these 108 seats were divided as follows: 50% Keren Hayesod, 30% UJA and 20% other organizations). Two institutions were elected by this assembly: the Executive Committee of the Jewish Agency, consisting of 10 members (and 21 associate members) and a 40-member Board of Governors. Since 1973 the President of Keren Hayesod has been a member of both institutions, reporting to the Chairman of the Jewish Agency's Executive Committee. Moreover, a Standing Committee for Fund-Raising has been set up to ensure the maximal income for the Jewish Agency. This committee reports to the Jewish Agency's Executive Committee, which in turn takes any necessary action, always conscious of the autonomy of Keren Hayesod and the UJA and of the differences in various Diaspora communities.

The functions of the Standing Committee are: (1) to define the goals of Keren Hayesod in each country according to its local potential; (2) to suggest leaders, speakers and functionaries for individual soliciting; (3) to encourage young women to take leadership roles wherever possible; (4) to train professionals in an Israel-based institute directed by the Executive Committee, (the training institute has applied the Keren Hayesod's training methods for professionals to the UJA. The committee decided to make this the general practice in all fundraising organizations); (5) to support and encourage local leadership; (6) to bring together community leaders from various countries in order to exchange views and experiences.

Approximately 100 officials serve in the Jerusalem office. Its activities are concentrated in four areas: (1) information--it is responsible for dispatching guest speakers and special representatives, organizing and accommodating survey missions in Israel, and preparing and supplying written and audio-visual material to the various countries; (2) staff training and professional counselling; (3) shaping, directing and controlling the overseas system by intensifying contacts between Jerusalem and active members and donors overseas, through conventions, meetings, and seminars; and (4) recruitment and placement of professionals.

The United Jewish Appeal

Established in 1939, the UJA is "the main [American] body in charge of raising funds for overseas and refugees' assistance." It receives a considerable part of its income (about 90 percent) from 225 "federations", the remainder through 800 independent fundraising campaigns conducted in the "non-federated" communities.

The term "federation" (or "welfare fund" or "Jewish community council") refers to communal bodies in 95 percent of American Jewish local communities responsible for: (1) raising funds for local, national and overseas services; (2) allocation and distribution of funds for these purposes; (3) coordination and central planning of local services; (4) direct administration of local social services in small and some medium-sized cities.

In principle, each federation and community is sovereign in determining the sums it transfers to the UJA (with the exception of the proceeds of "emergency" or "special" funds, which are transferred in toto to the UJA). Influential, however, in the decisions of the federations is the Council of Jewish Federations and Welfare Funds (CJFWF), a coordinating organization of all the federations, that makes annual recommendations for the amounts to be allocated for local, national and overseas needs.

Both the UJA and CJFWF are represented in various bodies of the Jewish Agency, its Assembly, Action Committee, and Executive.

To carry out its activities, the UJA has at its disposal a permanent administrative machinery (the number of professionals has been estimated at between 300-700), directed by an Executive Committee of about 100 people, in charge of stimulating activity and formulating propositions concerning the organization's policies and strategies.

The internal structure of this permanent body comprises: (1) Women's Division; (2) Young Leadership Cabinet (established in 1963); (3) Student Coordination Cabinet (established in 1969); (4) Rabbinical Advisory Council (established in 1961); (5) National Labor Council (established in 1953 to mobilize and coordinate the activity of 675 Zionist groups).

One of the major responsibilities of the Executive Committee is to set up "campaign cabinets" charged with leading the annual fundraising campaigns. The National Campaign Cabinet is responsible for organizing, leading, and stimulating the campaigns often run simultaneously throughout America. It is a body of more than 200 members chosen on a regional basis. At the head of each of the eight regions into which the UJA administratively divided the American Jewish community is a campaign cabinet of at least 20 members, with one chairman and several vice-chairmen. The National Campaign Cabinet is headed by 12 National Chairmen, who are responsible either for the conduct of the campaign in each of the eight regions, or for the implementation of special functions, such as the actual collection of "pledges", the guidance of the "pacemakers", the handling of the big donations, and the organization of study missions in Israel. The targets, slogans, and schedules of the campaigns, prepared by the Executive Committee, are reviewed and adopted by the National Chairmen. The structure of the UJA is outlined in diagram 1.

Diagram 1
The Dual Structure of the UJA

National General Chairmen of the UJA	
Executive Committee Director General	National Campaign Cabinet (12 National Chairmen)
Executive Vice-Chairmen	Local Campaign Cabinets (Cabinet Chairmen)

Of particular significance in considering the UJA decision-making process is its dual structure, namely, its permanent staff and the ad hoc cabinets responsible for the direction of the annual campaigns. In this dual structure, the professionals serve to ensure coordination and continuity. It is also important to note that the UJA is in fact a federation of independent funds throughout the country. At the same time, the UJA serves as a vital link with world Jewish organizations. This complex structure reflects the federative nature of the American Jewish community (which stems from the American Jews' geographic dispersion, the unique character of each community, and the federal tradition that characterizes the United States in general) and the complex socio-demographic features of the Jewish people. The problems of decision making and of incorporating professionals and determining their role in such a complex organization with multiple connections on various levels with individual contributors, funds and organizations (including volunteers and professionals) and with international Jewish organizations are immense.

The Common Features of UJA and Keren Hayesod

There are common features in the campaigns of almost all Jewish communities in the Diaspora. The similarity has been created by the accumulated experience exchanged between the various communities through either Keren Hayesod or the UJA. These exchanges were formally carried out by the organizations' leaders and informally through direct contacts between the organizations' rank and file.

In most of the communities, the campaign can be described in terms of a five-phase model:

Phase 1: Formulation and confirmation of campaign goals and general plans. The formulation of the annual campaign goals is carried out on three levels: (1) in the central offices of the UJA and Keren Hayesod; (2) on the national level (Keren Hayesod) and regional or state level (UJA); (3) on the local community level. In the US a considerable degree of freedom has been maintained by local offices and organizations in planning and implementing the campaign. Before formulating the campaign plans, surveys of the needs of Israel as well as of the local communities are conducted; the goals and themes of the campaign are set in accordance with these surveys.

Phase 2: Preparation of technical means for the campaign. During this phase, background material and propaganda aids are prepared and various tasks are assigned to both volunteers and professionals.

Phase 3: Laying the groundwork among the volunteers and "big" donors. Significant here are meetings with "pace-makers", within either professional or social frameworks. A great deal of effort goes into these meetings, since large sums of money are raised at this stage, and pledges made even before the official opening of the campaign. The purpose here is to create an atmosphere conducive to the general fundraising campaign.

Phase 4: The campaign. The campaign usually begins with a series of well-publicized events with the participation of guest speakers from Israel or local Jewish leaders. A lot of planning is put into this phase to ensure maximal response. Currently, there is a strong tendency to abandon large meetings in favor of smaller ones in which it is possible to exert individual pressure and influence, thereby obtaining better results. Face-to-face contact now also assumes an important place in the campaign.

Phase 5: Ensuring the fulfillment of pledges. Much effort is devoted to following up pledges, and soliciting donations and further pledges during each phase of the campaign. This is done with a close eye on the progress of the campaign.

THE CAMPAIGN FOCI. Keren Hayesod's campaign is planned by the permanent professional staff. The actual campaign plans are prepared by the regional and state offices. Those plans are reviewed by the Jerusalem headquarters. Jerusalem often modifies the plans, especially with regard to objectives and the feasibility of technical apparatus (lectures, written information, visits and meetings). In short, coordination is carried out by the central organization in order to direct and control the campaign. In the UJA, on the other hand, the local organizations have a greater degree of autonomy in planning and executing their campaign. Nevertheless, even here the influence of the center is noticeable, particularly through the influence of the professional staff on local leaders. Once the financial goals are set, the central organization supplies the main themes and ideas for the campaign. It also assists in professional counselling and, especially, in providing guest speakers for local organizations.

THE PARTICIPANTS IN PLANNING AND IMPLEMENTING THE CAMPAIGN. There are four main groups of participants: local leadership; permanent professional staff; volunteers; and Israelis. Understanding the methods and motivations of each group is vital for evaluating the performance and the politics involved.

THE LOCAL LEADERSHIP. This does not necessarily consist of the outstanding social or spiritual leaders of the respective communities, particularly in communities where Jewish activities are dynamic and are still undergoing change. In more conservative and established communities, the communal and campaign leadership is usually similar. Nevertheless, there still are powerful constraints on the merging of these two elites. The resistance to the merging of these elites comes especially from the well-established organizational leadership which understands the political power which can be achieved through the control of this activity.

In any case, the lay leaders head the committees and the meetings in the campaigns. The donors meet in various groupings in accordance with regional, professional, communal or social criteria.

THE PROFESSIONALS. The main occupation of the permanent professional staff is fundraising and its management. The permanent staff performs four functions: First, it is responsible for the establishment of data and information bases which are necessary for soliciting funds during the campaign. This information serves the community beyond the needs of the campaign, assisting, for instance, in the determination of educational needs and cultural services. Thus mutual interests are established between the professionals and the lay leaders of local organizations. Second, professionals organize special committees which individually assess veteran and potential contributors' means. This is the "tax base" for approaching donors. Third, they provide general and specific advice to all the participants in the campaign; for example, on optimal means of persuading donors to contribute, on the manner in which the donations are allocated, etc. Fourth, they are responsible for follow-up and persuasion of contributors to fulfill their pledges. This also requires updated information about contributors' financial situation.

The "personal approach" method which has been adopted by Keren Hayesod and UJA postulates a differential mode of contacts with each veteran and potential contributor. According to this approach, raising money should be the result of a psychological process which requires "professional" know-

ledge, understanding, sensitivity and toughness on
the part of the fundraiser. Moreover, fundraising
is now conceived by both professional and lay leaders as an "economic transaction." That is, the
contributor should be induced to "buy" a sense of
participation in the Jewish fate, a sense of satisfaction in helping the needy, and self-esteem,
pride and status within his peer group or community
because of the size of his donation. These are the
kind of "packages" "sold" to the contributors by
professionals and active volunteers who are in-
structed to conclude the "deals" during their face-
to-face meeting with contributors. It is also
emphasized that contributions smaller than previous
ones made by the person should not be accepted.
This is to prevent a general "deterioration" of
income. When the potential contributors' response
is negligible, there is a tendency to resort to
socio-psychological pressures.

Despite the desire to increase the rates of
personal donations, the exhaustion of given sources
is of course not encouraged: the pressures exerted
on "big givers" to increase their donations are
carefully calculated and measured so as to prevent
the total withdrawal of any contributor.

Thus, Jewish fundraising bears a similarity to
other administrative activities in its attempts to
optimize organizational efforts. In this instance
the preferred strategy of optimization is concentration on a small number of "big givers."

Data on New York UJA campaigns, for example,
highlight the fact that a small number of "big
givers" are responsible for the most significant
part of the annual contribution. In 1974, more
than 50% of the funds raised by the UJA came from
fewer than 0.5% of the donors. Also evident is a
decline in the number of contributors after peak
years. Although the declared aim of the UJA and
Keren Hayesod is to draw as many Jews as possible
into fundraising activity, it has been agreed to
focus first on "big-givers," who theoretically can
be persuaded to contribute large sums at low marginal organizational costs. This may prove a more
efficient way to optimize the results of the campaigns, but it certainly clashes with some of the
organization's basic ideological postulates.

THE ISRAELI PARTICIPANTS. Israeli political
figures (Meir, Begin, Eban, etc.), are recruited on
an ad hoc basis to solicit donations, particularly
in times of crises. The "Israeli side" also plays
an important role in the course of survey missions

to Israel, when volunteers and lay leaders are afforded a first-hand look at the country.

THE DYNAMICS AND IMPLEMENTATION OF THE CAMPAIGNS. Although formally fundraising planning and actual implementation should have been in the hands of the World Zionist Organization, the Jewish Agency and their respective volunteers, the truth of the matter is that the professional directors activate all other participants in the process. The main activities are guided by the professionals who, in addition to the functions mentioned above, undertake to plan the annual campaign and to draw the conclusion afterwards. It is especially evident in the national bureaus of Keren Hayesod and the UJA, where the following aspects are evident:

1. There is a clear tendency to reinforce the professional staff by the systematic accumulation of data and by recruitment of additional professionals. In June 1971, the General Assembly of the Jewish Agency decided to train professional manpower for campaigns in an institute in Israel, directed by the Executive and responsible for it. Accordingly, a joint training center has been established. Workers from various countries have been invited, seminars held, and information, opinions and evaluations concerning methods of fundraising exchanged.

2. There is an effort to increase the number of volunteers, which is carried out primarily through the formation of new action frameworks, e.g., university students and women. The latter have gradually emerged in almost all Jewish communities, where the intention was to offer a sphere of activity for many older and retired women, to increase the rate of donations from heads of families by introducing an element of competition within the family itself, and to influence the children by involving them in Jewish and Israeli affairs. The establishment of "young leadership" is yet another example of the attempt to enlarge the ranks of volunteers. In many countries, however, systematic attempts are made to avoid certain grouping in fundraising. This refers mainly to intellectuals and students who may express skeptical opinions and raise troublesome questions. In the more conservative communities, then, the patterns of leadership recruitment and of management of

the campaigns remain mostly unchanged; the
initiative to form new frameworks is ultimately determined by the professionals who
have their own organizational considerations.
3. Deliberate attempts to form a new leadership
have been made. From the professionals' point
of view, the recruitment of lay leadership is,
at least in part, the outcome of their own
efforts. The professionals have encouraged
what they regarded as the most suitable lead-
ers--the wealthy and influential members of
the local communities who are "disciplined"
and ready to identify themselves almost unre-
servedly with the State of Israel and its
policies. As we have observed, a recent development in this direction is the establishment of "young leadership", which, in addition
to facilitating the recruitment of wealthy
potential contributors, can also serve as a
framework for the creation of the future leadership of the campaign as well as of the
communities. Most of the efforts in this
sphere are directed at young people familiar
with and ready to conform to the traditional
established Jewish communal institutions.
4. Efforts have been made to develop and introduce new techniques for fundraising which can
be characterized as a tendency towards a more
aggressive and personal approach to fundraising. While in the past funds were raised
mainly at large meetings, the tendency today
is to raise money through face-to-face interaction and soliciting. Accordingly, a "tax"
based on reliable knowledge of the potential
donors' means is fixed and aggressively "imposed" on the contributor in the course of the
personal interviews.
5. When the means of persuasion fail and one is
confronted with a refusal on the part of a
potential contributor, pressures are sometimes
exerted. These may be very subtle, for example, through the rules of acceptance for new
members to Jewish clubs and the denial of
communal services. The pressures are directed
at emotional and personal factors as well as
at social and business weak points. There is
a danger, however, that such measures--which
of course deviate from "pure" voluntary fund-
raising--may elicit negative reactions from
potential donors who may entirely refuse to
participate in Jewish affairs.

Specific Problems Confronting the UJA
and Keren Hayesod

The UJA is now confronted by a number of issues
that might jeopardize its operations in the future.
The most critical are those connected to recruitment and allocation of available funds. The UJA
has experienced great difficulties in recruiting
volunteers for the implementation of the campaigns,
"big givers" for maintaining the given levels of
its income, and young leaders to replace the old
guard. Nobody foresees a dramatic positive change
in this respect in the near future. The UJA is
also confronted with a dilemma in regard to the
allocation of the available resources for domestic
and overseas needs. The dilemma has emerged as a
result of the worsening situation of local communities. This in turn caused a series of decisions
to direct more resources to local needs, and hence
less to Israel. If the present trend continues,
then the UJA leaders and professionals should expect mounting Israeli pressure to reverse their
decisions. Failure to respond to Israeli pressure
may create a crisis within the organization and
with Israel. Any solution of such a major crisis
would entail high domestic costs (Sheffer 1981).
Recently, in a closed seminar attended by its
professionals from all over the world, Keren Hayesod initiated a stock-taking of its activities
and performance. The participants in this seminar
delineated the common general problems facing the
organization. The list includes the following
"factors influencing the current situation: a considerable decrease in the number of volunteers as a
result of wider assimilation, weaker inclinations
to volunteer, and deterioration of fundamental
values and of the Zionist ideology; problems in
Jewish identification with Israel in the wake of
the war in Lebanon; and a change in the orientation
of the communities.[1] The communities are directing
their efforts to solve their own problems and
therefore they allocate more money for the solution
of these problems; the peace treaty with Egypt has
created an image that basically Israel's defence
problems have been solved and thus there is no
immediate need to increase the allocation for Israel; the natural process of the aging of lay
leaders and volunteers reduces the efficacy of the
organization; the deterioration of the campaign
committees; the inability of young people to find

their place in the system; the worsening economic situation in the West; the feeling that Israeli economic and social problems are insoluble in the near future; the tendency towards earmarked contributions; a growing and tougher competition among the various fundraising organizations." Special emphasis has been placed on the deterioration in the number of volunteers. The figures for 1982 are shown in table 7.

Table 7

Estimated Numbers of Volunteers in Keren Hayesod

Countries	Volunteers	Young Leaders	Women
English Speaking	4020	1140	2620
Europe	2200	230	385
Latin America	1200	580	500
Sub Total	7420	1950	3505

Total: 12,875

The participants analyzed the situation in Argentina (Keren Hayesod, n.d.). While they welcomed the legitimization of CUJA and its activities as well as the fact that the donations there are tax deductible, they attributed the difficulties in raising money to social pressures, political and economic instability, and spiraling inflation. The main result in Argentina is a diminishing number of contributors—16.7 percent out of all Jewish families. This is the lowest in Latin America. Furthermore, the situation regarding volunteers is also critical—there are only 250 in the large Jewish community. Consequently, Argentina has been defined as a crisis country and "was selected as a target country for campaign reorganization and endeavors to recruit new workers and leadership."
    Because of the inherent political instability in the host country and the relatively weak campaigns, South Africa has also been selected as a target country for reorganization. Keren Hayesod leaders felt that there is a great untapped potential for fundraising there. High hopes are placed on the recruitment of wealthy and active individuals to promote the campaign.
    The main difficulties in France are the demographic changes which have occurred in the wake of the influx of Jews from North Africa. The absorp-

tion and integration of these Sephardic Jews neces-
sitated an allocation of great resources. Since
Keren Hayesod deals now with both local and overseas needs and because of the stiff competition
with parallel organizations, it has been felt that
the income would be further diminished in the future. Keren Hayesod leaders expressed their hope
that revival would start with greater commitment to
fundraising coming from the Zionists in this country who until now concentrated on political activities.
    In Great Britain there are no inherent diffi-
culties. Donation is subject to the covenant system of tax rebates (to the extent of 30 percent),
the organization is strong, and there is a long
tradition of charity and fundraising. Therefore
the participants felt that the main problem is the
lack of adequate campaign themes. It seems that
behind this understatement there is a great deal of
criticism of Israeli behavior. Also in Britain
there is an acute shrinkage of the number of
donors. (During 1981 they lost 3200 donors.)
Since 8 percent of the donors contribute 83 percent
of the total income in the annual campaigns, the
inevitable decision was to concentrate their efforts on the recruitment of new "big givers."

Fluctuations in Fundraising for Israel

Table 8 and the graph on page 287 sum up the UJA
receipts (on a cash basis) from 1939 to 1982. From
these data, it is clear that increases occurred as
a result of events connected with Israel's security, and that the rate of increase stabilized on a
new level when Israel's security situation was not
in crisis. Therefore, the increase in the rate of
the income did not stem from planned action, but
rather from other factors. It is evident that
difficult economic conditions in Israel (such as
those of 1964-67) did not produce substantial increases in fundraising.
    Let us now examine the stabilization of income
following a crisis. According to UJA and Keren
Hayesod leaders, they worked hard during these
periods to maintain the rate of income received
immediately after a crisis in the Middle East.
Stabilization should be attributed more to "harping
on the same string"--Israel's defense situation--
and less to professionalization and the more "rational" approach. The levels of personal donations

Table 8
UJA Receipts and % of Annual Change, 1939–1982
(on a cash basis)

Year	Income (in million dollars)	Percent Change
1939	11.5	
1940	11.4	-0.1
1941	13.1	+14.9
1942	13.7	+4.5
1943	16.5	+20.4
1944	16.0	-0.3
1945	32.8	+100.0
1946	77.8	+137.2
1947	110.5	+42.0
1948	145.3	+33.3
1949	111.4	-24.4
1950	89.0	-20.1
1951	80.0	-10.1
1952	69.0	-12.7
1953	63.0	-9.9
1954	48.6	-22.9
1955	58.8	+21.0
1956	70.6	+20.0
1957	73.0	+3.4
1958	55.7	-23.7
1959	68.3	+22.9
1960	60.2	-11.9
1961	62.7	+4.1
1962	63.7	+1.8
1963	60.3	-5.4
1964	60.6	+0.5
1965	61.5	+1.5
1966	61.5	--
1967	233.8	+280.2
1968	122.4	-47.6
1969	150.0	+22.5
1970	176.5	+19.0
1971	212.2	+18.9
1972	230.5	+8.6
1973	564.0	+114.7
1974	222.0	-60.7
1975	193.0	-10.5
1976	228.0	+11.0
1977	222.0	-2.6
1978	225.0	+1.3
1979	224.0	-0.4
1980	214.0	-4.0
1981	232.0	+8.0
1982	255.0	+9.9

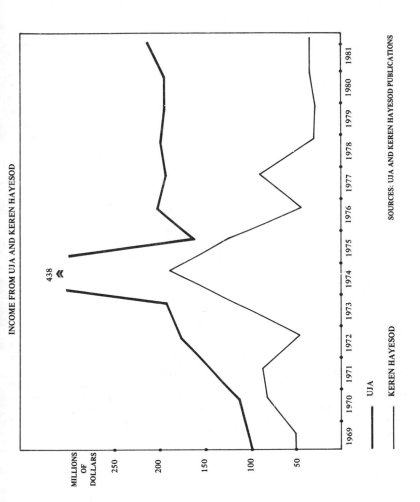

INCOME FROM UJA AND KEREN HAYESOD

MILLIONS OF DOLLARS

250
200
150
100
50

1969 1970 1971 1972 1973 1974 1975 1976 1977 1978 1979 1980 1981

438 «

UJA

KEREN HAYESOD

SOURCES: UJA AND KEREN HAYESOD PUBLICATIONS

depend to a very great extent on the economic situation prevailing in a certain country. This is especially pertinent in Argentina, South Africa, France and Great Britain.

On the basis of interviews with contributors, it seems that donors who have once decided to deduct their contributions from their income tax returns, will continue doing so. This is also a factor contributing to stabilization. Those who contribute for the first time during crises usually continue to contribute once the crisis has passed and deduct the contribution when declaring their income.

Thus, only in part can one attribute a stabilized increased level of income to the work of the institutions. They contribute to stabilization as follows: as a result of an impressive increase in receipts, new donors are added to the funds lists. For example, in France prior to the 1967 War, there were some 22,000 donors, about 16,000 contributing to the "Fonds Social" and 12,000 to Keren Hayesod. After the war, the number of donors was 80,000; but since some of the donors contributed to a number of funds, the net number of contributors in 1968 was about 32,000, a 50% increase. In such a situation the professionals can enlarge the base of activity by enlarging and updating the personal card index. But it is clear that stabilization occurs mainly as a result of the extended **amount** of donations rather than from an increase in the actual **number** of donors. Table 9, for example, illustrates the situation in France between the 1967 and 1973 wars. In other words, despite the 1972 drop, the general trend to donate increased, whereas the number of donors decreased.

Table 9

Year	Number of Donors		Amount	
1968		31,787		26.7 million Fr.
1969	(+)	39,018	(+)	33.1 million Fr.
1970	(-)	37,613	(+)	41.0 million Fr.
1971	(-)	35,401	(+)	49.1 million Fr.
1972	(-)	33,304	(-)	45.1 million Fr.

(+) = increase; (-) = decrease

Even if there are certain signs of change in this sphere, the inclination is still to neglect "smaller" contributors. For instance, 8 percent of the American contributors (those who give more than $1,000) are responsible for 77 percent of the total. In 1967, 5 percent of the donors in New York contributed 80 percent of the total. The situation in France is similar. There, 3.5 percent to 4.5 percent of the donors (those who contribute more than 5,000 Fr.) contributed between 65 percent and 70 percent of the total funds collected.

Thus, effort is focused on the "big" donors. Many individuals involved in fundraising contend that the greatest failure of the organizations is the minimal effort expended on "small" donors. Of course, concentrated effort directed towards big contributors means that the professionals can enlarge the scope of donations immediately and significantly, or at least maintain a given level. This is also the reason for the "aggressive" methods and for the new "professional" approach. The guiding idea is that concentrating on a relatively small and defined group, together with the application of adequate pressure based on up-to-date, accurate information, will ensure the success of fundraising. Theoretically, this should have supplemented the basic view of Keren Hayesod which regards donations as a self-imposed tax. Unfortunately, however, concentrating on a certain group does not serve to persuade the Jewish public that contributions are in effect a self-imposed tax.

The size of Jewish communities and their regional dispersal have direct effects on the rate of contributions. For example, if we compare the situation in the United States as a whole to that of New York, we find that in New York, with a population of 2,400,000 Jews, $75 million were raised in 1972 ($25 per Jew), whereas the estimated 3,400,000 Jews who live elsewhere in the United States contributed more than $100 per Jew. The same phenomenon occurs in other Jewish communities. The smaller and less dispersed the Jewish community, the larger the average rate of contributions per individual.

In many countries, a close connection exists between Jewish education and fundraising. The larger the scope of Jewish education, the stronger the inclination to contribute to Jewish funds. For instance, in Antwerp 90 percent of Jewish children received Jewish education in the sixties; in Mexico 85 percent in the sixties and 65 percent to 75

percent in the seventies, and in Chile, 60 percent.
These were countries with a high rate of per capital contribution to Jewish funds. On the other
hand, only 16 percent of Jewish children in England
and 10 percent in France received Jewish education
in the sixties. In the United States, however, in
communities where Jewish education is on the increase, the inclination is to set aside larger sums
of money for this purpose, at the expense of the
allocation for Israel's needs.

For the purpose of examining the connection
between Zionist activities and fundraising, one
indicator for Zionist activity, Jewish immigration,
and its relation to fundraising has been examined.
It turns out that there is a low correlation between periods which are marked by an increase in
immigration and those which are marked by an increase in income from fundraising activities. On
the contrary, there was, for instance, an increase
of immigration from the affluent countries (especially the United States) between 1968 and 1971.
During the same period, income was on the decrease
and then stabilized. On the other hand, since 1972
immigration has decreased while income has increased. This subject, however, requires a further
systematic and deep examination since Diaspora Jews
were not "required" to identify themselves with
Israel by immigrating to Israel; consequently, the
view of "Zionism through contributions" has become
increasingly dominant. The professionals, in fact,
rather than objecting to this view, are inclined to
use it and encourage it. They support methods
which seem more profitable for their organizations,
that is, they preserve the ratio of income and
thereby their professional pride and prestige.

The Autonomy of Jewish Communities in Fundraising

Extensive fundraising for Israel is conducted in
permanent, relatively affluent, highly organized
Jewish communities. According to any financial
criterion these fundraising endeavors are amazing
success stories. But when observed more closely
the social, political and organizational problems
involved become evident.

The basic features of the structure of fundraising for Israel were shaped by the Zionist movement in Western Europe and the US. When these
organizations were established they were merely an
addition to existing fundraising organizations for

other purposes. Therefore their structures and procedures were designed in view of communal conditions and needs. Hence the UJA reflects the structure of the American Jewish community and Keren Hayesod reflects the conditions in the other communities. Hence, Israel has "inherited" fully developed organizations with established practices. The only major structural change that has been introduced since the establishment of the State of Israel--and mainly as a result of its growing financial needs--is a high degree of professionalization. This means the use of aggressive methods for fundraising and the employment and reliance on full-time professionals.

The organization's performance in financial terms, however, is a function of the specific structure of each community, the levels of Jewish education, long-term involvement in Jewish affairs, and the given level of conflict in the Middle East. These are also indications about the relative autonomy in which fundraising develops.

There is cross-fertilization among the various communities in this sphere. But, by virtue of its size, well-established practices and reputation, the UJA leads in shaping new techniques and their introduction to the entire system. The contacts between UJA and Keren Hayesod are, however, mediated by their respective headquarters. And here it should be remembered that these are dominated by the Jewish Agency in which Israel and the American Jewish community play the major roles. Thus, there exists a cross-national network which is loosely coordinated and controlled by two centers. But this is balanced by other factors.

Although pro-Israeli sentiments serve as the main motivation for donation especially during periods of crisis and tension in the Middle East, and despite the fact that Israel has obtained a dominant position in the Jewish Agency, it can not fully control the development of the organizations, or determine their decisions concerning the allocation of money for various goals. This explains the reversal in the ratio of allocation for Israel and local needs.

The fundraising organizations also show a remarkable degree of autonomy in their relations with host governments and other communal organizations. They are so adaptable that they found ways to survive during the most difficult periods in Argentina and South Africa. The main reason for the high level of their ability to survive is the decision to provide money both for local and overseas needs. Thus, it is extremely difficult for any host government to stop their activities. In many of its aspects Jewish fundraising for Israel is politicized. Its lay leaders form in fact the established political leadership of the local community, or they are the aspiring young leaders. Intensive activity in these organizations is regarded as an essential step toward senior political positions on the local Jewish level or the national political level. Through their activities in these organizations, whether willingly or unwillingly, these leaders become involved in the endless process of shaping the host country's foreign policies. Furthermore, the planning of annual campaigns, their implementation, and especially the allocation of the money are parts of a continuous political process which is conducted through highly complex networks of communication. And in order to ensure their ability to continue with their missions the leaders are engaged in open and informal dialogues with the most important sectors of the host country and Israel.

And finally, the new internal problems confronting the Jewish communities in the diaspora (i.e., assimilation, aging, new dispersal, and the emergence of a new generation) on the one hand, and the growing image that Israel is militarily strong enough and that it is pursuing wrong foreign and domestic policies on the other hand, only enhance the autonomy of the Jewish communities in this sphere.

Note

1 Interviews with senior officals in Keren Hayesod main offices, conducted during February 1982.

References

Armstrong, J. A. 1976. Mobilized and Proletariat Diasporas. **APSR** 70, (June).

Bensimon, D. 1982. La Communaute Juives de France. In **Handbook of European Jewish Communities,** ed. E. Stock. Tel Aviv: Turtledove Press.

Bloom, M. 1982. The Missing Half Billion--On the UJA and its Future. **Tefuzot Israel** 20, (Spring).

Cohen, S. M. 1980. Trends in Jewish Philanthropy. **American Jewish Yearbook,** vol. 80, pp. 21-51.

Elazar, D. 1976. **Community and Polity, The Organizational Dynamics of American Jewry.** Philadelphia: The Jewish Publication Society of America.

Frankel, A. 1981. On British Jewry Today. **Tefuzot Israel** 19, no. 1 (Spring): 79-86.

Goldin, Milton. 1978. **Why They Give? American Jews and Their Philanthropies.** NY: Macmillan Publishing Co.

Keren Hayesod. n.d. The World of Keren Hayesod. Proceedings of Keren Hayesod Professionals Seminar, Jerusalem, September.

Manor, Y. and G. Sheffer. 1975. Problems in the Activities of the UJA and Recommendations for Their Change. Jerusalem: The Jerusalem Group for National Planning, The Jerusalem Van Leer Foundation.

-----. 1977. L'United Jewish Appeal' au la metamorphose du don. **Reveu Francaise du Sociologie** 18: 3-24.

-----. 1979. Fundraising: Money is Not Enough. In **Can Planning Replace Politics? The Israeli Case,** ed. R. Bilski et al. The Hague: Martinus Nijohff.

Maslow, W. The Structure and Function of American Jewish Community. **Tefuzot Israel** 13,(April-June): 5-44.

Schmeltz, U. O. and S. Della Pergola. 1982. World Jewish Population. **American Jewish Yearbook,** vol. 82, pp. 272-90.

Sheffer, G. 1981. The UJA Contributions to Israel. In **The Levi Eshkol Institute, A Study Day 1979.** Jerusalem: The Magnes Press.

Shimoni, G. 1980. **Jews and Zionism, the South African Experience, 1910-1967.** Oxford: Oxford University Press.

DIASPORAS AND COMMUNAL CONFLICTS IN DIVIDED SOCIETIES: THE CASE OF PALESTINE UNDER THE BRITISH MANDATE

Dan Horowitz

Trans-State Links and Intrastate Conflicts

Socially and politically distinctive diasporas create, by their very existence, noncongruent boundaries of state and community. As there are many such situations, there are few nation-states among modern polities (Connor 1972). However, diasporas are not the only source of intrastate communal divisions. The implications of the diaspora phenomena for communal conflicts are not necessarily confined to the host countries. In cases of twofold noncongruent boundaries of state and community, such as mandatory Palestine and Cyprus, where the diaspora's homeland is also divided into ethnic communities, the communal affiliation that cuts across state boundaries might have an impact also on communal relations in the homeland country.

This paper deals with the role of diasporas in conflicts rooted in communal divisions in the particular context of Palestine under the British mandate. The questions raised in the paper, however, have implications relevant to other cases as well.

Diasporas may relate to communal conflict and communal divisions in several ways:

1. A diaspora may be a party to a communal conflict due to its self-perception as an extension of the homeland. This category may be subdivided into diasporas struggling for territorial changes and diasporas struggling for the annexation of their present land of residence as a whole to the homeland. Irredentist aspirations of the first kind were common in Europe in the post-World War I period, particularly with the German minorities in Czecho-

slovakia and Poland, whose aspirations were among the causes of World War II. Irredentist aspirations of the second kind were the causes of the civil war in Northern Ireland. In Cyprus, Greek aspirations for **Enosis** (i.e., annexation to Greece) conflicted with Turkish aspirations for partition. However, none of these cases represents an undisputed case of a diaspora situation as each conflict was the outcome of aspirations to terminate the conditions which permitted the diaspora to exist.

2. A diaspora may also be a party to a communal conflict in the host country. The Chinese in Malaysia and the Palestinians in Lebanon were struggling for a dominant position in the host country rather than for unity with the homeland (in the first case there is no common border with the homeland, while in the second the homeland does not exist as an independent sovereign state).

3. A diaspora may provide resources and political support to a homeland community in a homeland country which is an arena for a political struggle between hostile ethnic communities. This was the situation of the Jewish diaspora regarding the Jewish-Arab communal conflict in Palestine (Horowitz 1957; Halevi and Klinov-Malul 1968).

This is also the role played by the Irish in the United States concerning the struggle in Northern Ireland, and in a way by the Palestinian refugee communities concerning the communal division resulting from the Israeli occupation of the West Bank and the Gaza Strip in 1967.

Looking at communal conflicts in divided societies (Nordlinger 1972; Lustick 1979), the most significant question is not whether the community party to a potential or actual communal conflict is an indigenous or diaspora community, but rather what is the role played by the cross-state link in the context of the intrastate and intercommunity relations. The primary concern of students of communal relations and communal conflict is therefore the impact of the trans-state link on the intrastate division. Hence, for example, in the Cyprus conflict the Greek and Turkish states played a role parallel to that of the Jewish diaspora in the Jewish-Arab struggle in Palestine under the British mandate. In Palestine the Jews relied on a diaspora for material and moral support while the Arabs, for their part, relied on the neighboring Arab countries whose role in the conflict can thus be described as a quasi-diaspora one. As this paper focuses on communal relations and communal conflict, for our purposes the distinction between "diasporas," and other forms of cross-state communal affiliations can, to a considerable extent, be ignored. However, the role of diasporas will be examined with reference to a conceptual framework developed for a previous study of the political implications of communal division in four deeply divided societies: Cyprus (Stephen 1967; Crashaw, Foley and Scotie 1975; Foley 1964; Salih 1978; Ehrlich 1974; and Stephens 1966), Northern Ireland (Rose 1976, 1970, 1971; Lijphart 1975; Bonito and Coster 1972, 1971; Foley 1962; Kane 1971; Hockey 1973; and Heslinger 1962), Lebanon (Binder 1966; Crow 1962; Dekmejian 1975, 1978; Hurewitz 1963; Hourani 1966; and Rondot 1966), and Mandatory Palestine. In this framework the latter case will be examined as an example of the crucial role that links with the diaspora may play in deciding the features and outcome of a communal conflict (Eisenstadt 1967).

Dual Authority and Conflict in Divided Societies

Common sense as well as theoretical considerations suggest that a propensity for communal conflict is inherent in divisions between politically mobilized communities sharing the same political-territorial system. The noncongruent boundaries of community and state tend to create problems of legitimation of government which lead, in deeply divided societies, to the emergence of communal conflict from systems of dual authority (Nordlinger 1972; Connor 1972; and Horowitz 1982).

A dual authority political system can be described as "a system of government consisting of at least two population groups possessing primordial communal identities that determine their respective political aspirations." Implied in this definition are: the noncongruent boundaries of community and state (a systemic dimension); the noncongruence of citizenship and communal affiliations as determinants of national identity (an individual dimension); the coexistence of an authority exclusive to the community and an "inclusive" state system shared by both communities (an institutional dimension); and divergent political aspirations (a value-orientation dimension).

The propensity for communal conflict in such systems is a consequence of the simultaneous attachment of individuals and groups to two centers of authority--state and the community--each of which derives its legitimacy from a different source. In divided political systems, individuals and groups may thus be simultaneously attached to two or more centers of authority (Horowitz 1982, pp. 331-32). The sphere of inspiration of each center can be conceived as a "field" of authority. Two main assumptions are at the root of this conception: (1) that the individuals and groups composing a society may exhibit different degrees of attachment to the center in the sense that they do not respond to the same degree to the authority of the center; and (2) that individuals, groups, and even societies at large may be attached to more than one center, thus creating overlapping "fields of authority" that are characteristic of all non-nation-states.

Responsiveness to communal authority may thus play a role in the context of intercommunity relations even where it is not sanctioned by the formal constitutional framework of the state authority system. The state center is comprised of those institutions and organizations that carry out the common political functions of the two communities. Therefore its center may be called "the inclusive center." The function of the inclusive center tends to be primarily instrumental (Parsons 1952, pp. 68-77).

The communal centers, on the other hand, derive their legitimacy from the primary allegiance of the communities' members and may thus be called "the primary centers" of the respective communities (Greetz 1963, pp. 105-57; Alter 1977, pp. 300-2, 335). On the symbolic level a primary center consists of the symbols that epitomize the core of the community's identity, be they ethnic, linguistic, or religious. On the structural level the primary center comprises all institutions and organizations that shape, maintain, and disseminate these symbols and values, thus providing for political mobilization based on affinity to the community.

Overlapping boundaries of state and community are an essential quality of the nation-state as an ideal type in the Weberian sense. Only in such a system are "national" in the sense of "nationality"

and "national" in the sense of "nationalism" one.[1]
In non-nation-state polities, state boundaries and
communal boundaries diverge. The boundaries of the
state are defined in terms of territory and citizenship which are not applicable to an ethno-
national community.[2] The community boundaries
cannot be defined easily as they reflect voluntary
affiliation to a collectivity rooted in primordial
sentiments. Communal consensus in divided societies is often a more powerful source of authority
than the constitutionally sanctioned sovereign
status of the state. The state's center of authority is the more institutionalized while the primary
allegiance of the individuals is more likely to be
given to the communal center. Thus, the status of
the "citizen" in the state is derived from the
system, while in the community the status of the
system is derived from the individual's commitment.
However, the state system cannot function without a
degree of legitimation by its citizens and such
legitimation is not received unless it is sustained
by communal identification. In this respect the
state's legitimacy in deeply divided societies is
conditional (Mischal 1978, pp. 12-13, 22-23, 47-
61). The state apparatus thus functions under a
constant threat of withdrawal of legitimacy by one
of the sectors of the population which might result
in a breakdown of the system.

Under these conditions, the normative basis of
the common state system tends to be unstable.
Since the legitimization of the common institutions
is derived from primary identification with the
constituent communities, the legitimacy accorded to
the polity by the population is often conditional
and may be perceived as temporary. Constituent
communities often aspire for changes in their position vis-à-vis rival communities which would eliminate the restrictions on self-determination that
result from the need to accept the plurality of the
system.

Conditional legitimation, a high degree of
internal autonomy of each community, a low normative status of the common institutions, and frequently the inability of the government to secure
monopolistic control of the means of violence in a
society, introduce into the system elements that
can be described as analogous in many respects to
international relations, rather than to relations
within an integrated nation-state.[3] This fragility
of the system implies a relatively high probability

of breakdown which may lead to communal conflict involving the exercise of violence.

The conditions which make dual authority systems so vulnerable to the effects of communal division are particularly manifested when one of the communal centers can rely on cross-state links for provision both of resources and political support.

In some cases of acute communal conflict the communal center is located abroad and may thus be referred to as a "diaspora center" of the homeland community. This is for example the situation with regard to the Palestinians in the West Bank since 1967. The diaspora center differs from a "government in exile" in two respects: (1) it represents one community and not the whole population of the homeland; and (2) it is associated with a diaspora which provides it with political and financial backing.

However, diasporas may have an influence on communal polities in the homeland even when the communal center is not located in the diaspora. In Palestine under the British mandate, for example, the link between the Jewish community and the Jewish diaspora played a central role both in the development of the political institutions of the Jewish community and in the outcome of the Arab-Jewish conflict.

The case of Palestine under the British mandate is unique in many respects. Nevertheless, it provides an example worth studying of a conflict between two communities whose outcome was decided by the capability of one of the rival communities to grow and accumulate power due to its association with a diaspora. In this respect the Jewish community of Palestine may serve as an example of a community which succeeded to utilize effectively resources originating in a diaspora in an acute conflict with a rival community (Horowitz 1957, pp. 65-68; Halevi and Klinov-Malul 1968, pp. 18-39).

Palestine Under the Mandate

The Jewish community in Palestine is identifiable in ethno-national, religious and linguistic terms, which overlap in this case. However, there is still ambiguity regarding the boundaries of the community. On the one hand one may distinguish between the "Yishuv" and the "Organized Yishuv." The Yishuv is the Jewish community in Palestine according to an inclusive definition which ignores the questions of consciousness and commitment. The term Organized Yishuv, on the other hand, relates only to those Jews living in Palestine who accepted the authority of the institutionalized political center of the collectivity and abided by certain rules of the political game upheld by a broad community consensus. The Organized Yishuv was therefore an institutionalized socio-political entity (Bernstein 1934) which, in spite of being based essentially on voluntary affiliation, developed quasi-state features as well as a common set of symbols rooted in the Zionist version of Jewish nationalism.

As a consequence of these characteristics of the Organized Yishuv, one sector--the ultra-orthodox elements of the so-called "Old Yishuv"-- had never been affiliated with the Organized Yishuv (Friedman 1978, pp. 129-45), while another sector--the Revisionist movement in Zionism-- refused to abide by the rules of the game and to comply with the communal center's institutionalized authority (Schechtman 1956; Lubotzky 1946). While certain sectors of the community did not participate in its institutionalized quasi-state system, there were formal as well as informal channels for active participation of Jews from the diaspora in the activities of the Organized Yishuv's central political institutions.

The ambiguity regarding the boundaries of the communal socio-political system was thus twofold: on the one hand, there was ambiguity about the attachment to the community of peripheral groups which seceded from the institutionalized communal organization,[4] and on the other hand, there was ambiguity due to the involvement of the diaspora in the life of the community. This involvement embraced the provision of manpower, and financial and political support, as well as participation in communal political processes.

Indeed, both parties to the conflict in Palestine under the British mandate relied on cross-state ethno-national ties for the provision of resources for the conduct of the conflict. Moreover, for Jews and Arabs alike, the cross-national ties implied ambiguity regarding ethno-national identity and the boundaries of the community.

The ambiguity in the Arab community concerned the meaning of "Palestinian identity" in the framework of "Arab identity." The issue was further complicated after the 1948 war when the West Bank was annexed to Jordan--thus adding a third component of national identity. The Arab countries surrounding Palestine were by no means a diaspora of the Palestinian Arabs. However, in the context of the Arab-Jewish struggle over the domination in Palestine, the role they played was parallel to the role played by the Jewish diaspora with regard to the Jewish community. In other words, in providing financial, political and, in 1936-39 and 1948, military support to the Arab community, the neighboring Arab countries played a quasi-diaspora role without ever being considered a diaspora (Porath 1977, pp. 238-58, Sheffer 1974).

On the Jewish side, it was not the status of the diaspora which was open to question, but rather that of the homeland community. It was a rare case of a community created by immigration from the diaspora instead of vice versa as in most cases of diaspora-homeland community relations. The Jewish community in Palestine was from its inception a community of immigrants and it continued to grow by immigration. Consequently the demographic ratio of population in Palestine continuously changed in favour of the Jews, who thus threatened to deprive the Arabs of their status as the majority community (see table 1).

Table 1

Population Increase 1922-1945

	Jewish Population	Non-Jewish Population	Total Population
1922	83,790	668,258	752,048
1945	554,329	1,255,708	1,810,037
% Growth 1922-45	569%	87%	140%

Calculated on the basis of Gertz, pp. 46-97.

As a result of this high rate of increase, the percentage of Jews in the total population grew from 11.2 percent in 1922 to 16.9 percent in 1931, 27.9 percent in 1939, and 33.2 percent in 1947 (Halevi and Klinov-Malul 1968, 1-15).

The need of the Jewish community for a continuous inflow of manpower and capital and for political support from the diaspora somewhat blur-

301

red the boundary between the community and the diaspora, rendering it permeable rather than integral.[5] This permeability of the boundaries between the Jewish community in Palestine and the Jewish diaspora has been demonstrated institutionally in the status of the Jewish Agency for Palestine--a corporate body representing the interest of world Jewry in the development of the Jewish "national home in Palestine." This status was internationally recognized in the mandate over Palestine granted to Britain by the League of Nations in 1922 (see **Palestine Royal Commission** Report, Cmd. 5479, July 1937). This recognition was reinforced by the authorization of the Jewish Agency to allocate immigration certificates granted by the Mandatory Government according to the Agency's own order of priorities.

The Jewish Agency has also controlled most of the channels for inflow of Jewish "public" (as distinct from "private") capital from the diaspora for Palestine (Elizur 1939). Consequently, this institution became the more powerful of the two major national institutions--the Jewish Agency and the Knesset Israel--which played the role of the political center of the Jewish community in Palestine. The Jewish Agency's status is significant with regard to the question of the boundary between the homeland community and the diaspora because the Jewish Agency's executive bodies were elected by both Palestinian and diaspora representatives in the framework of the Zionist Congress. These Congresses were assembled once in two years after popular elections were held both in Palestine and the diaspora (with a double vote for residents of Palestine). In this respect, the "Jewish Agency for Palestine" differed from the National Council of Knesset Israel, which represented the Jewish community in Palestine in accordance with "The Religious Communities Act" enacted by the Mandatory Government. Knesset Israel was the recognized communal framework of the Jews living in Palestine and the National Council was its executive body. The National Council, however, lacked the authority and material resources to play as central a political role in Palestine as played by the Jewish Agency.

Thus, the combination of international and British recognition of the link between the diaspora and the "National Home" community, and the National Institutions' control of resources which originated in the diaspora, enabled the Organized

Yishuv to function as an authoritative quasi-state even in the absence of sovereignty (Connor 1972). At the same time, the link between the Yishuv and the diaspora facilitated the involvement of the organized diaspora (in particular, of the Zionist movement in the diaspora) in the affairs of the community. For certain purposes, like the mobilization of political support, the diaspora was perceived as an extension of the community while for other purposes (such as political decision making at certain periods) the Organized Yishuv was treated as an extension of the world Zionist movement.

In terms of the functioning of the Yishuv as a socio-political system, the link with the diaspora was complementary to the participation in the bicommunal political system of Palestine under the mandate. The input of resources from the diaspora made it possible for the Jewish community to maintain partial autonomy within the mandatory system --in matters such as education, health services and even "communal" security (the equivalent of national security in fully fledged nation-states).

In other words, the input from the diaspora extended the Yishuv's capability for collective action which was particularly significant in the context of the Arab-Jewish communal conflict. The inflow of additional resources, due to the links with the diaspora, compensated the Organized Yishuv for its lack of the coercive capability available to sovereign political systems, and allowed the political system of the Yishuv to develop a mode of operation based on allocation without extraction (Horowitz and Lissak 1977, chap. 7, pp. 167-84, chap. 9, pp. 222-27). The pool of available resources created in this manner was utilized to secure the continued expansion of the politically-oriented settlement effort; Jewish workers were employed although cheap Arab labor was available, the Yishuv maintained an independent educational system instead of utilizing the mandatory educational system as the Arabs did, land was purchased in spite of high prices and, above all, a policy of self-reliance in matters of communal security was adopted (Kimmerling 1982; Szeresevski 1968)--leading to an allocation of scarce resources for maintaining an underground communal armed organization of the Organized Yishuv.[6]

The input of manpower and capital resources from the diaspora facilitated both the political status of the Yishuv as a quasi-state system and its conduct in the communal struggle with the Arab community to achieve a dominant economic and political position in Palestine. The internal political organization of the Yishuv was effective not only because of consensus over some basic goals but also because of the capacity for allocation without extraction, which facilitated the adoption of a "non-zero-sum" perception of internal politics within the Yishuv. (Non-zero sum is a term borrowed from Gain Theory and used in the study of politics and international relations to describe situations in which the gain of one party is always the loss of another--such situations occur when the overall resources available for allocation are fixed). As long as there was no need for internal mobilization of financial resources and the system appeared to be continuously expanding due to external input, there was a strong incentive for political movements and parties in the Yishuv to participate in the coalitionist political system of the Organized Yishuv. The result of this situation was a development of a consociation-like style of internal politics based on bargaining and compromise among political movements and parties each of which had relative autonomy in cultivating its own subculture (Lijphart 1969; Daalder 1971; Macrae 1974; Guttman and Lissak 1977, pp. 171-72). Consequently, the intensity of internal conflict within the community was reduced to a level which did not endanger the capacity for unified action vis-à-vis the Arab minority, (Kimmerling 1976, 35-6). The political system of the Jewish community could not, however, be defined as a full fledged consociated system as the Yishuv was not a state system but rather a quasi-state based on authority without sovereignty. Its political regime can therefore be labelled quasi-consociated.

This degree of unity and level of political organization was not reached by the Arab community, which thus failed to utilize its relative advantages, such as demographic quantitative superiority, in the conflict. The aid from neighboring Arab countries did not match the aid for the Jewish community except, perhaps, in terms of political support. The external aid for the Arabs included some aid in manpower and equipment after the outbreak of the so-called "disturbances" in 1936-1938 and 1948, and a very limited inflow of financial resources which were made available to political groups and factions within the Arab community rather than to any representative communal institutions. The Jewish advantage over the Arabs in regard to the relative volume of inflow of resources had a considerable impact on the development and eventual outcome of the communal conflict. A basic condition for relative stability in relations among rival communities in divided societies is an unchanging balance of demographic, economic and political power. Any shift in the balance of power between the communities tends to upset the stability of the system.

The undermining of existing ratios of population, economic welfare, political representation, or paramilitary capabilities implies an improvement in the disposition of one community vis-à-vis a rival community (or rival communities) and is therefore apt to provoke a counteraction. Indeed, such a shift in the balance of power is likely to result in the intensification of conflictual tendencies. The awareness of such an effect of shifts in the balance of power accounts for the tendency for fixed proportional arrangements in representation in certain divided societies. However, the implementation of such arrangements is conditional upon the adoption of a defensive posture by the rival communities. Only as long as both communities are oriented toward the status quo can they try to neutralize the effects of demographic or economic changes arising as a consequence of differential rates of birth or economic growth. This was not the case of Palestine under the British mandate. The offensive anti-status quo orientation was inherent in the Jewish community. Indeed, demographic expansion through immigration was the raison d'être of the Jewish community as a collective. Hence, while in other divided societies the change in communal political aspirations follows the change in the demographic or economic balance of power, in the case of Palestine under the mandate the change in the balance of power was intentional and resulted from political aspirations. The tendency towards escalation of the conflict was thus inherent in the basic dispositions of the rival communities. The change in the balance of power was not a consequence of internal factors within Palestine but rather of the Jewish community's relations with the diaspora. These relations facilitated the inflow of manpower, through immigration, and material resources, through importation of capital (Horowitz 1982, pp. 117-22).

Between 1930 and 1937, 80,000,000 Palestine pounds (one Palestine pound was equivalent to one

pound sterling) were invested in Palestine (Horowitz 1957, p. 13). This investment was made possible by capital import. Between 1932 and 1937, for
example, Jewish investment amounted to 52,800,000
pounds and Jewish capital imports to 60,060,000
pounds, (Halevi and Klinov-Malul 1968, p. 22).
The legitimacy of the Jewish communal organization was also rooted in the internal commitment
and external (British and international) obligations to promote the development of a "Jewish National Home in Palestine." In these conditions, a
modus vivendi based on fixed ratios of political
representation or other agreed-upon constitutional
rules of the game was impossible (Rose 1976, pp.
217-45).

Since Arab expectations were based on the existing balance of power and Jewish expectations
were based on the potential for asymmetrical
growth, the propensity for intensification of the
conflict was inherent in the situation. The drive
for immigration from the diaspora and the availability of financial resources from abroad were
beyond the mandatory system's control. However,
the amount of immigration and the extent to which
imported capital could be utilized for territorial
expansion through land purchases were politically
controllable. The British authorities could, and
did, regulate the flow of immigration and in later
stages also the volume of land purchases.

This link between demographic and economic
developments, on the one hand, and political decisions, on the other, increased the propensity for
communal conflict inherent in ethno-national, religious and linguistic division. The only measure
available to the Arabs to check the development of
the Jewish National Home was the exercise of political pressure (including the use of violence) in
order to increase the cost for the British in
maintaining their obligation to the Jewish cause.
In other words, escalation of the conflict was a
potentially effective Arab measure to induce the
British Government to impose constraints on the
process of Jewish settlement in Palestine.

These conditions may account for the timing of
the outbreaks of the Arab "disturbances" which
could usually be interpreted as responses to an
acceleration in the pace of Jewish colonization
(Porath 1977; Shimoni 1947). But, ultimately, the
belated Arab response failed to check the development of the Jewish National Home. "The Arab Revolt" of 1936-1939 brought about a political diplo-

matic achievement for the Arabs--the 1939 "White Paper" of the British Government--but destroyed the political center of the Arab community. Since 1939, the political struggle for the Palestinian Arab cause has been conducted mainly from the capitals of independent and semi-independent Arab countries whose leaders became the spokesmen for the Palestinians as well as their main source of political inspiration. This process culminated in the 1948 War when the local Arab forces collapsed before the official end of the mandate on 14 May 1948, and were replaced on the battlefield by the regular armed forces of Jordan, Egypt, Syria, Iraq and Lebanon. Jordan and Egypt remained in control of those parts of Palestine that were not captured by the Israelis in the course of the 1948 war.

In the Jewish community, by contrast, the political influence of the diaspora on the community's political center diminished in spite of the Yishuv's continued dependence on the inflow of financial and human resources from the diaspora. Zionist policy making was transferred from London to Jerusalem by the 1930s. Political leaders from the Zionist labor movement, whose political power base was in Palestine, took over from delegates of the diaspora Zionists the main positions of power in the Jewish Agency executive. David Ben Gurion, the chairman of the executive in Jerusalem since 1935, gradually became the leading figure in Zionist politics in general, and in the politics of the Organized Yishuv in particular. By contrast, the president of the World Zionist Organization, Dr. Chaim Weizmann, whose office was located in London, lost much of his personal power. The trend known in Zionist history as Palestino-centrism thus prevailed and the diaspora, while increasing its financial and political support for the Yishuv, lost influence over the conduct of its domestic politics and external policy alike.

The inflow of resources from the diaspora strengthened not only the material infra-structure of the Yishuv but also its institutional framework (Horowitz 1957, pp. 119-20). This quasi-state framework gradually became more independent not only vis-à-vis the mandatory authorities and the Palestinian Arab community but also vis-à-vis the organized diaspora Jewry in general and its Zionist component in particular.

The contrasting developments in the Jewish and Arab communities eventually played a central role in determining the outcome of the struggle over

Palestine. When the withdrawal of British rule
created a power vacuum in Palestine the Jews had an
institutional infrastructure which could take control of the Jewish dominated areas while the Arabs
had to turn to their neighboring Arab countries in
order to save what they could of the Arab-dominated
parts of Palestine.

It is worth noting that the Palestinian Arabs
have learned a lesson regarding the potential role
of a communal organization located in the diaspora
in the struggle for the self-determination of the
homeland community. The Palestine Liberation Organization owes much of its political strategy to
the lessons drawn from the mandatory period when in
the absence of sovereignty the Jewish community
succeeded in building an authoritative center with
quasi-state (or state-in-the-making) features re-
lying on the diaspora as a resource base.

The conditions of the Palestinian struggle
against Israel, however, differ from the conditions
of the Jewish community's struggle against the Arab
community in Palestine. The difference is a consequence of the transformation of the Jewish community in Palestine into the State of Israel as well
as of the Israeli occupation of the West Bank and
Gaza Strip in 1967. As a result of these conditions, the PLO is a diaspora-based communal organization whose attempts to create a territorial infrastructure have resulted in conflicts within its
host Arab countries while the community it aspires
to represent remains effectively under Israeli
rule. The PLO has twice been deprived of its
"extraterritorial" infrastructure in Arab host
countries, in Jordan in 1970, and in Lebanon in
1982, and is thus not a quasi-government of a
quasi-state communal organization, but rather a
quasi-government-in-exile with a diaspora power
base. Therefore, although the results of the 1967
War reintroduced elements of intercommunity struggle into the Arab-Israeli interstate conflict, it
remained essentially an interstate conflict. However, the PLO, as one of the expressions of the
communal elements of the conflict, deserves a separate study which, among other things, will touch
upon the similarities and dissimilarities with the
Jewish community pre- and post-1948.

Conclusions

The characteristics of the Arab-Israeli communal
division under the British mandate in Palestine are

unique and therefore do not permit broadly applicable conclusions. Nevertheless, some developments in communal relations in Palestine may cast light on some similar situations. The case of Palestine under the British mandate is compatible with the following propositions whose applicability to other cases of divided societies deserves examination:

1. The propensity for communal conflict is inherent in communal divisions, particularly when ethno-national, religious and linguistic divisions overlap and thus reinforce one another.
2. Cross-state links of the respective communities with organized diasporas tend to assist communal integration by providing the home communities with financial and political resources, which facilitate the building and institutionalization of an authoritative communal center.
3. The inflow of resources from diasporas tends to intensify communal conflict as it is apt to upset the existing balance of economic, political and even para-military power among the communities. Moreover, an asymmetrical inflow may decide the outcome of communal conflict.
4. The most prominent resource in the context of communal conflict is population. Therefore, immigration from a diaspora to the homeland which changes the demographic ratio among the communities is instrumental to one community and a cause for escalation of the conflict for the other.
5. A control of resources from a diaspora may provide a communal political center with extended capabilities and authority in three contexts: vis-à-vis its own communal periphery; vis-à-vis a rival community (or rival communities); and vis-à-vis the institutionalized leadership of its own diaspora whose status relates to its links with the homeland community.
6. The link between a diaspora and a homeland community may strengthen the position of an institutionalized diaspora center vis-à-vis its own periphery by contributing to the legitimation of its authority and providing it with a sense of purpose.

The case of the Jewish diaspora and its links with the Jewish community in Palestine is unique.

It may, however, serve as a point of departure for formulating research questions in other case studies of communal conflicts in divided societies where one or more of the constituent communities maintains cross-state links with a mobilized diaspora.

Notes

1 The use of "nation" in this context implies cultural affinity as a fundamental component of national identity. This usage is European in origin and has much in common with the English term "people." It is thus the "nation-state" rather than the "nation" that implies independence, cohesion, political organization, autonomy and internal legitimacy. These are considered the characteristics of a full-fledged nation by exponents of the "national building" school. See Friedrich 1966, pp. 27-32; and Deutsch 1968, pp. 1-14.

2 The division of political systems into ethno-national, religious or linguistic communities tends to entail predominance of primordial "vertical" cleavages over stratificational "horizontal" cleavages. See Horowitz 1982, p. 329.

3 Mandatory Palestine is an example of this perception, see Horowitz 1982, p. 342.

4 The ideological cleavages which led to cessation were particularly salient in a society whose formation was inspired by ideology. See Horowitz and Lissak 1977, pp. 120-56; and Eisenstadt 1967, chap. 3.

5 These terms have been borrowed from the vocabulary of political-sociological studies of civil-military relations. See Luckham 1971, pp. 5-35.

6 Although communal armed organizations in divided societies are never legally recognized, the State has often to comply with their existence. In such circumstances the toleration of their existence becomes part of the rules of the game of intercommunal politics. There are even examples of state authorities aided by such organizations in the imposition of law and order in periods of violent disturbances.

7 The asymmetrical relations between the communities are reflected in the volume of their inputs in relations to each other. For data, see Szeresevski 1968, table 1; and also Metzer 1982.

References

Alter, D.A. 1977. **Introduction to Political Analysis.** Cambridge, MA: Winthrop Publishers.

Bernstein, M. 1934. **Self Government of the Jews in Palestine Since 1900.** Tel Aviv: Hapoel Hatzair.

Binder, L. 1966. Political Change in Lebanon. In **Politics in Lebanon,** ed. L. Binder. New York: J. Wiley and Sons.

Bonito, D. and C. Coster. 1971. **Ireland's English Question.** New York: Schocken Books.

------. 1972. **The Northern Ireland Problem,** 2d ed. London: Oxford University Press.

Connor, W. 1972. Nation Building and Nation Destroying. **World Politics** 24, no. 3 (April): 319-55.

Crashaw, N. **The Cyprus Revolt--An Account of the Struggle for Union with Greece.** London: Allen & Unwin.

Crow, R. 1962. Religious Sectarianism in the Lebanese Political System. **Journal of Politics** 24 (August): 498-520.

Daalder, H. 1971. On Building Consociational Nations: The Case of the Netherlands. **International Social Science Journal** 23, no. 3: 355-70.

Dekmejian, R. H. 1975. **Patterns of Political Leadership: Lebanon, Israel, Egypt.** Albany, NY.

------. 1978. Consociational Democracy in Crisis: The Case of Lebanon. **Comparative Politics** 10, no. 2: 251-65.

Deutsch, K. W. 1968. **Nationalism and Social Communication.** New York: J. Wiley and Sons.

Ehrlich, T. 1974. **Cyprus 1958-1967: International Crises and the Role of Law.** Oxford University Press.

Eisenstadt, S. N. 1967. **Israeli Society.** London: Weidenfeld and Nicolson.

Elizur, A. 1939. **Ha'Hon Ha'Leumi Be'Binyan H'Aretz** (National Capital in the Building of the Land). Jerusalem: The Central Bureau of the Jewish Foundation Fund.

Foley, C. 1962. **Ireland in Revolt.** London: Longman.

------. 1964. Legacy of Strife. In **Cyprus from Rebellion to Civil War.** Baltimore: Penguin.

Foley, C. and I.W. Scotie. 1975. **The Struggle for Cyprus.** Stanford: Hoover Institution Press.

Friedman, M. 1978. **Hevra ve'dat--Ha'orthodoxia, Ha'Lo Zionit B'Eretz Israel 1918-1936** (Society and Religion--The Non-Zionist Orthodox in Israel 1918-1936). Jerusalem: Yad Ben Zvi.

Friedrich, C. J. 1966. Nation Building. In **Nation Building.** New York: Atherton Press.

Gertz, ed. **Statistical Handbook of Mandatory Palestine 1947.** Jerusalem: Jewish Agency Department of Statistics.

Greetz, C. 1963. The Integrative Revolution. In **Old Societies-New States,** ed. C. Greetz. New York: The Free Press of Glencore.

Guttman, E. and M. Lissak, eds. 1977. **Ha'Marechet Ha'Politit Be'Israel** (The Political System in Israel). Tel Aviv: Am Oved.

Halevi, N. and R. Klinor-Malul. 1968. **The Economic Development of Israel.** New York: F. D. Praeger in Cooperation with the Bank of Israel.

Heslinger, Marcus. 1962. **The Irish Border as a Cultural Divide.** New York: Humanities Press.

Hockey, Thomas E. 1973. One People or Two? The Origins of Partition and the Prospects for the Reunification in Ireland. **Journal of International Affairs** 27, no. 2: 232-46.

Horowitz, D. and M. Lissak. 1977. **Origins of the Israeli Polity.** Chicago: Chicago University Press.

Horowitz, Dan. 1982. Dual Authority Politics. **Comparative Politics** (April).

Horowitz, David. 1957. **Kalkalat Israel** (The Israeli Economy). Tel Aviv: Masada.

Hourani, A. 1966. Lebanon: The Development of a Political Society. In **Politics in Lebanon,** ed. L. Binder. New York: J. Wiley and Sons.

Hurewitz, J. C. 1963. Lebanese Democracy in its International Setting. **Middle East Journal** 17 (Autumn): 487-506.

Kane, John. 1971. Civil Rights in Northern Ireland. **Review of Politics** 33, no. 1 (January).

Kimmerling, B. 1976. Nihul Hasichsuch, Ha'Jehudi-Aravi Ve'Tahaliche Binuy Ha'Uma Be'Tkufat Hamandat (The Conduct of the Jewish-Arab Conflict and the Process of Nation Building During the Mandatory Period). **State and Government** 9 (May): 35-56.

------. 1982. **Zionism and Economy--Sociological Exploration into a Case of Economic Development.** Cambridge, MA: Schenkman Publishing Co.

Lijphart, A. 1975. The Northern Ireland Problem:
Cases, Theories and Solutions. **British
Journal of Political Science** 5: 83-106.
-----. 1969. Consociational Democracy. **World
Politics** 21, no. 2: 207-50.
Lubotzky, B. 1946. **Ha'zahar ve'Betar** (The
Revisionist Zionist Organization and Betar).
Jerusalem: The Small Zionist Library.
Luckhan, A. K. 1971. A Comparative Typology of
Civil-Military Relations. **Government and
Opposition** 6, no. 1 (Winter): 5-35.
Lustick, I. 1979. Stability in Deeply Divided
Societies--Consociationalism Versus Control.
World Politics 31, (3 April): 325-44.
Macrae, K., ed. 1974. **Consociational Democracy.**
Toronto: McClelland and Stewart.
Metzer, J. 1982. **Technology, Labor and Growth in a
Dual Economy's Traditional Sector: Mandatory
Palestine, 1921-1936.** Jerusalem: The Maurice
Falk Institute for Economic Research in
Israel, January.
Mischal, Shaul. 1978. **West Bank-East Bank: The
Palestinians in Jordan 1949-1967.** New Haven:
Yale University Press.
Nordlinger, E. A. 1972. **Conflict Regulation in
Divided Societies.** Occasional Papers in In-
ternational Affairs No. 29 (January). Cam-
bridge: Harvard University Center for Interna-
tional Affairs.
Palestine Royal Commission Report. Cmd. 5479.
July 1937.
Parsons, Talcott. 1952. **The Social System.** London:
Tavistock Publications.
Porath, Y. 1977. **From Risks to Rebellion: The
Palestinian Arab National Movement 1929-1939.**
London: F. Cass.
Rondot, P. 1966. The Political Institutions of
Lebanese Democracy. In **Politics in Lebanon,**
ed. L. Binder. New York: J. Wiley and Sons.
Rose, Norman. 1976. **Mechkarim Be'Toldot Am Israel
v'Eretz Israel** (Studies in the History of the
People of Israel and the Land of Israel), eds.
B. Rose, A. Rapaport, A. Shochat and Y.
Schultzmiller. Haifa: Haifa University Press.
Rose, R. 1970. The Dynamics of Divided Regime.
Government and Opposition 5, no. 2 (Spring).
-----. 1971. **Governing Without Consensus.**
London: Faber and Faber.
-----. 1976. **Northern Ireland--A Time of Choice.**
London: Macmillan Press.

Salih, I. M. 1978. **Cyprus--The Impact of Diverse Nationalism on State.** Alabama: University of Alabama Press.

Schechtman, J. B. 1956. **The Vladimir Jabotinsky Story.** New York: T. Yoseloff.

Sheffer, Gabriel. 1974. The Involvement of Arab States in the Palestine Conflict and British-Arab Relationship Before World War II. **Asian and African Studies** 10, no. 1: 59-78.

Shimoni, D. 1947. **Arviyey Eretz-Israel** (The Arabs of Palestine). Tel Aviv: Am Oved.

Stephen, A. G. 1967. **Cyprus: Conflict and Conciliation (1954-1958).** Ohio: Ohio State University Press.

-----. 1973. **Cyprus: Reluctant Republic.** The Hague: Mouton & Co. N.V.

Stephens, R. 1966. **Cyprus: Place of Arms-Power Politics and Ethnic Conflict in the Eastern Mediterranean.** London: Pall Mall Press.

Szeresevski, R. 1968. **Essays in the Structure of the Jewish Economy in Palestine and Israel.** Jerusalem: The W. Falk Institute for Economics in Israel.

THE PALESTINIANS IN THE DIASPORA

Iliya Harik

The Main Problems

The Palestinian diaspora is of recent origin. It resulted from the sudden upheaval and dispersal of the Arab population that was living in mandated Palestine. Being natives of Palestine, their uprooting and dispersal to other Arab countries turned them into a bitter and frustrated community living in the hope of returning home. Return was not so straightforward though, for what was their home had given birth to a newly settled community of Jews, mostly of European origin. Their new state was adamantly opposed to the return of the Palestinian refugees, seeing in them a threat to the realization of the Zionist ideal of the establishment of Israel as a Jewish state.

The long struggle between native Arab Palestinians and Jewish settlers lasted for the duration of the British mandate, from 1922 to 1948, ending in the defeat of both the Palestinians and the Arab states who went to their aid. Hundreds of thousands of Palestinians escaped the war and were not allowed to return home. Estimates of the number of Palestinians who became refugees in 1948 vary from 700,000 to 900,000. The 1967 War between the Arab states and Israel created a new wave of Palestinian refugees, many displaced for the second time. This was due to the Israeli occupation of the West Bank and Gaza, the last remaining parts of mandated Palestine inhabited by Palestinians and not under Israeli rule.

At present, the total Palestinian population in the world is estimated to be over 4 million, with more than half a million living in Israel itself. Jordan has the largest group of Palestinians living anywhere in the world, over one

million, followed by the West Bank with an estimated population of over 800,000. The Gaza strip
and Lebanon have over 400,000 each. Kuwait has
become the sixth largest center of Palestinians
with nearly 300,000, followed by Syria, Saudi Arabia and the United States. Over a 100,000 Palestinians, mostly professionals and small businessmen, now live in the United States. It is those
Palestinians who were displaced from their original
homes in Palestine into areas outside the state of
Israel who constitute the subject of this paper.

While it is a simple matter to identify the
Palestinians, agreement on their status is not that
easy to achieve. They are a diaspora in that they
are a population that lives outside the bounds of
its ancestral home. But given the definition of
diaspora in this volume as "a minority ethnic group
of migrant origin in a host country, which maintains sentimental or material links with its land
of origin," the Palestinians do not qualify, for
several reasons. First, they are not by origin
immigrants but war refugees; second, they are not
always a minority, for in the Kingdom of Jordan
they constitute a majority of the population, while
in Gaza until 1967 they constituted the entire
population. Third, they are not ethnically distinct from the population of their host countries,
but are Arabs like them. Fourth, they do not
maintain material relations with their land of
origin, being on hostile terms with the state now
in that land. Indeed, this last factor is the
major exception to our definition of a diaspora
because since their original exodus of 1948, the
Palestinians have organized themselves into a political and military movement whose purpose is to
fight and undo what the state of Israel has done.

These considerations make it difficult to deal
with the Palestinians under the framework adopted
by this volume, for it seems that they fit more
accurately into the category of "non-state actors"
aiming to become a nation-state. With this in mind
we may proceed to discuss their impact on their
host countries and the role they play in international diplomacy.

A number of variables become significant when
trying to explain Palestinian relations with host
countries. The symbiosis between the diaspora and
its host, the nature of the host's political system, and the population ratio of the diaspora to
the host are considered here the main factors in-

fluencing the Palestinian diaspora. I shall pro-
pose a number of hypotheses to guide the inquiry.
My first hypothesis is that the major successes of the Palestinian diaspora can be attributed to the cultural symbiosis between the Palestinians and Arabs in their host countries. My
second hypothesis maintains that the larger the
ratio of Palestinians to the host population the
greater their impact on the host's state affairs;
and my third, that the greater the limits on political freedom in the host society, the less effective is the diaspora organization.

A corollary to this last hypothesis is that
the political leverage that accrued to the diaspora
organization from the idealization of its mission
by rank and file Arabs failed to alter the authoritarian systems of host countries. This was a hope
expressed by many Arabs who saw in the Palestinian
resistance movement a countervailing force to the
all-powerful governments of their lands. On the
contrary, the resistance proved to encourage li-
cense in less authoritarian systems and proved a
threat to their continued existence. Finally,
Israeli military superiority and its retaliatory
strategy based on holding the host state responsible for the behavior of the Palestinians living
under its jurisdiction contributed in a major way
to the desire and ability of the host authorities
to curtail hostile Palestinian activities against
Israel and to reduce the Palestinians' autonomy, if
not to eliminate their political organization altogether. The fact is that it was the Arab host
states that originally aided and abetted Palestinian resistance and later forced them to desist. In
three out of four border states, the Arab authorities stopped the resistance, and in the fourth,
Lebanon, the Israelis moved in militarily and accomplished the same objective in 1982, after their
pressure on Lebanese state policy failed to produce
the desired results. Before I proceed to discuss
these points I shall first summarize the history of
the Palestinian diaspora.

The History of the Palestinian Diaspora

The large waves of Palestinian refugees fleeing to
neighboring Arab countries in 1948 were hastily
accommodated in camps in Lebanon, Syria and Jordan.
The West Bank and Gaza, which were the only remaining Arab-controlled portions of mandated Palestine,

faced different fates. The West Bank was annexed to the Kingdom of Jordan and the Gaza strip was put under Egyptian administration. The Palestinians who moved from territories under Israeli control to these two areas were also accommodated in refugee camps. The traditional inhabitants of the West Bank were given Jordanian citizenship as were the rest of the Palestinians who found their way into Jordan.

Since the Palestinians in the Kingdom of Jordan constitute the largest single diaspora group, it would be safe to say that most Palestinian refugees found their citizenship problem solved. A few Palestinians succeeded in acquiring citizenship in other Arab countries. At any rate, the acquisition of citizenship by the Palestinians did not solve their identity problem, for the spark of Palestinian nationalism had been kindled in them and drove them with almost a blinding force.

Palestinians in refugee camps were cared for primarily by the United Nations Relief and Works Agency (UNRWA). They were given food rations, medical care and schooling. Educational progress made at UNRWA schools has had a major effect on the Palestinian political struggle and on the roles the Palestinians played in Arab countries, with large numbers of Palestinians being employed in education. Middle class Palestinians found employment in professional pursuits and in business with remarkable success, especially in countries such as Lebanon and some Gulf states, where they enjoyed economic freedom.

Though resistance activities never quite stopped, it was not until the late 1950s that the Palestinians started to take their affairs into their own hands by organizing guerrilla groups. It was not until 1968 that they achieved a high degree of political autonomy.

Fatah, the major resistance group, was established in 1959 and was encouraged by some Arab states, particularly Syria. From the start it was conservative in orientation, drew its leaders from middle class Palestinians and projected a mixed ideological blend of Palestinian and Arab nationalism. Its objective was to fight the Israelis and make Palestine an Arab Palestinian state. In the mid-1960s, Fatah developed the idea of a democratic secular state for Palestinians, and Jews who had been there in 1948. Article six of the Palestinian National Charter states: "The Jews who had normally resided in Palestine until the beginning of the Zionist invasion will be considered Palestinians."

The second major resistance movement started by Palestinians in the diaspora was the Popular Front for the Liberation of Palestine (PFLP), which emerged from the bosom of the Arab nationalist movement started in Beirut. Its objectives were similar to those of Fatah, but were more clearly Arab nationalist in orientation. Its Arab nationalist ideology and later Marxist development attracted non-Palestinian Arabs to its ranks and led to interference in domestic Arab affairs in host countries. They considered this a national right, and sometimes an operational necessity.

The third major Palestinian resistance movement was an offshoot of the PFLP, the Popular Democratic Front for the Liberation of Palestine (PDFLP). It was similar to the PFLP in every respect except that it was more radically Marxist and ideological.

In terms of numbers, Fatah was the strongest movement, followed by the PFLP and the PDFLP respectively. All three recruited among the refugee camps while their leadership at various levels comprised of urban, settled, middle-class Palestinians. All three groups valued their organizational autonomy and resisted fiercely the patronage of Arab states, while accepting financial and military aid from them. All three established links with international groups, especially with developing countries and their liberation movements. Ties with communist regimes were also established.

Other resistance movements also developed in the diaspora but lacked the autonomy of these three. Notable was the Sa'iqa organization which owed its existence to the Syrian government until 1980 when, for many reasons, it declined in strength.

Another active resistance group, the Arab Liberation Front, was basically a Ba'thi organization with no independence from the Iraqi government. Smaller groups existed but were not of much importance.

In 1964, prompted by Nasser, the Arab League proclaimed the creation of a single Palestinian resistance movement to serve as an organizational umbrella for all the resistance groups. That is how the Palestine Liberation Organization (PLO) came into being. It has a chairman, an executive committee and a national council, whose members are coopted under conditions of extensive consultation

involving the various guerrilla organizations,
trade unions, professional groups and independent
leaders. In the first phase of its existence, the
organization was under Egyptian tutelage. In 1967
and subsequent to the demise of Nasser, the PLO
emerged out of the ruins of Arab defeat as an
independent body dominated by Fatah and with great
Arab popular support. In 1974 the Arab League
granted it the right to be the sole representative
of the Palestinian people and the United Nations
admitted it as an observer. In effect the United
Nations General Assembly recognized the PLO as the
representative of the Palestinian people, and King
Hussein of Jordan had to give up his claim to the
West Bank which had been occupied by and annexed to
Jordan from 1948 until 1967, when it was occupied
by Israel. PLO links with Third World countries
increased.

Relations with the Soviet Union, which eventually emerged as a major diplomatic, political and
military supporter of the PLO, developed slowly.
At first the Soviets showed no friendliness toward
the PLO, though they always expressed sympathy with
the rightful struggle of the Palestinian people.
Aid and recognition of the PLO by China did not
help to ease that position. By 1969 relations
between the Soviets and the PLO had thawed and
Arafat, the PLO chairman, headed a delegation to
Moscow at the invitation of the Afro-Asian Solidarity Committee. Arafat made several other unofficial visits to Moscow, but not until the summer of
1974 was he officially invited and a PLO office
opened in Moscow. Now Moscow recognizes the PLO as
the sole legitimate representative of the Palestinian people and has sided with it even against her
Arab allies such as Syria.

PLO relations with the United States remained
negative and the distance was formalized by the US
policy of no dealings with the PLO until the organization recognizes the state of Israel. This policy commitment was made to Israel by US Secretary
of State Henry Kissinger. However, during and
after the Carter administration, secret contacts
were maintained between the US government and the
PLO. The recognition by the US government of the
political rights of the Palestinians and their
legitimate claims to a homeland of their own was
not only a major reward for the PLO but also a
cause for improved relations with the US.

Perhaps the major successes of the PLO have
been diplomatic ones. In addition to progress in

its relations with the Soviet Union and the United States, the PLO succeeded in developing relations with many other countries including Austria, Spain, Portugal, Britain, France and Japan. In most of these diplomatic advances, the good offices of the Arab states as well as the desire of foreign governments to win favor with the increasingly influential Arabs were important for the PLO.

In the seventies, the PLO became a quasi-government of the Palestinian people, not only by representing them internationally and fighting their cause, but also by establishing services for Palestinians in various countries and refugee camps. For instance, the Social Affairs Department of the PLO was reported in 1981 to have a budget of more than $100 million to provide education, health care, pensions and other services.

It is true that the PLO could not reach all Palestinians, but it was able to reach a very large proportion of them and those most in need of help. The occupation of the West Bank and the Gaza Strip in 1967 and the expulsion of the PLO from Jordan in 1971 reduced the PLO's ability to affect large segments of the Palestinian people. Similarly, its defeat and exile from Lebanon cut it off from large sectors of its people. Nevertheless, most observers seem to agree that the majority of Palestinians, wherever they happen to be, consider the PLO as their legitimate representative, even when disagreeing with their policies.

Symbiotic Relations

Mention of the symbiosis between the Palestinian diaspora and its host countries brings up the regional aspect of the Palestinian-Israeli dilemma. Zionism targeted Palestinian lands and the population living there, but the problem was that the Palestinians could not be isolated from the broader question of Arab national identity of which they formed a part. By putting the Palestinians and their land in jeopardy, the Zionists were, consciously or not, provoking a reaction from a wider population which identified with the Palestinians as Arabs and Muslims too.

In the early period of the Palestinian-Zionist confrontation, Arab nationalism among the Palestinians was stronger than local Palestinian identity. The fac that the Palestinians shared a national identity with the rest of the Arabs made the local

Palestinian-Zionist quarrel a regional issue and
increased the dependency of the Palestinians on
outside forces for the resolution of their problem.
The implications of this fact may be summed up
as follows. First, the exodus of the Palestinians
under fire to the hinterland was a retreat into
areas where kith and kin lived and shared the sense
of their tragedy and defeat, and the objective to
continue the struggle.

Second, Arab states active in the Palestinian-
Israeli war manifested strong Arab nationalist
sentiments that drove them to become involved in
the Palestinian issue. In one sense, vis-à-vis
Israel, they were in a position almost identical to
that of the Palestinians in the diaspora. As a
corollary, it should be noted that the Arab states
later picked up a few causes of conflict with
Israel of their own in the process. By the early
1960s they were faced with the problem of having to
cope with a new state on their borders that was
foreign in origin and culture to theirs. Moreover,
it was a powerful state with strong ties to superpowers such as the United States and Western Europe. A security factor therefore arose for them,
which they couched in empty rhetoric; the Israelis
felt a similar insecurity from their presence in
the midst of a hostile environment.

The survival needs of the new state dictated
policies of adjustment in its environment which
under the prevailing conditions could be obtained
only by forceful and unilateral actions. This
enforced the fears of the border states. Having
drawn its borders as best it could subsequent to
the 1948 war, Israel needed a peaceful environment
ready to make concessions on vital issues for its
prosperity and security. Free passage in the Suez
Canal and the Straits of Tiran and a cooperative
attitude on water resource sharing and on settlement of the refugee question were uppermost in this
respect. Not being able to receive satisfaction on
any one of these issues by negotiation, Israel
opted for the use of force.

This brief historical statement shows the
extent to which the objectives of the Palestinian
refugees were part and parcel of the political and
cultural problems of the host countries. Both
logic and history compel us to view the Palestinians in the diaspora as part of a larger community.
For the Palestinians in the diaspora enjoyed a
symbiotic relationship with both the population
and the governments of their host countries. It

would be easy in the Middle East to distinguish between people and government, but in this case there was a convergence of views. Indeed, the public was bound culturally with the Palestinians and felt free from official restraints in supporting them against the Israelis. In this way, the people exerted pressure on their governments to identify more strongly and tangibly with the Palestinians in their struggle to recover their homes.

Caught up between reality and the ideal, many Arab leaders found themselves in a hypocritical position and many lost their positions and sometimes their lives on that account. The tension which existed between the Palestinians and Arab governments was due to the countries' leaders' fears of such a volatile population in their midst, and was rendered more acute by their inability to contain or satisfy Palestinian claims.

The tide of Arab nationalism was at its peak from the start of the Palestinian exodus until the 1970s. To the Arab people, the Palestinian issue became the conscience of their nationalism. The identification therefore between the Arab people and the Palestinian diaspora was almost complete.

The Palestinians and Authoritarian Arab Regimes

The national identification between the Arabs and the Palestinian diaspora was not free from problems. On a daily person-to-person basis, the Palestinians found that the status of an Arab refugee was indeed different from that of a native Arab citizen. The most serious tension, however, arose from the Arab regimes' fears of a discontented population in their midst whose demands were beyond their power to satisfy. Nevertheless, the similarity of their objectives vis-à-vis the Israelis drove Arab regimes to support Palestinian resistance. However, they made sure that the course of resistance activities remained within the confines of state policy and did not spill over into domestic life. In other words, Arab governments supporting the Palestinian resistance built barriers between it and their own subjects. The restrictions obviously limited the Palestinians' ability to organize and recruit freely. The resistance thus remained in the shadow of Arab regimes until 1967, when three of those regimes, Egypt, Syria and Jordan, were disgraced militarily at the hands of the Israelis. This gave the Palestinian resist-

ance, now organized under the PLO, the chance to
shed the burden of the Arab states' control.

In the first place, the PLO freed itself or-
ganizationally by rejecting leaders handpicked by
Arab regimes and electing its own. It was at this
time that Fatah gained ascendancy under the stew-
ardship of Yasser Arafat. Secondly, the PLO became
freer and more active in recruiting followers and
fighters among the Palestinian inhabitants of refugee camps and linked itself directly to the host
populations over the heads of their governments.
Thirdly, it sought to remove the restrictions
placed by Arab regimes on its military operations
against Israel.

Egypt was the first to impose these restrictions subsequent to the 1956 war. Having received
a military blow at the hands of the Israelis, part
of the price Egypt paid to the victor was to close
the Gaza strip to commando sorties against Israel.
Then came Syria's turn in 1967, when Israel defeated her army and occupied the Golan Heights.
Syria's encouragement of Fatah and other groups to
attack Israel in the period immediately before the
war did not pay off and the Syrians were compelled
by the Israelis to close their borders to the
guerrillas. It may be added that while both Egypt
and Syria continued to harbor Palestinian guerrillas inside their borders, to this day neither has
allowed them to attack Israel from its own
territory.

The third country to close its borders to
guerrilla activities was Jordan. In Jordan PLO
groups enjoyed greater freedom of action than in
Syria or Egypt and by 1968 the Jordanian border was
the most active in guerrilla activities against
Israel. Once again, Israeli military superiority,
proven beyond any doubt in 1967, forced the Jordanian government to clamp down on the Palestinian
resistance. The regime in Jordan had the option of
being invaded by the Israelis or closing its borders to PLO activities.

King Hussein also faced another problem. The
PLO was challenging his authority and had tried in
certain cases to establish itself as a state within
a state, concealing certain areas of its activities
to Jordanian officials and tightening its control
over the Palestinians of the Hashemite Kingdom.
The result was that Hussein took the bull by the
horns, fought the PLO and defeated it in battle.
The Jordanian borders have been closed to the PLO
since 1971. The Palestinians thus lost a great

opportunity, one of the best they and the Jordanian people had, to create middle level organizations to mediate between the authoritarian government and the people.

The Demographic Ratio

It should be no surprise that the border states (Egypt, Syria, Jordan and Lebanon) were the most affected by the Palestinian question. Not only had they security problems with Israel, but they were also host to the largest numbers of Palestinian refugees. The influx of Palestinians into these countries was sudden and under duress, whereas the Palestinian presence in Kuwait and in other Gulf countries came about slowly and in response to opportunities. Moreover, each immigrant was considered individually.

In Kuwait, the government recognizes the large resident Palestinian population socially but not politically. The Palestinians cannot organize themselves into political action groups, though it is well known and tolerated by the government that most subscribe to the PLO and support it discreetly. Most important is the fact that none of these Palestinians are armed or could function militarily against Israel from Kuwait. So the Kuwaiti government does not have to worry about retaliatory action from Israel or about having Palestinian guns fired against itself. Thus, Kuwait finds it possible to be financially very generous toward the PLO and can support it freely with impunity. In this way, it wins favor with its Palestinian residents who, though constituting nearly 21 percent of the Kuwaiti population, pose no serious threat to the regime.

It would be helpful here to take a quick look at the Palestinian minority in the United States. It was estimated at over 100,000 in 1981 but, as in Kuwait, each Palestinian entering the country was individually scrutinized and the majority are professionals and business people. The Palestinians in the US, more than any other Palestinians, constitute something close to a diaspora in the conventional sense. They are a cultural minority often acting on behalf of their people; and they have been given support by other and older Arab immigrants in the US with whom they now form a political lobby. The most well known and effective lobbies are the National Association of Arab Americans

325

and the Arab American University Graduates, a more professional group in which Palestinians predominate. Though these lobby groups have not succeeded in affecting official US policy toward the Palestinian problem, they have quite effectively brought the Palestinian issue to the attention of other Americans and filled the vacuum in Arab information in the United States. The Arab American University Graduates includes members who are also strongly linked to the PLO and are represented in the National Council, a sort of Palestinian parliament.

Turning once again to the border Arab states, historically the Palestinians played their most significant political role in Lebanon, Jordan, Syria and Egypt respectively. In Jordan this occurred because the Palestinians constitute the majority of the population, and the government was not as strong as Egypt's and Syria's. In post-1967 Jordan, the Palestinians still constitute more than fifty percent of the Kingdom's population. In contrast, in Egypt they constitute only one percent of the population, and live on the periphery in Gaza. Very few found their way into business and schools in Egypt itself. In Syria, they constitute only three percent of the population. While there is disagreement on their numerical strength in Lebanon, in 1975 they constituted no less than fourteen percent of the population, with 400,000 or more inhabitants.

Demographically, therefore, it seems clear that where the Palestinians were concentrated in the largest numbers they played the strongest political role, both in their host country and against Israel. But, in Lebanon in particular, they enjoyed something greater than numbers: freedom. In Jordan, where they boasted larger numbers, the Palestinians enjoyed less freedom than in Lebanon and their direct political links with the Jordanians and even with their own people were limited. The camps and Palestinian city quarters of Amman did not become centers of armed resistance against the regime, as happened in Lebanon. Moreover, the government of Jordan was more cohesive and stronger than Lebanon's and the Jordanian army stood up to the challenge from the PLO.

The Palestinians in Lebanon

Lebanon is a very good illustration of the thesis that the fortunes of a political movement, even

when not native, will flourish by virtue of the
leverage it is able to obtain through the use of
the freedoms the system allows it.

In Lebanon the PLO had some major advantages.
In the first place, it could operate in a politically free atmosphere among resident Palestinians
as well as Lebanese. This freedom to establish
links with the Lebanese people allowed the PLO to
avail itself of the political opportunities that
existed in the country to build up power over the
national government. As Lebanon is so pluralistic
in character, it was possible for the PLO to find
groups with whom to ally itself, regardless of the
sectarian divisions within the country.

The PLO could offer moral support and prestige
to groups that lacked these qualities, and indeed
it did attract as allies many small political
groups who could not succeed in normal parliamentary politics in Lebanon. But because of its prestige, it also attracted political leaders who were
part of the establishment. Kamal Jumblatt, for
example, one of the most talented and ambitious
political leaders in the country, reached the peak
of his power without ever occupying the presidential palace, as he was a Druze, one of the minority
groups. He called for secularization of the system
as a way of reaching supreme power, and quickly
appreciated the growing strength of the PLO after
its influx into the country from Jordan in 1970-71.
Allying himself with the PLO and championing its
cause was his best ticket to a secularized system
in which he could rise on Palestinian shoulders to
the presidency, over the heads of the Maronites,
Sunnis and Shiites. Such a step, though, proved
too much and eventually led to his death and the
relative isolation of his community.

Nevertheless, the coalition engineered by
Jumblatt and the PLO consisted of almost all the
small groups who were against the existing system
such as the Nasserists, Syrian nationalists, Muslim
extremists, communists, as well as leaders of conventional standing in the Muslim community. The
latter were a special case. The Jumblatt-PLO coalition presided over a large number of Muslims who
used to owe loyalty to their conventional leaders.
The PLO succeeded in undermining the authority of
these leaders and established sway over their followers who were then armed and trained by the
Palestinians.

The PLO hit the Muslim community in a second
way. Having undermined the power of establishment

leaders, it then forced them to join the coalition
by encouraging its small allies to champion the
cause of Muslim political rights in Lebanon. Once
the battle cry of sectarian rights was raised, no
Muslim leader could be left behind. This move had
the effect of splitting the traditional Maronite-
Sunni concordat upon which the system had rested
until then. The split widened as the Christians,
particularly the Maronites, disliked the changing
nature of the situation and started to arm themselves and build militias to face up to the armed
Palestinian presence.

The PLO strategy in Lebanon succeeded in undermining the system, weakening the national government to the point of paralysis and making violence a way of life.

On the face of it, the PLO gained politically
since the paralysis of the central government allowed them almost complete freedom of action and
even dominion over their Lebanese Muslim allies.
Since it was by far the largest, most cohesive and
best trained group, it took no special effort to
establish its dominion. In the long run, this was
a very poor strategy because the continued violence
deprived the PLO of the service Lebanon used to
provide it and prevented it from executing its main
objective, namely launching guerrilla attacks
against Israel from Lebanon.

Finally, PLO excesses invited outside forces
into the picture with the express purpose of check-
ing their free reign. First, the Israelis established contact with Christians and Shiites in South
Lebanon to serve as a buffer zone against the PLO.
This virtually stopped the guerrilla attacks. Second, Syria invaded Lebanon to prevent the emergence
of a radical state on its western flank dominated
by the Palestinians and free from Syrian control.
They succeeded in restraining the PLO and disposing
of Kamal Jumblatt who proved too independent an
ally for them. Finally, the Israelis invaded in
June 1982 in order to deal with the PLO in Lebanon.
The Israeli invasion succeeded in pushing the PLO
out of the south and Beirut. It was forced to
leave the country and was dispersed in North Africa
and Arabia. The remaining PLO units in the Bika'
valley in the east and in Tripoli in the north were
dealt their final blow the following year, when
Syria and Syrian-supported Palestinian units ousted
Arafat and his loyal troops from Lebanon. At present, the only organized Palestinian presence in

Lebanon is an anti-Arafat organization created and controlled by the Syrians. In effect, by weakening Lebanon and paralyzing its government, the PLO made it vulnerable to outside intervention which worked, above all, against itself. Instead of maintaining the system that provided it with shelter and freedom of action, the PLO contributed to its demise, a strategy which proved self-destructive. Moreover, by the time the PLO left Lebanon, there was hardly a Lebanese citizen left willing to stand up and support it.

Why the PLO could not satisfy itself with its status in Jordan and Lebanon is not clear to this writer. Some Palestinian intellectuals claim that the differences among the Lebanese drew the PLO into the fray. There seems to be some truth to this statement, but the fact remains that the PLO was also actively pursuing a policy of intervention in Lebanese affairs as it had done in Jordan.

It is true that at the time of the PLO influx Lebanon was going through a critical transition. Christian majority status was no longer defensible and the Muslims escalated their demands for the dominant political positions in the government. The arrival of the PLO into the arena at that critical time made a peaceful transition impossible, but the PLO was incapable of achieving this change militarily.

A Concluding Note

The Palestinians are not the only people who lost a homeland or a bid for one in the Middle East; the Armenians and the Kurds preceeded them on that route. The Armenians suffered a worse fate, and Kurdish casualties from wars with Turkey, Iran and Iraq were not fewer than those of the Palestinians. On a world scale, the Palestinian refugees may be the most noted, but not the most numerous or miserable. Why then does their problem defy a solution? The answer lies simply in the fact that the Palestinians are part and parcel of a larger, supportive community, the community of Arabs from the Gulf to the Atlantic Ocean. Not only do they owe their importance to their being Arabs, but also most of their important successes were earned for them by Arab diplomacy and other forms of support. Their own choice of armed struggle aggravated their problem and added to their tragedy, not to mention the trouble they brought upon their host countries.

The argument that armed struggle pushed others to act diplomatically on their behalf is neither to be dismissed nor accepted fully at face value. The Palestinians probably pushed their armed struggle too far and unwisely at critical times, and perhaps used it in the wrong way. Trying to seize power in two of the countries that were most hospitable to them could not be justified in any way, if they were actually operating on rational grounds.

Finally, it must be mentioned that while Arab support gave the Palestinians strength, endurance and world attention, it also gave them a sense of false security and power. They misunderstood their critical position and its limitations within the Arab world. Had they realized those limitations early on, they would have spared themselves and their friends a great deal of mistrust and acrimony.

References

Abu-Lughod, ed. **The Transformation of Palestine: Essays on the Origin and Development of the Arab-Israeli Conflict.** Evanston, IL: Northwestern University.

Avineri, Shlomo, ed. 1971. **Israel and the Palestinians: Reflections on the Clash of Two National Movements.** New York: St. Martin's Press.

Bertelsen, Judy. 1976. **The Palestinian Arabs: A Non-State Nations Systems Analysis.** Comparative Interdisciplinary Studies Section, vol. 4. Beverly Hills: Sage Professional Papers.

Buehrig, Edward H. 1971. **The U.N. and the Palestinian Refugees.** Bloomington, IN: Indiana University Press.

Cooley, John K. 1973. **Green March, Black September, The Story of the Palestine Arabs.** London: Frank Cass.

Dodd, Peter and Halim Barakat. 1968. **River without Bridges, A Study of the Exodus of the 1967 Palestinian Arab Refugees.** Beirut: Institute of Palestine Studies.

Girard, Chaliand. 1972. **The Palestinian Resistance.** London: Penguin Books.

Harik, Iliya. 1981. **Lebanon: Anatomy of Conflict.** American Universities Field Staff.

Harkabi, Yehoshafat. 1968. **Fedayeen Action and Arab Strategy.** Adelphi Papers No. 53. London: The Institute for Strategic Studies.

-----. 1972. **Arab Attitudes Toward Israel.** New York: Hark Publishing Co.

-----. 1977. **Arab Strategies and Israel's Response.** New York: Free Press.

Heller, Mark A. 1983. **Palestinian Political Elites: The West Bank Under Foreign Rule.** New York: Praeger.

Israeli, Raphael. 1983. **The PLO in Lebanon: Selected Documents.** London: Weidenfeld and Nicolson.

Khalidi, Walid. 1979. **Conflict and Violence in Lebanon: Confrontation in the Middle East.** Cambridge: Harvard University Press.

Khouri, Fred J. 1976. **The Arab-Israeli Dilemma.** Syracuse University Press.

Lesch, Ann Mosely. 1980. **Political Perceptions of the Palestinians on the West Bank and the Gaza Strip.** Washington, D.C.: Middle East Institute.

Mishal, Shaul. 1978. **The West Bank/East Bank: The Palestinians in Jordan, 1949-1967.** New Haven: Yale University Press.

Nadav, Safran. 1969. **From War to War: The Arab Israeli Confrontation 1948-1967.** New York: Pegasus.

O'Neill, Bard E. 1978. **Armed Struggle in Palestine: A Political Military Analysis.** Boulder, CO: Westview Press.

Peretz, Don. 1958. **Israel and the Palestinian Arabs.** Washington, D.C.: Middle East Institute.

Peretz, Don, Richard J. Ward and Evan M. Wilson. 1976. **The Palestine State: A Rational Approach.** New York: Kennikat Press.

Plascov, Avi. 1980. **The Palestinian Refugees in Jordan 48-57.** London: Frank Cass.

Porath, Yehoshua. 1974. **The Emergence of the Palestinian-Arab National Movement, 1918-1929.** London: Frank Cass.

Quandt, William. 1977. **Decade of Decisions: American Policy Toward the Arab-Israeli Conflict, 1967-1976.** Berkeley, CA: University of California Press.

Quandt, William, Fuad Jabber and Ann Mosely Lesch. 1973. **The Politics of Palestinian Nationalism.** Berkeley, CA: University of California Press.

Rouleau, Eric. 1978. **Abou Iyad, Palestinien sans Patrie.** Paris: Fayelle.

Schiff, Ze'ev and Raphael Rothstein. 1972. **Fedayeen--Guerrillas Against Israel.** New York, NY: McKay and Co.

331

Sharabi, Hisham. 1969. **Palestine and Israel: The Lethal Dilemma.** New York: Pegasus.
Tessler, Mark and Ann Mosely Lesch. 1983. **Israel's Drive into the West Bank and Gaza.** Universities Field Staff International.
Turki, Fawaz. 1972. **The Disinherited Journal of a Palestinian Exile.** New York: MR.
Waines, David. 1977. **A Sentence of Exile: The Palestine/Israel Conflict, 1897-1977.** Wilmette, IL: The Medina Press.
Ya'ari, Ehud. 1970. **Strike Terror--The Story of Fatah.** New York: Sabra Books.

DIASPORAS AND INTERNATIONAL RELATIONS

Milton J. Esman

The term "diaspora" has long been associated by historians and social scientists with the dispersal of the Jews from Palestine, their homeland, following their defeat by the Romans in 70 A.D. More recently, the concept has been generalized to refer to any population which has migrated from its country of origin and settled in a foreign land, but maintains its continuity as a community. Thus, our working definition of diaspora is "a minority ethnic group of migrant origin which maintains sentimental or material links with its land of origin." This definition excludes migrants who take over or form a state and become its dominant element, for example the British in Australia and New Zealand. It excludes groups such as the Afrikaners in South Africa who have severed their sentimental and economic ties with their country of origin. It explicitly excludes ethnic groups whose minority status results not from migration but from conquest, annexation or arbitrary boundary arrangements; such minorities as the Albanians in Yugoslavia or the Somali in Ethiopia may become involved in irredentist conflicts. These differ from diaspora politics and require separate treatment.[1]

Migration has been a continuous phenomenon throughout history, induced by political or religious oppression and, more frequently, by the search for improved economic opportunities. Migrations may be voluntary or compelled. The most conspicuous case of the latter was the transportation of Africans to slavery in the Americas, but the movement of contract labor to Malaysia, Fiji and the Caribbean plantations in the nineteenth century also had many features of compulsion. Rapid population growth, uneven economic development and greatly improved transportation, beginning in the mid-nineteenth century, have accelerated migratory movements. New, large-scale diasporas have appeared almost overnight: Turks in Germany; Jamaicans in Britain; Ghanians in Nigeria; Indians,Pakistanis, and Bangladeshis in the Persian Gulf states; Cubans and Vietnamese in the United States; Colombians in Venezuela. In every continent migrations are producing fresh diasporas and there is no reason to believe that this phenomenon will diminish in importance.

Nor do diasporas quickly assimilate into the receiving society. The "illusion of impermanence" has been shattered by the experience of the overwhelming majority of migrations during this century.[2] Through a combination of preference and social exclusion, they maintain their identity and solidarity over extended periods. After three generations the Armenian community in France, though French-speaking and well-established economically, retains its group solidarity and applauds, when it does not directly support, terrorist activities against Turkish targets. In many countries there are older diasporas and newer diasporas. Even within the same ethnic group mutual support and solidarity may be strained by tensions and conflicts between earlier and later arrivals.

Along with internal cohesion, migrant groups tend to maintain links with their country of origin. Communication with kinfolk and financial remittances to relatives are the most common form of exchange. Migrants may return to their home country for visits or for permanent repatriation; fresh flows of recruits may nourish the migrant community and help to maintain language, culture and personal contacts; nostalgic third generation migrants may visit their homeland to rediscover their roots. Migrant communities may look to the home country and perhaps to its government for cultural reinforcement in the form of teachers and religious leaders. They may take a vital interest in political developments in the home country and even try to influence them. Thus migrant communities not only retain their group identity and their institutions over extended periods, they also maintain continuing links, both material and sentimental, with their country of origin. These links become a dimension of international politics.

To most migrant groups, the concept of homeland is quite specific and clear. To Croats in Germany, Pakistanis in Kuwait, Koreans in Japan or Haitians in the United States, their homeland is unambiguous. Depending on historical experience, however, the "homeland" may be a less specific point of reference. Deprived by slavery of tribal solidarity, and of specific historical memories, American Blacks tend to identify with all of Black Africa, rather than with a particular territory or cultural community. For centuries, Jews in the diaspora identified with historical memories of Jerusalem and the land of Israel, to which the Messiah would lead them on the day of redemption, but they had few, if any, live contacts with that land and no affinities with its governors. Most diaspora Jews now identify sympathetically with the State of Israel, though Palestine has not been the actual homeland of their fathers for nearly two millennia. To diaspora communities the homeland may be an ideological construct or myth, but no less significant to them than specific homelands to which other migrant communities relate.

The continuing links between diasporas and homelands can be politicized, and this is their major significance in the study of international relations. Diaspora solidarities can be mobilized and focused to influence political outcomes in the home country, to provide economic, diplomatic and even military assistance to the home country or to seek protection and help from its government. Likewise, the government of the home country may call on the diaspora community for economic or political support, and the host country's government may attempt to use the diaspora community to promote its interests vis-à-vis the home country. With their variable capacities, opportunities and propensities to exert influence on behalf of their domestic or external interests, diaspora communities can be regarded as interest groups and as political actors. When diasporas are involved in issues that extend beyond the borders of their country of residence, the significant actors, aside from the diaspora communities, are the host government and, to a lesser degree, transnational and international institutions.

In some situations, however, the option of politicization is foreclosed for diaspora communities. The Persian Gulf countries exemplify this situation. The very existence of large foreign communities is regarded by these wealthy, but weak, authoritarian regimes as an unfortunate economic necessity and a potential political danger. They thus insist on the complete political neutralization of their immigrant communities. Nevertheless,

international transactions between the home governments, which provide the labor force, and the host
governments are necessary to regulate the flow and
status of the migrants for whom their home governments act in the internationally recognized role of
protectors. Though these diasporas are required to
be entirely passive, their presence and activities
are subjects for interstate relations. This article will deal with such situations only in passing.
It will concentrate on the more common and more
interesting cases where diaspora communities can
themselves be actors in international exchanges.

The scope and intensity of diaspora activities, including those that affect international
relations, are determined by three factors: the
material, cultural and organizational resources
available to them; the opportunity structures in
the host country; and their inclination or motivation to maintain their solidarity and exert group
influence.

The Resources and Skills Available
to the Diaspora

In his treatment of migrant communities in the
Ottoman, Romanoff and Hapsburg empires, one scholar
distinguishes between mobilized and proletarian
diasporas (Armstrong 1976, pp. 393-408). Proletarian or labor diasporas have no economic resources
other than their labor, few communication skills
and limited organizational experience. They are
incapable of articulating their group interests in
their new environment and they have no access to
decision-making circles. They are relegated to the
bottom of the income, occupational and status hierarchies. Gradually, as they become proficient in
the local language, begin to acquire occupational
skills and economic resources, form their own organizations for mutual assistance, and develop
cadres of locally-educated leaders who know how to
exert influence on the political structures of
their adopted country, labor diasporas can begin to
impress their needs on the public agenda. The
great majority of migrant communities begin as
proletarian diasporas. Before they develop the
skills, capabilities and access needed to promote
their domestic or international group interests,
at least one or perhaps several generations may be
required.

In contrast, Armstrong speaks of mobilized diasporas--those which bring occupational or communication skills that are in short supply in their adopted country. Because these skills are valuable to the dominant native elites, the leading elements of the diaspora communities can enjoy material rewards and sometimes the social status that these scarce resources command; they gain access to the native elites, securing their patronage and protection. Because of their cosmopolitan contacts and their language skills, they are often prominent in diplomatic roles, though as foreigners with another homeland they may not be fully trusted by the patrons they are serving. In time, as social mobilization occurs in their host country and indigenous groups acquire these skills, the diaspora becomes less valuable to the native elites. Yielding to competitive domestic pressure, the native elites eventually withdraw their patronage and protection; the diaspora is then exposed to the fate of privileged but unpopular foreigners.

"Middleman minorities," that is immigrant communities that fill economic niches in pre-modern societies between the peasantry and the ruling elites, represent a more contemporary version of Armstrong's mobilized diaspora. Among the larger and better known middleman minorities are the Chinese in Southeast Asia, Asians in East Africa and Lebanese in West Africa. Their economic skills were valued, both by colonial governments and by successor indigenous regimes. But, as highly visible, economically successful, non-assimilating foreigners, they become vulnerable targets for emergent nationalist, populist and Marxist intellectuals and for potential economic competitors. By partnership arrangements, in effect by sharing their wealth with local elites--e.g., the Chinese in Southeast Asia--they may buy protection and continue to prosper. With modernization, however, Armstrong predicts that local elites will eventually be forced to abandon them as undesirable or even subversive foreigners. Do the recent disasters visited on the Asians in Uganda and the Chinese in Vietnam presage similar consequences for the Asians in Kenya and the Chinese in Indonesia, as well as for all middleman diasporas in modernizing societies?

Like most dichotomies, the division between mobilized and proletarian diasporas is too crude. It would be more accurate to visualize a continuum between the two poles. Migrant communities have

greater or lesser ability to influence their new
environment according to the economic resources,
occupational skills and communication capabilities
they bring with them. Their integration varies
with their original endowments and with the rate at
which the migrants and their descendants acquire
these capabilities. Contrast the experience of
migrant communities that arrived in the United
States during the same period: the Irish, a proletarian diaspora and the Germans, a relatively mobilized community. The Irish struggled over many
decades to accumulate the necessary resources to
exercise influence beyond their localities; the
Germans moved much more rapidly. A similar contrast can be drawn between Iraqi and Moroccan communities in Israel, both of which immigrated in
large numbers shortly after the independence of the
State in 1948. The Iraqis were soon absorbed into
the Israeli establishment; the Moroccans after 35
years remain the most depressed and discontented
group among Israeli Jews.

Opportunity Structure in the Host Country

The second factor affecting the ability of diasporas to function as an interest group is the
opportunity structure in the host country. This
denotes the degree of freedom available to them to
organize and to promote their group interests.
Some political systems tolerate the organization of
interest groups, including ethnic minorities, and
the exercise of influence on their behalf. Others
discourage it or forbid it entirely. In the relatively open political system of the United States,
ethnic interest groups are free to organize and
operate in the political market place; in the
Soviet Union, they are not. Jews in the US have
taken advantage of the opportunity to organize and
promote their domestic and international interests;
in the Soviet Union, similar activities by Jews or
any other ethnic group would be considered sedi-
tious. Migrant communities in France are relatively free to organize and promote their collective
interests; in the Persian Gulf states, political
or organizational activity, even by fellow Arabs,
is categorically proscribed and punished by deportation.

Opportunities in some countries are not equally available to all migrant groups. Some minorities

may encounter severe constraints, while others are
free to pursue their interests, even on international issues. Blacks in South Africa are completely circumscribed, while Jews are highly organized.
The main point is clear: activities by diaspora
communities, including those that relate to international affairs, vary as much with the opportunities available to them in their host country as
with their skills and resources.

Motivation to Maintain Group Solidarity

Diaspora activities also depend on their varying
inclination or motivation to maintain group solidarity and to promote their interests by political
means. Where cultural differences are minor, where
there is no sense of discrimination or deprivation,
and where the host society encourages assimilation,
migrant communities may feel no compelling interest
to bind them together; they may blend into the
host society as individuals and cease to function
as separate communities. This has been the experience of the Dutch in the US and the Javanese in
Malaysia. Where cultural diferences are greater,
especially if ethnic identities are reinforced by
minority religious solidarity, as with the Greeks,
Irish and Jews in the United States, then communal
distinctiveness and solidarity are likely to be
longer-lasting. Social marginality is likely to
support that solidarity, and communities will organize for self-maintenance, defense and advocacy.
    Diaspora communities that feel culturally
superior to their host society tend to resist assimilation and insist on self-maintenance even when
assimilation is an option. During the half-century
before World War I, Germans in the US maintained an
elaborate and vigorous network of institutions to
promote what they considered to be their superior
culture. The Chinese in Southeast Africa and
Asians in East Africa display the same evidence of
cultural superiority toward their host societies
and the same disinclination to assimilate as did
the Jews and Greeks in Eastern Europe two centuries
ago. The Chinese, whose cultural pride is legend-
ary, are far more prone to come to terms with
American culture which they respect than with cultures of Southeast Asia, to which they feel im-
mensely superior.
    A review of diasporas discloses seven classes
of activity that implicate them in international

relations, in which initiatives may be taken by the home government, the host government or the diaspora community.

1. The diaspora may attempt directly to influence events in the home country. The methods they employ may be economic, political or military. Overseas Chinese provided vital economic help and facilitated the supply of military equipment to the successful revolution led by Dr. Sun Yat-sen against the C'hing regime in 1911. In contemporary Germany Turkish guest workers provide financial support to competing political parties in Turkey while Croats smuggle weapons to support Croat dissidence in Yugoslavia. Factions of the Irish diaspora in the United States supply weapons to the IRA terrorists (freedom fighters) in Northern Ireland to the dismay of the British government and embarrassment of the governments of the United States and Ireland and of prominent leaders of the Irish diaspora in the United States. Direct action by diaspora groups may create serious tensions between host and home governments, the latter accusing the former of tolerating and even abetting hostile activities which they are believed to have the power to suppress. Under Japanese pressure, the British colonial government in Malaya did embargo financial help from local Chinese to the Chinese government which was resisting Japanese invasion in the 1930s. Economic assistance from diaspora Jewry has been important to Zionist settlement in Palestine and Israel. Arab states have accused European governments and the United States of supporting the Zionist enterprise--and of hostility to the Arab cause--by tolerating these financial flows and by granting them tax-exemption status.

2. Diasporas may use their influence with their host governments to act on behalf of the interests of the home government. These activities can be quite consequential. The Greek diaspora in the United States was successful in inducing the Congress in the face of strong opposition from the State and Defense Departments and from the White House itself to embargo military assistance to Turkey in protest against Turkey's invasion and partition of Cyprus. On the other hand, Blacks

have been less successful in inducing the
United States to take effective measures
against South Africa's racist policies and its
continued retention of Namibia. Malaysia's
Chinese used their limited opportunities to
exert influence on their government's foreign
policy by facilitating the establishment of
normal diplomatic relations with the Peoples'
Republic of China in 1972. They were, however, completely unsuccessful in inducing
their government to accept any of the ethnic
Chinese "boat people" as refugees. The success of the Jewish diaspora in the United
States in committing its government to far-
reaching diplomatic, economic and military
support for Israel is the most prominent example of a diaspora's influence on its host
government on behalf of its homeland.

3. Home governments may attempt to use their
diaspora in pursuit of their own goals. The
intended benefits may be economic or political. The governments of South Asia realize
vital economic benefits from financial remittances from their nationals working as guest
laborers in the Persian Gulf states. These
governments are interested in maintaining
these important flows of funds and are prepared to exert themselves diplomatically to
facilitate the supply of docile labor on terms
that are satisfactory to the host governments.
They appear to be more concerned with satis-
fying the requirements of the Gulf states than
with protecting the interests of their nationals. The Chinese government operates
large networks of educational, tourist and financial services to facilitate these flows,
similar to those that have been established by
Israel and the Zionist movement to lure funds
from diaspora Jewry.

Home governments may also attempt to
induce their diasporas to act politically in
their support. The imperial government of
Germany made an all-out effort to mobilize the
large and influential German community in the
United States to prevent the United States'
entry in World War I on the side of the Allies. At the same time the British government
invested heavily, and more successfully, to
encourage persons of British extraction to
prompt US participation on the side of the
Allies. There is often a symbiotic relation-

ship between a home government that needs help and a diaspora community that is eager to act, as in the case of US Jewry and the state of Israel. More problematic are efforts by a home government to manipulate a reluctant, insecure, unsympathetic, or divided diaspora community; witness the failure of Hitler's Germany to mobilize German-Americans on behalf of the Third Reich.

4. The diaspora may seek protection from the home government when it is threatened with mistreatment. Sympathy notwithstanding, the response of the home government in such cases is likely to be problematic. The doctrine of noninterference in the internal affairs of a sovereign state is still a powerful norm in interstate relations. When combined with their limited capacity to be effective and the diplomatic costs of intervention, home governments tend to be cautious in response to requests to act or to speak out on behalf of their diasporas. India has done nothing to protect its hard-pressed diasporas in East Africa, nor has China found it expedient to champion its ethnic brethren in Southeast Asia, except in Vietnam where it had other scores to settle with Hanoi. Diasporas under stress are inclined to turn to their country of origin for help; the latter seldom respond effectively.

5. The host country government may attempt to use a resident diaspora community in pursuit of its external political or economic goals. The diaspora may be a convenient and low-cost resource for the host government, while by supporting its government, the diaspora enhances its own status and security. The US government encouraged Italian Americans and their organizations in 1948 to conduct a propaganda and letter-writing campaign to persuade Italians to vote against the Communist Party in the critical 1948 election. From time to time the US government has attempted to use prominent American Jews to influence the behavior of the government of Israel. Southeast Asian governments work with local Chinese businessmen to facilitate arrangements for investment by Chinese transnational firms, investments in which the native elites and local Chinese entrepreneurs often emerge as "partners".

6. Diaspora communities may attempt to influence international organizations on behalf of their homeland. The most conspicuous case has been the success of the Palestinians in embarrassing and isolating Israel in the UN and its agencies. Success in such a campaign depends entirely on active patronage and support among member governments; the Palestinians have successfully mobilized Arab and Moslem governments, as well as the Soviet bloc. Efforts by the Kurdish, Armenian, Croatian, South Moluccan and other diasporas to invoke UN support have failed entirely because they lack the patronage and support of member governments.

7. The home governments may ask the host government to influence, usually to restrain what it perceives to be the hostile or embarrassing activities of sections of its diaspora. Dublin has asked the United States to restrain the movement of weapons from sympathizers in the United States to the IRA. Peking has asked governments in Southeast Asia to block the flow of funds and other support from sections of its diaspora to the regime of Taiwan. Yugoslavia has asked the Federal Republic of Germany to control the activities of Croat nationalist organizations which it considers subversive. Such requests usually involve activities by diaspora groups which the home government considers to be hostile. The responses are seldom likely to satisfy the home government unless the actions in question are perceived as a danger to the host government.

It is misleading, of course, to speak of diaspora communities as if they were united or monolithic in their orientation to their domestic situation or to international affairs. They may be divided by class interests, by the longevity of their residence in the host country, by subethnic, regional or caste origins. There may be conflicts both in goals and tactics. For example, the Chinese in Malaysia can be divided into three groups: the communists, who combine ethnic chauvinism with Marxist ideology and revolutionary tactics; the capitalist establishment and their client networks which would defend Chinese interests by pragmatic accommodation and quiet bargaining with the governing Malay elites; and the urban middle class professionals who favor the end of Malay privileges and the incorporation of all Malaysians as individuals into a secular, non-ethnic Malaysian Malaysia. Because of such differences Malaysia's Chinese, despite their large numbers (35 percent), do not function as an effective political force or interest group in that country. In the pre-Hitler period in the United States, Jews were divided into Germans (the earlier arrivals) and East Europeans; into Orthodox, Conservative and Reform religious movements; and into a Zionist minority (itself split along ideological and religious lines), the non-Zionist majority and important anti-Zionist groups among the ultra-Orthodox and ultra-Reform.

Careful observation of any diaspora community is likely to disclose divisions such as those that exist in any society. Those internal divisions affect the group's appreciation of its situation, definition of its interests, both domestic and international, and choice of tactics. Representatives of these competing orientations vie for leadership and influence within the diaspora and for the right to represent it to outsiders. These orientations are dynamic and subject to changes in circumstances. Among American Jews, rapid social and economic mobility have blurred earlier differences between Germans and East Europeans, while the European holocaust converted the great majority to the support of Israel. It is predictable that the Turkish diaspora in contemporary Germany will not disappear, that there will be internal divisions and competition for leadership and influence, and that the second and third generations will shape their goals, tactics and relations with both the home and host governments differently from those that seemed feasible to the immigrant generation. The goals and tactics that diasporas adopt are influenced by their internal divisions as well as by changing circumstances.

Host governments and home governments likewise have varying capacities, opportunities and inclinations to become involved in activities that affect diaspora communities. Each party has its own distinctive interests and these interests seldom coincide, indeed they are often in conflict with one or both other parties. Internal divisions may be present in governments and especially within diaspora communities, further complicating an inherently complex set of relationships. Because of changing circumstances and the numbers and interests of the parties involved, any assessment of the factors involved in a specific instance of diaspora politics must depend on inductive analysis.

Such analysis can be facilitated by a number of orienting propositions that are warranted by the evidence reported in this book. Both on a global and on a regional scale, the influence of diaspora on interstate politics can be consequential. The status and rights of Soviet Jewry have further aggravated relations between the two superpowers. The entry of the United States into World War I was affected by the competitive mobilization of the German and British diasporas and the strenuous efforts of their homeland governments to manipulate them. The Palestinian diaspora has been at the heart of Middle Eastern politics and its global ramifications for two generations. China's relations with the states of Southeast Asia have been greatly complicated by the conspicuous presence of overseas Chinese in the region, their continuing links with the homeland and the deep suspicions of their dual loyalty among both native elites and masses.

The implications of diasporas for interstate relations are dynamic due to the continuing migration, new distribution, influence, and new patterns of diaspora organization. Uneven economic development generates international migratory movements on a very large scale, witness the labor migrations to Western Europe and the post-World War II economic boom which have left large permanent diaspora communities in all Western European countries. Like the earlier movement of Chinese into Southeast Asia and the more recent migrations from South Asia to the Persian Gulf states, these diaspora communities have become essential to the economic structures of their host countries. As they are unlikely to disappear, their presence has and will continue to provide the ingredients of interstate transactions and in many cases of tensions between the host and home governments and between third parties as well. New patterns of organization and of influence may be innovated by diaspora communities to promote and protect their interests. The large transnational economic enterprises recently created by overseas Chinese capitalists in Southeast Asia represent a new force in the economy of that region which governments must take into account in their economic planning and in their behavior towards the ethnic Chinese communities in their midst.

Diasporas may be a foreign policy or economic asset which home governments are eager to exploit. The most conspicuous contemporary case is the dip-

345

lomatic, economic and military support that the state of Israel receives from the United States, resulting in no small measure from the activities of the Jewish diaspora. The financial remittances provided by the various South Asian migrant communities are vital to the balance of payments of India, Pakistan, Bangladesh and Sri Lanka. Because they represent real and potential assets, home governments often find it useful to invest in the maintenance of close and friendly relations with diaspora communities, fostering cultural ties, providing political propaganda supportive of the home country regime, promoting return travel to the homeland, facilitating financial remittances, and neutralizing dissidence within the diaspora community. Despite such careful cultivation, a diaspora may nevertheless prove to be a burden or even an embarrassment to the home country. China's efforts since 1955 to normalize relations with the governments of Southeast Asia have been inhibited by the presence in these countries of Chinese communities which are suspected by the local elites of dual loyalty, but which Peking cannot disown. The supply of arms to the IRA by militant Irish groups in the US has been an embarrassment to the government of Ireland. Home governments invest in their diasporas not only for the support they may provide, but also to maintain sufficient influence to prevent them from acting counter to the interests of the home government.

Diasporas are inclined to act in the interest of the home government on matters affecting interstate relations. But because their interests may differ they can be influenced, but not easily manipulated by the home government. Normally a diaspora community which has the capability and the opportunity will also have the inclination to sympathize and support the government that speaks for the homeland. However, when vital interests are at stake, they may act independently. Diasporas may distinguish between the homeland and its current government. They may love the homeland but despise its regime, like the overseas Chinese who financed and supported the overthrow of the Ch'ing dynasty by the republican, revolutionary forces of Sun Yet-sen. Since the late 1940s the Eastern European diasporas in the US have opposed the Soviet-imposed regimes in their homelands and encouraged the US government to do likewise. Since diaspora communities are seldom homogeneous, important elements may be offended by the behavior or policies of the

home government, oppose it actively, or withhold
their support. An example is the increasing hostility of growing sections of US Jewry to the
creeping annexation of the West Bank by the Likud
government of Begin and Shamir.
More fundamentally, diaspora communities have
their own vital interests to defend in their adopted countries. They are especially sensitive and
vulnerable to charges of "dual loyalty" which may
threaten their status and security. The dominant
elements among the Chinese in Southeast Asia could
not support the Maoist cultural revolution. The
charges of disloyalty and dual loyalty leveled
against German-Americans during World War I produced a wave of hostility that permanently destroyed their morale and cohesion. The higher the
cost to their status and security in their adopted
country, or to their ideological commitments, the
greater the prospect that the community will split,
fail to support the home government or even turn
against it. One of the motives of home governments
in cultivating their diasporas is to diminish this
possibility.
Diasporas will attempt to reconcile their
security needs and economic interests with the requirements of the homeland and its government.
When these conflict, the diaspora's domestic security needs are likely to take precedence. The weaker a diaspora's capabilities, and the more limited
its opportunities, the less it will be inclined to
take risks on behalf of its homeland.
Homeland governments are not reliable cham-
pions or defenders of the interests of their diaspora communities. Other things being equal, homeland governments are inclined by reasons of empathy
or by domestic political pressures to speak out in
defense of their diasporas when they are threatened
with mistreatment. Thus President Lopez Portillo
of Mexico threatened to reduce Mexico's oil exports
to the US if the employment opportunities of illegal Mexican immigrants in the US were jeopard-
ized by the actions of the US government. Normally, there are severe limitations on what a home
government can do. Israel, which does not depend
on the Soviet Union for diplomatic, military, or
economic support, can protest the persecution of
Jews in the Soviet Union and the denial of their
right to emigrate, and can attempt to mobilize
international support. India, which depends on
the Gulf states to accept Indian workers, can nego-
tiate quietly for its diaspora but has little bar-

gaining power and cannot protest publicly. Because it would not be effective and because it wishes to protect its position as a champion of Third World solidarity, India does not protest the mistreatment of its diasporas in East Africa, even when whole communities are despoiled and expelled, as in Uganda in 1968. To state the relationship bluntly, the foreign policy interests of states supersede their commitments to their diasporas. China invaded Vietnam in 1978 in part to avenge the mistreatment and pillaging of the large Chinese minority which the Vietnamese regarded as a potential fifth column. The main reason for the invasion was that Vietnam had become China's enemy because of its alignment with the Soviet Union. In neighboring Cambodia, thousands of ethnic Chinese had been slaughtered by the genocidal Pol Pot government, but Peking emitted not a word of protest. Cambodia was a client state of China, and the exigencies of foreign policy required unqualified support of its government. To cite more subtle cases: because of its desire to normalize relations with Indonesia in the late 1950s, China abandoned many of the claims it had previously made to represent and protect the Chinese diaspora; Israel has been accused of turning a blind eye to the mistreatment of Jews in Argentina in order not to jeopardize military sales to that country.

In international politics, reasons of state normally take precedence over other claims, including the status of diaspora communities. States will not risk important security or economic interests for the sake of diaspora communities.

The presence of a diaspora may constrain the freedom of action of a host government on internationally significant issues. Because of the presence of a Chinese diaspora, which is widely distrusted and is presumed to be vulnerable to subversive manipulation by the government of its homeland, Indonesia's elites have refused to normalize relations with the PRC. Many students of US foreign policy believe that US policy toward the Arab states of the Middle East has been distorted by the unrelenting influence of the Jewish lobby. Though their objections were eventually overridden, Greek-Americans for several years were successful in blocking the transfer of weapons to an important US ally in the Eastern Mediterranean.

The considerable scholarship and writing on ethnic pluralism and conflict which has appeared in recent years in comparative politics and political sociology have tended to assume closed political systems and to neglect external influences on domestic ethnic politics. Academic writers on international relations, on the other hand, have focused mainly on political and economic transactions among states. They have paid little attention to non-state actors, including ethnic minorities and their influence on foreign policy and international affairs. Only recently have transnational corporations been recognized as significant non-state participants in international affairs.

Diasporas based on enduring ethnic affinities are the components of another set of transnational networks that influence both the internal politics and external relationships of contemporary states. Their impacts may be consequential both on a global and a regional scale. Since migrations are likely to be a continuing phenomenon and since migrant communities tend to maintain themselves, to develop distinctive interests and to retain material and sentimental links with their homelands, and since these interests and relationships can be politicized, the ingredients of expedient cooperation as well as of tension and conflict are inherent in the triadic networks between diaspora, homeland and host government.

Notes

1 Though diasporas originate in migration, their termination is more problematical. When its members assimilate into their host society to the point that the group loses its coherence and its interest in its land of origin, or becomes estranged from its former homeland, they cease to function as a diaspora community.

2 I owe this term to Myron Wiener.

Reference

Armstrong, John. 1976. Mobilized and Proletarian Diasporas. **American Political Science Review** 70, no. 2 (June): 393-408.